W9-AVX-116

SURVIVING
MANIC DEPRESSION

ALSO BY E. FULLER TORREY, M.D.

The Invisible Plague (2001, Senior Author)

Out of the Shadows (1997)

Schizophrenia and Manic-Depressive Disorder
(1994, Senior Author)

Freudian Fraud (1992)

Criminalizing the Seriously Mentally Ill
(1992, Senior Author)

Frontier Justice:
The Rise and Fall of the Loomis Gang (1992)

Nowhere to Go:
The Tragic Odyssey of the Homeless Mentally Ill (1988)

Care of the Seriously Mentally Ill (1986, Senior Author)

Witchdoctors and Psychiatrists (1986)

Surviving Schizophrenia: A Family Manual
(1983, 1988, 1995, 2001)

The Roots of Treason:
Ezra Pound and the Secret of St. Elizabeths (1983)

Schizophrenia and Civilization (1980)

Why Did You Do That?
Rainy Day Games for a Postindustrial Society (1975)

The Death of Psychiatry (1974)

SURVIVING
MANIC DEPRESSION

A Manual on Bipolar Disorder for
Patients, Families, and Providers

E. Fuller Torrey, M.D.
and
Michael B. Knable, D.O.

BASIC
BOOKS

A Member of the Perseus Books Group

Published by Basic Books,
A Member of the Perseus Books Group

Designed by Jeffrey P. Williams
Set in 12-point Bulmer MT Regular by Perseus Publishing Services

A cataloging-in-publication record for this book is available from the Library of Congress.
ISBN 0-465-08663-2

MV 02 03 04 05 10 9 8 7 6 5 4

To Torrey Gane,
for her kindness and caring

To my parents, John and Patricia Knable,
for their constancy and courage

Of all the afflictions to which human nature is subject, the loss of reason is at once the most calamitous and interesting. Deprived of this faculty, by which man is principally distinguished from the beasts that perish, the human form is frequently the most remarkable attribute that he retains of his proud distinction. . . . The figure of the human species is now all that remains to him, "and like the ruins of a once magnificent edifice, it only serves to remind us of its former dignity and grandeur," and to awaken our gloomiest reflections—our tenderest regret for the departure of the real and respectable man.

PHILIPPE PINEL,
A TREATISE ON INSANITY (1806)[1]

CONTENTS

PREFACE:

Manic Depression or Bipolar Disorder?

Until the early years of the twentieth century, people with manic-depressive illness were part of a large group of people called insane. The term *insane* (from the Latin *insanus,* meaning unsound of mind) had been widely used for four hundred years to designate those who had delusions, hallucinations, disordered thinking, bizarre behavior, excess mood swings, or some combination thereof. *Insanity* was largely synonymous with the terms *madness* and *lunacy.*

In the early twentieth century, the term *insanity* was replaced by *psychosis,* which in turn became associated with an increasing number of subcategories. Some cases of psychosis were found to be caused by medical conditions, such as syphilis or vitamin deficiencies; these cases were separated out and given names appropriate to their cause. The remaining cases of psychosis were divided into dementia praecox, which became known as schizophrenia, and affective psychoses, which included manic-depressive illness, psychotic depressive reactions, and involutional melancholia.

Until 1980, the people said to be suffering from manic depression in the United States included those with depression only (manic-depressive illness, depressed type), mania only (manic-depressive illness, manic type), or both (manic-depressive illness, circular type). But in fact 80 percent of the people diagnosed with manic-depressive illness at that time had depression only.[1] Including people with depression alone under the definition of manic-depressive illness makes it very difficult to compare current studies, in which such individuals are not counted as having manic-depressive illness, with past studies, in which they were counted.

A new definition of manic-depressive illness was introduced in the United States in 1980. According to this definition, a person had to have experienced at least one episode of mania and the episode had to have lasted for at least one week. This new category was christened *bipolar disorder* by the American Psychiatric Association's advisory committee, which formulated the definitions for the third edition of the *Diagnostic and Statistical Manual of Mental Disorders,* referred to as DSM-III.

Bipolar disorder was an unfortunate selection as a name for manic-depressive illness, and it has never completely caught on. The dictionary defines *bipolar* as "having two poles" and "involving both of the earth's poles or polar regions," thus connoting a geographic entity. The word *pole* is derived from the Latin *polus,* meaning "pole of the heavens," and the Greek *polos,* meaning "firmament," but there is nothing heavenly about this disease. *Poles* also refer to the two ends of a battery, suggesting electrical overtones. The term *bipolar disorder* is thus quite unsatisfactory compared to *manic-depressive illness,* the term it was supposed to replace.

The DSM-III definition of manic-depressive illness did accomplish one thing, however: Individuals with depression alone no longer qualified for the diagnosis. The category of manic-depressive illness (bipolar disorder) now included individuals with manic episodes alone as well as those with a mixture of manic and depressive episodes. As the new definition of manic-depressive illness is much more restrictive than the old definition, it is the one used throughout this book.

Since 1980, American psychiatry has continued to tinker with the definition of manic-depressive illness, causing further confusion. DSM-III-R (revised), introduced in 1987, omitted the requirement of a one-week minimum duration for a manic episode but raised the threshold by specifying that the person had to be socially or occupationally impaired or in need of hospitalization. DSM-IV, introduced in 1994, reinstated the requirement that a manic episode must last for at least one week but subdivided the category of bipolar disorder into *bipolar I* (had a full manic episode) and *bipolar II* (had an episode of hypomania, i.e., did not quite meet the criteria for mania). The concept of bipolar II had previously been lurking in the diagnostic shadows under the heading "cyclothymic disorder" in DSM-III and the heading "bipolar disorder, not otherwise specified" in DSM-III-R. "Cyclothymic disorder" and its DSM-III cousin "dysthymic disorder" evolved into "cyclothymia" and "dysthymia" in DSM-III-R and back into "cyclothymic disorder" and "dysthymic disorder" in DSM-IV, but with continuously modified definitions. And if that did not sufficiently confuse everybody, DSM-IV added other caveats. For example, a manic episode precipitated by the taking of an antidepressant medication, which had qualified the person for a diagnosis of bipolar disorder under DSM-III and DSM-III-R, no longer did so under DSM-IV.

In short, psychiatric attempts to define manic depression should be viewed as works in progress. As the term is used in this book, *manic depression* describes a mood disorder that includes at least one episode of mania or at least one period of severe depression plus one period of mild mania (hypomania, or bipolar II) or severe mania (bipolar I). The periods of severe depression or mania may or may not be accompanied by symptoms of psychosis, such as delusions and hallucinations, in addition to the mood symptoms. Cyclothymic disorder is characterized by periods of mild mania (hypomania) and mild depression. Slightly fewer than 1 percent of the adult population in the United States suffer from manic-depressive illness (bipolar I or II) in any given one-year period.

ACKNOWLEDGMENTS

We are grateful to Jo Ann Miller, executive editor at Basic Books, who conceived the book and provided it with excellent prenatal care. Judy Miller at the Stanley Foundation Research Programs proved to be a careful and diligent midwife, and we are deeply indebted for her assistance. Copyeditor Christine Arden conducted a detailed and skillful postnatal examination. Thanks also to Khoi Nguyen and Shen Zhong, who checked the vital signs throughout as needed.

Dr. Maree Webster kindly provided the picture of the glia. Brief passages in Chapters 4 and 11 as well as Appendix A were taken from the fourth edition of *Surviving Schizophrenia*, by E. Fuller Torrey, M.D. In addition, we gratefully acknowledge the following:

Harvard University Press and the trustees of Amherst College, for permission to reprint four lines from Emily Dickinson's poem "After Great Pain."

The American Psychiatric Association, for permission to include information from the *Diagnostic and Statistical Manual of Mental Disorders*, Fourth Edition (DSM-IV).

Random House, for permission to reprint excerpts from *A Brilliant Madness: Living with Manic-Depressive Illness*, by Patty Duke and Gloria Hochman (New York: Bantam Books, 1992).

Random House, for permission to reprint excerpts from *An Unquiet Mind*, by Kay Redfield Jamison (New York: A. A. Knopf, 1995; paperback by Random House, 1997).

Houghton Mifflin Company, for permission to reprint twelve lines from Anne Sexton's poem "The Sickness Unto Death."

Sterling Lord Literistic Inc., for permission to reprint twelve lines from Anne Sexton's poem "The Sickness Unto Death" in the United Kingdom and British Commonwealth.

Houghton Mifflin Company and Little, Brown and Company (U.K.), for permission to reprint excerpts from *Daughter of the Queen of Sheba: A Memoir*, by Jacki Lyden (New York: Houghton Mifflin, 1997; paperback by Penguin Books, 1998).

Hodder Headline Australia, for permission to reprint excerpts from *Daughter of the Queen of Sheba: A Memoir*, by Jacki Lyden (New York: Houghton Mifflin, 1997; paperback by Penguin Books, 1998) in Australia.

Grove/Atlantic, Inc., for permission to reprint a portion of *Not I*, by Samuel Beckett (New York: Grove Press, 1984).

1

DIMENSIONS OF
MANIC-DEPRESSIVE ILLNESS

Why those suffering from a disorder, the most terrible to which the human race is liable, which the world regards with fear and horror, which affixes a stigma on the sufferer for life . . . should be branded with vagrant and the mendicant, thus exposed to a degradation . . . which even the committed criminal is spared, appears to me to be an evil which requires amendment.

JOHN MILLAR,
*advocating for the building of an asylum
to treat insane persons in Buckinghamshire* (1846)[1]

Manic-depressive illness, like other severe psychiatric disorders, has come out of the closet. Once relegated to the dark recesses of the family, it is now openly discussed as a brain disease—frequently a tragic disease, to be sure, but a disease nonetheless, like multiple sclerosis, Parkinson's disease, or Alzheimer's disease. The devils and demons once suspected of lurking in the brains of those afflicted have been permanently banished by the power of magnetic resonance imaging and molecular neuroscience. We are left with a brain disease whose precise cause is unknown, but for which effective treatment is, in most cases, available.

Among the many public figures who have openly acknowledged that they suffer from manic depression are Congresswoman Lynn Rivers, astronaut Buzz Aldrin, musician Charley Pride, humorist Art Buchwald, singer Rosemary Clooney, and a host of actors, among them Ned Beatty, Robert Downey Jr., Patty Duke, Carrie Fisher, Margot Kidder, Kristy McNichol, and Spike Milligan. Also included are many athletes,

such as professional golfers John Daley and Muffin Spencer-Devlin, former tennis player Ilie Nastase, former baseball player Jimmie Piersall,
and professional football players Alonzo Spellman and Dimitrius
Underwood.[2] Even as we write this, Underwood is in the news, identified as having an illness (rather than as being possessed by demons,
which would have been the case in the past):

> The Cowboys were reeling Saturday after learning that police said
> defensive tackle Dimitrius Underwood tried to kill himself Wednesday
> by twice running into traffic on a busy suburban highway in Coral
> Springs, Fla.
>
> Underwood, 23, pleaded with startled motorists that he "wanted to
> go to Jesus," and asked passersby for a gun, according to the police
> report.
>
> Underwood, who describes himself as having "acute bipolar disor-
> der," has a swollen scar at the base of his neck from a jagged steak knife
> that he used in a September 1999 suicide attempt in East Lansing,
> Mich., while a member of the Miami Dolphins.
>
> The deeply religious Underwood, who has one year remaining at
> $275,000 on a two-year contract signed in March, has taken medication
> for his disorder during his nine months with the Cowboys.[3]

How Many People in the United States
Have Manic-Depressive Illness?

Ascertaining the prevalence of manic-depressive illness is not an easy
task. Prevalence figures vary widely, depending on the definition of the
disease being used (as discussed in Chapter 3). In the United States,
two large studies are commonly cited: the Epidemiologic Catchment
Area (ECA) survey, carried out at five sites from 1980 to 1985, and the
National Comorbidity Survey (NCS), which utilized a national sample
from 1990 to 1992.

The ECA study reported that 1.0 percent (10 per 1,000) of all adults
(ages 18 and over) met diagnostic criteria for manic-depressive illness
(bipolar I and II) in a one-year period. A further 1.2 percent (12 per
1,000) of children (ages 9 to 17) met these criteria.[4] However, the ECA

Fact Sheet

- Approximately 1.9 million Americans are found to have manic-depressive illness (bipolar I and II) in any given year. This figure amounts to 6.8 cases per 1,000 people.

- Approximately half of these people are not receiving any treatment for their illness at any given time. Many such individuals end up homeless or in jail.

- Men and women are equally susceptible to manic-depressive illness.

- There appear to be regional differences in the prevalence of manic-depressive illness both in the United States and elsewhere in the world.

- Blacks and whites appear to be equally susceptible, whereas Mexican-Americans may have a lower-than-average prevalence. The prevalence is also lower among the Amish and very low among the traditional Hutterites.

- Manic-depressive illness may have been much less common prior to the nineteenth century.

- Manic-depressive illness may be increasing in prevalence.

- The total annual cost of manic-depressive illness in the United States has been estimated at approximately $45 billion.

study has been widely criticized on methodological grounds for over-diagnosing mania and thus exaggerating the prevalence of manic-depressive illness.[5]

The National Comorbidity Survey, carried out on a sample of adults ages 15 to 54 a decade after the ECA study, originally reported that 1.3 percent (13 per 1,000) of adults had experienced a manic episode in a one-year period.[6] A clinical reappraisal later concluded that the survey questionnaire used in the NCS study "wildly overdiagnoses mania."[7] Subsequently, the lead researchers on the NCS published a revised estimate indicating that 0.75 percent of the U.S. population (7.5 per 1,000) have manic-depressive illness (bipolar I) in any given one-year period.[8]

A more recent study of the prevalence of manic-depressive illness was carried out in Washington state in 1998.[9] Among 294,284 individuals enrolled in the Group Health Cooperative of Puget Sound (an HMO), a total of 1,236 individuals, or 0.42 percent (4.2 per 1,000), were diagnosed with manic-depressive illness (bipolar I and II) in one year. This figure included only those individuals being treated. Since, as noted below, it is known that approximately half of all individuals with manic-depressive illness are untreated at any given time, it seems reasonable to approximately double the 0.42 percent; this produces a prevalence figure of 0.84 percent (8.4 per 1,000), consistent with the revised NCS prevalence rate of approximately 0.75 percent for bipolar I only.

Based on the limited and imperfect data available, it appears that approximately 0.85 percent of adults (8.5 per 1,000) are affected with manic-depressive illness (bipolar I and II) over a one-year period. In 2000, there were an estimated 221.6 million people in the United States ages 15 and over. *Thus there are approximately 1.9 million individuals in the United States who have manic-depressive illness (bipolar I and II) in any given one-year period, yielding a rate of 6.8 cases per 1,000.* An unknown number of children under age 15 also have this disorder, as discussed in Chapter 12.

How Many People Are Being Treated?

The question of how many people with manic-depressive illness are being treated is an important one. The ECA study reported that 61 percent of such individuals (bipolar I and II) were receiving treatment in a one-year period; conversely, 39 percent were not receiving treatment.[10] Approximately half of those receiving treatment were being treated by "specialty mental services" (e.g., psychiatrists or psychologists); the remaining half were being treated by "general medical services" (e.g., internists or family practitioners).[11]

The NCS study reported a lower treatment rate. Among those with narrowly defined manic-depressive illness (bipolar I), only 45 percent were receiving treatment and 55 percent were not receiving treatment in a one-year period.[12] The authors of the NCS study speculated that the ECA study treatment rate was higher because all five ECA sites were in cities or suburbs, where individuals were more likely to be able to access treatment. They also claimed that the NCS study, which sampled more widely, was more representative of the general population. *Nevertheless, it appears that approximately half of all individuals with manic-depressive illness are not receiving treatment at any given time.*

Why are so many individuals not being treated? Some are not receiving treatment because they are currently in remission from their symptoms and have stopped their medication. Others refuse to be treated, often because they lack awareness of their illness (see Chapter 2). Still others are not receiving treatment because they lack health insurance coverage or because treatment facilities are too far from where they are living.

The implications of this finding are profound. As discussed in Chapter 13, many such individuals end up homeless or incarcerated in jails on misdemeanor charges. Others are victimized or, because of their untreated symptoms, commit suicide. A small number of individuals with untreated manic-depressive illness commit violent acts, thereby markedly increasing the stigma against all individuals with mental illness. Still others turn to alcohol or street drugs as a form of self-medication. Indeed, the consequences of the failure to treat individuals with manic-depressive illness are often tragic.

Do Some Groups Have More Than Others?
The Hutterites and the Amish

Men and women are equally susceptible to manic-depressive illness, as confirmed by the ECA and NCS studies as well as by previous research. This equality of gender for manic-depressive illness stands in contrast to the female predominance for episodes of depression alone; the reason for the sex difference is not understood, however.

Somewhat more is known about the geographical distribution of manic-depressive illness in the United States. In the five-site ECA study, which attempted to use the same diagnostic criteria and methodology at each site, the lifetime prevalence of manic-depressive illness (bipolar I) varied from highs of 1.2 percent in New Haven and 1.0 percent in St. Louis to lows of 0.6 percent in Baltimore and Los Angeles and 0.4 percent in Durham. (This last figure represents a three-fold difference.) The ECA findings for bipolar II at the five sites were all between 0.4 and 0.6 percent.[13] Another geographical difference in the distribution of manic-depressive illness in the United States—the urban-rural contrast—will be discussed in Chapter 5.

Ethnicity has also been examined to determine whether some racial groups are more predisposed to manic-depressive illness than others. Past studies suggested that blacks were less likely to be diagnosed with manic-depressive illness, and conversely more likely to be diagnosed with schizophrenia, because of racial bias (either conscious or unconscious) on the part of mental health professionals. But neither the ECA survey nor the NCS found this to be the case; both reported that blacks and whites had approximately the same prevalence of manic-depressive illness.

The ECA study further reported that the lifetime prevalence of manic-depressive illness (bipolar I) for Hispanics is 0.7 percent,[14] just under the lifetime prevalence for whites (0.8 percent), whereas the prevalence for the Mexican-American subset of Hispanics is much lower. The prevalence rates for manic episodes among Mexican-Americans in Los Angeles are less than one-third the six-month and lifetime prevalence rates for whites in that area. The rates for major depressive episodes among Mexican-Americans are lower as well.[15] This finding is especially interesting in light of the fact that the ECA study and others have reported a low prevalence rate of schizophrenia among Mexican-Americans. The reason for these comparatively low prevalence rates is not known.

The Hutterites and the Amish have also become prominent in prevalence studies of manic-depressive illness. The Hutterites are descendants of a Central European Anabaptist sect that migrated to the United States in the 1870s and settled in the northern prairie states and the Canadian prairie provinces. They currently number approximately 40,000, live communally in small, isolated colonies, and raise most of their own food. They are said to be the most inbred population in North America.

In the early 1950s, the prevalence of mental illness among the Hutterites was studied by Joseph Eaton and Robert Weil.[16] They reported a very low prevalence of schizophrenia but a higher-than-average prevalence of old-definition manic-depressive illness (i.e., including cases of depression alone). In the 1990s, when the original case material from the 1950s study was reanalyzed using DSM-III-R criteria, almost all of the Hutterites originally diagnosed as having manic-depressive illness were found to have had depression only.[17] The prevalence of new-definition manic-depressive illness (bipolar disorder) in the 1950s sample was only 0.6 per 1,000, thus confirming that the Hutterites had a very low prevalence of both manic-depressive illness and schizophrenia at that time. A new study of mental illness among the Hutterites was also carried out in the 1990s by Vish Nimgaonkar and his associates at the University of Pittsburgh; among these associates was Joseph Eaton, who had directed the original 1950s study. They confirmed that the traditional Hutterites continue to have a very low prevalence of both manic-depressive illness and schizophrenia. Their prevalence rate for manic-depressive illness and depression with psychosis was only 1.5 per 1,000, less than one-fourth the rate found among non-Hutterites living in the same area.[18]

The Old Order Amish are another Protestant sect with a very conservative lifestyle. Approximately 15,000 Old Order Amish in southeastern Pennsylvania have been intensively studied since 1976 by Janice Egeland and her colleagues. This study became well known for its attempts to identify genes that predispose individuals to or cause manic-depressive illness.

Less well known are the prevalence data from this study. Although these Amish people had been exhaustively studied for more than fifteen years in efforts to identify all individuals with severe psychiatric disorders, as of 1990 the researchers had identified only sixty-three cases of manic-depressive illness (bipolar I and II), six cases of atypical manic-depressive illness, sixteen cases of schizoaffective disorder, and five cases of schizophrenia.[19] Even if all atypical cases of manic-depressive illness are included in the category of manic-depressive illness and all cases of schizoaffective disorder are included in the category of schizo-phrenia, the prevalence of manic-depressive illness is still only 4.6 per 1,000 and the prevalence of schizophrenia only 1.4 per 1,000—both figures being markedly below national prevalence estimates derived from surveys such as the ECA and the NCS. Speculations about the reasons for these low prevalence rates have included genetics, psychosocial factors, and differential exposure to infectious agents. If we could understand why groups such as the Hutterites and the Amish have such a low prevalence of manic-depressive illness, we would be much closer to understanding this disease.

What Is the Prevalence of Manic-Depressive Illness in Other Countries?

Given the shifting diagnostic criteria for manic-depressive illness at different time periods and in different countries, it is not surprising that comparisons of prevalence rates among different countries are suspect. Add to this the known cultural differences in the expression of manic and depressive symptoms, the known differences in the availability of psychiatric services, and other methodological considerations, and one may understandably conclude that cross-national data on manic-depressive illness are of limited value.

The most serious attempt to compare prevalence rates of manic-depressive illness across countries was the Cross-National Collaborative Group organized by Myrna Weissman and her colleagues in 1970. Research groups in ten countries carried out community surveys using similar survey instruments and diagnostic criteria. Twenty-six years later, in 1996, Myrna Weissman et al. reported the lifetime prevalence rates of manic-depressive illness (bipolar I) among adults (ages 18 to 64) in seven of these counties, using an average of the ECA five-site data as the rate for the United States:[20]

New Zealand (Christchurch)	15 per 1,000 adults
United States (ECA's five sites)	9 per 1,000 adults
Canada (Edmonton)	6 per 1,000 adults
Puerto Rico	6 per 1,000 adults

West Germany (Munich)	5 per 1,000 adults
Korea (Seoul and rural areas)	4 per 1,000 adults
Taiwan	
(Taipei, towns, and rural areas)	3 per 1,000 adults

A previous publication by this group had reported a one-year prevalence rate of manic-depressive illness in Italy (Florence) of 17 per 1,000.[21] Despite the researchers' use of common methodology and diagnostic criteria, the lifetime prevalence rates for manic-depressive illness varied from 3 per 1,000 in Taiwan to 15 per 1,000 in New Zealand. (The one-year prevalence rate in Italy was 17 per 1,000.) There was also variability within these studies; an example is the aforementioned three-fold difference found by the five-site ECA study in the United States. Moreover, within the three sites in Taiwan (city, town, and rural), the prevalence rates varied more than two-fold.

There have been reports of other unusual prevalence rates of manic-depressive illness, although the lack of standardized methodology and diagnostic criteria makes comparisons difficult. For example, in Israel, the prevalence of manic-depressive illness appears to be high among Ashkenazic Jews (born in Europe or the Americas) compared to Sephardic Jews (born in Asia or Africa).[22] On the other end of the prevalence spectrum, a community survey of 12,000 adults (ages 18 to 64) carried out in Hong Kong using sophisticated methodology reported a lifetime prevalence for manic-depressive illness of only 1.5 cases per 1,000 adults; the prevalence rate for schizophrenia was 1.8 per 1,000, also very low.[23] Most surveys of manic-depressive illness in other countries have reported lifetime prevalence rates in the median range of those reported by the Cross-National Collaborative Group—namely, 6 to 9 per 1,000.[24]

Has Manic-Depressive Illness Always Existed?

In one sense, we must answer "yes" to this question: The symptoms of mania and depression have always existed, because head trauma, encephalitis, and other medical conditions that can cause mania and depression have always existed. But did this particular clinical *combination*—periods of mania and depression in the same person—exist in the past? And, if so, did the illness occur at approximately the same prevalence rate as it now does in the United States: 6.8 cases per 1,000 people?

The syndrome of depression was clearly described in Mesopotamian tablets in the second millennium B.C., as well as by Hippocrates and Galen in later years. The modern syndrome of mania, however, is more difficult to identify in ancient texts because the term *mania* was previously used much more broadly, roughly equivalent to the use of *insane* or *psychotic* today. And nowhere in the ancient texts is there a clear linking of periods of depression and mania in the same individual.

After the collapse of the Roman Empire in the fifth century, the study of medicine went into decline. For the next ten centuries, most discussions of psychiatric symptoms assumed the validity of the Greek humoral hypothesis, which taught that "melancholia" (depression) was caused by black bile and "mania" (insanity) by yellow bile. There were occasional discussions regarding the relationship of the two conditions but still no description of a case that today would be called manic-depressive illness.

The seventeenth century contains further evidence. For example, Richard Napier, a medical practitioner in England during that century, wrote detailed descriptions of patients with psychiatric symptoms. In recent years, English psychiatrist Michael Shepherd reanalyzed Napier's case records and concluded that a few of the patients probably had manic-depressive illness.[25]

By the end of the eighteenth century, manic depression had clearly emerged. In 1795 essayist Charles Lamb experienced an episode of mania and was hospitalized for six weeks. During this episode he had grandiose delusions that he later described to his former schoolmate and close friend, Samuel Taylor Coleridge: "But mad I was—and many a vagary my imagination played with me, enough to make a volume if all told. . . . For while it lasted I had many many hours of pure happiness. Dream not, Coleridge, of having tasted all the grandeur and wildness of Fancy, till you have gone mad. All now seems to me vapid; comparatively so."[26]

In September 1796, eight months after Charles Lamb had recovered from his insanity, his older sister, Mary, killed their invalid mother with a carving knife as the family prepared to eat dinner in their London home. Mary "had been once before, in her earlier years, deranged," and "for the few days prior to this [murder] the family had observed some symptoms of insanity in her." Charles "was at hand only in time enough to snatch the knife out of her grasp," and Mary was immediately taken to a local madhouse.[27]

Within a few weeks Mary had recovered. Charles petitioned the court to become her guardian and removed her from the madhouse. For the remainder of his life he cared for her despite her continuing, and increasingly prolonged, episodes of violent mania followed by "a succeeding dreadful depression." Between episodes, Mary was a successful author; her work included an 1807 children's book, *Tales Founded on the Plays of Shakespeare,* which she wrote jointly with Charles.

By the early nineteenth century, the clinical pattern of manic-depressive illness had been described in medical textbooks, most prominently in Philippe Pinel's *Treatise on Insanity* (1806) and John Haslam's *Observations on Madness and Melancholy* (1809). Haslam, a physician at Bethlem Hospital, also described patients with postpartum psychosis, childhood-onset psychosis, and syphilis of the brain and gave the first unequivocal account of adolescent-onset schizophrenia.

Individuals with mania, said Haslam, "get but little sleep, . . . are loquacious, and disposed to harangue, and decide positively upon every subject that may be started." Those with melancholia "wear an anxious and gloomy aspect, . . . are little disposed to speak, . . . lie in bed the greatest part of the time, . . . and endeavor by their own hands to terminate an existence which appears to be an afflicting and hateful incumbrance." Haslam argued that mania and melancholia were often found in the same patients, adding that "I would strongly oppose their being considered as opposite diseases." At Bethlem Hospital, "every day [we] see the most furious maniacs suddenly sink into a profound melancholia, and the most depressed and miserable objects become violent and raving."[28]

Haslam cited examples of manic-depressive illness among thirty-seven clinical cases, which he described in detail. One man "had been in the hospital three times before, and had each time been discharged well. His disorder usually recurred every seven or eight years. . . . When admitted he was very talkative, although his natural character was reserved. . . . He ornamented his person and apartment in a very whimsical manner."[29] Haslam also described cases involving rapid cycling (see Chapter 6) and mania that proceeded to exhaustion and death.

By the middle of the nineteenth century, manic-depressive illness was well established as a clinical entity. Consider, for example, French physician Jules Baillarger's 1854 description of *la folie à double forme:* "There exists a special type of insanity characterized by two regular periods, the one of depression and the other of excitement. . . . This type of insanity presents itself in the form of isolated attacks; or, it recurs in an intermittent manner; or, the attacks might follow one another without interruption."[30] Another French physician, Jean-Pierre Falret, published similar accounts of a type of insanity he called *la folie circulaire,* characterized by a "succession of mania and melancholia." It remained for German psychiatrist Emil Kraepelin to provide a definitive clinical description in his 1896 textbook and to baptize the disorder *manicdepressive insanity*—a name that, in a slightly different form, is widely used to this day: "Manic-depressive insanity . . . includes on the one hand the whole domain of so-called periodic and circular insanity, on the other hand simple mania, [and] the greater part of the morbid states termed melancholia."[31]

By Kraepelin's time, the increasing prevalence of insanity in most European countries as well as in Canada and the United States had become a prominent concern. For this reason, the 1880 U.S. census included a special count of all insane persons, both those institutionalized and those living at home. It was, in fact, the most complete enumeration of insane persons ever carried out in the United States, either before or since. The census reported a total of 91,997 insane persons, or 1.83 per 1,000; less than half of them were in psychiatric hospitals. Pliny Earle, a prominent American psychiatrist, concluded that "all the known data . . . very clearly lead to the inference that insanity in the United States is increasing, not merely absolutely in correspondence with the increase of population, but relatively as compared with the number of inhabitants."[32]

In sum, occasional cases of depression and mania can be found in the distant past, but true manic-depressive illness, if it existed at all, appears to have been comparatively rare. From the eighteenth century onward, manic-depressive illness was clearly described, and in the nineteenth century it was recognized as a separate clinical syndrome. The nineteenth century also witnessed an apparent increase in the prevalence of insanity in general, but what part manic-depressive illness played in this increase is not known.

Is Manic-Depressive Illness Increasing?

In the first half of the twentieth century, the prevalence of insanity in general increased rapidly. In the United States, the number of hospitalized insane persons more than doubled from 74,028 to 187,791 between 1890 and 1910, during which time the general population increased just 46 percent. This more than three-fold difference in rates was described as an "extraordinary increase" and "phenomenal accumulation" in the official 1910 U.S. Census.[33] In 1870 there were only two American psychiatric hospitals with more than 1,000 patients; in 1910 there were seventy-five such hospitals.

The number of hospitalized insane persons continued to grow steadily throughout World War I, during the 1920s when immigration to the United States was being severely restricted, and during the Great Depression—apparently unaffected by any of these events. From 1880 to 1940, the rate of hospitalized psychiatric patients in the total population almost tripled, from 1.2 per 1,000 to 3.2 per 1,000. This outcome was partly due to the increasing number of elderly patients with dementia who were being admitted, but the majority of the new patients were diagnosed with schizophrenia or manic-depressive illness.

The high-water mark for hospitalized psychiatric patients in the United States was reached in 1955, when the count was 558,922—a rate of 3.4 per 1,000 in contrast to 0.2 per 1,000 a hundred years earlier.

With the introduction of effective antipsychotic medication and lithium as a mood stabilizer, it became possible to discharge many patients who suffered from schizophrenia and manic-depressive illness, and deinstitutionalization of these patients began. Since that time, there has been virtually no mention of possible increasing insanity. In 1967 the National Institute of Mental Health even stopped collecting its annual hospital census data, which had been the main source of information for assessing psychiatric hospital trends.

Suggestions have been made in recent years, however, that severe psychiatric disorders, including schizophrenia, manic-depressive illness, and severe depression, are on the rise. The high prevalence of these disorders reported by both the Epidemiologic Catchment Area survey, done in the early 1980s, and the National Comorbidity Survey, done in the early 1990s, surprised many people, despite the methodological limitations of both surveys. The ECA study claimed that 3.6 million adults had schizophrenia or manic-depressive illness, a rate of 15.9 cases per 1,000 people. One hundred years earlier, the 1880 census of insane persons, both hospitalized and living in the community, had found 91,997 such individuals, a rate of 1.8 cases per 1,000 people. The 1880 census counted some individuals who would not have been included in 1980 (e.g., those suffering from epilepsy with insanity), and the 1980 study counted some individuals who would not have been included in 1880 (e.g., bipolar II and hypomania with depression). But even allowing for such differences between the two surveys, the nearly nine-fold greater prevalence in 1980 is impressive.

Other recent American studies have also suggested that manic-depressive illness increased in prevalence in the second half of the twentieth century. In 1987, for example, Elliot Gershon et al. reported that "people born in the decades starting approximately in 1940 have a higher lifetime prevalence of affective disorders than people born earlier."[34] By examining the decade of birth of individuals specifically diagnosed with manic-depressive illness, they found that "the total lifetime prevalence appears to be much higher in the cohorts born since 1940." They concluded that "when these data are combined with other reports, an ominous trend may be present, leading to an increase in prevalence of a broad spectrum of familial affective disorders in the coming decades."

In 1990 Kathryn Lasch et al., using the ECA survey data, similarly showed that the prevalence of mania increased among individuals born between 1935 and 1964 compared to those born earlier. They concluded that "the results support the hypothesis that birth cohort changes have occurred in the risk of mania and that the risk was greatest in the post-1935 cohorts."[35]

There are methodological problems with these studies, including the fact that people born more recently are more likely to recall their past psychiatric histories—a situation referred to as *recall bias*. In addition, these studies involve comparatively small numbers of affected individuals. Nonetheless, they provide cause for concern, especially since a study in Switzerland also demonstrated an increase in hospitalizations for mania between 1950 and 1980.[36] Moreover, several studies have demonstrated that the prevalence of depression increased after World War II both in the United States and in other countries.[37]

The possibility that manic-depressive illness may be increasing in prevalence should be considered an open question, since definitive data are lacking. Of major concern, however, is the fact that the National Institute of Mental Health collects virtually no data with which to answer such a question. Manic-depressive illness could be rapidly increasing or decreasing in prevalence, and we would not know it. Even more remarkable is the fact that there appears to be no interest in studying this question. Given the magnitude and expense of the disorder, such official negligence is incomprehensible. (For further discussion of this issue, see Chapter 16.)

What Is the Cost of Manic-Depressive Illness?

The greatest cost of manic-depressive illness is the personal toll it takes on affected individuals and their families. It is also incalculable. How, for example, do you calculate the cost of small daily trade-offs made by family members so as to not irritate an individual with hypomania or depression? How do you calculate the cost of repairing the consequences when a family member with mania depletes the family's savings account, purchases three cars, and publicly announces he is going to marry a prostitute? How do you calculate the cost of what happens to young children when their mother experiences prolonged, severe, untreated episodes of depression, or the cost of a suicide, which is much greater than merely "lost wages"? And how do you calculate the cost to the family when the police must be summoned to take a psychotically manic individual from the home for involuntary hospitalization? All such costs cannot be reduced to dollars; rather, they are costs to one's heart, soul, and memory that continue indefinitely.

However, we live in a democratic society in which resources are not unlimited. Decisions about resource allocation depend partly on costs to society, and it is therefore important to calculate the costs of manic-depressive illness in purely fiscal terms.

The only major study that has attempted to calculate the fiscal costs of manic-depressive illness in the United States was that done by Richard Wyatt and Ioline Henter[38] using 1991 data. They estimated the direct annual costs of the illness at $7.6 billion, including $2.4 billion in hospitalization costs, $3.0 billion in nursing home costs, $0.3 billion in outpatient costs, and $0.7 billion in substance abuse costs. In addition to the direct costs, they estimated that individuals with manic-depressive illness incurred $37.6 billion annually in indirect costs, including $17.6 billion in lost compensation, $7.8 billion in lost wages due to suicide, and $6.2 billion in lost productivity among family members who had to provide care for relatives with manic-depressive illness. Thus, the total costs, both direct and indirect, of manic-depressive illness over one year were said to be more than $45 billion.

Professionals who provide care for individuals with manic depression are aware that many such costs would not be necessary if an adequate treatment system existed. This point was illustrated by a study done between 1991 and 1996 at a state psychiatric hospital in Kentucky.[39] The researchers identified four people with manic-depressive illness who responded very well to medication, but "due to lack of insight, all four had a history of noncompliance and lengthy hospitalizations." The average per-year costs of hospitalization for all four individuals over the six-year period was $98,532, or approximately $24,600 each. Yet if the these same four individuals had been compliant with their medications, the average annual costs for their outpatient treatment would have been only $5,068. The noncompliance of just four individuals essentially cost the state of Kentucky approximately $93,000 per year.

Still another way to calculate the costs of diseases like manic-depressive illness is to look at expenditures by federal, state, and local governments to subsidize the living expenses of affected individuals. The two large programs that provide such subsidies are Supplemental Security Income (SSI) and Old Age, Survivors, and Disability Insurance (OASDI, also known as SSDI), as further discussed in Chapter 11. Although data are available regarding the SSI and SSDI costs for the category of disability labeled "mental disorders other than mental retardation," there is no diagnostic breakdown for specific types of mental disorders. This category primarily comprises individuals with schizophrenia, manic-depressive illness, and severe depression, but a small number of individuals with severe obsessive-compulsive disorder and severe anxiety disorders are also included.

In 1998 the federal costs (not including state SSI supplements) of SSI and SSDI for individuals with mental disorders other than mental retardation totaled $18.4 billion, compared to only $4.6 billion in 1985.[40] This amounts to a fourfold increase over thirteen years—an increase that should alarm federal officials.

In short, manic-depressive illness is an extremely expensive disease. Its costs to individuals and their families are incalculable. Its costs to federal, state, and local governments, which can be calculated, are exceedingly high. Moreover, these costs appear to be increasing rapidly.

2

THE INNER WORLD: MANIA AND DEPRESSION FROM THE INSIDE

Retaining his original sensibility he gives himself up to all the extrava-
gances of maniacal fury, or sinks inexpressibly miserable into the lowest
depths of despondence and melancholy. If the former, he resembles in
ferocity the tyger, and meditates destruction and revenge. If the latter, he
withdraws from society, shuns the plots and inveiglements which he
imagines to surround him, and fancies himself an object of human perse-
cution and treachery, or a victim of divine vengeance and reprobation.

PHILIPPE PINEL,
A Treatise on Insanity (1806)[1]

Understanding the symptoms of manic-depressive illness is essential for
surviving this disease. For those affected, the knowledge that others have
experienced similar symptoms provides not only consolation but also
some perspective on their disease: "If others have experienced what I am
experiencing and have survived, then perhaps I can, too." Reading about
the symptoms of mania, depression, and mixed states as experienced by
other people may also increase one's understanding that the symptoms
are part of a biologically based disease process.

THE SYMPTOMS OF MANIC-DEPRESSIVE ILLNESS

Mania
- Mood: overly happy to euphoric; possible enhancement
  of one's senses; may be irritable; moods may shift
- Thoughts: distractible, difficulty concentrating;
  accelerated thoughts and speech
- Self-esteem: decreased inhibitions; increased sense of
  importance; grandiose delusions; paranoid delusions

- Activity: increased physical activity; decreased need for sleep; spending sprees; increased sexual activity; increased alcohol and drug use; excessive writing; risky and bizarre behaviors

Depression
- Mood: depressed, empty, hopeless, painful; unable to experience joy or pleasure
- Thoughts: impaired thinking, concentration, and memory; preoccupied by death and suicide, which become increasingly attractive
- Self-esteem: preoccupied by shortcomings and sin, feelings of worthlessness and inadequacy, and self-hatred
- Activity: diminished movements; sleep disturbances and exhaustion; stupor

Mixed States
May include any combination of the above, and may last for varying lengths of time. Agitated depression (depression with restlessness and anxiety) and dysphoric mania (mania with depressed mood and/or thoughts) are examples of mixed states.

Awareness of Illness
Approximately one-third of those with manic depression have significant impairment in awareness of their illness. In most cases, the awareness improves when they are treated.

For families and friends, understanding the symptoms of manic-depressive illness will improve their ability to diagnose the disease earlier in the course of the illness and thus help the affected individual seek psychiatric treatment. All of us who work in this field are constantly surprised to observe otherwise intelligent family members and friends sit back for weeks, months, or even years while the person with obvious manic-depressive illness creates chaos. Looking back, these people say, "I didn't realize he was sick" or "I thought those were just her ups and downs." The general public's widespread ignorance about this illness is truly remarkable.

For families and friends, understanding the symptoms of manic-depressive illness may also increase sympathy for the person affected. True sympathy requires that we be able to put ourselves into the other person's place. That is relatively easy to do when a flood or earthquake takes place, because we can imagine ourselves in rising waters or trembling houses. But it is much more difficult for us to imagine ourselves in advanced mania or profound depression.

It should be clearly stated, however, that the disease is not the person. The symptoms of manic-depressive illness are merely symptoms and are distinct from the person's underlying personality. Manic depression is an equal opportunity disease: It may affect those whose underlying personality is shy or outgoing, altruistic or narcissistic, responsible or spoiled, kind or cruel. The symptoms of mania and depression then interdigitate with the person's underlying personality to create a unique medley that differs not only from person to person but even from day to day within a single person as the disease process evolves. It is this interaction of disease symptoms with underlying personality that makes manic-depressive illness so difficult to comprehend for most people.

Mania

The symptoms of mania can be categorized in terms of their effects on mood, thoughts, self-esteem, and activity.

Elevated *mood* is the signature disability of mania; it is what most people think of first when asked to describe manic-depressive illness. Emil Kraepelin, in his classic textbook, noted that "mood is mostly exalted in mania, and in lively excitement it has the peculiar colouring of unrestrained merriment."[2] Psychologist and writer Kay Jamison, as she was becoming manic, described her mood as follows: "The world was filled with pleasure and promises; I felt great. Not just great, I felt *really* great. I felt I could do anything, that no task was too difficult."[3] Jamison also quotes painter Benjamin Hayden, who described his euphoric mood as being "like a man with air balloons under his armpits and ether in his soul."[4]

There are, of course, many degrees of euphoric mood, ranging from Kraepelin's "quietly happy" or "over merry"[5] to the exuberant exalta- tion of full-blown mania. Psychiatrists label the lesser degrees of euphoric mood *hypomania*. Filmmaker Bill Lichtenstein described his hypomania as follows:

> Normal people have this thing called adrenaline that comes on and off
> and it's a switch. . . . And they feel it, and they're pumped up, and that's
> the normal, healthy way. And then it goes away. . . . But for people that
> have the illness and are in that hypomanic state that doesn't go away, it's
> just there. It's there when you go to sleep and you're trying to close your
> eyes and sleep, but your thoughts are still going. You can't even sleep.[6]

Many books speak of hypomania and mania as if they are two distinct states, but of course they are merely two points on a spectrum of eupho- ria; an individual may shift up and down this spectrum from day to day, hour to hour, or even minute to minute.

One of the most important aspects of euphoric mood in mania is the degree to which it includes an enhancement of the senses. John Cus- tance, who suffered from manic-depressive illness, described in *Wis- dom, Madness, and Folly* how "the outer world makes a much more vivid and intense impression on me than usual." He noted that "the ordinary beauties of nature, particularly, I remember, the skies at sunrise and sunset, took on a transcendental loveliness beyond belief." Lights were "deeper, more intense. . . . Coloured objects make a particularly vivid impression" and "faces seem to glow with a sort of inner light." Sounds, Custance noted, were sometimes magnified "almost as though I were in a gallery with supernatural powers of resonance." Smell and taste were also enhanced:

> I have often in manic states eaten ordinary cabbage leaves or new Brus-
> sels sprouts picked straight off the plants with such relish that they
> appeared to me the greatest delicacies—a kind of manna from Heaven.
> Even common grass tastes excellent, while real delicacies like strawber-
> ries or raspberries give ecstatic sensations appropriate to a veritable food
> for the gods.

This enhancement of the senses, combined with euphoria, sometimes produces in the individual "a sense of communion, in the first place with God, and in the second place with all mankind. . . . I feel a mystic sense of unity with all fellow-creatures and the Universe as a whole."[7]

Others, too, have described enhancement of the senses and mystical fusion with God and nature. Actress Margot Kidder said that "when you listen to Beethoven's ninth, you get pleasure; a manic-depressive gets rapture! . . . Sometimes I go soaring up to a place of incredible illumination and wonder. . . . I have mood swings that knock over entire cities."[8] Writer Theodore Roethke claimed that when manic "he knew what it was like to be a tree or a flower or a blade of grass, or even a rabbit."[9] And Kay Jamison observed: "Individual notes from a horn, an oboe, or a cello became exquisitely poignant. I heard each note alone, all notes together, and then each and all with piercing beauty and clarity." Jamison also experienced "a marvelous kind of cosmic relatedness" in which her "sense of enchantment with the laws of the natural world caused me to fizz over."[10]

It is this enhancement of the senses and the sense of spiritual communion that makes manic episodes so attractive to individuals thinking back on their manic experiences. Jamison articulates this lyrically:

> Long after my psychosis cleared, and the medications took hold, it became part of what one remembers forever, surrounded by an almost Proustian melancholy. Long since that extended voyage of my mind and soul, Saturn and its icy rings took on an elegiac beauty, and I don't see Saturn's image now without feeling an acute sadness at its being so far away from me, so unobtainable in so many ways. . . . And I miss Saturn very much.[11]

This is indeed the seduction of mania, as further discussed in Chapter 13.

Although a euphoric mood usually accompanies mania, the person's mood may also be irritable. As described by Kraepelin:

> The patient is dissatisfied, intolerant, fault-finding, especially in intercourse with his immediate surroundings, where he lets himself go; he

becomes pretentious, positive, regardless, impertinent and even rough, when he comes up against opposition to his wishes and inclinations; trifling external occasions may bring about extremely violent outbursts of rage.[12]

Irritability was also a hallmark of manic episodes for baseball player Jimmy Piersall. As he recalled in his autobiography: "I had countless arguments with the umpires. I was thrown out of half a dozen ball games and suspended four different times. I baffled my teammates, infuriated my manager, insulted the umpires, squabbled with opposing ballplayers and delighted the sports writers and fans."[13] Although at first glance it seems illogical, euphoria and irritability may occur simultaneously in the same person, a manifestation of the mixed states to be described below. Or the euphoria and irritability may alternate, in what is called a *labile mood*. When relatives of individuals with manic-depressive illness were asked which symptoms of the illness were the most burdensome to them, labile moods were one of the three most highly ranked.[14]

The second major manifestation of mania is its effects on the person's *thoughts*. Being distractible and unable to concentrate is one symptom. John Haslam, in his 1809 book *Observations on Madness and Melancholy*, noted that "on the approach of mania, they [the patients] first become uneasy, are incapable of confining their attention, and neglect any employment to which they have become accustomed."[15] Kraepelin similarly commented on the "extraordinary distractibility of attention . . . each striking sense-stimulus obtrudes itself on them with a certain force, so that they usually attend to it at once."[16] This distractibility often makes it difficult for the person to remember what he or she is doing. Mathematician Norbert Wiener exhibited this symptom, according to one account: "He hardly seemed to know where he was. He would ask, for example, '[w]hen we met, was I walking to the faculty club or away from it? For in the latter case I've already had my lunch.'"[17]

One especially common effect of manic-depressive illness is that it speeds up a person's thoughts. Indeed, accelerated thoughts and speech are hallmarks of mania. Kraepelin said his patients observed that "thoughts come of themselves, obtrude themselves, impose upon the patients." His patients complained: "I am not master over my thoughts" and "one thought chases the other; they just vanish like that."[18] Jamison similarly noted that "the ideas and feelings are fast and frequent like shooting stars. . . . There was a neuronal pileup on the highways of my brain, and the more I tried to slow down my thinking the more I became aware that I couldn't."[19]

When the person's thoughts become very accelerated, the condition is called a *flight of ideas*. As described by Kraepelin:

> In states of excitement they are not able to follow systematically a definite train of thought, but they continually jump from one series of ideas to a wholly different one and then let this one drop again immediately. Any question directed to them is at first perhaps answered quite correctly, but with that are associated a great many side remarks which have only a very loose connection, or soon none at all, with the original subject.[20]

Kraepelin further cited a study by Isselin showing that normal individuals change the direction of their thinking every five to six seconds, whereas a patient with mania may change the direction in less than two seconds.[21] Jacki Lyden, describing her mother's manic-depressive flight of ideas, summarized it as follows: "Her brain is a bubbling Molotov cocktail. When it explodes, my mother raves."[22]

Accelerated speech follows logically and inevitably from accelerated thoughts. Isselin's study, cited by Kraepelin, reported that "the number of syllables spoken in a minute by a manic patient amounted to 180 to 200, while the normal control produced not more than 122 to 150." Such speech is often a pastiche of "silly joking, puns, violent expressions, quotations, scraps of foreign languages . . . and occasionally violent abuse and swearing or emotional weeping intervenes." [23] Actress Patty Duke recalled that during her manic state "my speech was so fast . . . I was saying everything that was coming over the radio, seemingly at the same time it was being said. . . . I was bursting with ideas and I kept interrupting whatever conversation was going on."[24] Indeed, listening to the speech of a person in extreme mania is an unforgettable experience.

It is important to note that there is often an involuntary aspect to the pressured speech of mania. Custance, in a memoir about his mania, wrote: "My pen can scarcely keep up with my rapid flow of ideas."[25] One of our research subjects stated that he believed his thoughts were normal (though in fact they were quite accelerated), "but my mouth doesn't keep up." And Samuel Beckett in *Not I*, his 1963 play about a woman who is manic, clearly expresses this involuntary aspect:

> . . . lips . . . cheeks . . . jaws . . . tongue . . . never still a second . . . mouth on fire . . . stream of words . . . in her ear . . . practically in her ear . . . not catching the half . . . not the quarter . . . no idea what she's say-ing . . . imagine! . . . no idea what she's saying! . . . and can't stop . . . no stopping it . . . she who but a moment before . . . but a moment! . . . could not make a sound . . . no sound of any kind . . . now can't stop . . . imagine! . . . can't stop the stream . . . and the whole brain begging . . . something begging in the brain . . . begging the mouth to stop . . . pause a moment . . . if only for a moment . . . and no response . . . as if it hadn't heard . . . or couldn't . . . couldn't pause a second . . . like maddened . . . all that together . . . straining to hear . . . piece it together . . . and the brain . . . raving away on its own . . . trying to make sense of it . . . or make it stop.[26]

Increased *self-esteem* is the third major manifestation of mania. In the hypomanic state, according to Custance, "the normal inhibitions disap-pear."[27] Jamison remembers this condition as follows: "Shyness goes, the right words and gestures are suddenly there, the power to captivate oth-ers a felt certainty."[28] In 1809, Haslam also noted that individuals with mania "are divested of all restraint in the declaration of their opinions."[29]

If the mania progresses, the person's increased self-esteem develops into frank grandiosity. As professional golfer Bert Yancey described it:

> I had just left Hawaii on the way to Japan where I was to promote golf clubs and do seminars and make videos for instruction. Somewhere on my way to Japan, there was a six-hour time change. Something began to happen. I began to think that I was not only a professional golfer, but I was some sort of messiah that would rise out of the PGA of America and make the world safe for democracy. I would eliminate all Communism from the Oriental world. It was my job to do that.[30]

It is a short step from grandiosity to outright delusions, often accompanied by auditory hallucinations. Patty Duke recalled:

> I was on the freeway, on my way from a tennis lesson, when I began to hallucinate. This is something I've not talked about before because I was afraid of being judged as someone who was truly crazy. Voices talked to me through my car radio. Bizarre headlines spoke to me personally in the form of a news report. The voice told me someone was taking over the White House, and that I could be of assistance in this matter. I had to get to Washington! I was on a mission. I *did* call people before I left and say, "Have you been listening to the radio? There's been an invasion of the White House. . . . " And of course what could anyone say to that except, "Gee, I think you'd better calm down."[31]

Kraepelin noted that grandiose delusions may vary from those that are "less nonsensical" ("a great artist or author, a baron [or] . . . honorary doctor of all sciences") to those that are patently absurd ("the Christchild, the bride of Christ, Queen of Heaven, Emperor of Russia, Almighty God").[32] Indeed, grandiose delusions often merge with the person's sense of relatedness to nature or to the universe.

The increased self-esteem and sense of importance that accompany mania is another aspect of its seductiveness. Imagine the disillusionment experienced by a person who for weeks has believed she is a queen but is slowly realizing she is merely Jane Doe confined to a psychiatric ward. As Jacki Lyden noted when discussing the effect of this problem on her mother: "Delusion is a pretty thing. It keeps molecules afloat, pulling lives forward to a shining distant point. To the thorny gates of heaven, perhaps, if the delusion is great enough."[33]

Although most maniacal delusions are grandiose, they may also be paranoid in content. Many psychiatric professionals mistakenly assume that the presence of paranoid delusions automatically qualifies the person for a diagnosis of paranoid schizophrenia. As early as 1973, a study of patients with mania reported that 60 percent had grandiose delusions, 42 percent had paranoid delusions, and many had both.[34] It is a relatively short leap, after all, from believing that you are the president of the United States to also believing that foreign agents are after you.

Other researchers, too, have reported that paranoid delusions are commonly found in manic-depressive illness.[35] (The relationship of manic-depressive illness and paranoid disorders are discussed further in Chapter 3.)

Cases of fully developed mania are relatively easy to distinguish from cases of schizophrenia. Although some individuals with schizophrenia may be hyperactive and grandiose, they almost always exhibit a pronounced disorder of thought processes as well. However, early in the course of the illness there may be more overlap between symptoms of mania and schizophrenia, making it difficult to determine the correct diagnosis.

Increased *activity* is the fourth major manifestation of mania. Often, such activity is a direct outgrowth of the person's euphoric mood, accelerated thoughts, and grandiose thinking; although outsiders may find it bizarre, to the person it is completely logical. Prior to the availability of effective medication, the increased activity in mania sometimes proceeds to exhaustion and death.

In the early stages of mania, according to Kraepelin, "increased busyness is the most striking feature. . . . As he is a stranger to fatigue, his activity goes on day and night; work becomes very easy to him."[36] Also striking is the person's decreased need for sleep; Patty Duke noted that "this is not an exaggeration—at least two weeks went by without sleep."[37] In the more advanced stages of mania, the person's repertoire of activity often becomes remarkable. As Kraepelin described it:

> The patient sings, chatters, dances, romps about, does gymnastics, beats time, claps his hands, scolds, threatens, and makes a disturbance, throws everything down on the floor, undresses, decorates himself in a wonderful way, screams and screeches, laughs or cries ungovernably, makes faces, assumes theatrical attitudes, recites with wild passionate gestures.[38]

Certain kinds of activity are especially common during manic episodes. Buying sprees may bankrupt the person and his or her family. We know of one individual, a physician, whose mania became obvious when he purchased three new automobiles in one day. Kay Jamison went on a book-buying spree while visiting London: "I spent several pounds on books having titles or covers that somehow caught my fancy: books on the natural history of the mole, twenty sundry Penguin books because I thought it could be nice if the penguins could form a colony."[39] And Patty Duke saw a dune buggy she liked, so she bought it, even though it had a stick shift that prevented her from driving it. She recalled:

> I don't know why I bought it. Like Mount Everest, it was there. That's the childlike part of the mania. It's whatever you see you want, that's it, it's yours, with no thought, not the slightest anxiety about what it takes to get it or how you're going to pay for it. It really is like believing that the money's all growing on trees.[40]

Increased sexual activity is also common. As Jamison observed, "sensuality is pervasive and the desire to seduce and be seduced irresistible."[41] Sexual thoughts and feelings often become intermingled with the person's euphoria and delusional thinking. John Custance, for example, recalled how in England "religious feelings and emotions eventually combined with sexual impulses to cause me to give away some three hundred pounds, which I could ill afford, to ladies of easy virtue." For Custance, "the sexual symptoms of the manic state seem to be the most powerful and important of all. . . . Sexual activity, instead of being placed, as in our Western Christian civilization, in opposition to religion, becomes associated with it."[42] Sexual escapades by individuals with mania often result in divorce, pregnancy, and venereal disease—including AIDS.

Another common activity among individuals experiencing mania is increased alcohol and drug use, as further discussed in Chapter 13. Russian writer Maxim Gorky described this phenomenon in a short story titled "Foma Gordeyev":

> And another spirit awoke within him—the fierce, lustful spirit of a hungry beast. He was rude to people and profane in his speech; he drank, indulged his coarse instincts, and got others to drink with him, enjoying a very frenzy of excess, as though a volcano were erupting filth inside

him. . . . Dirty, unkempt, his face swollen with drink and lack of sleep, his eyes wild, his voice hoarse and bellowing, he went from one brothel to another, taking no account of the money he squandered.[43]

The man would "go on in this way for weeks at a time," then come home "subdued and depressed."

Excessive writing is yet another common behavior, as noted by Krae-pelin: "Many patients develop a veritable passion for *writing*, cover innumerable sheets with very large fantastic calligraphy, the words crossing one another in all directions."[44] Most of us who provide care for individuals with severe psychiatric disorders have received letters in which the envelopes are covered with various messages, often written with different colored pens, at odd angles, and with messages on top of each other. Mania is the only psychiatric diagnosis that can be deter-mined with 99 percent certainty without even opening one's corre-spondence.

Risky and bizarre behaviors are also common in mania. Poet Robert Lowell, during episodes of mania, "ran about the streets of Blooming-ton, Indiana, crying out against devils and homosexuals and believed he could stop cars and paralyse their forces by merely standing in the mid-dle of the highway with his arms outspread."[45] Patty Duke recalled hav-ing become "absolutely maniacal about safety-deposit boxes": "I kept putting stuff in safety-deposit boxes all over town. I'm talking about a Kleenex in one, an earring in another. But, boy, they thought I was very busy at those banks."[46] And Kraepelin described a patient who dresses in a bizarre manner, "takes a bath with his clothes on, [and] performs military exercises with a broom."[47]

Jimmy Piersall, playing baseball while in a manic state, created a pub-lic spectacle. When at bat, "he stood in the batter's box, dropped his bat and imitated the pitcher as he wound up. . . . He pulled the stunt two or three times each time he came up." During one game, when he was called out on strikes, "I pulled a water pistol out of my pocket, squirted the plate with it and said, 'Now maybe you can see it.'" Then, when he got on base, he "flapped his arms like a chicken and made noises like a pig."[48] The fans, of course, loved this display until it became obvious that Piersall was psychiatrically ill. At that point, he was hospitalized.

Depression

The symptoms of depression can also be categorized in terms of their effects on mood, thoughts, self-esteem, and activity. As noted in Chapter 3, the clinical symptoms of the depressed phase of manic-depressive illness and those of major depression are virtually identical.

Depressed *mood* is, of course, the hallmark of depression. As described by Kraepelin:

> The patient's heart is heavy, nothing can permanently rouse his interest, nothing gives him pleasure. He has no longer any humour or any religious feeling, —he is unsatisfied with himself, has become indifferent to his relatives and to whatever he formerly liked best. Gloomy thoughts arise, his past and even his future appear to him in a uniformly dim light.[49]

The onset of the depressed mood is often subtle. Writer William Styron, whose *Darkness Visible* contains a poignant description of this illness, recalled the early manifestations as follows: "It was not really alarming at first, since the change was subtle, but I did notice that my surroundings took on a different tone at certain times: the shadows of nightfall seemed more somber, my mornings were less buoyant, walks in the woods became less zestful."[50] In the early stages of depression, there are frequently also somatic components, as Styron noted: "I felt a kind of numbness, an enervation, but more particularly an odd fragility—as if my body had actually become frail, hypersensitive and somehow disjointed and clumsy, lacking normal coordination. And soon I was in the throes of a pervasive hypochondria."[51] Martha Manning, in *Undercurrents,* said that the early stages of her depression felt "like my old Ford Escort when the transmission started slipping."[52] Kay Jamison also noted this aspect of depression in *An Unquiet Mind:* "There is nothing good to be said for it [depression] except that it gives you the experience of how it must be to be old, to be old and sick, to be dying."[53]

The next stage of depression slowly abolishes all pleasures in life. As Jamison described it: "From the time I woke up in the morning until the time I went to bed at night, I was unbearably miserable and seemingly incapable of any kind of joy or enthusiasm."[54] Kraepelin invoked Goethe's novel *The Sorrows of Werther,* in which the increasingly depressed Werther says: "'O, when this glorious nature lies before me so rigid, like a little varnished picture, and all the joy of it cannot pump a drop of bliss from my heart up to my brain.'"[55] Manning recalls being "seized with the most piercing sadness—that I have lost that capacity, for playing, for creating, for relishing beauty."[56] In an effort to reverse this condition, she pushed herself to do the pleasurable things she had always wanted to do. However: "The continuous editorial commentary in my brain says, 'This is wonderful. You've always wanted to do this, stupid. Enjoy it.' But the circuits must be blown, because the message never reaches the destination where pleasure is experienced."[57] And writer Percy Knauth, in his autobiographical *A Season in Hell,* likened this aspect of depression to an empty village:

> There was a real world all around me, but I seldom saw it. I walked familiar streets in the lovely Connecticut village where I lived, but I saw no friendly houses and heard no children's cries; there was only the echo of my own footsteps in an empty gloom. Even the sea, beating in restless rhythm against the breakwater, stretching away in ranks of blue or gray or whitecapped waves toward Europe, seemed a desolate wasteland to me, a repository of whitened bones and blasted hopes.[58]

As the mood of depressed persons continues to deepen, they progressively withdraw from all activities and all social relations. One woman described the descent as follows:

> It is like falling into a deep black pit; or being drawn down into a dark vortex led by only a pinpoint of light, which, growing smaller and smaller, finally flickers and goes out. With it goes all feeling. There is no despair for there is no meaning; all is as white as the absence of color, as black as all color. It is a state of nonbeing; there is no cure, there is no illness. I was convinced that I was dead, emotionally dead.[59]

Lewis Wolpert, a scientist who became severely depressed, emphasized the difference between sadness and true depression:

That's the thing I want to make clear about depression: it's got nothing at all to do with life. In the course of life, there is sadness and pain and sorrow, all of which, in their right time and season, are normal—unpleasant, but normal. Depression is in an altogether different zone because it involves a complete absence: absence of affect, absence of feeling, absence of response, absence of interest.[60]

Manning also compared sadness and depression:

In the psychological literature, depression is often seen as a defense against sadness. But I'll take sadness any day. There is no contest. Sadness carries identification. You know where it's been and you know where it's headed. Depression carries no papers. It enters your country unannounced and uninvited. Its origins are unknown, but its destination always dead-ends in you.[61]

Poet Randall Jarrell sounded a similar theme when trying to describe his depression: "It was so queer . . . as if the fairies had stolen me away and left a log in my place."[62]

Poet Anne Sexton suffered from severe depression and committed suicide at age forty-six. Following are some lines from her poem "The Sickness Unto Death."

> God went out of me
> as if the sea dried up like sandpaper,
> as if the sun became a latrine.
> God went out of my fingers.
> They became stone.
> My body became a side of mutton
> and despair roamed the slaughterhouse. . . .
> I did not hear the bird sounds.
> They had left.
> I did not see the speechless clouds,
> I saw only the little white dish of my faith
> breaking in the crater.[63]

In the deepest stages of depression, those who have experienced it
find it difficult to describe. Lewis Wolpert quotes a physician in England who, having experienced a heart attack, the severe pain of renal
colic (kidney stones), and severe depression, said that the depression
was the most painful of the three.[64] Journalist Tracy Thompson in *The
Beast* likened severe depression to feeling "as if my brain were a lump of
protoplasm with tiny circuits embedded in it, and some of the wires
keep shorting out."[65] And writer William Styron said that "the pain is
most closely connected to drowning or suffocation—but even these
images are off the mark."[66] Martha Manning invoked a similar image:
"My world is filled with underwater voices, people, lists of things to do.
They gurgle and dart in and out of my vision and reach. . . . I can't
believe that a person can hurt this bad and still breathe."[67]

Styron also ridiculed the term *depression* itself as being hopelessly
inadequate to convey the gravity of this condition. It is, he said, "a noun
with a bland tonality and lacking any magisterial presence, used indif-
ferently to describe an economic decline or a rut in the ground, a true
wimp of a word for such a major illness."[68] Styron's descriptions of the
depths of depression are unsurpassed:

> I had now reached that phase of the disorder where all sense of hope had
> vanished, along with the idea of a futurity; my brain, in thrall to its out-
> law hormones, had become less an organ of thought than an instrument
> registering, minute by minute, varying degrees of its own suffering.[69]

In addition to mood, depression affects a person's *thoughts*. Indeci-
sion, slowed thinking, poor concentration, and impaired memory are all
common. One of Kraepelin's depressed patients complained: "I cannot
think any longer. I cannot imagine anything any more, cannot reflect any
more, my head is empty." Another commented: "Like a mist, it lies over
everything."[70]

Styron said his mind was "dominated by anarchic disconnections,"[71]
whereas Wolpert recalled: "My thought processes were often confused
and I could think of nothing but my own terrible condition."[72] And as
Thompson put it: "Depression robs the mind of its normal power to
concentrate and analyze. . . . To the sufferer [the effects] are as devas-

tating as if a knitting needle had sliced 20 IQ points from his frontal lobe while he slept."[73]

Increasingly, as depression deepens, the person's normal thoughts are blocked by the shadow of death. For Percy Knauth, this phase began when he came across a dead man in a park:

> If I joined him, might I find my answer, too? This was the night that marked the beginning of my deadly argument with the dark power of suicide. It was a terribly unequal struggle, and there were times when I was more than ready to give in. Death seemed to hold all the cards of logic and persuasion; I had nothing on my side beyond the fact that I was still alive.[74]

Thompson compared it to being "like someone in the last stages of cancer" in which death seems like the ultimate narcotic: "And it was necessity I felt—not hostility, as psychiatric texts would say, or vengeful rage, or a desire for attention. This was done in secret, out of a need to alleviate pain which was as implacable as thirst."[75]

Writer Van Wyck Brooks recalled being "possessed now with a fantasy of suicide that filled my mind as the full moon fills the sky. . . . I could not expel this fantasy that shimmered in my brain and I saw every knife as something with which to cut one's throat and every high building as something to jump from."[76] Styron, as his depression worsened, similarly noted that death "was now a daily presence, blowing over me in cold gusts." The attic rafters, the garage, the kitchen knives all "had but one purpose for me." Death was not a fearful or unpleasant thought; on the contrary:

> These thoughts may seem outlandishly macabre—a strained joke—but they are genuine. They are doubtless especially repugnant to healthy Americans, with their faith in self-improvement. Yet in truth such hideous fantasies, which cause well people to shudder, are to the deeply depressed mind what lascivious daydreams are to persons of robust sexuality.[77]

Russian novelist Leo Tolstoy, who became severely depressed at age 50, also observed the seductive quality of death for those who are depressed: "The force that drew me away from life was stronger, fuller, and concerned with far wider consequences than any mere wish; it was a force like that of my previous attachment to life, only in a contrary direction. The idea of suicide came as naturally to me as formerly that of bettering my life."[78]

English poet and critic Alfred Alvarez likewise noted how suicide totally dominated his thinking as he became increasingly depressed:

> It was the one constant focus of my life, making everything else irrelevant, a diversion. Each sporadic burst of work, each minor success and disappointment, each moment of calm and relaxation, seemed merely a temporary halt on my steady descent through layer after layer of depression, like a lift stopping for a moment on the way down to the basement. At no point was there any question of getting off or of changing the direction of the journey.

He likened such depression to "a kind of spiritual winter, frozen, sterile, unmoving," in which "suicide becomes a natural reaction to an unnatural condition." Alvarez, who made a serious suicide attempt himself, added that what finally makes a man kill himself "is not the firmness of his resolve but the unbearable quality of this anguish which belongs to no one, of this suffering in the absence of the sufferer, of this waiting which is empty because life has stopped and can no longer fill it."[79]

Emily Dickinson captured much the same feeling in her poem "After Great Pain":

> *This is the Hour of Lead—*
> *Remembered, if outlived,*
> *As Freezing persons, recollect the Snow—*
> *First—Chill—then Stupor—then the letting go—*[80]

A third major manifestation of depression is the loss of *self-esteem*. Kraepelin noted that his depressed patients became preoccupied with their shortcomings or sins: "Frequently the self-accusations are connected with harmless occurrences which have often happened long before."[81] Similarly, Knauth recalled: "In long night sessions, I reviewed my life and saw everything that I had done wrong. Not even the most triv-ial detail escaped this deadly scrutiny."[82] Styron described it as follows:

Of the many dreadful manifestations of the disease, both physical and psychological, a sense of self-hatred—or, put less categorically, a failure of self-esteem—is one of the most universally experienced symptoms, and I had suffered more and more from a general feeling of worthless-ness as the malady had progressed.[83]

And Jamison put it this way: "I seemed to myself to be dull, boring, inadequate, thick brained, unlit, unresponsive, chill skinned, bloodless, and sparrow drab."[84]

The fourth major manifestation of depression is diminished *activity*. According to Kraepelin, "all isolated movements, so far as they require volitional impulse, are carried out with more or less reduced speed and without vigor; hands and feet obey no longer. . . . The patients lacks spirit and willpower, like a wheel on a car which simply runs but in itself has no movement or driving power."[85]

Manning recalled: "It is all I can do just to empty the dishwasher and sweep the floor. Then I lie on the couch and stare into space, vacant and deadened."[86] One reason for this diminished activity is exhaustion. Sleep is commonly disturbed in depression, such that the person is unable to get to sleep initially or awakens in the early morning hours and is unable to get back to sleep. Consequently, depressed persons often spend much of their days in bed but get very little sleep. For Styron, this was a major component of his depression: "It had become clear that I would never be granted even a few minutes' relief from my full-time exhaustion."[87] And for Wolpert, "the days were interminable and I wanted to remain curled up in bed all day."[88]

Another reason for diminished activity in depression is that volun-tary activity requires making decisions. Writer Andrew Solomon recalled lying in bed thinking about taking a shower, but as he thought about each step that would be required, "they became like 14 steps as painful and difficult as the Stations of the Cross."[89] Similarly, Dru Ann McCain wrote of lying in bed for hours because to do otherwise seemed unbearably taxing:

Since making one choice inevitably leads to the next, over time the depressive is so sapped of energy they may in effect choose not to even get out of bed because the prospect of all the choices that will follow is too overwhelming. The biochemical process of free will is so slowed down that to the depressive it is like having to wade through hip-deep mud every step you take. You cannot get very far, very fast and eventually lose the strength to take one more step.[90]

Three months after writing this, Ms. McCain committed suicide.

In earlier years, before effective antidepressant medications were available, some cases of depression became so severe that activity ceased altogether. As described by Kraepelin:

In the most severe *stuporous* forms every volitional expression of the patient may be arrested, so that he is only able to lie still and can scarcely open his eyes. He is unable to show his tongue, to take his meals, to give his hand, or even to leave his bed and relieve nature. Although he perhaps understands quite well what he is told to do, yet at most a few weak, trembling attempts at the required movements follow.[91]

These depressive stupors may be so severe that patients "often do not defend themselves from pinpricks."[92] Such cases are almost never seen today, since they can be treated with antidepressant medication or electroconvulsive therapy (ECT).

Mixed States

It is relatively easy to understand that a person may have *either* manic *or* depressive symptoms, because we view these as polar opposites. A person may be *either* happy *or* sad. The reality, however, is more complicated, in that individuals with manic-depressive illness may be *both* manic *and* depressed at the same time. These combinations are called *mixed states*, and they have given rise to much confusion and controversy among psychiatric professionals.

Kraepelin was the first to attempt a systematic categorization of mixed states. Noting that there could be any combination of manic and depressed moods, thoughts, and activity, he labeled the various possible combinations *anxious mania, mania with poverty of thought, inhibited mania, manic stupor, excited depression,* and *depression with flight of ideas.* Kraepelin emphasized that most mixed states were "temporary phenomena in the course of the disease" and were seen "in the transition periods between the two principal forms of the disease"[93]:

> Rather do some morbid symptoms of the earlier period vanish more quickly, others more slowly, and at the same time some or other phenomena of the state which is now developing are already emerging. If one examines more precisely those transition periods, one is astonished at the multiplicity of the states which appear; some of them scarcely seem compatible with the orthodox attacks. Nevertheless I believe that we can understand these states better, if we assume that they proceed from a mixture of different kinds of fundamental disorders of manic-depressive insanity.[94]

The clinical manifestations of mixed states are indeed varied. All combinations of euphoria, irritability, and depression are seen, often with varying levels of anxiety as well. As Kraepelin observed, "Manic patients may transitorily appear not only sad and despairing, but also quiet and inhibited; depressive patients begin to smile, to sing a song, to run about."[95] Such mixed states may kaleidoscopically merge from one to another; alternatively, they may remain static for varying periods of time.

The current official terminology for mixed states is almost as confusing as the mixed states themselves. The American Psychiatric Association's current *Diagnostic and Statistical Manual* (DSM-IV) recognizes mixed states as occurring only when the full diagnostic criteria for a manic episode and a major depression are simultaneously met. This condition, of course, occurs rarely, whereas mixed states with varying degrees of mania and depression are comparatively common.

In recent years, two forms of mixed states have become diagnosed with increasing frequency: *agitated depression* and *dysphoric mania.* Agitated depression is synonymous with Kraepelin's category of "excited depression," in which patients "display, on the one hand,

extraordinary poverty of thought but, on the other hand, great restlessness."[96] Jamison described such a state in *An Unquiet Mind:*

> On occasion, these periods of total despair would be made even worse
> by terrible agitation. My mind would race from subject to subject, but
> instead of being filled with the exuberant and cosmic thoughts that had
> been associated with earlier periods of rapid thinking, it would be
> drenched in awful sounds and images of decay and dying: dead bodies
> on the beach, charred remains of animals, toe-tagged corpses in
> morgues. During these agitated periods I became exceedingly restless,
> angry, and irritable, and the only way I could dilute the agitation was to
> run along the beach or pace back and forth across my room like a polar
> bear at the zoo.[97]

Dysphoric mania, in turn, resembles what Kraepelin called "anxious
mania":

> The patients display a more or less lively restlessness, cannot sit still, do
> not remain in bed, run about, hide in corners, try to escape. They whim-
> per, groan, sigh, scream, wring their hands, tear out their hair, beat their
> head, pluck at themselves and scratch themselves, cling to people, pray,
> kneel, slide about on the floor, beg for mercy, for forgiveness.[98]

In current clinical practice, however, the term *dysphoric mania* is used
rather broadly—in reference to patients whose activity is manic but
whose mood is not euphoric. For example, according to Steven Dilsaver
et al.,[99] "dysphoric mania can also describe patients regarded as primarily irritable and paranoid as opposed to those who are euphoric and
grandiose." Sheila La Polla, a former schoolteacher, described what it
was like to experience dysphoric mania:

> I desperately needed to understand what was happening to me. I was
> supercharged. I experienced intense psychomotor agitation and was
> immersed in a sea of irritability. I experienced an exaggerated startle
> response and jumped at the slightest noise; a slice of toast popping up,
> a phone ring, a gentle voice. I was bombarded with stimuli. . . . I stut-

tered for the first time in my life. It was as if I got stuck on a word . . . a concept . . . while a whole story was whirling in my mind, urgently trying to get out. Hundreds of sentences lined up, scrambling, trapped. My thoughts raced. My speech came faster and faster. I could see the look in people's eyes, but I couldn't slow down.[100]

Much work remains to be done regarding the mixed states of manic-depressive illness. Are there clear mixed-state syndromes, or are the various states merely random clusters of mood, thought, and activity on a three-dimensional continuum? The question can also be posed metaphorically: When moving along the spectrum from one state to another, where does red-orange end and orange-red begin?

Clinically, the mixed states are important because they appear to include more severe forms of manic-depressive illness. As a rule, individuals with mixed states take longer to recover, relapse more quickly, are more resistant to medications, and are more likely to commit suicide. They also tend to receive inferior psychiatric care because mixed symptoms make it more difficult to arrive at a correct diagnosis. Finally, mixed states are said by some researchers to occur more commonly in individuals with rapid-cycling manic-depressive illness, a particularly malignant form of the disease that is further discussed in Chapter 6.

Awareness of Illness

An important but often neglected aspect of the inner world of manic-depressive illness is the degree to which sufferers are aware of their illness. Impaired awareness of illness—or *lack of insight*, as it is commonly called—has been associated with insanity for at least four hundred years. In Thomas Dekker's seventeenth-century play *The Honest Whore*, for example, a character says: "That proves you mad because you know it not."[101] And a nineteenth-century article in the *American Law Review* noted: "Generally, insane people do not regard themselves as insane, and, consequently, can see no reason for their confinement other than the malevolent designs of those who have deprived them of their liberty."[102]

In recent years, many studies have focused on awareness of illness in schizophrenia. At least eight studies have also been carried out on awareness of illness in manic depression.[103] All of these report that some individuals with manic-depressive illness are relatively or completely unaware that they are ill and rationalize their symptoms in a variety of ways. Moreover, studies that have compared patients with schizophrenia and those with manic-depressive illness describe the former as having more impaired awareness of their illness; however, they also point out that patients who are actively manic at the time of testing experience impairment almost as great as that of patients with schizophrenia. And one study that assessed awareness of illness among individuals with bipolar I and those with bipolar II found, surprisingly, that the latter had more impairment that the former.[104] Overall, it appears that when not being treated, at least one-third of individuals with manic-depressive illness have significantly impaired awareness of their illness compared to approximately one-half of individuals with schizophrenia.

Medication improves awareness of illness in the majority of patients with manic depression.[105] The improvement in such cases is usually considerably greater than that which occurs when patients with schizophrenia are treated. Thus, if one compares awareness of illness in individuals with manic-depressive illness and schizophrenia who are not being treated, the difference between the groups will be relatively small whereas if they are being treated, the difference will be much greater. Practically, this means that if treatment is given to people with manic-depressive illness who do not know they are sick, they stand a reasonable chance of being more aware of their illness after treatment. This is not surprising since evidence strongly suggests that impaired awareness of illness is associated with impaired function of the prefrontal and anterior cingulate areas of the brain; as the illness is treated, brain function improves—more so in a person with manic-depressive illness than in a person with schizophrenia.

Impaired awareness of illness in individuals with mania was described by Kraepelin as follows: "In manic states the patients mostly reject with emphasis the suggestion of mental disease. . . . With extraordinary acuteness the patient can find a reason for all his astonishing and nonsensical doings; he is never at a loss for an excuse or explanation."[106]

Impaired awareness of illness in individuals with depression has also been described. Thompson, for example, compared her awareness to that of "a psychic sleepwalker, going through the motions of wakefulness without the self-consciousness that attends normal wakefulness, only vaguely aware that something is wrong."[107]

Clinically, awareness of one's illness is of crucial importance (as further discussed in Chapter 13): People with manic depression who believe that there is nothing wrong will not seek psychiatric care or accept it if it is offered. Awareness of illness is therefore one of the most significant determinants of long-term prognosis—if not *the* most significant. By the same token, impaired awareness of illness is a major problem for family members of individuals with manic-depressive illness. In one study, relatives of individuals with manic depression rated "no insight" as by far the most troublesome symptom in a list of twenty symptoms that such individuals may exhibit.[108]

3

THE OUTER WORLDS:
MANIC-DEPRESSIVE ILLNESS DEFINED

> The slighter shades of this disease [insanity] include eccentricity, low
> spirits, and oftentimes a fatal tendency to immoral habits, notwithstand-
> ing the inculcation of the most correct precepts, and the force of virtuous
> example.
>
> JOHN HASLAM,
> *On Madness and Melancholy* (1809)[1]

Because the boundaries of manic-depressive illness have shifted substantially over the years and are continuing to shift, the current definition should be regarded as merely a temporary way station. Biological
markers will almost certainly be needed to arrive at the ultimate definition. These are currently being developed, but the relative lack of
research is largely responsible for our contemporary confusion.

Official Definitions

The current official definition of manic-depressive illness in the United
States is in the fourth edition of the American Psychiatric Association's
Diagnostic and Statistical Manual of Mental Disorders (DSM-IV), published in 1994.[2] To qualify for a diagnosis of manic-depressive illness
(called *bipolar disorder* in DSM-IV), a person must have had a manic
episode but not necessarily a depressive episode, although most persons so diagnosed have had both. As indicated in the accompanying
box, the diagnosis is then further qualified by (1) whether it was a single episode or is recurrent and (2) by its severity, including whether or

DSM-IV Mood Disorders

296.00	major depressive disorder
296.2	single episode
296.3	recurrent
296.31	mild
296.32	moderate
296.33	severe, without psychotic features
296.34	severe, with psychotic features
296.35	in partial remission
296.36	in full remission
300.4	dysthymic disorder
311.0	depressive disorder NOS (not otherwise specified)
296.00	bipolar disorders
296.0	single manic episode
296.4	recurrent, most recent episode hypomanic or manic
296.5	recurrent, most recent episode depressed
296.6	recurrent, most recent episode mixed
296.7	recurrent, most recent episode unspecified

(The fifth digit is the same as for major depressive disorder, above.)

296.89	bipolar II disorder
301.13	cyclothymic disorder
296.80	bipolar disorder NOS (not otherwise specified)
293.83	mood disorder due to a medical condition, e.g., hypothyroidism
296.90	mood disorder NOS (not otherwise specified)

Mood disorders caused by alcohol or street drugs are coded under substance-abuse disorders (e.g., 291.8, alcohol-induced mood disorder, and 292.84, amphetamine-induced mood disorder).

not the person has had psychotic features such as delusions and hallucinations.

The numbers to the left of each category are codes used for identification only.

DSM-IV Symptoms of Mania

At least three of the following symptoms must be present with the "elevated, expansive, or irritable" mood; if the mood is only irritable, four symptoms must be present.

1. inflated self-esteem or grandiosity

2. decreased need for sleep (e.g., feels rested after only three hours of sleep)

3. more talkative than usual or pressure to keep talking

4. flight of ideas or subjective experience that thoughts are racing

5. distractibility (i.e., attention too easily drawn to unimportant or irrelevant external stimuli)

6. increase in goal-directed activity (at work, at school, or sexually) or psychomotor agitation

7. excessive involvement in pleasurable activities that have a high potential for painful consequences (e.g., engaging in unrestrained buying sprees, sexual indiscretions, or foolish business investments)

The DSM-IV criterion for a manic episode is "a distinct period of abnormally and persistently elevated, expansive, or irritable mood, lasting at least 1 week (or any duration if hospitalization is necessary)." During that period, at least three symptoms of mania must be present, as listed in the accompanying box. The symptoms must be "sufficiently severe to cause marked impairment in occupational functioning or in usual social activities or relationships with others, or to necessitate hospitalization." Furthermore, the symptoms must not be due to a medical condition or substance abuse, both of which have their own official code numbers.

Bipolar II disorder was added in 1994 to label persons who had manic-like episodes that were not as severe. To qualify for this diagnosis, a person must meet the criteria listed under "symptoms of mania." However, the symptoms need not be "sufficiently severe to cause marked impairment"; they must merely involve "an unequivocal change in functioning that is uncharacteristic of the person" and is "observable by others."

If the person has had one or more episodes of depression but no episode of mania, under the current diagnostic system he or she does not qualify for a diagnosis of manic-depressive illness (bipolar disorder). Rather, the person is diagnosed with major depressive disorder, often referred to as unipolar depression. The criterion for this diagnosis is having had at least five symptoms of depression (see accompanying box) for at least two weeks. The symptoms must "cause clinically significant distress or impairment in social, occupational, or other important areas of functioning" and must not be due to a medical condition or substance abuse.

If the person is chronically depressed but does not meet the full criteria for major depressive disorder, he or she may be diagnosed as having a *dysthymic disorder*. These criteria are similar to those used for a major depressive disorder, except that only three symptoms, including the first, must be present. In addition, the symptoms must have been present almost all the time for a period of two years.

Cyclothymic disorder is a DSM-IV category introduced to cover individuals who have "a chronic, fluctuating mood disturbance involving numerous periods of hypomanic symptoms and numerous periods of depressive symptoms." Neither the hypomanic nor depressive symptoms are severe enough to meet criteria for mania or major depression. This pattern must have been present "for at least 2 years," and during that time "any symptom-free intervals last no longer than 2 months." In addition, "although some people may function particularly well during some of the periods of hypomania, overall there must be clinically significant distress or impairment in social, occupational, or other important areas of functioning as a result of the mood disturbance."

Of course, many individuals have symptoms of mania and/or depression but do not fit neatly into one of these official pigeonholes. DSM-IV

DSM-IV Symptoms of Depression

At least five of the following symptoms must be present for at least two weeks, and one of the symptoms must be either symptom 1 or symptom 2.

1. depressed mood most of the day, nearly every day, as indicated by either subjective report (e.g., feels sad or empty) or observation made by others (e.g., appears tearful). Note: In children and adolescents, can be irritable mood.

2. markedly diminished interest or pleasure in all, or almost all, activities most of the day, nearly every day (as indicated by either subjective account or observation made by others)

3. significant weight loss when not dieting or weight gain (e.g., a change of more than 5% of body weight in a month), or decrease or increase in appetite nearly every day. Note: In children, consider failure to make expected weight gains.

4. insomnia or hypersomnia nearly every day

5. psychomotor agitation or retardation nearly every day (observable by others, not merely subjective feelings of restlessness or being slowed down)

6. fatigue or loss of energy nearly every day

7. feelings of worthlessness or excessive or inappropriate guilt (which may be delusional) nearly every day (not merely self-reproach or guilt about being sick)

8. diminished ability to think or concentrate, or indecisiveness, nearly every day (either by subjective account or as observed by others)

9. recurrent thoughts of death (not just fear of dying), recurrent suicidal ideation without a specific plan, or a suicide attempt or a specific plan for committing suicide

covers them by including categories of depressive disorder NOS (not otherwise specified), bipolar disorder NOS, and mood disorder NOS. These categories are essentially diagnostic receptacles into which can be placed all individuals who do not meet the official criteria, including those with minor depression and those with recurrent episodes of hypomania but no episodes of major depression.

Europe and most countries other than the United States use the International Classification of Diseases (ICD), developed by the World Health Organization. The most recent classification is ICD-10, which closely follows the DSM-IV classification. Thus, manic-depressive illness is divided into those cases in which there has been a single manic episode or in which mania is recurrent, and then further subdivided on the basis of whether the most recent episode involved mania, depression, or a mixed state and whether or not psychotic symptoms were present.

It should be obvious that the present official definition of manic-depressive illness (bipolar disorder) is arbitrary. The definition depends upon the presence of a specific cluster of symptoms that achieve a specific level of severity and last for a specific minimum period of time. Consider, however, the ways in which a group of Martian psychiatrists with no knowledge of the official diagnostic criteria might define manic-depressive illness after examining earthlings with this disorder:

Symptom cluster: They might decide that individuals with an elevated mood should be grouped separately from those whose mood is only irritable, or that those with mixed states are different from those with pure mania or pure depressive episodes.

Severity: They might decide that individuals who have symptoms that are below the threshold for official hypomania and/or dysthymia nonetheless have a minor form of the same disease.

Period of time: They might decide that individuals who have exhibited the requisite symptoms but for an insufficient length of time nonetheless qualify for the diagnosis.

Pattern of episodes: They might decide that individuals who have a manic episode at the beginning of their illness are different from those who have a depressive episode at the beginning of their illness.

Intervals between cycles: They might decide that individuals with years between episodes are different from those with weeks between cycles (called rapid cyclers) or even days between cycles (ultra-rapid cyclers).

Course: They might decide that those who recover completely between episodes are different from those who do not completely recover or who slowly become more disabled over time.

Age of onset: They might decide that individuals whose illness begins in childhood or adolescence are different from those whose illness begins in their thirties.

Family history: They might decide that those individuals who have a family history of manic-depressive illness are different from those who do not. (The latter are often referred to as "sporadic" cases).

Associated symptoms: They might decide that those individuals who have associated psychotic symptoms (e.g., delusions or auditory hallucinations) are different from those who do not.

Response to treatment: They might decide that those who respond to lithium, or another drug, are different from those who do not.

In fact, all of these criteria have been proposed for defining manic-depressive illness by one or more researchers. Any or all of them could be important. Our main reason for listing them is to emphasize that the present official definition is relatively arbitrary and subject to change as more research information becomes available.

One other problem must be considered: People with manic depression often display different symptoms during different periods of their illness. For example, they may cycle rapidly for two years and then have no further episode for five years. Or they may have psychotic symptoms (e.g., delusions and auditory hallucinations) early in the course of their illness but no such symptoms later on. Such exceptions further confuse most diagnostic schemes, which assume that individuals continue to display the same symptom patterns over time.

Are Unipolar Depression and Manic-Depressive Illness One Disease or Two?

Among the many questions to be answered before manic-depressive illness can ultimately be defined is whether unipolar depression (i.e., depressive episodes only) and manic-depressive illness (bipolar disorder) are one disease or two. Until 1980, in the United States, it was generally accepted that these were one disease and, therefore, that a person qualified for the diagnosis of manic-depressive illness by having depressive episodes only (without any manic episodes). Studies of manic-depressive illness conducted prior to 1980 reported that only 20 percent of individuals diagnosed with manic-depressive illness had had manic episodes; thus, four out of five individuals diagnosed with manic-depressive illness prior to 1980 had suffered from depression only.[3]

As early as the 1960s, however, a few researchers in Europe and the United States had questioned whether individuals who experienced just depressive episodes had the same disease as those who experienced both depressive and manic episodes. These researchers proposed dividing what was then called manic-depressive illness into two diseases: major depressive disorder (also called unipolar depression) for those who had depressive episodes only, and bipolar disorder for those who had both depressive and manic episodes. This suggestion was incorporated into DSM-III, published in 1980, and has continued to be the official diagnostic policy of American psychiatry. (Note: As mentioned in the Preface, this book uses the term *manic-depressive illness* to refer to the post-1980 entity *bipolar disorder*. Thus, unless otherwise indicated, *manic-depressive illness* refers to individuals who have had a manic episode or some combination of depressive and manic or hypomanic episodes.)

Although most North American and European psychiatrists now assume that unipolar depression and manic-depressive illness (bipolar disorder) are two different diseases, the evidence supporting this dichotomy is mixed. Some researchers have argued that many individuals with recurrent depressive episodes have the same disease as those with recurrent manic, or manic and depressive, episodes. Such researchers have suggested that those with recurrent depressive episodes should be labeled as having "pseudounipolar depression" or "bipolar III."[4] And as recently as 1999, Canadian researcher Russell Joffe and his colleagues published a review arguing that "the current notion of bipolar disorder as a discrete disease entity distinct from unipolar illness may be neither clinically nor theoretically useful and is not wholly supported by the literature."[5]

What does the evidence show? Are unipolar depression and manic-depressive illness one disease or two? The evidence can be examined in terms of epidemiological factors, family history, clinical symptoms, course of the illness, biological aspects, and response to treatment.

Epidemiologically, unipolar depression is much more common than manic-depressive illness; in the United States, the lifetime prevalence for the former is approximately 5 percent and for the latter, approximately 1 percent. More women are affected by unipolar depression, whereas men and women are approximately equally affected by manic-depressive illness. Also of interest is the fact that unipolar depression is associated with an excess of births in March, April, and May, whereas manic-depressive illness is associated with an excess of births in December, January, February, and March.[6]

In terms of family history, according to psychiatric researcher Samuel Barondes, "more than a dozen independent studies of first-degree relatives of hundreds of index cases with unipolar or bipolar disorder . . . show that these two forms of mood disorder generally run in different families."[7] Barondes, however, also acknowledges that there is much overlap: Relatives of individuals with manic-depressive illness develop unipolar depression and vice versa. Thus, depending on the research orientation of the person looking at the data, the proverbial glass supporting a genetic interpretation is either half full or half empty.

The clinical symptoms of unipolar depression and those of the depressed phase of manic-depressive illness are virtually identical. It has been claimed that individuals with unipolar depression are more likely to have decreased sleep, psychomotor agitation, and weight loss, whereas those with depressive episodes in manic-depressive illness are more likely to have increased sleep, psychomotor slowing, and weight gain; however, these differences do not appear to be impressive.

Regarding the course of illness, manic depression is characterized by an earlier average age of onset, shorter intervals between episodes, and thus more episodes within a given time period. In short, as psychiatrist Charles Bowden has observed, manic-depressive episodes "occur more frequently and occupy a greater percentage of a person's chronological life than do episodes of major depression."[8] Conversely, individuals with unipolar depression are more likely to recover completely and to have a more benign, long-term course. It is unclear, however, whether the two disorders are associated with different suicide rates.

Evidence for biological differences between unipolar depression and manic-depressive illness is just now emerging from research conducted by the Stanley Foundation Neuropathology Consortium (discussed further in Chapter 7). Past studies had reported some differences in various neurotransmitters (especially norepinephrine and serotonin), in intracellular calcium, and in various components of the intracellular (second messenger) signaling system, but in general these differences were not impressive. However, the Consortium's more recent research, involving neurochemical and neuropathological measures in postmortem brain tissue, suggests that, in the frontal lobe, the differences between manic-depressive illness and unipolar depression are much greater than the similarities. In fact, the findings for manic-depressive illness more closely approximate those for schizophrenia than those for unipolar depression.[9]

The response to treatment also differentiates the two disorders. Lithium is effective for treating many cases of manic-depressive illness but only some cases of unipolar depression. Antidepressant drugs, on the other hand, are effective in treating most cases of unipolar depression but will induce mania in some individuals with manic-depressive illness. For preventing recurrences of the illness, lithium is said to be equally effective for both disorders.

The majority of evidence thus appears to support the current dichotomy between manic-depressive illness and unipolar depression as separate diseases. A summary is provided in the accompanying box.

Are Unipolar Depression and
Manic-Depressive Illness One Disease or Two?

They are one disease:

- There is much overlap of family history for both diseases.
- The clinical symptoms of unipolar depression and those of the depressed episode of manic-depressive illness are virtually identical.
- Lithium is an effective treatment for preventing recurrences of both disorders.

They are two diseases:

- Unipolar depression is approximately five times more common.
- Unipolar depression is more likely to affect women.
- Unipolar depression is associated with an excess of births in March through May, whereas manic-depressive illness is associated with an excess of births in December through March.
- Relatives of individuals with manic-depressive illness are more likely to have this illness than are relatives of individuals with unipolar depression.
- Manic-depressive illness is characterized by an earlier average age of onset and shorter intervals between episodes, thus occupying more of the person's life course.
- On average, unipolar depression has a more benign long-term course.
- Postmortem neurochemical and neuropathological measures indicate more dissimilarities than similarities.
- Lithium is more effective for treating manic-depressive illness, but antidepressants are more effective for treating unipolar depression.

Where Does Manic-Depressive Illness End and Normal Mood Swings Begin?

Another important question that must be answered before manic-depressive illness can ultimately be defined concerns its outer boundaries. Everyone has good days and bad days, ups and downs. How up do the ups have to be, and how down do the downs have to be, before they qualify as a disease? DSM-IV states that the mood disturbance must be "sufficiently severe to cause marked impairment in occupational functioning or in usual social activities or relationships with others," but such criteria are subjective. "Marked impairment" to one person may appear to be an insignificant problem to another.

The idea of minor degrees of mania or depression is as old as the concept of temperaments in ancient Greece. The belief is that some individuals are born happy, with much energy (hyperthymic); others are born sad, with little energy (dysthymic); and a few cycle between these two temperaments (cyclothymic).

In recent years, interest in temperaments has been revived by psychiatrists such as Hagop Akiskal in San Diego and Athanasio Koukopoulos in Rome. Akiskal, in particular, has argued for official recognition of what he calls "bipolar III disorder," which is recurrent depression alternating with a hyperthymic temperament.[10] Both psychiatrists also talk about "subsyndromal depression" and "minidepressions" as part of a manic-depressive spectrum. Akiskal estimates that "3 to 6 percent of the general population, possibly worldwide, seem to exhibit temperamental instability along hypomanic or cyclothymic lines," adding that if cases of overt manic-depressive illness are included, "we would arrive at an estimate of 5 to 7 percent for the entire spectrum of bipolar disorder."[11] Peter Whybrow similarly estimates that "behaviors characteristic of the bipolar spectrum of temperaments occur in . . . perhaps twelve to fifteen million citizens in America alone."[12]

However, a major problem with studies of the manic-depressive spectrum is that many of them have been funded by the pharmaceutical industry, which has a vested interest in promoting antidepressant drugs for individuals with dysthymia or "subsyndromal depression" and mood stabilizers for individuals with hyperthymic temperaments. In recent years, advertisements for antidepressants and mood stabilizers in medical journals have increasingly implied that these medications are useful for individuals with minor mood changes.

The concept of a manic-depressive spectrum, moreover, has been extended even beyond the realm of moods. For example, some researchers have speculated that borderline personality disorder is a form of rapid-cycling manic-depressive illness, that attention deficit hyperactivity disorder (ADHD) and manic-depressive illness are closely related (see Chapter 12), that some cases of anxiety disorders, panic attacks, and obsessive-compulsive disorder are forms of manic-depressive illness, and that the manic-depressive spectrum may explain many cases of substance abuse. Other researchers are severely critical of such diagnostic hegemony, claiming that the "trend toward expanding the bipolar disorder concept . . . bears ominous parallels to the broadening of 'major depression' so as to risk clinical and scientific meaninglessness."[13]

This debate points up the importance of defining the outer boundaries of manic-depressive illness. Chronic laziness with low energy is not the same as depression. And "workaholism" with high energy is not the same as hypomania. As Patty Duke correctly noted in *A Brilliant Madness:* "Many people are compulsively driven, can get along on just a few hours' sleep, and can function at a very high energy level, but are not mood-disordered and do not come from a family that is."[14]

What Is the Relationship of Manic-Depressive Illness to Schizoaffective Disorder and Schizophrenia?

The third major question that must be resolved before manic-depressive illness can ultimately be defined is the relationship of manic-depressive illness to schizoaffective disorder and schizophrenia. Ever since the early years of the nineteenth century, when Emil Kraepelin categorized individuals with psychoses in terms of those with schizophrenia (*dementia praecox*) and those with manic-depressive illness, there have been ongoing arguments regarding the validity of what has become known as the "Kraepelinian dichotomy."

The problem concerns the fact that many people have a mixture of symptoms said to be characteristic of both schizophrenia and manic-depressive illness: They experience episodes of mania and depression that meet the criteria required by DSM-IV, as outlined above; but they also have prominent disorders of thinking, delusions, and auditory hallucinations, which are characteristic of schizophrenia. When these mixed symptoms occur simultaneously, the diagnosis is manic-depressive illness with psychotic features. However, when the delusions or hallucinations occur "for at least 2 weeks in the absence of prominent mood symptoms," the diagnosis, according to DSM-IV, should be *schizoaffective disorder*, a term introduced in 1952.

The dividing line is, of course, entirely arbitrary. People who have symptoms of mania or depression but do not meet the full criteria required by DSM-IV cannot be diagnosed with schizoaffective disorder. Conversely, people with schizophrenia can also have prominent symptoms of mania or depression; but unless those symptoms meet the full criteria for a manic or depressive episode and are "present for a substantial portion of the total duration of the active and residual periods of the illness," they, too, cannot be diagnosed with schizoaffective disorder.

The reality, well known to clinicians, is that there are many admixtures of symptoms characteristic of schizophrenia and manic-depressive illness. These admixtures form a diagnostic spectrum along which a small number of people in the middle are designated as having schizoaffective disorder. Even more confusing is the fact that many individuals with schizophrenia and manic-depressive illness have different constellations of symptoms at different times during the course of their illnesses. The Kraepelinian dichotomy is thus not truly a dichotomy at all but, rather, a spectrum.

This raises the fundamental question we posed earlier: What is the relationship between schizophrenia and manic-depressive illness? It is a question that, for many decades, has generated more heat than light. As early as 1935, for example, it was known that a single infectious organism—the spirochete that causes syphilis—is capable of causing the symptoms of mania, depression, *and* schizophrenia.[15] Indeed, a definitive answer regarding the relationship between schizophrenia and manic-depressive illness is unlikely to be found until we have more studies of brain structure and function comparing individuals on all points of this diagnostic spectrum.

Are Schizophrenia and Manic-Depressive Illness One Disease or Two?

How are the two alike?

- Both disorders are associated with an excess of affected people who were born in the winter and spring.

- Both disorders are associated with an excess of admissions and readmissions in the summer.

- Both disorders involve an excess of perinatal complications and dermatoglyphic (fingerprint) abnormalities, suggesting an *in utero* origin in some cases.

- Genes on similar chromosomes (e.g., 10, 13, 18, 22) are suspected of being involved in both disorders.

- Both disorders are associated with increased developmental abnormalities in some individuals, including delayed motor and language milestones, educational problems, and neurological signs such as poorer coordination, although these abnormalities are more marked in schizophrenia.

- MRI studies indicate enlarged cerebral ventricles and basal ganglia abnormalities in both disorders, although these are generally more marked in schizophrenia.

- Both conditions frequently involve prominent psychotic features such as delusions and hallucinations.

- Both conditions respond to antipsychotic medication.

How are the two different?

- Manic-depressive illness is more prevalent in upper socioeconomic groups.

- Schizophrenia affects men earlier and more severely, whereas manic-depressive illness affects both sexes equally.

- Genetic factors are more prominent in manic-depressive illness.

- Individuals with manic-depressive illness are found more commonly in families with other members so diagnosed, and those with schizophrenia are found more commonly in families with other members so diagnosed; but exceptions to this rule are also found.

- Geographic, perhaps genetic, clustering of cases is more prominent in manic-depressive illness.

- Schizophrenia produces more marked and more generalized neuropsychological dysfunction, especially on tests of memory and frontal lobe function.

- Many people with manic-depressive illness have achieved fame for their creativity in the arts.

- MRI studies indicate that schizophrenia is associated with decreases in brain volume and medial temporal lobe structures (e.g., hippocampus), and that manic-depressive illness is associated with increases in white-matter hyperintensities.

- Although many neurotransmitters are believed to be involved in both disorders, manic-depressive illness is thought to involve serotonin more prominently.

- Clinically, manic-depressive illness is much more likely to have a relapsing and remitting course with periods of normality.

- Affective (mood) symptoms (e.g., depression, mania) are much more common in manic-depressive illness.

- Manic-depressive illness can successfully be treated by mood stabilizers (e.g., lithium) and, often, no other medication, but the same is usually not true for schizophrenia.

- ECT is more effective for manic-depressive illness.
- Calcium channel blockers (e.g., verapamil) sometimes improve the symptoms of manic-depressive illness but may worsen the symptoms of schizophrenia.

On April 17, 1999, in Santa Fe, New Mexico, a presentation of current research findings on this question was given at a one-day symposium in conjunction with the International Congress on Schizophrenia Research.[16] The findings are summarized in the accompanying box. Briefly, schizophrenia and manic-depressive illness appear to share many similarities in the *antecedents* of the disorders, such as susceptibility genes on similar chromosomes and an excess of winter-spring births. However, schizophrenia and manic-depressive illness do not share many aspects of the *expression* of these disorders, such as clinical manifestations, course, and neuropsychological and neuroimaging findings.

As this chapter makes clear, defining manic-depressive illness with any level of certainty is impossible at present. But the situation should improve in the near future with increased research on this disorder, especially with more studies directly comparing individuals with manic-depressive illness and individuals with schizophrenia and other disorders. For the moment, we should assume that manic-depressive illness includes individuals with manic or hypomanic episodes, combined with episodes of major depression.

The ultimate definition of this disease entity may conceivably encompass almost any possible combination of the categories discussed. Indeed, given the paucity of present research knowledge, we should not prematurely come to closure on any one definition.

4

CONDITIONS SOMETIMES CONFUSED WITH MANIC-DEPRESSIVE ILLNESS

Demonic frenzy, moping melancholy, and moon-struck madness.

JOHN MILTON,
Paradise Lost (1667)[1]

In 1978, an important paper titled "Secondary Mania" was published in the *Archives of General Psychiatry*. Its first author was Charles Krauthammer, then a young psychiatrist and now a prominent columnist and news analyst. By "secondary mania" the authors meant mania that could be caused by drugs, toxins, infections, epilepsy, or other conditions. This may look clinically identical to primary mania, but there's one difference: In secondary mania the cause of the mania is known, whereas in primary mania it is not.

The concept of secondary mania is widely used by clinicians, even though it is not included in the official DSM-IV classification system. This chapter reviews some known causes of secondary mania, including street drugs; prescription, over-the-counter, and herbal medications; infections; head injuries; other brain disorders; and other illnesses. It also briefly reviews manic-like behavior that occurs in other countries as an aspect of culture-bound syndromes.

Mania Caused by Street Drugs

People with manic depression frequently engage in alcohol and drug abuse. This unfortunate situation makes the illness and its treatment unpredictable. Many street drugs not only worsen the symptoms of

---

Causes of Secondary Mania

- street drugs, especially cocaine and amphetamines
- prescription, over-the-counter, and herbal medications
- infections
- head injuries
- other brain disorders (e.g., strokes, tumors, epilepsy, multiple sclerosis, Huntington's disease)
- other illnesses (e.g., hyperthyroidism, vitamin B–12 deficiency, kidney dialysis)

---

mania and depression but can also produce manic or depressed states in people who are not predisposed to having manic-depressive illness. Thus, a history of exposure to these drugs is an important factor to consider when sorting through the differential diagnosis of "secondary mania." Further complicating matters is the fact that the street drug scene is an ever-changing one. Many drugs of abuse can be synthesized quite easily; they vary dramatically in purity and potency, sometimes containing impurities that are in themselves able to produce psychiatric symptoms. In addition, medical tests for many street drugs are often not widely available.

Cocaine and Stimulants: Stimulants or "uppers"—cocaine, amphetamines, methylphenidate, and MDMA ("Ecstasy")—are the drugs most likely to produce effects reminiscent of mania. Cocaine may be used intranasally as a powder, smoked in a pipe, or injected intravenously. The other stimulants are usually taken orally.

Stimulants produce a sensation of euphoria, increased energy, sleeplessness, and feelings of power, grandiosity, or superiority. In some individuals, these symptoms can be severe enough to resemble mania. Stimulants can also produce hallucinations, paranoia, and other delusions. In contrast to the typical auditory hallucinations seen in mania, visual and tactile hallucinations are commonly associated with stimulant intoxication. A manic state brought on by stimulants is likely to have other physiological effects as well, such as dilated pupils, increased blood pressure, and increased heart rate; moreover, these drugs can be detected in the urine and the blood.

Stimulant intoxication can sometimes paradoxically induce a state of sadness, crying, and anxiety. This state can be confused with typical depression but is usually more acute and associated with noticeable agitation and changes in vital signs. People who abuse stimulants heavily may experience a severe "crash" during withdrawal from stimulants that is indistinguishable from major depression.

The long-term effects of stimulant abuse on mood and cognitive performance have been much debated in the medical literature. Some researchers believe that heavy users of stimulants can develop a chronic state of mood instability even after they have stopped taking the drugs. There is increasing evidence from animal experiments that "Ecstasy" can permanently damage parts of the brain that synthesize serotonin, leading to chronic problems with mood, anxiety, and memory.

Hallucinogens: The classic forms of hallucinogens are LSD (lysergic acid diethylamide) and various types of mushrooms (e.g., peyote and psilocybin). These drugs commonly cause visual hallucinations but may also induce auditory, tactile, olfactory, or gustatory hallucinations. In addition, they may bring about *synesthesia*, in which one sensory modality is mixed with another. For example, music may be perceived as colorful or as having a particular smell. Hallucinogens may also produce intense anxiety, panic, agitation, and catatonic states. Chronic users of these drugs may experience "flashbacks," brief hallucinatory experiences reminiscent of acute intoxication that occur days or months after use of the drug. Flashbacks, though rare, can be mistaken by patients and physicians for a primary psychosis.

Phencyclidine: Phencyclidine (PCP) is sometimes considered a hallucinogen, but its use has a number of distinct features that distinguish it from those drugs. PCP is a cheap and easily synthesized liquid that can be added to marijuana or tobacco cigarettes. PCP intoxication can look like mania; patients may be talkative, hyperactive, aggressive, even violent. Because PCP is an anesthetic, patients often do not notice the physical pain associated with their actions. One patient who had ingested PCP became angry with his father and decided to try to destroy the father's car with his bare hands. He was able to keep punching despite broken bones and lacerations. PCP can also cause hallucinations. Most people who use PCP become "spaced out" and appear mute, inactive, or even catatonic. PCP does not produce dilated pupils but does produce unsteadiness of gait and an involuntary jerking of the eyes known as nystagmus.

Inhalants: Inhalation of airplane glue and other hydrocarbons such as gasoline can produce irritability, euphoria, paranoia, and hallucinations. More commonly these substances cause somnolence and sedation. Since there is no good laboratory test for the presence of these drugs, the diagnosis can be difficult.

Alcohol Intoxication: Some patients who are intoxicated with alcohol can become talkative, uninhibited, and overly active, but these behaviors are rarely confused with the symptoms of primary mania. Heavy drinkers who suddenly stop drinking can develop delirium tremens. This state often includes agitation, sleeplessness, and hallucinations, but patients are also disoriented and can have severe memory and attention problems. Some heavy drinkers may continue to experience hallucinations even after acute alcohol withdrawal has ceased. This condition is known as alcohol hallucinosis, and it can become chronic. Alcohol-related symptoms are usually quite easy to differentiate from primary mania, in that there is evidence for damage to other organs from alcohol (especially the liver) and the vital signs are abnormal during withdrawal.

Opiates: People who abuse narcotic pain killers and illegal opiates (such as heroin) frequently develop depression. Manic states during withdrawal or intoxication are uncommon, but patients may be irritable, anxious, and restless.

Marijuana: Although marijuana intoxication does not usually produce a classic manic state or psychosis and is not often confused with primary mania, it can cause anxiety, restlessness, and paranoid thoughts. It can also worsen preexisting psychosis. Chronic heavy users may develop a lethargic state reminiscent of major depression.

Benzodiazepines and Barbiturates: Patients who are dependent on central nervous system depressants such as benzodiazepines or barbiturates may develop agitation, anxiety, and hallucinations when withdrawing from these drugs. They do not experience euphoric mood states but can be irritable and depressed. These patients will exhibit abnormal vital signs similar to those seen in alcohol withdrawal.

Mania Caused by Prescription, Over-the-Counter, and Herbal Medications

The average American uses large numbers of medications, both prescription drugs and over-the-counter substances. The media is saturated with advertisements for medications, and the bathroom cabinets in many American homes look like mini–commercial pharmacies.

Some medications cause severe depression or mania as side effects. Reserpine, widely used in the past for high blood pressure, is an example of a medication that occasionally produces severe depression. Many people are aware that if they become depressed after starting a new medication, they should stop taking it. Fewer people are aware that some medications can also cause mania, leading to a mistaken diagnosis of manic-depressive illness.

The following is an example of mania caused by a prescription medication:

> Mellanie was a successful 41-year-old lawyer in a prestigious D.C. firm. Over a period of two weeks her husband noticed that she was speaking increasingly rapidly, undertaking several large new projects, and sleeping only three to four hours a night. When asked about this, she denied anything was wrong and said she had never felt better. Mellanie's family members suspected that she was becoming manic and were not surprised, since Mellanie's mother was known to have had episodes of severe depression and one sister was said to be "not quite right." Mellanie agreed to see the family physician, who diagnosed manic-depressive illness and referred her to a psychiatrist. The psychiatrist's first question was: Has she taken any new medications recently? In fact, Mellanie had been started on clarithromycin (Biaxin) for an infection one week prior to the onset of her symptoms. When the clarithromycin was stopped, the symptoms of mania immediately went away.

Mania can also be induced by over-the-counter and herbal medications, as the following cases illustrate:

A 62-year-old woman was admitted to a hospital with symptoms of mania. She had chronic bronchitis and had been using two over-the-counter medications (Tedral and Primatene), both of which contained theophylline, for many months. Five days after withdrawal of the theophylline and treatment with haloperidol, she was well.[2]

A 39-year-old construction worker ingested large amounts of Herbalife, a mixture of herbs and seeds, in an attempt to lose weight. Three days later he became classically manic, spending lavishly, talking rapidly and incoherently, not sleeping or eating, and experiencing delusions and hallucinations. He was arrested when he ran his car into a police car and was then hospitalized and diagnosed with manic-depressive illness. Within one day following cessation of Herbalife, he had completely recovered and had no recurrence.[3]

Histories like these are more common than most people realize. *In fact, whenever a person develops severe depression or mania for the first time, a newly started medication should always be suspected as the possible cause.* The list of medications that can cause depression is very long. The list of those that can cause mania is somewhat shorter but still impressive. Many of these adverse reactions are comparatively rare, but if you are the one person in 10,000 who gets the adverse reaction, it will not seem rare to you.

Be Suspicious

Whenever a person develops symptoms of mania or depression for the first time, always ask whether he or she has recently started taking any new medication. Many medications can cause such adverse effects. The treatment in these cases is to stop the new medication.

Medications That May Cause Mania

The following medications have been reported to occasionally cause extreme euphoria or mania. The omission of a medication from this list does not mean that it cannot cause these reactions; most adverse reactions are not reported.

amitriptyline (Elavil, Endep)
anabolic steroids
anticonvulsants
antidepressants (tricyclics)
baclofen (Lioresal)
barbiturates
benzodiazapines
bromide
bromocriptine (Parlodel, Ergoset)
bupropion (Wellbutrin, Zyban)
buspirone (BuSpar)
captopril (Capoten)
chloroquine (Aralen)
cimetidine (Tagamet)
clarithromycin (Biaxin)
corticosteroids
corticotropin (Acthar)
cortisone (Cortone)
ACTH
dapsone
deet (Off)
digitalis glycosides
disulfiram (Antabuse)
fenfluramine (Pondimin)
fluoxetine (Prozac)
fluvoxamine (Luvox)
histamine H$_2$-receptor antagonists

isoniazid (Nydrazid, Rifater)
levodopa and carbidopa (Sinemet)
levodopa (Dopar)
methandrostenolone (Dianabol)
methylphenidate (Ritalin, Concerta, Methylin)
methyltestosterone (Android, Oreton M, Testred)
metoclopramide (Reglan)
monoamine oxidase inhibitors
naproxen (Anaprox, Naprosyn, Aleve, Naprelan)
nortriptyline (Aventyl, Pamelor)
oxandrolone (Anavar, Oxandrin)
oxymetholone (Anadrol)
paroxetine (Paxil)
phenmetrazine
phencyclidine
phenelzine (Nardil)
phentermine (Fastin, Adipex P)
phenylpropanolamine (Dexatrim)
procainamide (Pronestyl, Procan SR, Procanbid)
procarbazine (Matulane)

procyclidine (Kemadrin)	sulfonamides
propafenone (Rythmol)	theophylline (Respbid, Theo-
pseudoephedrine (in Sudafed,	Dur, Theobid Dura, and
Robitussin, and others)	others)
selective serotonin reuptake	thyroid preparations
inhibitors (SSRI antidepres-	tranylcypromine (Parnate)
sants	trazodone (Desyrel)
selegiline (Eldepryl, Carbex)	

Reporting Adverse Drug Reactions to the FDA

If you experience, or become aware of, a medication that causes mania or any other serious adverse drug reaction, you should immediately report it to the Food and Drug Administration (FDA). This can be done through the Internet: Simply go to the FDA MedWatch website at *www.fda.gov/medwatch* and follow the instructions for submitting a report by consumers. Also ask your physician to submit a report. To obtain a reporting form to take to your physician, print it off the website above or call MedWatch at 1-800-332-1088.

Mania Caused by Infections

It is widely known that systemic infections can cause depression as well as other changes in brain function. Influenza is probably the best example. A study of Israeli teenagers with documented cases of influenza within the preceding six months reported that they "had more difficulty remembering, concentrating and making decisions" and "almost all had clinical signs of depression such as poor appetite, lack of interest in what was going on around them, and continual thoughts of death and dying."[4] Depression is also a prominent symptom in mononucleosis, a systemic infection caused by the Epstein-Barr virus, a member of the herpes family. In most such cases, the depression is recognized as being part of the systemic infection and is not confused with the depressed phase of manic-depressive illness.

Less acknowledged is the fact that systemic infections can also cause mania through their effects on the brain. In such cases, the mania is sometimes mistaken for manic-depressive illness. How often this occurs is not known, but it is clear that a wide variety of infectious agents are capable of inducing mania.

Influenza can also cause a syndrome resembling schizophrenia, as was well documented following the 1918–1919 influenza pandemic. Occasional such cases continue to be reported:

> A 21-year-old woman developed influenza, documented by laboratory studies. Two weeks after the onset she became depressed, then began having symptoms of mania. These included "pressure of speech, flight of ideas, distractibility, and over-responsiveness to trivial environmental cues" as well as grandiose delusions. Over a period of six months she slowly returned to normal.[5]

Mania can also be caused by the virus that causes mononucleosis. One 22-year-old college student developed excitement, pressure of speech, flight of ideas, and auditory hallucinations a week after the onset of mononucleosis. Studies of her cerebrospinal fluid were consistent with a viral infection in her brain.[6] The herpes simplex virus, which usually causes just lesions of the lips, can also result in infections of the brain with symptoms of mania:

> A 41-year-old factory worker developed a severe headache, stiff neck, and herpes lesions on his lip. Shortly thereafter "a massive depressive mood change was obvious" and this "severe depression lasted for about 3 weeks." He then suddenly switched to mania with elevated mood and grandiosity. "His general activity was also greatly increased and he rushed about the village, meddling in the affairs of others; all the while he talked excessively and his ideas were hard to follow since they slipped from one theme to another in rapid fashion." When admitted to the hospital "he proceeded to dance around the room . . . [and] insisted that he was now the chief of the clinic . . . [and] an international star." Serial

spinal fluid examinations documented that he had herpes simplex virus encephalitis. He was treated with antipsychotic medication and completely recovered in six months.[7]

Several other infectious agents have been suspected of causing mania, although laboratory evidence has not always definitively proved causality. These agents include other viruses such as St. Louis encephalitis,[8] coxsackie virus,[9] human immunodeficiency virus (HIV),[10] mycoplasma infections,[11] fungi such as cryptococcosis,[12] spirochetes such as that causing syphilis,[13] and bacteria such as that causing Q fever.[14]

Two important questions about the relationship between infections and the symptoms of depression and mania remain unresolved. First, how much evidence is necessary to establish cause and effect? When, for example, the onset of manic-depressive illness follows the onset of infectious mononucleosis six weeks later, one must determine whether the mononucleosis caused a manic-depressive illness that otherwise would not have occurred, whether it precipitated a manic-depressive illness that would have occurred anyway, or whether the two illnesses are unrelated and merely coincidental. The second question is how frequently infectious agents cause depression and/or mania in cases where no accompanying neurological symptoms are present. The infectious disease theory of manic-depressive illness (discussed in Chapter 7) maintains that infectious agents may cause many cases of this illness, but proof has not been obtained. This possibility is all the more intriguing when one realizes that many antipsychotic, antidepressant, and mood stabilizer medications also have anti-infectious properties.

Mania Caused by Head Injuries

Occasional cases of head injury causing severe depression or mania have been reported in the psychiatric literature for almost one hundred years. In cases of severe depression, it is especially difficult to differentiate the physical effects of the head injury from the person's psychological reaction to it. Indeed, for both depression and mania, it is difficult to assess whether the head injury was directly causal, how much time could have elapsed between the injury and the psychiatric symptoms, and whether the head injury merely precipitated a reaction that was about to occur even if the injury had not taken place.

Sashi Shukla and his colleagues[15] studied twenty cases of mania following head injuries, almost all of which were associated with motor vehicle accidents or falls. In thirteen of the twenty cases, the trauma was severe, in four cases moderate, and in three cases mild. In thirteen of the twenty cases, the interval between the injury and the onset of mania was two years or less, and in three cases it was between eight and twelve years. Irritability was a prominent component of the mania in these patients, several of whom had been assaultive. A 1992 review of psychiatric sequelae of head injuries further noted that "mania is reported in association with the full range of injury severity including some cases of very mild trauma with brief or no loss of consciousness. . . . The full spectrum of manic syndromes can be seen [including] rapid cycling variants."[16]

There is general agreement that cases of mania due to head injuries exist; there is much less agreement regarding how frequently they occur. In a study of head injuries sustained by 3,552 Finnish soldiers in World War II, 44 developed symptoms of severe depression but "only 3 were typically manic-depressive."[17] On the other hand, a study of 66 consecutive admissions with head injuries to a trauma unit reported that 6 patients (9 percent) developed symptoms of mania within the following year.[18] The average duration of the manic episodes was two months. Another study of 144 individuals with head injuries noted that 10 (7 percent) had subsequent periods of euphoria.[19]

Rather than asking how often people with head injuries develop mania, one can ask how often people with manic-depressive illness have a history of head injuries. A study of 122 individuals with manic depression reported that 5 percent had a history of head trauma in childhood; by contrast, 11 percent of individuals with schizophrenia and fewer than 1 percent of normal controls had such a history.[20] A recent study using the national case register in Denmark found that individuals with manic-depressive illness, compared to normal controls, had three times more head injuries in the year preceding the onset of their illness and two times more head injuries in the first through fifth years preceding their illness; however, their head injuries were no more numerous than those of the controls during the period greater than five years prior to the onset of their illness.[21]

Thus it appears that head injuries can at least occasionally either cause or precipitate episodes of mania and the full syndrome of manic-depressive illness. How often this occurs remains to be determined.

Mania Associated with Other Brain Disorders

Symptoms of depression or mania occasionally develop in individuals with other brain disorders, including strokes, brain tumors, epilepsy, multiple sclerosis, and Huntington's disease. In most cases, the primary disease is obvious, although occasionally the psychiatric symptoms become apparent before the primary disease does. As with head injuries, it is very difficult to ascertain how many of the person's depressive or manic symptoms are caused by the brain disorder and how many are psychological reactions to the brain disorder.

Although depression is common following strokes, mania was found in only 3 of 700 patients in a study of psychiatric sequelae.[22] Mania may also follow bleeding in the brain caused by a subarachnoid hemorrhage:

> A 59-year-old man with no previous psychiatric problems developed mania two months after treatment for a subdural hematoma caused by a fall. He was elated, irritable, had pressured speech and flights of ideas, and exhibited reckless behavior and buying sprees. He was successfully treated with lithium but had two subsequent manic episodes over the following two years after discontinuing his medication.[23]

Mania also occasionally occurs in association with brain tumors, either those found initially in the brain or those that have spread from elsewhere in the body (metastases):

> A 40-year-old woman was hospitalized for mania and successfully treated with haloperidol. When she relapsed a brain scan was done and revealed a brain tumor on the right side, which was then surgically removed.[24]

A 45-year-old man was hospitalized for symptoms of mania and neurological problems. He was found to have a metastatic right brain tumor, which was unsuccessfully treated with surgery and radiation. His mania, however, responded well to lithium therapy.[25]

Mania in association with epilepsy is a relatively rare occurrence. According to a review by Janice Stevens, it occurs in approximately 1 percent of cases of partial complex epilepsy and even less frequently in grand mal epilepsy.[26] Of particular interest is the 1969 study in which Pierre Flor-Henry showed that "epilepsy of the non-dominant temporal lobe is associated with manic-depressive [symptoms]; of the dominant temporal lobe with schizophrenic disturbances."[27] We will return to the issue of brain localization below.

Multiple sclerosis is often associated with severe depression, both as part of the illness and as a reaction to it. A 1987 study of 100 patients with multiple sclerosis reported that 13 had also had episodes of hypomania and therefore met diagnostic criteria for manic-depressive illness.[28] Another study of 2,720 admissions to psychiatric hospitals identified 10 patients with concurrent multiple sclerosis; in 4 of the cases, the patient had initially been hospitalized with symptoms of mania or hypomania before the multiple sclerosis was diagnosed.[29]

Huntington's disease is another disorder of the brain commonly accompanied by depression and occasionally by mania or hypomania. One study of 88 patients with Huntington's disease reported that 28 had a history of major depression and another 8 had a history of mania or hypomania and met diagnostic criteria for manic-depressive illness.[30]

Mania Associated with Other Illnesses

In addition to brain disorders, mania or hypomania may accompany a variety of other disorders of the body. In most cases, the diagnosis will be obvious because of the patient's delirium and the mania merely an incidental finding. Occasionally, however, mania will be the presenting symptom and may initially confuse the clinical picture.

Three systemic disorders that may be accompanied by mania are hyperthyroidism, vitamin B-12 deficiency, and kidney dialysis. Examples of such cases follow:

A 43-year-old woman presented with classic symptoms of mania as well as with an enlarged thyroid, eye changes, weight loss, and other symptoms of hyperthyroidism. Laboratory studies confirmed the diagnosis and her mania resolved as her hyperthyroidism was successfully treated.[31]

An 81-year-old man presented with hyperactivity, decreased sleep, agitation, grandiosity, and hypersexuality. Vitamin B-12 deficiency was diagnosed. Administration of vitamin B-12 led to a rapid resolution of the mania.[32]

A 35-year-old woman developed symptoms of hypomania after being on kidney dialysis for 13 months. Her mania was successfully treated with antipsychotic medication.[33]

Other systemic conditions that may cause secondary hypomania or mania include pellagra, uremia, and the postoperative state.

What Does Secondary Mania Tell Us About Brain Localization?

The most interesting aspect of secondary mania, from the standpoint of studying manic-depressive illness, is what it may tell us about brain localization in this disease. As noted above, in 1969 Flor-Henry reported an association between temporal lobe epilepsy occurring on the right side of the brain and the presence of symptoms of mania. Since that time, there has been additional evidence linking mania to the non-dominant hemisphere (right brain in right-handers and in 90 percent of left-handers).

Much of the work on this question was carried out by Robert Robinson and his colleagues at Johns Hopkins University School of Medicine. In 1987 they published a study of eleven patients with mania secondary to a brain lesion. In seven of the patients the lesion was exclusively on the right side, in two it was in the midline, and in two it affected both sides of the brain. Subsequent studies of additional patients, which involved the use of CT scans and MRI to localize the lesions, found that "patients with [secondary] bipolar disorder [i.e., both mania and depression] had lesions restricted to the right hemisphere, which involved the head of the caudate or thalamus." Patients with pure mania, by contrast, were said to have lesions involving the right orbitofrontal and right inferior temporal regions.[34] A study of the location of the lesion in individuals with secondary mania following head injuries also pointed to the inferior temporal region.[35]

This association of mania with lesions in the nondominant side of the brain is considered to be controversial and has been replicated by some, but not other, researchers. Stephen Strakowski and Kenji Sax, for example, reported on the localization of eight cases of secondary mania; in six of the cases (all involving right-handers), the lesion was in the right hemisphere, and in the other two cases (both involving left-handers) it was in the left hemisphere.[36]

An appealing possibility is that the symptoms of manic-depressive illness will ultimately be explainable in terms of the part of the brain affected. This finding might account for why some individuals have predominantly manic episodes and others have predominantly depressive episodes. It may also explain why some individuals have mixed states, in which two brain areas appear to be simultaneously affected. But such ideas are still just speculation.

Given the complexity and interconnectedness of the brain, however, it is unlikely that researchers will find a single brain area to be responsible for a single psychiatric symptom. Indeed, the greater likelihood is that specific brain *circuits* will be associated with specific symptoms. Given the ongoing improvements in brain imaging technology, this is an area of promising research.

Manic-Like Behavior in Culture-Bound Syndromes

Many cultures have developed culture-specific means for expressing anxiety, fear, enthusiasm, and joy—expressions that may appear strange to individuals from other cultures. Imagine, for example, what a suddenly transplanted Kalahari Bushman from Namibia or a Kukukuku tribesman from central New Guinea would think of a Friday-night pep rally preceding a college football team's big game.

Many culture-bound syndromes involve frenzied, agitated, and euphoric behavior that may appear briefly and superficially to resemble mania. Outside observers, if they witness such behavior without understanding its cultural context, may erroneously conclude that mania is common in that culture.

An example is *amok*, which occurs in many cultures throughout Southeast Asia and involves a trance-like state in which the person becomes very talkative and physically active. In its fully developed form, amok "is characterized by automatism, amnesia, sudden outbursts of motor action and screaming, along with violent attacks on people, animals and inanimate objects; it is followed by exhaustion, calm, depression and the return of consciousness."[37]

Behavior similar to amok may be observed in other culture-bound syndromes, such as *boufée delirante* in West Africa and Haiti, *negri-negri* in parts of Papua New Guinea, and *piblokto* among the Arctic Eskimos. In all such cases, the manic-like behavior usually terminates after a few hours or days, and there is no known association of the behavior with true manic-depressive illness.

What Is an Adequate Diagnostic Workup?

Given the existence of certain conditions that may sometimes be confused with manic-depressive illness, these conditions clearly need to be ruled out. What, then, would constitute an adequate diagnostic workup? The following measures are those we would personally want taken if one of us or a member of our families was admitted to a hospital with symptoms of manic-depressive illness for the first time.

1. *History and Mental-Status Examination:* During this phase of the diagnostic workup, headaches, recent head injuries, and the presence of visual hallucinations should be asked about, since all suggest the possibility of organic factors. A general review of organ systems may also turn up symptoms suggesting diseases such as hyperthyroidism. Perhaps the single most important question the examining physician can ask is: "What drugs are you using?" This is a two-pronged question

intended to elicit information about street drug use, which may be producing or exacerbating the symptoms, as well as prescription drug use, which may be producing manic or depressive symptoms as side effects. Since acutely manic patients often cannot give a coherent history, family members and friends play an essential role in providing the needed information.

Interestingly, certain aspects of the history may be more suggestive of secondary mania. One study, for example, reported that patients with secondary mania, compared to those with manic-depressive illness, were likely to be older at the time of the first onset, to have less family history of depression or manic-depressive illness, and to have had more manic and fewer depressive episodes.[38]

2. *Physical and Neurological Examinations:* These are sometimes done superficially, with the consequence that many physical and neurological diseases are missed. A careful neurological examination is especially important, as patients with manic-depressive illness may occasionally have neurological abnormalities (see Chapter 7). A useful part of the neurological exam, which can be taught to nonphysicians who must screen psychiatric patients, is a series of pencil-and-paper tests such as write-a-sentence and draw-a-clock; as Robert Taylor describes in *Distinguishing Psychological from Organic Disorders,*[39] such tests can help identify patients who initially present with the symptoms of manic-depressive illness but have other brain diseases such as brain tumors or Huntington's disease.

3. *Basic Laboratory Work Involving Blood Count, Blood Chemical Screen, and Urinalysis:* These tests are also routine, although abnormal results are sometimes not noticed or followed up. Blood chemical screens, for example, have become widespread. They involve many different tests on a single sample of blood, including those designed to detect endocrine or metabolic imbalances. A thyroid function test is important; if it is not included in the routine blood chemical screen, it should be ordered separately. A routine test to screen for syphilis should also be included. Urinalysis should include screening tests to detect street drugs in the urine. A useful and cost-effective diagnostic algorithm for detecting physical disease in psychiatric patients has been developed by Harold Sox and his colleagues.[40] For some patients, a

baseline electrocardiogram (EKG) is also useful; since some drugs used to treat manic-depressive illness affect the heart, having a baseline EKG done prior to starting medication may be helpful in future assessments of such side effects.

4. *Psychological Tests:* Psychological tests are useful both in cases where the diagnosis is not clear and in cases involving unusual cognitive deficits. The choice of psychological tests varies from hospital to hospital and depends on the psychologist. Such tests can be useful in making the diagnosis of manic-depressive illness in early or borderline cases and can also point the examiner away from manic-depressive illness and toward other brain diseases. Note, however, that many acutely manic patients are unable to concentrate long enough to undergo psychological tests.

5. *MRI Scans:* Magnetic resonance imaging (MRI) is now widely available and, with improving technology, should become less expensive. An MRI scan should be done on every individual who presents with manic-depressive illness for the first time, especially if the person also has delusions or hallucinations. Diseases that may cause secondary mania and that may be detected by MRI scans include brain tumors, Huntington's disease, subdural hematomas, and strokes. On the other hand, a scan probably is not justified diagnostically for persons who have had symptoms of manic-depressive illness for many years, given that the diseases the procedure is capable of detecting would have become evident over time because of other signs or symptoms.

Computerized tomography (CT) scans, though less sensitive for detecting most brain pathology, can be used in place of MRI scans if the latter are not available.

6. *Lumbar Puncture:* Despite the stereotype to the contrary, a lumbar puncture (also known as a *spinal tap*) is a simple procedure that typically produces little more discomfort than the drawing of blood. In this procedure, cerebrospinal fluid is withdrawn by a needle from a sac in the lower back; since the sac is connected to fluid channels in the brain, examination of the cerebrospinal fluid often provides clues (e.g., antibodies to viruses) about events in the brain. Lumbar punctures are routinely used in the diagnosis of brain diseases. They are capable of detecting a variety of such diseases, especially multiple sclerosis and

viral diseases of the central nervous system. Indications for their use in patients admitted for a first episode of manic-depressive illness include those listed in the accompanying box.

7. *Electroencephalogram (EEG):* The indications for an EEG are symptoms suggesting the possibility of a seizure disorder, including symptoms that are episodic but of brief duration. Patients who have a history of brain injury or neurological findings that suggest a focal lesion are also candidates for an EEG.

8. *Other diagnostic tests:* Though not routine, other diagnostic tests may be indicated by specific findings. Examples include newer brain scans (e.g., functional MRI scans and PET scans), whose use is still experimental, and the dexamethasone suppression test (DST), which at one time was thought to be useful for differentiating between certain kinds of patients but has not proven to be so. As technology improves, the diagnostic workup of manic-depressive illness will become increasingly complex and sophisticated.

Indications for Lumbar Puncture in First-Episode Manic-Depressive Illness

- Patient's complaints of headache or stiff neck with nausea or a fever

- Fluctuations in patient's orientation (e.g., patient knows where he is one day but does not know the next day)

- Rapidly deteriorating course, with prominent symptoms of dementia

- Neurological signs or symptoms suggesting central nervous system disease other than manic-depressive illness (e.g., nystagmus of the eyes in which the gaze moves rapidly from side to side)

5

RISK FACTORS FOR DEVELOPING
MANIC-DEPRESSIVE ILLNESS

Hence, loathed Melancholy,
Of Cerberus and blackest Midnight born,
In Stygian cave forlorn,
'Mongst horrid shapes, and shrieks, and sights unholy.

JOHN MILTON,
L'Allegro (1631)[1]

The line between risk factors for manic-depressive illness and the causes of manic-depressive illness is much like that between twilight and dusk—we cannot tell where one ends and the other begins. Are risk factors such as pregnancy and birth complications or viral infections in infancy, which occur years prior to the onset of the disease, really just risk factors? Or are these really causes that we fail to recognize as such because of the latent period between the occurrence of the risk factor and the onset of the disease?

Genes are a good example of this problem. They are such a clearly established risk factor that most researchers consider them to be an actual cause of manic-depressive illness. But, in fact, we do not know for certain whether genes are a true cause, or whether they merely act as predisposing agents for another cause. If the latter is true, then genes are risk factors and not causes.

This chapter will discuss risk factors other than genes (see Chapter 7) or head injuries (see Chapter 4). The evidence supporting their possible role as risk factors varies considerably, as indicated in the accompanying chart.

Risk Factors for Developing Manic-Depressive Illness: How Strong Is the Evidence?

genes	very strong
winter birth	strong
summer onset	strong
urban birth	weak
pregnancy and birth complications	moderate
prenatal famine	weak
prenatal exposure to influenza	negative
severe stressors in childhood	
• physical or sexual abuse	weak
• loss of parent	weak
head injuries	
• within five years of onset	moderate
• in childhood	weak
social class	moderate

Winter Birth

Being born in the winter months slightly increases a person's chance of having manic-depressive illness later in life. This risk factor has been demonstrated in large studies of individuals both with mania and with the modern version of manic-depressive illness (bipolar disorder). It has been a consistent finding in all large studies done to date, which include countries as geographically diverse as Sweden, England, Japan, and the United States.

Studies in the 1970s in Sweden[2] and England[3] reported that individuals with mania were more likely to be born in the winter. The largest study of birth patterns for individuals with the modern version of manic-depressive illness (bipolar disorder, DSM-III-R) was carried out by E. Fuller Torrey et al. utilizing data from Ohio, Pennsylvania, Virginia, and North Carolina. Comparing the birth dates of 18,021 individuals with manic-depressive illness and the birth dates of all persons born in these same states, the researchers found that December, January, February, and March were each associated with a 5–6 percent excess number of births of individuals who had been diagnosed with manic-depressive illness; every other month showed a deficit of such births. The winter excess of births of individuals with manic-depressive illness was statistically highly significant (p < 0.0001).[4]

When the same study examined individual states, the results for North Carolina were especially notable. In that state, there was an 18 percent excess of manic-depressive births in February and a 22 percent excess in March. The study also examined the birth pattern of individuals with schizophrenia (both paranoid schizophrenia and undifferentiated or "process" schizophrenia), schizoaffective disorder, and major depression. For North Carolina, the results were as follows:

North Carolina:
Percentages of Excess or Deficit Births

	Dec.	Jan.	Feb.	Mar.
manic-depressive illness	–5%	+5%	+18%	+22%
schizoaffective disorder	–13%	+7%	+28%	+22%
paranoid schizophrenia	–6%	+10%	+6%	+17%
undifferentiated schizophrenia	+8%	+7%	–16%	–3%
major depression	–4%	+3%	–2%	+7%

The similarity between the seasonal birth patterns for manic-depressive illness and schizoaffective disorder is striking, suggesting that they might be related (see Chapter 3). Though much smaller, other studies of the seasonal birth pattern for manic-depressive illness—including those conducted in Japan,[5] Ireland,[6] Taiwan,[7] France,[8] and Hungary[9]—have also reported trends toward an excess of winter and/or spring births.

The cause of the winter birth excess for manic-depressive illness is not known. For schizophrenia, however, a winter and spring birth excess is clearly established. Many explanations have been offered. These include a genetically related factor that might make some newborns more likely to survive or not survive in certain seasons; seasonal variations in pregnancy and birth complications (see below); seasonal variations in light and internal chemistry; and seasonal variations in toxins, nutritional deficiencies, infectious agents, and temperature or weather effects. Two other explanations—that seasonal birth excess is a statistical artifact and that it is caused by a seasonal pattern of procreation by the parents of those affected—have been largely disproven.

Summer Onset

For individuals who are inclined to get manic-depressive illness, the summer months are a risk factor for developing mania. Thus, this disease is associated with a seasonality of onset effect that is entirely separate from the seasonality of birth effect described above.

Summer as a risk period for the onset of insanity was observed two hundred years ago. In the early nineteenth century French physicians Philippe Pinel and Jean Esquirol both described it, and Esquirol, in particular, showed that admissions between 1806 and 1814 to a Paris psychiatric hospital were approximately 20 percent higher in the summer months than in the winter months.[10] In England, William Hood noted a similar summer increase in admissions to Bethlem Hospital between 1846 and 1860,[11] whereas John Bucknill and Daniel Hack Tuke recorded an 18 percent increase in summer admissions to the York Retreat.[12]

In the twentieth century, however, these earlier observations were largely forgotten until the 1970s, when studies in England brought renewed attention to this phenomenon. One study examined the month of hospital admission for 125,207 individuals with schizophrenia and 19,134 individuals with mania. Both groups showed a significant peak in admissions in June and July, with that for mania (10 percent excess) greater than that for schizophrenia.[13]

Another study looked at the month of admissions of 17,770 individuals with schizophrenia and 20,845 with affective disorders, including 4,423 diagnosed with mania. Those with mania showed a significant increase in June and July admissions. Those with schizophrenia also showed a June and July peak, but it was less prominent than that for mania.[14] More recently, a large study carried out in Ireland involving 2,654 individuals with first-episode manic-depressive illness (bipolar disorder, ICD-10) reported a 15 percent excess of admissions from June through September.[15]

A confirmatory test of seasonal phenomena is whether they are also observable in the Southern Hemisphere, where the seasons are reversed. Five studies on the seasonal admissions of individuals with mania were carried out in Australia and New Zealand between 1982 and 1995. The four largest, involving between 1,876 and 5,160 patients, each reported a spring-summer excess of admissions for mania of between 10 and 12 percent.[16]

The reason for this summer peak in onset of manic-depressive illness is not known. Researchers have speculated about such biological factors as longer days (thereby affecting the light and melatonin cycle), temperature, humidity, atmospheric pressure, ionization of the air, latitude, and seasonal infectious agents, and about such social factors as summer holidays and hospital-bed availability. What has been documented are seasonal differences in some body chemicals, including serotonin, which is linked to severe psychiatric disorders; but what role, if any, these chemicals play in the observed seasonality of onset remains to be ascertained.

Urban Birth

The tendency for more individuals with insanity to be born in urban areas than in rural areas has been noted for almost two centuries. In 1848, for example, Dorothea Dix observed: "There are, in proportion to numbers, more insane in cities than in large towns, and more insane in villages than among the same number of inhabitants dwelling in scattered settlements."[17]

In the early twentieth century, it was consistently observed that more first admissions for both schizophrenia and manic-depressive illness (old definition) came from urban rather than rural areas. Until recently, the assumption was that this urban-rural disparity in admission rates simply reflected the propensity for individuals who were in the early stages of their illness to migrate from rural to urban areas; thus, when finally hospitalized, they were counted as "urban" in origin. This is certainly the case, but recent studies of schizophrenia have led researchers to question whether migration is the whole story. Since 1992 eight separate studies have reported that being born, or raised, in an urban area doubles one's chances of being diagnosed with schizophrenia later in life, compared to individuals who are born or raised in a rural area.[18]

The data regarding manic-depressive illness are less clear. Studies in the United States[19] and the Netherlands[20] suggest that being born or raised in an urban area modestly increases a person's chances of being later diagnosed with manic-depressive illness. On the other hand, a study in Denmark did not find any increased risk.[21] Thus, additional research is needed to answer this question.

Pregnancy and Birth Complications

Multiple studies of mothers who gave birth to individuals who later developed schizophrenia or manic-depressive illness have found that these mothers had more birth complications than did mothers of normal controls, although the differences were small and no one complication stood out. For example, one study that compared individuals with manic-depressive illness and their well siblings in terms of pregnancy and birth histories (ascertained by both hospital records and maternal recall) reported more complications among the former.[22]

One other piece of evidence supports the fact that something is going wrong prenatally among at least some people who later develop manic-depressive illness—namely, fingerprint and palmprint patterns, which are formed during the first half of pregnancy and thereafter cannot be altered. Many studies have shown that some individuals with schizophrenia have minor abnormalities in their fingerprints and palmprints compared to normal controls. Recently, two studies of individuals with manic-depressive illness (bipolar disorder) also reported such minor abnormalities.[23] Of these two studies, the one that included people with schizophrenia among its participants (N. Jelovac, J. Milicic, M. Milas, et al.) found very similar fingerprint and palmprint abnormalities in both diagnostic groups.

What do these pregnancy and birth complication studies tell us? They suggest that some individuals with manic-depressive illness experience a biological process during pregnancy and/or birth that puts them at greater risk for developing manic-depressive illness later in life. The studies do not identify that biological process or tell us how important it is. It could theoretically be the effect of genes, infections, or some environmental factor.

Prenatal Famine

In late 1944 and early 1945, during World War II, the German army blockaded the western part of the Netherlands, allowing virtually no food to get through. The consequence was widespread famine and high mortality.

Recent studies that examined the psychiatric outcomes for children who were *in utero* during the famine months and are now almost 60 years of age reported an increase in schizophrenia among the offspring who were in the first three months of *in utero* development during the famine—approximately twice the rate that would be expected.[24] They also reported twice the expected rate of manic-depressive illness (bipolar disorder) and three times the expected rate of major depression among offspring who had been in the second and third trimesters of development during the famine.[25]

The researchers themselves suspect that some nutritional deficiency contributed to this increase in severe psychiatric disorders. The puzzling thing about their findings, however, is that severe famines have occurred widely in history and still occur in some countries on a regular basis, yet nobody has previously observed any increase in psychiatric disorders among the offspring of women affected by such famines. Clearly, these findings need to be replicated in another famine group.

Prenatal Exposure to Influenza

There have been a few reports suggesting that if pregnant women are exposed to influenza, there is an increase in the likelihood that their offspring will later develop schizophrenia, especially if the exposure takes place during the middle three months of pregnancy. Other studies of schizophrenia, however, have not replicated this finding.

Several of these studies also looked at manic-depressive illness, usually as part of the broader diagnostic category of affective psychosis, which includes individuals with major depression with psychotic features. To date, six separate studies have looked for a possible association of exposure to influenza during pregnancy and the later development of affective psychosis.[26] These studies were carried out in England, the Netherlands, Finland, and Australia, and all except one reported negative results. Exposure to influenza in pregnancy thus does not appear to be a risk factor for later developing manic-depressive illness.

Severe Stressors in Childhood

Recent years have witnessed a resurgence of interest in investigating severe stressors in childhood as possible risk factors for developing manic-depressive illness. The assumed existence of this relationship, though a prominent part of Freudian theories in the mid-twentieth century, was later largely discredited. Recent interest has been stimulated, however, by animal studies showing that severe stressors to infant rats and monkeys can cause changes in neurochemistry and the later behavior of the animal. The childhood stressors that have received the most attention are physical and/or sexual abuse as well as parental loss.

Physical and/or sexual abuse as a risk factor was evaluated in two large studies conducted in the 1990s. First, Mina Hyun et al.[27] compared the histories of 142 outpatients with manic-depressive illness with the histories of 191 outpatients with depression. Among those with manic-depressive illness, 32 percent claimed to have been physically and/or sexually abused in childhood, compared to 25 percent of those with depression. Second, Gabriele Leverich et al. ascertained the histories of 298 outpatients with manic-depressive illness and compared the clinical histories of 124 (42 percent) who claimed to have been physically or sexually abused with the 174 (58 percent) who said they had not been abused. Those who said they had been abused were found to have had an earlier onset of illness, more severe mania, and more alcohol and drug abuse. The researchers concluded: "These data suggest that a history of early abuse in patients with bipolar disorder is associated with earlier onset and a more severe course of illness."[28]

This conclusion seems premature, however. Neither study included a non-ill control group. And both studies collected their histories of abuse retrospectively from patients during a period when childhood sexual abuse was being widely reported as having been suggested by therapists to patients—a phenomenon labeled *false memory syndrome*. As Paul McHugh described the situation in 1992: "We have an epidemic right now of people being persuaded that they were abused as children."[29]

Alternative explanations of this association seem more likely than the conclusion that abuse in childhood in some way causes manic-depressive illness, or accounts for an earlier onset or more frequent symptoms. For example, it is probable that families with a child who later develops manic-depressive illness have other mentally ill or substance-abusing family members who may be abusing the child. Substantial support for this explanation is found in the aforementioned study by Leverich et al. in which the children who reported having been abused came from families with significantly more alcoholism, drug abuse, and other psychiatric disorders than those of controls. Thus the children were genetically predisposed to develop manic-depressive illness and, because of their family constellation, more likely to be abused. However, there was no evidence that the abuse *caused* the manic-depressive illness.

The other severe stressor in childhood that has been studied as a risk factor for manic-depressive illness is the loss of a parent. Ever since Sigmund Freud published his *Mourning and Melancholia* (1917), psychologists have expressed interest in the effects of the childhood loss of a parent on later mental health. This interest was heightened in the 1950s when Harry Harlow and John Bowlby demonstrated that both infant monkeys and children appeared to be profoundly affected by the loss of their mothers.

Evidence of parental loss as a risk factor for developing manic-depressive illness is mixed, with two studies supporting such an association and four not supporting it. A study in Israel reported that 12 of 79 individuals with manic-depressive illness had lost a parent in childhood, compared to only 5 of 79 controls. In five cases, the death took place before the child was age 9; and in the remaining seven, when the child was between ages 9 and 16.[30] In Denmark a case-register study of 2,299 indi-viduals with manic-depressive illness similarly reported that the death of a parent, especially if it occurred before the child's fifth year, was a sig-nificant risk factor for developing manic-depressive illness.[31] By contrast, four other studies, carried out in Sweden, Norway, Japan, and the United States, reported no association between parental loss in childhood and the later development of manic-depressive illness.[32]

Social Class

The possible relationship between social class and manic-depressive ill-ness has intrigued researchers since the early years of the twentieth cen-tury, when manic-depressive illness was first defined as a disease different from schizophrenia. The 1990 edition of Frederick Goodwin and Kay Jamison's textbook, *Manic-Depressive Illness,* reviews thirty-four different studies of this question, dating back to 1913.[33]

Such research, however, is fraught with methodological problems—one of which, of course, is the shifting definition of manic-depressive ill-ness over time. Another concerns differences in how social class is defined: Should this definition reflect the economic status of one's par-ents, one's own economic status, one's occupation and educational achievement, or some combination thereof? A third major problem is diagnostic bias; for many years, it was said that people who have psy-chosis and are rich will be diagnosed with manic-depressive illness, but those who have the same symptoms of psychosis and are poor will be diagnosed with schizophrenia. In more recent times, it has become politically incorrect in America to imply that any social or racial group experiences manic-depressive illness or some other psychiatric disor-der to a greater or lesser degree than any other group—and that mind-set currently holds sway.

In addition to diagnostic bias, a possible explanation of the associa-tion between higher social class and manic-depressive illness is that per-sonality traits associated with manic-depressive illness may lead to greater economic and social success and thus to higher social class. An alternate assumption is that the stresses of living in a higher social class may predispose some individuals to manic-depressive illness, although there is no evidence to support such causality.

What can we conclude about the relationship of social class to manic-depressive illness? In their textbook, Goodwin and Jamison concluded that "the majority of studies report an association between manic-depressive illness and one or more measures reflecting upper social class. . . . Considered in its entirety, the literature is highly suggestive of an association."[34] Since the textbook's publication, this conclusion has been tempered by the failure to find such a correlation in the Epidemiologic Catchment Area (ECA) study,[35] but the assumption that such a correlation exists is still generally accepted.

6

ONSET, COURSE, AND OUTCOME

My cue is villainous melancholy, with a sigh like Tom o' Bedlam.

WILLIAM SHAKESPEARE,
King Lear (1605-1606)[1]

Pinpointing the onset of manic-depressive illness is much like ascertaining the beginning of day. Does day begin when the first faint hints of light appear on the horizon, when enough daylight is present that streetlights automatically go off, or when the sun becomes visible? Similarly, does manic-depressive illness begin with the first hint of symptoms, when symptoms have become severe enough that psychiatric help is sought, or when the person is first hospitalized?

Past studies of manic-depressive illness measured onset in terms of when psychiatric help was sought or when the person was hospitalized. The median age of onset was thus reported to be between 25 and 30 years of age. Recent studies, using similar criteria, have reported the median age of onset to be between 20 and 25 years; whether this finding is based on more efficient diagnoses or reflects a genuine decrease in age of onset is uncertain.

In most cases, however, the symptoms of manic-depressive illness begin years before psychiatric help is sought. Janice Egeland and her research colleagues demonstrated this fact in their study of manic-depressive illness among the Amish. The mean age of first hospitalization for those affected was 25.8 years and the mean age of first psychiatric treatment was 22.0 years—but the mean age of the onset of major symptoms was 18.7 years and the mean age of "first impairment associated with affective symptoms" was 15.5 years.[2] In short, there was an average period of ten years between the initial symptoms of manic-depressive illness and the first hospitalization.

An early age of onset of manic-depressive illness is statistically associated with having a family history of this disorder. It is also associated with having more severe symptoms and a poor long-term course. These associations are merely statistical, however; many individuals with an onset at age 16 do very well, whereas many with an onset at age 35 do poorly.

Beyond age 40, the onset of manic-depressive illness becomes increasingly unusual. Anyone presenting with the onset of mania over age 40 should be closely examined for underlying medical conditions that may be causing the symptoms (see Chapter 4).

Headaches sometimes accompany the onset of a manic or depressive episode. Emil Kraepelin described them as being like "attacks of migraine, dull oppression, the feeling of a band round the forehead, of a heavy helmet, of a lead plate."[3] And Michael Cunningham gave this account of the onset of Virginia Woolf's episodes:

> First come the headaches, which are not in any way ordinary pain.
> . . . They infiltrate her. They inhabit rather than merely afflict her, the way viruses inhabit their hosts. Strands of pain announce themselves, throw shivers of brightness into her eyes so insistently she must remind herself that others can't see them. Pain colonizes her, quickly replaces what was Virginia with more and more of itself.[4]

Factors Affecting Course

Manic episodes usually begin more abruptly than depressive episodes, the former becoming apparent in a matter of days and the latter often taking weeks or months. Kraepelin described the onset of depressive episodes as follows: "Not infrequently their development is preceded by fluctuating, nervous disorders and slight irritable or depressive moodiness for years before the more marked morbid phenomena begin."[5]

Gender plays a role in the onset and course of manic-depressive illness. Women are more likely to present with depressive episodes, whereas men are more likely to have manic episodes. During the course of the illness, women are also more likely to have mixed states (see Chapter 2) and periods of rapid cycling (see below). The reasons for these gender differences are not yet known.

The type of initial episode—either manic or depressive—partially determines the predominant episodes for the subsequent course of illness. Thus, if one's initial episode is manic, episodes of mania are more likely to predominate in subsequent years.

The average duration of a single episode of mania or depression, if untreated, is three to twelve months, although episodes may last from a few days to a few years. Depressive episodes have a longer average duration than do manic episodes. The average duration between the first and second episodes is approximately three years, and between the second and third episodes, two years. Thereafter, the duration between episodes averages between one and two years but varies widely. The decreasing duration of time between initial episodes has been widely observed and is cited as major support for the *kindling hypothesis of manic-depressive illness* (see Chapter 7).

The course of manic-depressive illness is also highly variable. The classic course involving mania followed by major depression followed again by mania occurs in fewer than 20 percent of cases. Indeed, mania, hypomania, major depression, dysthymia, and mixed states may occur in virtually any sequence. Some people experience a highly predictable sequence that does not change over the course of the illness, whereas others have a sequence that varies widely over time.

Two life events have been found to be triggers that may precipitate the onset and/or relapse of mania: childbirth and loss of sleep. Of the two, childbirth is the better studied and more clearly established. One study reported that almost all cases of postpartum major psychiatric disorders met the diagnostic criteria for mania or depression.[6] A second study found that 20 percent of women with manic-depressive illness had developed mania following childbirth.[7] It is widely assumed that hormonal changes following childbirth may initiate the manic or depressed phase of the illness. A recent study also identified a gene associated with serotonin (see Chapter 7) as a risk factor predisposing some women to develop mania following childbirth.[8]

As noted, loss of sleep also appears to be a trigger for precipitating mania. Anecdotally, this outcome is well known to many individuals with manic-depressive illness who have developed hypomania or mania following prolonged trans-oceanic flights; these are cases of what might be called jet-lag mania. In one study, observations of a 59-year-old woman demonstrated that "mania could repeatedly be induced experimentally by depriving her of sleep for one night."[9]

Large studies of individuals with manic-depressive illness have also indicated the importance of sleep deprivation. One study of 34 inpatients with manic episodes found that the intensity of their manic symptoms was inversely correlated with the duration of their sleep.[10] And in a study of 206 individuals with manic-depressive illness who were in a depressed phase, sleep deprivation had the effect of switching 12 percent of them into a hypomanic or manic phase.[11] Clearly, the expression "get a good night's sleep" has special meaning for individuals with manic-depressive illness.

Rapid Cycling and Seasonal Affective Disorder

When episodes of mania, depression, or mixed states occur at a frequency of four or more per year, the condition is called *rapid cycling*. Although there has been much recent interest in this phenomenon, it is not new. John Haslam described it in *Observations on Madness and Melancholy*, published in 1809: "When the furious state is succeeded by melancholy, and after this shall have continued a short time, the violent paroxysm returns, the chance of recovery is very slight. Indeed, whenever these states of the disease frequently change, such alteration may be considered as very unfavorable."[12]

Rapid cycling is known to occur in 10 to 20 percent of individuals with manic-depressive illness. A small number of these, whose episodes occur much more frequently, are called *ultra-rapid cyclers*. Rapid cycling occurs much more commonly in women than in men and is also said to occur more frequently in individuals who have manic-depressive illness with co-occurring mental retardation. For most individuals with manic-depressive illness, rapid cycling is a transient phenomenon, occurring at some periods during the course of their illness but not continuously.

There are three major questions regarding rapid cycling in manic-depressive illness. First, is it related to hypothyroidism or other aspects of thyroid dysfunction? Second, is it caused by the use of tricyclic antidepressants or monoamine oxidase inhibitors? And third, what is the role of concurrent alcohol or drug abuse in causing rapid cycling? Evidence regarding all three questions is unclear, and the answers await additional research.

There are suggestions that rapid cycling is a bad prognostic sign and that individuals with this condition tend to have a more severe course. Lithium is said to be a less effective treatment for such patients, while carbamazepine and valproate are more effective treatments (as noted in Chapter 8).

Seasons are another factor affecting the course of manic-depressive illness for some people. As noted in Chapter 5, summer is clearly established as a risk factor for hospital admissions for mania. Seasons may also affect the subsequent course of the illness, with some individuals more likely to be depressed in the winter and hypomanic or manic in the summer.

The pattern of winter depression is widely referred to as *seasonal affective disorder*. Typically, the person becomes more depressed, sleeps more, and may also crave carbohydrates and gain weight. Some individuals with seasonal affective disorder have normal mood during the summer, while others feel especially good (hyperthymic).

Seasonal affective disorder varies in severity from mild winter blues to major depression. Individuals with marked seasonal mood swings, which include both major depression and hypomania or mania, meet diagnostic criteria for manic-depressive illness (bipolar I or bipolar II). Those with severe depression in the winter but normal moods in the summer may meet diagnostic criteria for major depressive disorder (unipolar depression). The majority of individuals who experience seasonal mood changes, however, have lesser degrees of symptoms and do not meet diagnostic criteria for either of these.

The relationship between seasonal affective disorder and manic-depressive illness is widely debated. One small study of individuals with seasonal affective disorder claimed that 93 percent met diagnostic criteria for manic-depressive illness. Conversely, a study of people with

manic-depressive illness found that 28 percent "report seasonal variation in their mood states."[13] Peter Whybrow, in *A Mood Apart,* claims
categorically that "SAD [seasonal affective disorder] appears to be a
special version of bipolar disorder."[14] By contrast, Trish Suppes and her
colleagues note that "multiple studies assessing this relationship have
resulted in either insignificant or conflicting reports of a relationship
between season and mood state."[15]

The neurochemical mechanisms underlying seasonal affective disorder have been widely debated as well. The hypothalamus and pineal
gland are thought to be involved because they control circadian
rhythms. Serotonin and melatonin are also under study (see Chapter 7).
If seasonal affective disorder is closely related to manic-depressive illness, understanding the neurochemistry of the former should also elu-
cidate the latter.

Outcomes and Their Predictors

Manic-depressive illness is characteristically a relapsing and remitting
disorder. During the periods between episodes of mania, depression, or
mixed states, some people are completely symptom-free, whereas others continue to have symptoms of varying severity.

For some, episodes of illness become less common as they age. For
others, there appears to be no change. The following case, recently
described to one of the authors, is illustrative:

At age 86, Ms. J. has been on lithium and stable for many years with no
episodes of either mania or depression. Because of her age, her psychiatrist decided that it was appropriate to stop her medication. Within
three weeks, she had become manic, whereupon she purchased a
$96,000 Mercedes convertible. She then drove it to the home of her
parish priest and demanded that he accompany her on a ride, threatening to disinherit the church in her will if he did not. Shortly thereafter,
Ms. J. and the priest were stopped by the police for driving 100 miles
an hour.

Studies of the long-term outcome of manic-depressive illness have yielded more pessimistic conclusions over the past century. Emil Krae-pelin claimed that the majority of his patients eventually returned to a normal level of function;[16] and Thomas Rennie, examining the outcome of 208 cases of manic-depressive illness hospitalized between 1913 and 1916, reported that only 8 percent of the cases became chronic and 32 percent had "remissions of 10-20 years."[17] By contrast, a recent one-year study of 134 patients admitted to the hospital for mania or mixed states reported that only 24 percent had completely recovered and returned to their baseline level of function.[18] Another study of 51 patients assessed 4.5 years following admission found that 15-20 percent were in com-plete remission, an additional 10-15 percent showed "consistently poor outcome at multiple follow-up assessments," and the remaining 65-75 percent had a variable outcome with "some degree of work impairment, subsyndromal affective symptoms, or occasional rehospitalizations."[19]

Long-Term Outcome of Manic-Depressive Illness

- 25 percent recover completely

- 55-65 percent recover partially

- 10-20 percent have continuing symptoms with a poor outcome

The latter two studies are representative of research reported in the past decade on the long-term outcome of manic-depressive illness. On average, approximately 25 percent of the patients have fully recovered, 10-20 percent have a chronic illness with poor outcome, and the remain-ing 55-65 percent have partial recovery, often able to work but not at the level they would have achieved had they not become sick. On neuropsy-chological tests, many individuals in this partial-recovery group show subtle deficits such as impairment on measures of sustained attention.

Whether the long-term outcome of manic-depressive illness has actu-ally worsened over the past century is not resolved. Those who doubt it point to the fact that individuals with unipolar depression, which has a better outcome, were included in the earlier samples. They also point to shifting definitions of "recovery" and "function" and to the inclusion of more individuals with schizoaffective forms of manic-depressive illness, which has a worse outcome, in the recent studies. In addition, many of the recent studies were carried out at university research centers, which tend to selectively attract the more severely ill patients.

Nevertheless, it is surprising that the long-term outcome for manic-depressive illness is not currently better than it is, given the availability of mood stabilizers and other medications that were unavailable in earlier years. It is possible that these medications, while helping to control the symptoms of the illness, have not truly changed the long-term outcome. It is also possible that the disease itself has changed over time and is now a more severe and chronic illness.

What are the best predictors of outcome for individuals with manic-depressive illness? There is widespread agreement that compliance with medication is the single best predictor of level of function; no matter how many symptoms individuals have at any point in their illness, those who adhere to their prescribed medication will do better. The presence of delusions is a bad sign, as is a diagnosis of schizoaffective disorder. Prominent rapid cycling and mixed states are also worrisome, although the data to support this conclusion are less strong than those supporting delusions or a schizoaffective diagnosis as bad prognostic signs.

In recent years researchers have also speculated that long periods of manic-depressive illness without medication may contribute to poor long-term outcomes. The period of nontreatment at the onset of the illness is often five to ten years, and many researchers have theorized that during this period irreversible brain changes take place consequent to the illness. If this is true, then beginning treatment more quickly at the beginning of the illness should improve the long-term outcome. Although this assumption seems logical, there are no hard data to support it; in fact, studies to date have yielded contradictory results. Furthermore, outcome studies carried out before pharmacological treatments were available did not appear to reveal outcomes any worse than those observed in studies conducted since such treatments were used. Additional research is clearly needed to resolve this issue.

Predictors of Outcome of Manic-Depressive Illness

Compliance with medications is a good prognostic sign.

The presence of delusions is a bad prognostic sign.

A diagnosis of schizoaffective form is a bad prognostic sign.

Prominent rapid cycling and mixed states are bad prognostic signs.

Stress as a Risk Factor for Relapse

It is widely accepted that stress may play a role in precipitating relapses of manic-depressive illness, thus affecting the course of the illness. Much less clear, however, is how severe such stressors must be to have an effect and what their relative importance is in determining the overall outcome.

Despite widespread acceptance of the importance of stress in precipitating relapses, empirical evidence is surprisingly thin. Almost all studies claiming to show an association have been retrospective, and some have asked about stressful events from up to ten years earlier. As noted in a review of this literature, "memory for minor events decreases within a year and . . . memories become more systematically biased over time to fit the patients' personal understanding or schema of the disorder."[20] Retrospectively, there is also the perpetual problem of sorting out cause and effect: Did the interpersonal stress cause the person to relapse, or did the person's recurrent symptoms cause the interpersonal stress?

Prospective studies on stress as a cause of relapse are divided in their outcomes. Those by Kathleen Hall et al.[21] (who followed thirty-eight patients for seven months) and Heather McPherson et al.[22] (who followed fifty-eight patients for two years) reported no association between stress and relapse. On the other hand, studies by Aimee Ellicott et al.[23] (who followed sixty-one patients for two years) and Neil Hunt et al.[24] (who followed sixty-two patients for two years) did report an association. The Ellicott et al. study is especially interesting in that it related only the most severe stressors to relapses: "The patients with low and average levels of stress did not have a greater risk of relapse than those without stress, but those with the highest levels had a risk 4.53 times higher than the patients without stress."[25] As examples of severe stressors, the authors listed "a major estrangement from [a patient's] live-in girlfriend" and "employment-related changes that jeopardized his job."

The mechanism by which stressors may help to precipitate relapses is not clear. It could simply involve interruption of the sleep cycle, which, by itself, is known to be a risk factor for relapses. Or it could involve neurochemical mechanisms of the hypothalamic-pituitary-adrenal (HPA) axis (see Chapter 7) or other systems.

Insofar as stress does play a role in precipitating relapses of manic-depressive illness, the implications are clear: Stress should be minimized to the extent possible. (See Chapter 11.) Unfortunately, severe stressors (such as the death of a relative or the loss of a job), though probably the most important, are the least able to be controlled.

Causes of Death

It is well established that individuals with manic-depressive illness have an increased mortality rate compared to individuals who do not have this disorder. Prior to the introduction of lithium and antipsychotic medications, the increased mortality rate was primarily attributable to suicide, exhaustion from mania, and infectious diseases such as tuberculosis.

According to an extensive review of contemporary studies, the current mortality rate for individuals with manic-depressive illness is approximately 2.3 times the rate in the general population.[26] In addition, a recent study of premature deaths among individuals with serious mental illness (37 percent of whom had "a major affective disorder") reported that the life expectancy of seriously mentally ill men was reduced by an average of 14.1 years and that of seriously mentally ill women, by 5.7 years.[27]

The most important cause of premature death in individuals with manic-depressive illness is suicide (discussed in Chapter 13). Approximately 25 percent of individuals with manic-depressive illness attempt suicide, and 10 percent successfully complete the act. The fact that many of these individuals are taking lithium or tricyclic antidepressants is a facilitating factor, since both types of medications are comparatively lethal when taken in overdose by people attempting to kill themselves.

Accidental deaths are also more frequent among individuals experiencing manic episodes, although the magnitude of this increase has not been quantified. Grandiosity and delusions may lead the person to drive 100 miles an hour, challenge a police officer holding a gun, or try to leap between the rooftops of buildings, often with fatal consequences.

In addition, studies have shown that individuals with manic-depressive illness have a greater-than-expected mortality from cardiovascular, endocrine, and respiratory diseases.[28] Part of the reason for this outcome is the comparatively high incidence of smoking among these individuals. Exactly why else is not certain. The higher mortality could be an effect of the psychiatric disease itself or a side effect of the medications used to treat it. It could be related to the fact that individuals with manic-depressive illness are less likely to seek medical care or to the fact that medical care is less available to them. And given the high rate of co-occurring alcohol and drug abuse among individuals with manic-depressive illness (as described in Chapter 13), the substance abuse itself could be the cause of the increased mortality associated with this medical condition.

Finally, individuals with manic-depressive illness tend to experience an increased rate of infections, some of which may be fatal. AIDS is one such example (see Chapter 13). Individuals who are living on the streets or in public shelters are also more exposed to infectious diseases, including tuberculosis.

7

CAUSES

Madness has many colours, and colours have many hues; . . . it very frequently occurs that the descendants from an insane stock, although they
do not exhibit the broad features of madness, shall yet discover propen-
sities, equally disqualifying for the purposes of life, and destructive of
social happiness.

JOHN HASLAM
(1809)[1]

The 1990s, officially designated "The Decade of the Brain," witnessed
an outpouring of research on basic brain function and specific brain diseases. Manic-depressive illness was included in this research. By the
end of the decade, knowledge regarding brain dysfunction in manic
depression had more than doubled. This chapter will review what is
known about brain abnormalities in this disease and discuss the major
theories regarding its cause.

The principal government agency charged with the responsibility for
supporting research on manic-depressive illness is the National Institute
of Mental Health (NIMH). Yet, despite some modest improvements in
recent years, NIMH has largely failed to do so (see Chapter 16). Part of
its failure has been offset by research support from private foundations,
especially the Stanley Foundation and the National Alliance for Research
on Schizophrenia and Affective Disorders (NARSAD). If NIMH had
supported research on manic-depressive illness commensurate with the
importance of this disorder, our knowledge of its causes would be much
more developed than is described in this chapter.

A major confounding factor in all research on causation is sorting
out cause and effect. In a given case of manic-depressive illness, is a

malfunctioning neurotransmitter, an underproducing endocrine organ, or an elevated viral antibody the cause of the illness or merely a secondary effect of something else that is the true cause? Questions like this one constantly bedevil researchers who study manic depression.

Of course, theories of causation are not mutually exclusive: there are proponents for almost all combinations of possibilities, such as genetic and neurotransmitter dysfunction, stress and immune dysfunction, and disturbances in body rhythm and endocrine dysfunction. Moreover, no serious researcher would claim that his or her particular theory accounts for all individuals affected by this disease. On the contrary, researchers acknowledge the existence of subgroups of manic-depressive illness, and the term *heterogeneity* has become a virtual mantra. The magnitude of the heterogeneity and the relative importance of various subgroups, however, continue to be subjects for spirited debate.

Studies of Brain Structure

One way to understand how psychiatric symptoms relate to the brain is to study brain structure. It is now possible to measure the volume of the brain and its component parts in patients exhibiting symptoms of manic-depressive illness. Volumetric studies of such patients have been conducted by means of computerized axial tomography (CAT) scans and magnetic resonance imaging (MRI). For schizophrenia, hundreds of studies have now been completed, clearly establishing that it is a brain disease. For manic-depressive illness, however, similar research has lagged behind, and far fewer studies specifically designed to examine brain structure in this illness have been completed. Furthermore, most of the studies that have been done have compared normal controls with patients who have "affective disorders," thus including patients with major depression as well as those with manic-depressive illness.

The spaces between the folds of the brain (known as cortical sulci) and the cerebral ventricles carry cerebrospinal fluid through and around the brain and become enlarged if the brain has not developed properly or has been damaged. These areas have been measured repeatedly because they are easy to identify and quantify with CAT and MRI technologies. The interpretation of these studies, however, can be difficult. A useful approach is to "synthesize" numerous studies by statistically combining the results obtained by different investigators, a procedure known in the medical literature as *meta-analysis*. The most complete meta-analysis available has shown that there is an enlargement of the cortical sulci and lateral ventricles of patients with affective disorders in general.[2] These areas are about 15 percent larger in such patients compared to normal controls, but the average enlargement is not as great as in patients with schizophrenia. Only five of the studies involved in this meta-analysis specifically looked at patients with manic-depressive illness and also included a normal control group; four of these reported enlarged ventricles in patients with manic-depressive illness, and one study was negative.

It should be emphasized, however, that the cerebral ventricles in manic-depressive illness are not as enlarged as those found, for example, in neurologic disorders such as Alzheimer's disease or hydrocephalus. The difference in the size of the ventricles in individuals with manic-depressive illness compared to normal controls is about 18–20 percent. This difference can be seen in Figure 7.1, which shows MRI scans of the ventricles in identical twins, one with manic-depressive illness and the other without. One study in the meta-analysis conducted on patients in their first episode of mania[3] showed a statistical trend toward enlarged lateral ventricle volume and enlarged third ventricle volume in manic-depressive illness. This finding suggests that structural brain changes are present at the time of illness onset and are not caused by exposure to medications. More careful research will be needed to fully understand the effects of medication on brain volumes, but at least one recent study suggests that lithium treatment may increase the volume of brain grey matter and decrease the volume of the cerebral ventricles.[4]

Although many volumetric studies of other brain regions have been performed, only one meta-analysis is available.[5] This showed that the total brain volume is not altered in manic-depressive illness. It is possible, however, that specific regions of the brain are damaged—an outcome that would account for the enlargement of the ventricles. Some studies have found abnormalities in the temporal lobe, the cingulate gyrus, and the cerebellum; other studies of these areas have not found

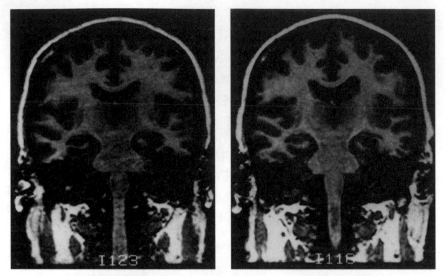

Well Twin   Affected Twin

FIGURE 7.1   Manic Depression and Ventricular Size

Shown on this MRI scan of 52-year-old female identical twins are modestly larger cerebral ventricles (black areas in the middle) in the affected twin compared to the well twin. The affected twin, who initially became sick at age 32, had experienced three episodes of mania and one episode of severe depression.

abnormalities.[6] More studies on this question are thus needed to refine our understanding of which specific brain areas are involved in manic-depressive illness.

In MRI studies of this illness, one abnormality that has been widely reported is an excess number of small, white areas in the brain, usually referred to as "white matter hyperintensities," as shown in Figure 7.2. Multiple studies involving a total of more than 300 patients have reported that these occur approximately three times more frequently in manic-depressive illness than in normal controls.[7] In addition, a recent study reported that certain types of white matter hyperintensities occur more frequently in individuals with a poor clinical outcome of their manic-depressive illness.[8] They also occur much more commonly in people with manic-depressive illness than in those with schizophrenia. What causes these lesions in manic-depressive illness is still unknown, but one hypothesis is that they may be caused by the blockage of small

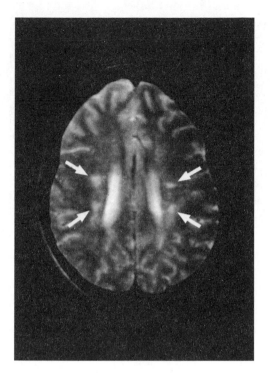

FIGURE 7.2   White Matter
Hyperintensities

This MRI scan of a 30-year-
old female identical twin
shows white matter hyperintensities (arrows) near the
ventricular area. The woman's
diagnosis at age 24 was manic-
depressive illness with psychotic features.

blood vessels, by inflammation, or by abnormalities of glial cells (as discussed below). It is also possible that such lesions are caused by lithium
or other medications taken by individuals with manic-depressive illness.

Studies of brain structure can also be carried out on a smaller scale—
specifically, on brain cells, using postmortem specimens. Few studies
using postmortem brain tissue from individuals with manic-depressive
illness had been done until recently. Since 1998, however, researchers
have had access to tissue from the Stanley Foundation Neuropathology
Consortium; samples from this collection, which includes matched
postmortem brains from individuals with schizophrenia, manic-depressive illness, major depression, and normal controls, have been made
available without charge to more than eighty research laboratories
around the world. The results of studies on these brains are just starting to become available, and much more should be learned in the next
few years.[9]

One of the most interesting findings to emerge from these studies
is a decrease in glial cells in the frontal lobes of individuals with

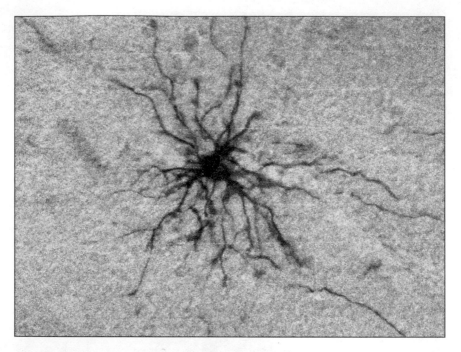

FIGURE 7.3   Glial Cells

Shown here is a glial cell in the brain. Recent studies suggest that glial cells, as well as neurons, do not function normally in individuals with manic-depressive illness.

manic-depressive illness.[10] As shown in Figure 7.3, glial cells support the neurons, supplying them with oxygen, glucose, and other nutrients and protecting them from infectious agents and toxins carried by the blood. Until recently, it was assumed that diseases like manic-depressive illness and schizophrenia were diseases of neurons; hence the supporting glial cells were relatively ignored. That assumption is now being reconsidered. In one study, for example, patients with a family history of manic-depressive illness showed a 17 percent reduction in the density of glial cells in part of the prefrontal cortex.

In all such studies of brain abnormalities in manic-depressive illness, it is important to consider the possible effects of medications as well as street drugs or alcohol abuse. In the aforementioned study of glial cells, for example, these effects could not be completely ruled out but appeared unlikely to fully explain the findings.

Studies of Brain Function

As we have seen, studies of brain structure suggest that there is something wrong with the brain in individuals with manic-depressive illness. Studies of brain function lead to the same conclusion. Brain function can be examined by means of functional brain imaging as well as through neurological, neuropsychological, and electrophysiological procedures.

Functional brain imaging is one of the newest technologies for studying the brain and can be done in several different ways; examples include positron emission tomography (PET) and single photon emission computed tomography (SPECT), which use radioactive tracers, and functional MRI (fMRI), which does not. All three techniques measure the metabolic rate of brain regions by examining the rate at which the brain extracts oxygen or glucose from the blood. Methods for measuring specific neurochemicals in the brain are also now available, as described in the section on neurochemistry.

Compared to work that has been done with schizophrenia and major depression, functional imaging of people with manic-depressive illness is still in its infancy. Only a small number of studies are available, and it is difficult to make generalizations about them. Patients included in these studies are often in different stages of their illness; they may be manic, depressed, or in normal mood states. In addition, they may also be taking different kinds of medications, which can alter the scan results. The research design of the studies also varies widely; some patients have been studied at rest, and others have been studied while performing neuropsychological tests.

Using techniques designed to measure the metabolic rate of the brain, researchers studying manic-depressive illness have found abnormalities in areas of the brain important for regulation of mood and for logical connections between language and memory.[11] Most commonly, such abnormalities have been reported in parts of the frontal lobes, especially the cingulate gyrus and orbitofrontal cortex. Parts of the temporal lobes and the cerebellum may also be abnormal. These findings, however, need to be replicated in additional studies that better control for medications and other sources of possible error.

Neurologically, it is known that some people who have neurological diseases, such as multiple sclerosis and Huntington's disease, develop symptoms of mania more often than would be expected by chance. It is also known that lesions in particular brain areas, including the cerebral cortex, basal ganglia, thalamus, and brain stem, may produce symptoms of mania.[12]

Multiple studies of neurological exams done on individuals with manic-depressive illness have reported an excess of neurological abnormalities, especially abnormalities referred to as "soft" neurological signs because they cannot be localized to a single brain area. For example, in a study of twenty-eight patients with mania, forty-four patients with schizophrenia, and twenty-nine normal controls, the patients with mania and schizophrenia both showed significantly more soft neurological signs than the normal controls, and there were only minor differences between the two patient groups.[13]

Neuropsychological abnormalities are also found in manic-depressive illness. Neuropsychology involves the quantitative testing of mental processes such as intelligence, psychomotor speed, attention, memory, visual-spatial skills, and executive functions (the ability to make complex plans and rapidly shift strategies). Although many more neuropsychological studies have been done on individuals with schizophrenia, there is also convincing evidence for neuropsychological abnormalities in those with manic-depressive illness, especially in visual processing and executive functions. However, as in other fields of research on these diseases, complex methodological problems make the interpretation of such studies difficult.

In comparison to normal controls and patients with major depression, patients with manic-depressive illness exhibit several reproducible neuropsychological findings.[14] Consistent with the classical clinical symptom of *flight of ideas*, patients with manic-depressive illness show an increased speed of associations between thoughts. In computer models of mental functioning, increased association speed can be explained by random activity of neurons, which allows memories to be inappropriately connected to each other.[15] Similarly, reaction time and rate of speech are increased during manic states. Studies have also shown that patients with manic-depressive illness may have subtle deficits in short- and long-term memory, attention, and executive functions, although these results are less clearly established. In studies comparing identical twins, the ill twins were only subtly worse than well twins on general intelligence, memory, attention, and executive functions.[16] The ill twins were, however, significantly more impaired on visual processing. This finding is consistent with the notion that the nondominant hemisphere (the right hemisphere, which is more concerned with visual-spatial skills) is more impaired in those with manic-depressive illness.

Compared to patients with schizophrenia, those with manic-depressive illness appear to have more deficits related to the nondominant hemisphere, whereas patients with schizophrenia appear to have more deficits related to the dominant hemisphere (the left hemisphere, which is more concerned with language). In general, patients with schizophrenia perform worse than patients with manic depression on a wide variety of tests. However, the differences are not yet clear enough for the development of a neuropsychological profile that can discriminate the two disorders accurately.[17]

Electrophysiological abnormalities are another example of abnormal brain function in individuals with manic-depressive illness. Electrophysiological approaches, among the first biological studies conducted on mental illnesses, date to the beginning of the twentieth century. Peripheral nervous system measures include electrical conductance of the skin, electrical aspects of the cardiovascular system, and electrical tracking of eye movements. However, studies of these parameters have rarely separated manic-depressive illness from major depression, and, in any case, they vary so widely in their methods and findings that definitive conclusions cannot be drawn.

Central nervous system electrophysiological measures include the electroencephalogram (EEG) and the event-related potential (ERP), in which the EEG pattern is recorded in response to a variety of stimuli. Manic-depressive illness is associated with a number of EEG abnormalities; however, the EEG findings are nonspecific in that they do not pertain to particular regions of the brain and are often associated with other brain illnesses. The EEG changes observed in people with manic-depressive illness are not characteristic of patterns seen in epilepsy[18] and are probably not due to treatment with lithium. Moreover, although abnormalities in ERPs have been consistently demonstrated in schizophrenia, the findings on manic-depressive illness are equivocal. Recent studies have suggested that abnormalities can be demonstrated, but they may occur in brain regions different from those involved in schizophrenia or only during particular states of the manic-depressive illness.[19]

Genetic Studies

It has been known for more than two centuries that manic-depressive illness tends to run in certain families, and genetic theories of this illness continue to be dominant among researchers. The major evidence in support of genetic theories are studies of twins, adoptees, and family pedigrees.

Twin studies have been the cornerstone of genetic theories of manic-depressive illness. Typically, researchers identify a group of twins, determine how many have manic-depressive illness, and then ascertain by blood studies which twins are identical (monozygous) and which are fraternal (dizygous). Identical twins share 100 percent of their genes; fraternal twins, only 50 percent. The seminal question is this: If one twin develops manic-depressive illness, what is the likelihood that the second twin will also develop manic-depressive illness? The answer, referred to as the *concordance rate*, is a measure of the degree of genetic heritability. In a completely genetic disease, the concordance rate among identical twins should be 100 percent.

The major study done on twins with manic-depressive illness was carried out in Denmark in 1977 by Axel Bertelsen and his colleagues.[20] Virtually every textbook of psychiatry quotes their pairwise concordance rate for identical twins of 74 percent for probable or certain diagnoses. According to Bertelsen et al., when other psychosis, "pronounced affective personality disorder," and suicide were also counted, the pairwise concordance rate for identical twins increased to 96 percent.[21] These data have been used to support claims that the cause of manic-depressive illness is predominantly, if not exclusively, genetic in origin.

Subsequent develop.
Examining the Bertelsen e have cast some doubt on these claims.
twin pairs in which at least on study closely, we find that there are 27
pairs) or depression and hypoma had both depression and mania (22
the co-twins also had depression ana pairs). Among these, only 14 of
pairs). Thus, the true pairwise concorda (11 pairs) or hypomania (3
sive illness (bipolar I or II) in the Bertelsen et . classical manic-depres-
percent. The co-twins in the other 13 pairs W. dy was 14/27, or 52
depression only (7 pairs), "affective" or "hypomani. diagnosed with
pairs), epilepsy with depression (1 pair), psychosis with u. rsonality" (3
case), or as being normal but dying at an early age (1 case). A u. ression (1
aspect of the Bertelsen et al. study was that almost half the twins. ad ubling
died before the study began, so that diagnoses had to be ascertained
through interviews with relatives. In addition, all diagnoses were done
by a single person, and that person was apparently aware of whether the
twin was an identical or a fraternal twin, thus introducing the possibility of unconscious bias.

Twin studies done more recently have confirmed the lower concordance rate for manic-depressive illness if strict diagnoses are adhered
to. A study in England of 25 identical twins in which one had been diagnosed with mania or hypomania reported a concordance rate for these
diagnoses of 11/25, or 44 percent.[22] And a study in Finland of 7 identical twin pairs in which one had manic-depressive illness (bipolar I)
reported a concordance rate of 3/7, or 43 percent, for bipolar I or
schizoaffective disorder, bipolar type.[23]

In sum, twin studies have clearly established that genes are important
in the causation of manic-depressive illness. In addition, they suggest
that depression and other psychiatric disorders may be inherited in
families with manic-depressive illness. At the same time, however, they
have established that nongenetic factors are important as well, since the
concordance rate is far short of 100 percent.

Adoption studies also suggest that genes are important.[24] The bio-
logic parents of adopted-away children who do *not* have manic-depressive illness have a 2 percent chance of having this disease—a probability
just slightly higher than the prevalence of manic-depressive illness in

the general adult population. The biologic~ness, by contrast, have a
children who later develop manic-depres~is rate is similar to the rate
31 percent chance of having the disea~nts of children who develop
of manic-depressive illness amon~adopted, suggesting that genes (or
manic-depressive illness but a~been transmitted to the children prior
some other causative agent~
to their adoption.

Studies of famil~ ~digrees further indicate that genes play a role.[25]
Studies of ove~ ~000 relatives of individuals with manic-depressive
illness rep~ ~that, on average, about 8 percent of first-degree relatives al~ ~have manic-depressive illness, compared to about 1 percent
of ~~e general population. An additional 12 percent of the relatives
~ave major depression, compared to about 5 percent of the general
population.

First-degree relatives of individuals with manic-depressive illness
also have an increased risk for schizoaffective disorder as well as for
manic-depressive illness and unipolar depression. This finding suggests that there is some overlap between the genetic susceptibility for
schizoaffective disorder and the genetic susceptibility for manic-depressive illness, and that attempts to discriminate between these two
disorders on purely clinical grounds may not always be possible[26] (see
Chapter 3).

In an effort to determine which abnormal genes may transmit the
risk for developing manic-depressive illness, two main types of molecular genetic studies have been done: linkage studies and association
studies. In *linkage studies*, researchers try to determine if particular regions of chromosomes (which are composed of DNA) are associated
with manic-depressive illness in families with many ill members. In
such studies, the genes contained in the chromosomal segments associated with manic-depressive illness are not necessarily identified.
However, it may be assumed that some important gene is located
within the linked segment, and the search can then be narrowed more
closely by sequencing those segments. Areas of chromosomes 4, 12,
18, 21, 22, and X (one of the sex chromosomes) have been linked to
manic-depressive illness in replicated studies.[27] As in the aforemen-

tioned genetic studies, which suggest an overlap in the risk of schizo-affective disorder and manic-depressive illness, linkage to chromosomes 18 and 22 have also been reported for schizophrenia, thus supporting the idea that these disorders have some shared genetic susceptibility.

Association studies attempt to show that known genes that are of special interest occur more frequently in individuals or families with manic-depressive illness. Although a large number of such studies have been carried out, none has been clearly positive. The genes that have been most widely studied to date are those known to regulate specific neuro-transmitters and their receptors. However, now that the full sequence of the human genome is available, it should become easier to pinpoint specific genes from additional biological systems that confer risk for developing manic-depressive illness.

Relatively few researchers now believe that manic-depressive illness is caused by a single gene. The majority agree that multiple genes are involved, and an increasing number of researchers suspect that the genes interact with environmental factors. Some researchers have focused on the maternal X chromosome or maternal mitochondrial DNA as the mode of transmission. Another genetic theory postulates that periodic genetic mutations cause the disease. One type of mutation being studied involves *trinucleotide repeat sequences;* the main evidence offered to support this theory is that the disease occurs at an earlier age and more severely in successive generations of affected families, although such evidence remains controversial.

Many genetic researchers also point to the possible evolutionary advantage of having mild cases of manic-depressive illness. Samuel Barondes, in his *Mood Genes,* describes this advantage as follows:

> It is, in fact, easy to make the case that the milder form of mania, called hypomania, has many adaptive aspects. With it comes optimism, enthusiasm, charisma, confidence, boldness, decisiveness, risk-taking, and the uninhibited thinking that sometimes leads to creative ideas. These are attributes that are not only useful to the individuals but also attractive to others, ensuring social position and reproductive success.[28]

Kay Jamison, in *Night Falls Fast*, makes a similar argument:

> The elements that in part define mania—fearlessness, a fast and broad scattering of thoughts, an expansiveness of moods and ideas, utter certainty, the taking of inadvisable risks—often carry with them the power both to destroy and to create. . . . The boldness and violence of the manic temperament may come at a cost, but there is strong evidence that manic-depression and its milder forms can provide advantages to the individual, his or her kin, and society at large.

Jamison says that she was once asked whether a person with mania "was not perhaps the first to throw a spear into the heart of a mastodon."[29]

Ronald Fieve, in *Moodswing*, claims that many of the most successful Wall Street stock traders have a form of manic-depressive illness. He cites Ted Turner as an example of someone "who through his vision changed the face of global awareness and created a multibillion-dollar empire in communications" because of this "classic energy, charm, and intuition that distinguishes many successful hypomanic creative geniuses."[30] A business magazine even called manic-depressive illness the "CEO disease."[31] Many individuals with manic-depressive illness have found this evolutionary perspective attractive, elevating, as it does, the status of those affected.

Although genetic theories of the cause of manic-depressive illness continue to be compelling, their shortcomings have become increasingly apparent. Increasing skepticism has come, in part, from multiple failures to replicate the reported linkage studies. As two genetics researchers summarized the situation in 1996:

> In no field has the difficulty been more frustrating than in psychiatric genetics. Manic depression (bipolar illness) provides a typical case in point. Indeed, one might argue that the recent history of genetic linkage studies for this disease is rivaled only by the course of the illness itself. The euphoria of linkage findings being replaced by the dysphoria of nonreplication has become a regular pattern, creating a roller coaster–type existence for many psychiatric genetics practitioners as well as their interested observers.[32]

Given the uncertainty of the outer clinical limits of manic-depressive illness (as defined in Chapter 3), precisely what is theoretically being inherited also remains unclear. Are the genes specific for classic manic-depressive illness (bipolar I), or do they also include bipolar II? Do the same genes cover unipolar depression? Or are the genes less specific such that they also cover schizophrenia and schizoaffective disorder, thus accounting for the clinical overlap in some families? What is the relationship of these genes to other conditions that frequently accompany manic-depressive illness, including substance abuse, attention deficit hyperactivity disorder (ADHD), and anxiety disorder? And what is the relationship, if any, of these genes to individuals with chronic low-grade depression (dysthymia) or high energy (hyperthymia)? At this time, it is much easier to pose such questions than to answer them.

Another major limitation of genetic theories of the cause of manic-depressive illness is the problem of restricted procreation. From the mid-nineteenth century to the late twentieth century, most individuals with severe forms of this disease were confined to state psychiatric hospitals for much of their reproductive years and thus had little opportunity to pass on their genes. Yet during those years, there is no evidence that manic-depressive illness became less common; in fact, as discussed in Chapter 1, what evidence exists suggests the opposite. To account for this apparent pattern, then, one must postulate either continuing genetic mutations or a great evolutionary (and procreational) advantage for individuals with milder forms of manic-depressive illness.

Finally, it is useful to remember that not every disorder that runs in families is necessarily genetic. Members of families are more likely than nonmembers to share exposure to a multitude of nongenetic factors such as diet, toxins, allergens, and infectious agents, as well as to familial habits and lifestyles such as cigarette smoking.

Neurochemical Studies

Neurochemical theories of manic-depressive illness rank just behind genetic theories in terms of popularity and allocation of research resources. They can be categorized in terms of their emphasis on neurotransmitters, intracellular second messengers, and neuropeptides. Hormone irregularities, which

Hormone irregularities, which are another type of neurochemical abnormality, will be considered below in the discussion of endocrine dysfunction.

Neurotransmitters

Neurotransmitters are chemicals that carry messages between brain cells. Abnormalities affecting neurotransmitters may involve not just a transmitter itself but also the antecedent chemicals needed to manufacture the neurotransmitter, the enzymes needed for the manufacturing process, the intracellular transporter that carries the neurotransmitter to the periphery of the cells, and the receptor on the target cell that receives the neurotransmitter.

Among the approximately 100 known neurotransmitters, the ones that have been most thoroughly studied for possible involvement in the causation of manic-depressive illness are dopamine, norepinephrine, serotonin, GABA, glutamate, and acetylcholine. Researchers study them in four different ways:

1. By measuring the concentration of these neurotransmitters in body fluids such as blood (e.g., platelet cells), urine, or cerebrospinal fluid (CSF)

2. By measuring the enzymes that are essential for making these neurotransmitters

3. By measuring the receptors to which these neurotransmitters bind

4. By giving drugs that are known to affect these neurotransmitters and then observing the behavioral effects that follow

Each of these approaches is complicated by methodological problems; for example, the measurement of a substance in the blood does not necessarily correlate with its measurement in the brain.

At a theoretical level, research on neurotransmitters in manic-depressive illness is attractive. It is known, for example, that some agents that increase dopamine (e.g., L-dopa, bromocriptine, cocaine) may induce mania, that some agents that block dopamine (e.g., haloperidol) may decrease mania, and that several neurotransmitters (e.g., serotonin,

GABA) appear to be decreased in depression. It seems likely, therefore, that neurotransmitters are involved in some way in the manic-depressive disease process.

Many studies have been carried out measuring the concentrations of norepinephrine and serotonin in various body tissues from patients with manic-depressive illness and depression. The findings from these studies are, unfortunately, contradictory and do not allow for straightforward interpretation. Nevertheless, one of the more consistent observations has been that decreased metabolites of dopamine in the spinal fluid may be related to the slowing of movements seen in depression and that increased metabolites may be present in mania.[33] There is also support for the observation that GABA levels are decreased in the blood and spinal fluid of patients with manic-depressive illness and that blood levels of GABA may predict responsiveness to valproic acid.[34] However, given the experimental problems with these techniques, and the fact that the variability in the measurements is so great, little research of this kind is currently under way, and it is doubtful that such measurements will emerge as a laboratory test for manic-depressive illness.

The same conclusions apply to research on neurochemicals in blood cells, such as platelets and leukocytes. Platelets contain many of the same neurotransmitters, receptors, and enzymes found in neurons, but the relationship of the platelet findings to brain function is not known. Measurements of platelet chemicals have not developed into reliable clinical tests because of significant methodological problems and extensive variability between individuals. Despite these caveats, however, it should be noted that abnormalities in several enzymes and receptors have been reported in platelets from individuals with manic-depressive illness.[35]

Other studies on manic-depressive illness have been done using drugs that are known to affect neurotransmitters. Amphetamine is an example of a drug that increases the concentration of neurotransmitters such as norepinephrine, serotonin, and dopamine in the brain by blocking their reuptake. Older tricyclic antidepressants also block the reuptake of norepinephrine and serotonin, but they affect many other transmitter systems. In recent years, new antidepressants that specifically affect serotonin or norepinephrine have become available. Given that amphetamine, tricyclic antidepressants, and selective reuptake blockers improve the symptoms of depression and may provoke symptoms of mania, the implication is that the chemical systems they affect are involved in the development of manic-depressive illness. The older tricyclic antidepressants block the actions of acetylcholine as well. These and other drugs acting on acetylcholine may elevate mood or cause mania, and drugs that mimic the actions of acetylcholine may produce symptoms of depression. Drugs that mimic the effects of GABA, the major inhibitory neurotransmitter in the brain, are also used in the treatment of mania. However, this effect may be mostly nonspecific and due to sedation.

In recent years, methodologies for measuring neurotransmitters and other brain chemicals more directly have improved markedly, thus producing many new findings on individuals with manic-depressive illness. These methodologies include brain imaging and postmortem studies.

Brain imaging, as noted previously, can be used to study brain structure (e.g., via MRI scans) and brain function (e.g., via PET scans), including neurochemicals. PET and SPECT, which use radioactive tracers, can measure receptors and other proteins associated with neurotransmitters. Magnetic resonance spectroscopy (MRS) uses MRI methodology, without radioactive tracers, to measure a variety of important neurochemicals. MRS studies of people with manic depression have shown, for example, reductions in N-acetyl aspartic acid (NAA), a chemical that is specific for healthy neurons.[36] This finding may be consistent with observations of cortical atrophy in manic-depressive illness. But further study is necessary to determine whether these scans can be used to clinically diagnose patients with manic-depressive illness or predict patients' response to medications.

Research on neurotransmitters in manic-depressive illness is, as noted, plagued by methodological problems. First, many medications used to treat the illness can themselves cause changes in some neurotransmitters, so it is difficult to separate the medication effect from the disease effect. Second, many of the neurotransmitters interact with other neurotransmitters or with other brain chemicals such as serotonin and dopamine, glutamate and norepinephrine, GABA and somatostatin, acetylcholine and the hormones of the hypothalamic-pituitary-adrenal (HPA) axis, creating an extremely complex interactive system. Third, since much of the research to date has been carried out on rat brains or with animal models of depression, the applicability of the results to humans is problematic. And, finally, many of the neurotransmitter abnormalities described are not specific to manic-depressive illness but are also found in unipolar depression and schizophrenia.

Intracellular Second Messengers

Research on the *second messenger system* in manic-depressive illness, also referred to as the *signal transduction system*, is relatively recent. In contrast to neurotransmitters, which carry messages *between* brain cells, the second messenger system carries messages *within* the cell. Much of the research on the second messenger system has been stimulated by the fact that lithium and valproate, the principal mood stabilizers used to treat manic-depressive illness, both affect the second messenger system. The components of the second messenger system that have received the most research attention in manic-depressive illness are choline, myo-inositol, phosphomonoesters, G-proteins, protein kinase C (PKC), and cyclic adenosine monophosphate (AMP). The majority of this research has focused on the blood (white blood cells and platelets), has involved postmortem brain tissue from individuals with this illness, and has entailed the use of MRS.[37]

As with the neurotransmitter research discussed earlier, several confounding factors add to the difficulty of studying the second messenger system. Not the least of these is the fact that many neurotransmitters and hormones affect the second messenger system, thereby confusing cause and effect. The study of blood cells is convenient, but there is no guarantee that what occurs in the peripheral blood also occurs in the brain. And the use of postmortem brain tissue carries its own set of problems, since medications taken by the person before death as well as postmortem cell changes may alter the second messenger system.

Neuropeptides

More than thirty *neuropeptides* have been identified in the brain. Some of these function as neurotransmitters, but the role of others is not yet well understood. Several neuropeptides are now being studied in patients with depression and manic-depressive illness. Those of greatest interest include endorphins, somatostatin, vasopressin, oxytocin, substance P, cholecystokinin, neurotensin, and calcitonin. Other neuropeptides are involved in the regulation of the thyroid gland and the HPA axis (as discussed below). There is much overlap between the neuropeptides and the neurotransmitters; as a result, they influence each other (e.g., somatostatin and GABA) and, in some cases, are even found in the same neurons (e.g., cholecystokinin and dopamine). Such overlap makes research on neuropeptides very difficult.

The neurochemical studies currently under way are likely to produce a significant increase in our understanding of the brain chemistry of manic-depressive illness. This understanding, in turn, should lead to medications that are more specific to the treatment of the illness.

Studies of Infections and Immunological Factors

Studies of infectious and immunological aspects of manic-depressive illness are among the newest areas of research on causes of this disease. Interest in such studies has been spurred by markedly improved techniques for studying infectious and immune phenomena. The recent finding that gastric ulcers are caused by an infectious agent as well as the increasing suspicion that some cases of strokes and heart attacks are also caused by infectious agents have led researchers to reevaluate the possible role of infections in manic-depressive illness, schizophrenia, and other chronic diseases of the central nervous system.

In theory, infectious agents are attractive as possible causal factors for manic-depressive illness. Most attention to date has focused on viruses, but bacteria, protozoa, and fungi also warrant consideration. Almost all infectious agents are known to be associated with a genetic predisposition, such that individuals with specific genes are more likely to become infected; this could account for the genetic aspect of manic-depressive illness, too. Also of interest is the fact that retroviruses can integrate themselves into human genes and thus be passed on from generation to generation, just like a genetic disease.

In addition, many of the known risk factors for manic-depressive illness are consistent with an infectious cause. The fact that many infectious agents have a seasonal occurrence may account for the known winter birth excess and/or summer onset excess described in Chapter 5. Infections during pregnancy or around the time of birth could also account for the excess of pregnancy and birth complications.

Known infections of the brain can also cause symptoms of mania and depression and appear clinically indistinguishable from manic-depressive illness. For example, influenza, mononucleosis (caused by the Epstein-Barr virus), and infections caused by the herpes simplex virus may all produce symptoms of either mania or depression. Moreover, some drugs that are effective in treating manic-depressive illness are known to be effective against some infectious agents; for example, lithium has been shown in several studies to inhibit the growth of the herpes simplex virus,[38] and some mood stabilizers have been shown to inhibit the growth of the toxoplasmosis parasite in culture.

Recent studies of infectious agents in manic-depressive illness have been promising. For example, researchers have found that Borna disease virus antibodies are increased in the serum of individuals with both depression and manic-depressive illness.[39] Studies from the Stanley Laboratory of Developmental Neurovirology at Johns Hopkins University Medical Center, a laboratory specializing in investigating infectious causes of manic-depressive illness and schizophrenia, have reported increases in certain retroviruses in postmortem brain tissue from individuals who had manic-depressive illness.[40] Another study from this laboratory reported increased levels of antibody to toxoplasmosis, a common parasite carried by cats, in the serum of pregnant women who have given birth to children who later developed manic-depressive illness and schizophrenia.[41]

The number of immunological studies of manic-depressive illness has also increased in recent years. The immune system, which defends the body against infectious agents and other foreign toxins, is almost as remarkable in its complexity as the central nervous system. Increasingly, there is an appreciation for the interactions of the immune system, the brain, and behavior. The immune system can be thought of as having two basic components: cellular immunity and humoral immunity. *Cellular immunity* concerns the direct actions of immune cells (such as lympho-cytes, macrophages, and leukocytes) and the products they secrete (cytokines) on foreign substances. *Humoral immunity* concerns the pro-duction of proteins known as antibodies or immunoglobulins that act on other cells of the immune system.

Several studies have described abnormalities in cellular immunity in manic-depressive illness that may fluctuate according to the state of the ill-ness.[42] A recent review of these studies concluded that there is evidence of abnormalities both in cellular immunity (e.g., increased activated T-lymphocytes, increased B-lymphocytes, and increased proinflammatory cytokines) and in humoral immunity (e.g., increased acute-phase proteins such as IgG, IgM, and haptoglobins).[43] Not yet clear, however, is whether these abnormalities are secondary to the effects of lithium or other med-ications. In addition, such research must be carefully controlled for the age, gender, and smoking habits of those being studied.

The other aspect of the immune system that has received considerable attention in manic-depressive illness concerns autoantibodies (i.e., anti-bodies made by the body and directed against itself) against the thyroid gland.[44] Since many researchers suspect that thyroid abnormalities may be involved in the phenomenon of rapid cycling (see Chapter 6), this is an area of considerable research interest. As in other studies of immune processes in manic-depressive illness, however, the role of lithium or other medications in producing the autoantibodies is not yet clear.

The main shortcoming of infectious and immunological theories of manic-depressive illness is the limited hard data in support of them; but this scenario may change in the future, since there are many related studies under way. A second shortcoming is the unknown role of med-ications in producing the abnormalities being described. Yet another is the problem of cause and effect: Do the infectious abnormalities pro-duce the immunological abnormalities, or is it the other way around? Or are both produced by a third factor? The close relationship and interaction of the immune system with neurotransmitters and neu-ropeptides, as well as with the hypothalamic-pituitary-adrenal (HPA) axis and other aspects of the endocrine system, make determination of cause and effect an ongoing challenge.

Disturbances in Body Rhythms

For many years researchers have theorized that disturbances in body rhythms and patterns of metabolism are important in the causation of manic-depressive illness. Such theorizing is readily understandable since manic-depressive illness itself is, by definition, a disturbance of rhythms. Indeed, the term *bipolar* evokes images of cycles and oscillating patterns, and these patterns have attracted much research attention.

The cyclical aspects of manic-depressive illness have led naturally to theorizing about disturbances in body rhythms. Of particular interest is the fact that mania occurs more commonly in the summer (see Chapter 5) and suicide occurs more commonly in the spring and autumn (see Chapter 13). One form of mood disorder is known as seasonal affective disorder (see Chapter 6). And sleep disturbances are prominent in episodes of both mania and depression. Sleep deprivation precipitates episodes of mania in some individuals, whereas in others it has been used therapeutically to improve the symptoms of depression. These findings have led researchers of manic-depressive illness to study sleep patterns, circadian rhythms, internal biological clocks, and the regulation of rhythms by melatonin and other neurochemicals.

Research findings, however, are sparse in support of the idea that disturbances in body rhythms are of primary importance in causing manic-depressive illness. Rat models have been developed using cocaine to approximate oscillations in neurochemistry, but their relevance to manic-depressive illness is unknown. Studies of sleep EEG patterns in patients with manic-depressive illness have produced inconsistent results. And studies of various neurochemicals that may affect rhythms, especially those that interact with melatonin, have not been promising.

Theories about disturbances in body rhythms have also led to attempts to improve the symptoms of manic-depressive illness by synchronizing the rhythms. Light therapy, which has proven to be effective in some cases of seasonal affective disorder, is one example. Another is social rhythm therapy, developed by Ellen Frank and her colleagues at the University of Pittsburgh (see Chapter 11).[45]

Endocrine Dysfunction

Dysfunction of the endocrine system is one of the oldest theories regarding causation of both manic-depressive illness and depression. Most of the research attention in this area has centered on the thyroid gland and the HPA axis. The reason for such attention is that diseases of the thyroid and adrenal gland may produce symptoms of depression, hyperactivity, or mood elevation. For example, hypothyroidism is frequently accompanied by a depressed mood, and an overactive thyroid may produce increased energy levels and euphoric states. Indeed, both depression and mood elevation have been reported in patients with Cushing's disease, in which the adrenal gland releases too much cortisol, and in patients who have received cortisol treatments for other illnesses.

It would not be surprising to learn that the endocrine system is involved in manic-depressive illness, since many aspects of the endocrine system are regulated by the hypothalamic area of the brain, an area closely connected to brain areas thought to be involved in this illness. The hypothalamic area also regulates functions such as sleep, appetite, and sexual drive, functions that are often affected in people with manic depression. In addition, the secretion of hormones by the hypothalamus depends on the levels of hormones secreted by the pituitary, thyroid, adrenal, and sex glands (testes and ovaries). Thus, this complex feedback system could theoretically be affected at any one of several levels.

The main problem in studies of the endocrine system's role in manic-depressive illness is determining cause and effect. Are mania and depression caused by abnormalities of the hypothalamus and/or various components of the endocrine system? Or are the endocrine abnormalities merely incidental manifestations of the underlying brain dysfunction that is causing the illness and affecting the hypothalamus as well? Such research is made even more difficult by the fact that many of the neurotransmitters thought to be relevant to manic-depressive illness, including norepinephrine, serotonin, acetylcholine, and GABA, are also necessary for proper function of the hypothalamus. The relationship between endocrine abnormalities and neurotransmitter abnormalities is thus very complicated. It is also only partially understood.

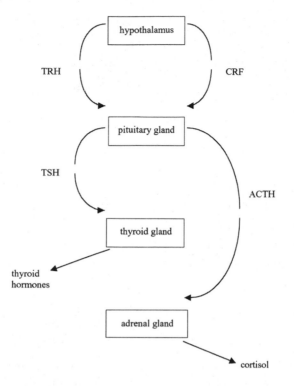

FIGURE 7.4   Control of the Thyroid and Adrenal Endocrine Glands

The hypothalamic (H), pituitary (P), adrenal (A) axis, thought to be abnormal in some individuals with manic-depressive illness. Research on endocrine dysfunction in the disorder has focused on the HPA axis and thyroid gland.

The thyroid gland is part of an endocrine circuit. The hypothalamus secretes thyrotrophin-releasing hormone (TRH), which stimulates the pituitary gland to release thyroid-stimulating hormone (TSH), which in turn stimulates the thyroid gland to release its thyroid hormones (see Figure 7.4). In cases of manic-depressive illness, abnormalities from all three parts of this circuit have been observed. There have also been reports that thyroid hormone is an effective treatment in manic depression. In addition, it is known that lithium can produce hypothyroidism (see Chapter 8). About 10–15 percent of patients with manic-depressive illness have the "rapid cycling" form of the illness (more than four mood episodes per year); some studies suggest that up to half of these patients also have hypothyroidism. While low thyroid function has been observed in rapid cycling patients who have not been treated with lithium, it is also possible that some of these patients have increased sensitivity to lithium-induced thyroid damage.[46]

The adrenal gland is part of another endocrine circuit. The hypothalamus secretes corticotrophin-releasing factor (CRF), which stimulates the pituitary gland to release adrenocorticotrophin (ACTH), which in turn stimulates the adrenal gland to release cortisol and other adrenal hormones (again, see Figure 7.4). Abnormal measurements from all three parts of this circuit have repeatedly been reported in patients with major depression and less frequently reported in patients with manic-depressive illness.[47]

Endocrine glands other than the thyroid and adrenal gland circuits have also been investigated. For example, abnormalities in growth hormone, which is secreted by the pituitary gland, have consistently been reported in manic-depressive illness.[48] The complexity of such abnormalities is suggested by two observations: Growth hormone release is stimulated by neurotransmitters such as dopamine and norepinephrine and by a hypothalamic growth hormone releasing hormone; and growth hormone release is inhibited by somatostatin, a hypothalamic peptide that has been reported to be abnormal in individuals with manic-depressive illness. Somatostatin is currently of great interest to researchers.

Sex hormone levels are also regulated by a circuit of endocrine glands. The hypothalamus produces gonadotrophin-releasing hormone (Gn-RH), which stimulates production of luteinizing hormone (LH) and follicle-stimulating hormone (FSH) from the pituitary. These pituitary hormones regulate the production of testosterone and estrogen in the gonads. Although it is an established fact that mood and behavioral problems accompany fluctuations in gonadal hormone levels (premenstrually, during menopause, after childbirth, and after changes in testosterone levels), there has been remarkably little research on the roles of these hormones in manic-depressive illness. Nevertheless, it is possible to cite one study showing that plasma levels of LH were increased in patients recovering from a manic episode.[49]

Kindling and Stress

Kindling is a model for the causation of manic-depressive illness popularized by Robert Post and Susan Weiss. The term refers to the phenomenon observed when a fire is being started and a series of small flames suddenly burst into a large flame at the point where a critical temperature is reached.

Two animal models illustrate the principle of kindling in behavioral disorders. In rats, a series of small electrical stimulations to the brain's amygdala will eventually induce a seizure. Once one seizure has occurred, subsequent seizures take place with progressively less electrical stimulation; eventually almost no stimulation is required to produce a seizure. The other animal model involves cocaine administration to rats. The initial dose of cocaine produces apparent euphoria, but repeated doses produce other behavior. This phenomenon is cited as an example of behavioral sensitization. According to Post and Weiss, "understanding the neurobiological mechanisms underlying the progressive increases in behavioral responsivity to the same dose of cocaine . . . may thus provide a useful paradigm for elucidating progressive alterations in manic symptomatology."[50] Their research has explored the effects of kindling on the neurochemistry of the brain, including changes in neurotransmitters, the second messenger system, and specific genes that become activated.

Although kindling is a useful model for thinking about causative pathways for manic-depressive illness, it does not by itself identify a cause. What is the flame that kindles the fire? The answer, according to Post and Weiss, may be stress; thus the kindling model of manic-depressive illness is a stress model of causation. As outlined by Post and Weiss: "The postulate is that, as in sensitization and kindling, appropriate psychosocial stressors may . . . reach a threshold for inducing full-blown episodes of affective illness."[51] The nature and timing of the stressors are not spelled out but are said to include "initial stressors early in development [which] may be without effect but predispose to greater reactivity upon rechallenge."[52] These "initial stressors" presumably include severe stressors in childhood, as discussed in Chapter 5.

The kindling-stress model of manic-depressive illness has many attractive features. It accounts for animal models in which repeated severe stressors have been shown to alter neurotransmitters, the second messenger system, and specific genes. It fits neatly with theories of endocrine dysfunction, since stress is known to affect CRF, ACTH, cortisol, and other aspects of the hypothalamic-pituitary-adrenal (HPA) axis. It is also compatible with a genetic predisposition that renders some individuals more susceptible to stress. And it is consistent with the established fact that some cases of unipolar depression are caused by severe stressors, especially those involving the death of a loved one or another severe loss.

Despite its attractiveness, however, the kindling-stress theory of manic-depressive illness is supported by few data. First, there is no evidence that individuals with manic depression are exposed to excess stress *prior to their initial episode* of mania or depression (although stress as a risk factor for *relapse* of symptoms is reviewed in Chapter 6). Second, studies of stress as a cause of the illness have been compromised by retrospective bias, confusion of cause-and-effect, or both. As summarized by a review of these studies by S. L. Johnson and J. E. Roberts, retrospective bias arises because "when a first break occurs, both the patient and his or her family are likely to be highly motivated to favor explanations that imply less risk for recurrence, and hence they will search for an environmental culprit."[53] In other words, if a patient's onset of manic-depressive illness was caused by his divorce, he and his family will be relatively less concerned about its recurrence as long as he avoids similar stressful situations. (Until recently, it was widely assumed that manic-depressive illness and other severe psychiatric disorders *were caused* by life events, so in the past both those affected and treating clinicians assiduously tried to identify the putative causal life events.)

Confusion about cause and effect is also ubiquitous in studies of stress and manic-depressive illness. Specifically, many of these studies focus on patients' life events in the weeks immediately preceding their hospitalization. However, given that manic-depressive illness usually begins slowly, over many weeks, the events of the weeks immediately preceding hospitalization are at least as likely to be *effects* of a patient's initial symptoms as *causes* of it. During those preceding weeks, for example, "[h]ypersexuality, irritability, and grandiosity may all create significant interpersonal difficulties."[54]

Readers should know that it is important to carefully analyze studies of stress and manic-depressive illness, because many books state, explicitly or implicitly, that a causal relationship has been established. One such book is Francis Mondimore's *Bipolar: A Guide for Patients and Families* (1999), in which the author states that "initial and early mood episodes in patients with bipolar disorder are often related to psychological stressors."[55] To date, there are no research data to support such statements.

8

MEDICATIONS: MOOD STABILIZERS

A strange and horrible darkness fell upon me. If it were possible that a heavy blow could light on the brain without touching the skull, such was the sensation I felt.

POET WILLIAM COWPER (1816),
describing the onset of his manic-depressive illness[1]

Medications are the single most important aspect of the treatment of manic-depressive illness. Medication treatment has two main goals: first, to alleviate or shorten the duration of an acute episode of mania, hypomania, or depression and, second, to maintain the improvement obtained in the acute phase and prevent further cycles of mania or depression. The main types of medications prescribed for manic-depressive illness are mood stabilizers, antidepressants, antipsychotics, and benzodiazapines.

Mood stabilizers are the mainstay of treatment for manic-depressive illness. An ideal mood stabilizer should alleviate acute symptoms and recurrences of both mania and depression. It should also exhibit a low tendency to increase the frequency of cycling (as, for example, antidepressants may do). Three drugs are used widely in the United States as mood stabilizers: lithium, valproate, and carbamazepine. Several other drugs are under active investigation; these are discussed below.

Lithium

Lithium was one of the first drugs shown to have an effect on psychiatric symptoms. The revelation of lithium's efficacy was due to a rare combination of serendipity and elegant clinical observation—an outcome for which biological psychiatrists continue to hope and dream. The effects of lithium were discovered in 1949 by John Cade, a mental hospital psychiatrist in Victoria, Australia. Cade thought that mania might be caused by imbalances in protein metabolism, which could be evaluated by studying uric acid and urea (breakdown products of proteins) obtained from the urine of manic patients. Cade wanted to inject these compounds into guinea pigs, but since the compounds are not soluble in water, they had to be conjugated to an element such as lithium prior to injection. After observing that lithium urate—and, later, lithium carbonate—produced calming effects in the guinea pigs, he decided to test the efficacy of lithium in humans. This he did in 1948 and 1949 by administering lithium to ten manic patients, most of whom experienced a dramatic recovery.[2]

Nearly twenty years passed before official application for lithium's clinical use was made. This was the case for two reasons: Cade's discovery remained relatively unknown, and lithium, as a naturally occurring and plentiful salt, could not easily be marketed for commercial gain. On the eve of the approval of lithium for clinical use in the United States, psychiatrist Nathan Kline wrote: "Lithium, the 20-year-old Cinderella of psychopharmacology, is at last receiving her sovereign due. . . . The modest proclamation of its use for manic and other excitement states in a journal of limited circulation in a remote country was to pass almost unnoticed."[3] One wonders how many other substances may exist that hold promise for the treatment of psychiatric illness but are not investigated because they have limited profit potential.

Efficacy of Lithium.   According to practice guidelines issued by the American Psychiatric Association, lithium is the treatment of choice for manic-depressive illness.[4] In a recent survey of the prescribing practices of expert psychiatrists,[5] lithium and valproate (see below) were ranked equivalently as first-line treatments for mania. These guidelines are based on a series of controlled studies that have convincingly demonstrated the efficacy of lithium.

Between the 1950s and the 1970s, researchers conducted four placebo-controlled studies that looked at the effects of lithium on acute mania.[6] These studies involved a total of 116 patients, of whom 78 percent had a good response to lithium (compared to only 40 percent of patients receiving placebo). In a larger study[7] comparing lithium, valproate, and placebo, about 50 percent of patients receiving lithium or valproate experienced a 50 percent reduction in symptoms, whereas only 25 percent of patients receiving placebo improved to this degree. From these studies, one can conclude that lithium treatment brings about a significant resolution of manic symptoms at least two times more often than would occur without treatment.

Lithium is rarely used as a sole treatment for acute mania, however. The reason is that there is a "lag time" from the first administration of lithium until its full therapeutic efficacy is observed. This lag time ranges from a few days to two or three weeks in duration. Therefore, lithium is often combined with other drugs in the acute stages of mania.

Regarding the use of lithium for depression, most early studies did not distinguish patients with manic-depressive illness from those with major depression. Although the results of the studies did not strongly endorse the use of lithium as an antidepressant, later analyses of these data have shown that lithium is more effective than placebo, equally as effective as tricyclic antidepressants, and especially helpful during the depressed phase of manic-depressive illness.[8] The response rate is 60 to 80 percent, and full response may take as long as four weeks. If patients presenting with acute depression are known to have manic-depressive illness, then lithium treatment may be better than treatment with an antidepressant alone, since antidepressants may induce mania in some patients (see below).

At least ten controlled studies have been conducted to determine if lithium can prevent mania and depression over the long term. Although there has been considerable debate about the appropriate design of these studies and the conclusions that can be drawn from them, lithium is now generally believed to be an effective prophylactic medication. Over 200 patients have been studied for periods ranging from four months to three years. About 35 percent of patients receiving lithium and about 80 percent of patients receiving placebo experienced a relapse during the study period. It appears that lithium is equally effective in preventing episodes of mania or depression. Lithium lessens the severity of mood symptoms that appear in a relapse and also reduces the frequency of relapses. Again, although we can conclude that lithium doubles the chances of improvement, we must also acknowledge that lithium is not completely effective for a substantial minority of patients.

Prediction of Response to Lithium.   As stated above, about one-third of patients enrolled in clinical trials relapse with lithium treatment. In naturalistic treatment settings (simple observation of treatment without a placebo control), the rate of relapse during lithium treatment may be even higher.[9] Because substantial numbers of patients with manic-depressive illness do relapse during lithium treatment, it is of great usefulness to both clinicians and patients to predict the chances for good response. So far, the best predictors of response to lithium can be obtained in a good clinical interview by the treating physician. The clinical predictors of lithium response are listed in the accompanying box.[10]

Scientists have also tried to identify molecular, genetic, and brain-imaging predictors of lithium response. The results of these studies have generally been negative or equivocal. However, the ability to predict responsiveness to psychotropic drugs may improve dramatically in the coming years as technology designed to rapidly screen large numbers of genes affected by psychotropic drugs becomes available.

Administration of Lithium.   Lithium is available by prescription in several forms. Lithium carbonate, the most common form, is very inexpensive and is marketed as a generic drug by several different companies. Lithium citrate, another inexpensive form of the drug, is marketed as a liquid. These forms of lithium have a half-life (the time required for the body to remove half of the drug from the blood) of about twelve hours and should be administered twice per day. Two "sustained-release" preparations (Eskalith CR and Lithobid) provide lithium carbonate mixed in coated tablets, but because they are unavailable as generic medications, they are more expensive. With these preparations, the rate at which lithium enters the blood is more constant. Thus, there is less of a "peak" blood level soon after taking one of these preparations and, theoretically, fewer immediate side effects. There is also evidence that the sustained-release forms of lithium produce better and more

Clinical Predictors of Lithium Response

Associated with good response to lithium prophylaxis:

- Typical manic-depressive illness (as opposed to mixed or schizoaffective types)
- Complete resolution of symptoms between episodes
- Family history of manic-depressive illness
- First episode was mania rather than depression
- Family history of good response to lithium

Associated with poor response to lithium prophylaxis:

- Family history of schizophrenia
- Delayed initiation of mood stabilizer between the first several episodes
- First episode was depression rather than mania
- Neurologic signs
- Rapid cycling
- Frequent noncompliance with medication
- Drug abuse
- Large number of previous episodes

even brain concentrations of lithium.[11] These forms of lithium, too, should be taken twice per day. The usual dose of lithium is 600–1,200 milligrams (mg) per day, although a few patients will require 2,100 mg or more to achieve a therapeutic blood level.

Laboratory Monitoring of Lithium Treatment. Prior to starting a patient on lithium therapy, the treating physician will ensure that several basic tests have been completed. These are listed in the accompanying box.

> **Laboratory Tests Required Before
> Starting Lithium Treatment**
>
> - Complete blood count
> - Serum creatinine and electrolytes
> - Thyroid hormones
> - Urinalysis

Other tests may also be necessary depending on one's general health. These might include an electrocardiogram and more detailed tests of kidney function. All such tests should be repeated regularly (usually every six to twelve months) during lithium maintenance therapy.[12]

Because the blood level of lithium needs to be maintained within a fairly narrow range to avoid toxicity and side effects, blood lithium levels may need to be measured frequently in the early stages of treatment and every three to six months thereafter. The blood for the determination of the lithium level should be drawn about twelve hours after the last oral dose of the medication. The blood lithium level should be maintained at between 0.8 and 1.0 millimoles (mmol)/liter for most patients. Some studies suggest that lower levels, between 0.6 and 0.8 mmol/liter, may be sufficient during maintenance treatment. It is recommended that lower blood levels (around 0.5 mmol/liter) be used for elderly and physically unwell patients; occasionally, other patients can successfully be maintained at this level as well.

Side Effects of Lithium.   Lithium treatment reduces *thyroid* function.[13] Although the underlying mechanism is not completely understood, lithium is known to prevent the release of thyroid hormones and to inhibit the uptake of iodine into the thyroid. It may also induce the formation of antibodies that adversely affect the thyroid. Patients taking lithium need to have their thyroid hormones checked on a regular basis.

Thyroid stimulating hormone, or TSH, (see also Chapter 7), offers the most sensitive test for damage. The TSH becomes elevated in about 23 percent of patients on lithium, but medically significant hypothyroidism develops in only 5 to 10 percent of patients. Many patients who develop abnormal thyroid tests decide to continue lithium if they have had a good response to treatment. In this case, thyroid hormones can be replaced by an oral preparation, with very few side effects. If patients have not had a good response to lithium, then valproate or carbamazepine can be substituted.

The *kidneys* are the only mechanism for removing lithium from the bloodstream (most other medications, by contrast, are metabolized at least in part by the liver). Lithium has gained a reputation for causing damage to the filtration system of the kidneys, but this reputation is unfair because damage to the kidneys from lithium is rare. Kidney damage may occur when lithium toxicity or prolonged periods of very high blood levels have occurred. For most patients who monitor their lithium therapy carefully with regular blood level measurements, however, the risk of kidney damage is probably not greater than the naturally occurring rate of kidney failure due to other diseases such as diabetes and hypertension.[14] It is probably best to avoid lithium treatment among patients with pre-existing kidney disease; but if lithium treatment is essential, it can be accomplished with lower doses and more frequent monitoring of the blood level.

About 23 percent of patients treated with lithium may develop a syndrome of excessive urination and thirst known as *polyuria-polydipsia*. If this occurs, kidney function should be checked carefully and the lowest possible therapeutic dose of lithium should be used. Taking lithium in a once-daily dose regimen or using a sustained-release preparation may also help. And again, if lithium treatment is essential, the problem can be helped with the prescription of a diuretic such as furosemide or amiloride. Valproate or carbamazepine can be substituted for lithium if necessary.

Patients who are on a salt-restricted diet or taking diuretics for high blood pressure tend to develop higher lithium levels and an increased chance of toxicity. Lithium levels need to be monitored closely in these patients.

Lithium can cause a fine tremor of the hands that is most evident when the arms are held in a sustained posture; hence the term *postural tremor*. This occurs in about a third of patients and can be helped by using the lowest effective dose of lithium or by adding propranolol. Antidepressants and valproate, as well as antipsychotic drugs used in combination with lithium, make postural tremor worse. Lithium can also aggravate some of the movement disorder side effects associated with antipsychotic drugs (see Chapter 9).

In general, lithium does not impair coordination at therapeutic blood levels, but early in the course of treatment many patients complain of *decreased coordination*. Usually, coordination improves as treatment continues, but athletes, musicians, and others who require a high degree of fine motor coordination may continue to notice an unpleasant effect. One does not have to give up driving or other physical activities while taking lithium.

Many patients taking lithium complain of *reduced memory and concentration*. Neuropsychological studies do show an adverse effect of lithium in these areas, although the magnitude of the effects is not well understood and there are complicated methodological problems associated with the studies designed to evaluate this question. Like many of the other side effects of lithium, these impairments are dose-related; thus, the lowest effective dose of lithium should be used. Some patients feel that lithium diminishes the capacity for creative thought, but many patients elect to continue lithium because it confers better long-term productivity (see Chapter 14).

Lithium has subtle effects on the electrical system that generates the *heart rhythm*. These effects can be seen on electrocardiograms but usually do not imply serious heart problems and in themselves are not a reason to discontinue lithium. Lithium is contraindicated, however, in patients with unstable congestive heart failure or the "sick sinus node syndrome." For older patients and those with a history of abnormal heart rhythm, an electrocardiogram should be obtained prior to lithium treatment. Abnormal heart rhythms as a direct consequence of lithium treatment are now believed to be very rare.

Skin reactions are frequently reported in association with lithium. The most common reaction is a fine rash that appears early in treatment. The rash dissipates if lithium is discontinued and often does not occur again if lithium is restarted. More rarely, acne-like reactions and other skin lesions may appear. These reactions usually improve on their own and do not necessarily require lithium discontinuation. On the other hand, pre-existing psoriasis may become worse, or psoriasis may appear for the first time. The latter outcome is most common among patients with a family history of psoriasis and usually improves if lithium is discontinued.

Some patients, especially women, complain of *hair loss* or change in the texture of the hair. In one survey,[15] 42 percent of patients who were questioned said that they had experienced some change in their hair. However, patients rarely volunteer complaints about hair problems or require lithium discontinuation because of them.

About 25 percent of patients taking lithium gain more than ten pounds. Still unknown is whether this is due mainly to increased consumption of food and sweetened drinks or to altered metabolism of sugars and insulin. For most patients, this level of *weight gain* is not medically dangerous. But for some patients with medical conditions made worse by weight gain, and in those already overweight at the start of treatment, this can be a significant concern. Unfortunately, other mood stabilizers also cause some degree of weight gain. An intense search for drugs that do not cause weight gain is under way. Patients should be very cautious about taking drugs to induce weight loss, as these often have significant side effects of their own, including worsening of psychiatric symptoms in some cases.

Weight gain can also be caused by *fluid retention*, which most often appears as swelling around the ankles. This condition is usually not medically serious. Patients should be very careful about seeking diuretics for fluid retention without first consulting with their treating physician, as these drugs may cause an elevation of lithium levels. Weight gain can also be a symptom of hypothryoidism (see above).

Lithium can be irritating to the stomach and the intestine and may produce *nausea* or *diarrhea*. Taking lithium with a meal can considerably relieve these problems. Divided doses or sustained-release preparations may help with nausea, but sustained-release preparations may make diarrhea worse. Severe or persistent diarrhea may indicate toxic blood levels (see below).

Decreases in sexual desire, arousal, and ejaculation have been reported for lithium, but these are rare and usually transient.

Patients with *chronic lung disease* (emphysema, bronchitis, or severe asthma) should take lithium with care, since high blood lithium levels can be associated with respiratory depression.

Lithium sometimes induces an *increase in the white blood cell count*, but it is usually transient and not of major concern.

Lithium Toxicity. Lithium toxicity is the most worrisome side effect of lithium treatment. It is usually associated with blood levels greater than 1.5 mmol/liter. However, lithium toxicity can occur in some patients who have therapeutic blood levels. Therefore, the treating physician needs to be very aware of lithium toxicity and to make decisions based on the entire clinical picture rather than just the blood level. Lithium toxicity often develops in stages and involves three main types of symptoms: gastrointestinal complaints, incoordination, and altered clarity of thought.

TABLE 8.1   Lithium Toxicity

	Gastrointestinal	Coordination	Thought
Mild toxicity	Nausea Diarrhea	Severe fine tremor	Poor concentration
Moderate toxicity	Vomiting	Coarse tremor Unstable gait Slurred speech	Drowsiness Disorientation
Severe toxicity	Vomiting Incontinence	Involuntary movements Muscle twitching Spastic muscles Seizures	Apathy Coma

If lithium toxicity is suspected, the patient must go to the emergency room, and lithium treatment should be stopped immediately. Sometimes intravenous fluids and electrolytes are necessary. For patients with very severe toxicity, dialysis may be required to rapidly remove lithium from the body.

Lithium toxicity is more likely to occur in patients who are in the midst of another medical illness, especially one that alters the fluid and salt balance of the body. For example, any condition that causes dehydration (such as pneumonia, diarrhea, excessive vomiting, or excessive sweating due to fever or overexercise) can lead to high lithium levels. Patients taking lithium are advised to discontinue it until they check with their doctor whenever they experience these symptoms. Drugs that reduce the blood level of lithium are also a risk factor (see below).

Patients who experience repeated bouts of lithium toxicity have a greater chance of suffering permanent damage to the kidney and the brain (especially the cerebellum).

Risks of Lithium Discontinuation.   If lithium needs to be discontinued—because of side effects, lack of efficacy, or sustained periods of normal mood—the discontinuation must be gradual. The sudden withdrawal of lithium is a major risk factor for further episodes of illness. Approximately 50 percent of patients who stop lithium abruptly will have a significant mood episode (usually mania) within five months.[16] Although some reports suggest that the sudden withdrawal of lithium may lead to recurrent episodes that are less responsive to treatment, this outcome has not been confirmed in other controlled studies and is still an open question.[17]

It is recommended that lithium be discontinued by one-eighth to one-quarter of the original dose every two months to reduce the risk of "withdrawal mania."

Interactions of Lithium with Prescription Drugs.   There are many possible interactions of lithium with other prescription drugs. Whenever a new drug treatment is anticipated for someone already taking lithium, this treatment should be reviewed with the treating physician. Some examples are listed in the accompanying box.

Drugs That May Interact with Lithium

Drugs that may cause increased lithium blood levels:

1. nonsteroidal anti-inflammatory drugs
   - indomethacin
   - phenylbutazone
   - naproxen
   - diclofenac
   - ibuprofen

2. anti-hypertension drugs
   - thiazide diuretics
   - methyldopa

3. antibiotics
   - tetracycline
   - metronidazole
   - erythromycin

Drugs that may cause decreased lithium blood levels:
   - verapamil
   - osmotic diuretics (mannitol)
   - carbonic anhydrase inhibitors (Diamox)
   - valproate
   - caffeine
   - theophylline

Drugs that may work less well during lithium treatment:
   - clonidine
   - insulin and oral hypoglycemics
   - digoxin
   - quinidine

Few interactions of lithium with other drugs are known to cause direct and lasting damage to organ systems. It has been proposed that the combination of lithium and antipsychotic drugs (especially haloperidol) may increase the chance of damage to the brain; however, brain injury from the combination of these medications is probably seen only with very high doses of neuroleptics or toxic blood levels of lithium. Careful clinical use of lithium in combination with antipsychotics is quite safe and, indeed, routinely practiced.

Valproate (Depakote, Depakene)

The development of valproate for the treatment of epilepsy and manic-depressive illness also occurred by accident. Valproate is a fatty acid similar to those found in animal and vegetable oils. It was first used as a solvent for other drugs that are insoluble in water. Scientists working to identify new drugs for epilepsy noticed that when valproate was used as a solvent, epileptic activity decreased. The first report of effectiveness in manic-depressive illness appeared in 1966.[18] Although valproate is now widely prescribed, research is still being conducted to determine if this drug fully meets the criteria for mood stabilization.

Efficacy of Valproate.   Valproate has been shown to be effective in the treatment of acute mania in six separate studies and is approved by the FDA for this use.[19] It is superior to placebo and approximately equal to lithium in efficacy. However, it may take less time to work than lithium and in some studies has been given in a "rapid loading" design to achieve adequate blood levels in a short period of time. Valproate may be more effective than lithium in patients with mania who have a history of rapid cycling or mixed states (depressive symptoms occurring simultaneously with mania).

Although relatively few controlled studies have looked at valproate in depression, the available data suggest that it is not very effective in this regard,[20] thus posing a considerable disadvantage in comparison to lithium.

There is still controversy concerning the effectiveness of valproate as a prophylactic treatment for future episodes of manic-depressive illness.

Several open studies suggest that valproate is effective as a maintenance treatment, but the only controlled study of this question found that the relapse rate for valproate was no different than that for placebo.[21] However, this study may have contained an unusual population in the placebo group that was less likely to have suffered a relapse.

Prediction of Response to Valproate.   Researchers know that about 50 to 65 percent of patients respond well to valproate, but they are not yet able to accurately predict which patients are in this group. Patients with accompanying neurologic abnormalities may respond better than those without abnormalities.[22] It has been suggested that valproate may be helpful in patients for whom lithium is often inadequate. Among such patients are those experiencing rapid cycling or mixed states and those with a significant history of impulsiveness or aggression.

Administration of Valproate.   Abbott Laboratories produces Depakote, which is a mixture of sodium valproate (the ionized form of valproic acid) and valproic acid. This mixture is also referred to as divalproex sodium. Depakote is available either as tablets or as capsules containing coated particles ("sprinkles") that can be mixed with food. Abbott also markets Depakene, which is pure valproic acid in the form of capsules or syrup. A generic preparation of valproic acid is available as well. The usual dose of valproate is 500–3,000 mg per day.

Laboratory Monitoring of Valproate Treatment.   The most worrisome adverse effects of valproate are liver damage and a decreased number of blood platelets (the blood cells that promote clotting). At the onset of treatment with valproate, the treating physician should assess liver enzyme function and do a complete blood count. These tests should be repeated every three to six months during treatment with valproate. If valproate has been administered safely for a prolonged period, these tests can be done on an annual basis.

The level of valproate in the blood can also be measured. Blood levels of 50–100 micrograms (mcg)/ml are usually sought. Side effects are more common if the blood level is greater than 125 mcg/ml. The blood level of valproate is usually measured several times early in the course of treatment, until a therapeutic blood level is achieved. Thereafter, it can be checked periodically along with the other laboratory tests mentioned above or more frequently if there is a change in symptoms.

Side Effects of Valproate.   Although valproate has significant side effects, it has fewer than lithium and is less likely to produce toxicity. The most common side effect is *nausea,* or upset stomach. Nausea is less frequent with divalproex sodium than with pure valproic acid. Serious abdominal pain may indicate *inflammation of the pancreas,* which is a rare but very serious side effect. *Sleepiness* may occur, especially in the early phase of treatment. Some patients complain of *decreased concentration,* but in formal studies this effect appears to be quite mild.[23] Valproate may cause *hair loss* by decreasing the absorption of zinc and selenium in the diet. This can be treated by taking valproate separately from meals, or by adding a multiple vitamin containing these trace elements. *Weight gain* and *increased appetite* are relatively common. Some patients develop a mild *postural tremor.*

As mentioned above, the most serious adverse events associated with valproate are *liver damage* and *decreased platelet count.* Serious liver damage is rare in adults but can be more common in children. Extended therapy with valproate in women may be associated with the formation of *ovarian cysts.*

Interactions of Valproate with Prescription Drugs.   Patients taking other anticonvulsants that activate the liver enzymes used to metabolize valproate may develop lower blood levels of valproate. These anticonvulsants include diphenylhydantoin (Dilantin), carbamazepine, and phenobarbital. Aspirin may cause increased levels of valproate.

The addition of valproate may cause elevated concentrations of other drugs such as lamotrigine, warfarin, and zidovidine. Care should be taken when combining valproate with these medications.

Carbamazepine (Tegretol)

Efficacy of Carbamazepine.   Carbamazepine, like valproate, was originally developed as a medication for epilepsy. In early studies with carbamazepine, patients with epilepsy exhibited improvements in mood. The first successful carbamazepine study involving patients with manic-depressive illness was performed in Japan.[24] Carbamazepine has fallen out of favor as a first-line treatment for manic-depressive illness, mainly because of side effects and interactions with other medications; however, it still plays a role for some patients.

In one study, carbamazepine was observed in comparison to placebo, to lithium, and to chlorpromazine (an antipsychotic).[25] This study suggests that carbamazepine is more effective than placebo and is approximately equivalent to lithium and chlorpromazine for acute mania. Similar to lithium and valproate, carbamazepine elicits a good response from about 60 percent of patients.

The specific effects of carbamazepine on depression have not been studied extensively, but in two controlled studies,[26] carbamazepine produced significant improvement in depressive symptoms.

Early studies of carbamazepine for prophylaxis of manic-depressive illness generated considerable controversy due to unusual trial designs. More recently, two controlled studies have evaluated carbamazepine in comparison to lithium for maintenance treatment.[27] These studies have shown that the efficacy of carbamazepine is similar to that of lithium overall. However, lithium may be more effective for "classic" manic-depressive illness, and carbamazepine may be more effective in cases involving mixed states, rapid cycling, or schizoaffective disorder. In the two studies just mentioned, more patients withdrew from trials due to side effects if they were taking carbamazepine.

Predictors of Response to Carbamazepine.   Predictors of response to carbamazepine have not been clearly defined in research studies. As noted above, however, "nonclassic" forms of mania may respond better to carbamazepine than to lithium.

Administration of Carbamazepine.   Tegretol (manufactured by Novartis) is available in 100 mg chewable tablets, in 200 mg tablets, and in a suspension. Because the half-life of carbamazepine is relatively short and varies depending upon how long one has been taking the drug, these forms of carbamazepine should be taken three or four times per day in order to maintain a consistent blood level. Generic preparations are available.

There are two sustained-release preparations available. Carbatrol (Shire) is available in 200 and 300 mg capsules, whereas Tegretol XR (Novartis) is available in 100, 200, and 400 mg tablets. The half-life for these preparations is twelve to seventeen hours, so they can be taken twice a day. The average dose of carbamazepine is 600–1,200 mg per day.

Laboratory Monitoring of Carbamazepine Treatment.   At the beginning of treatment, the treating physician should do a complete blood count and check liver enzyme levels; these should be rechecked every three to six months. In addition, a blood level should be checked five to seven days after the dose of carbamazepine has been determined. The blood level should be taken about ten hours after the last dose. Therapeutic blood levels are 6–10 micrograms (ug)/ml for epilepsy, and this level is usually sought for manic-depressive illness as well. However, a relationship between clinical efficacy and blood level is not well established for manic-depressive illness.

Side Effects of Carbamazepine.   Carbamazepine commonly causes the sensation of *sleepiness* or *dizziness* early in the course of treatment. These symptoms usually resolve within a few weeks; however, if they persist, or emerge after chronic treatment, they may indicate that the blood level of carbamazepine is too high. *Headache* is also a transient side effect. In elderly patients, *decreased mental concentration* or *confusion* may sometimes occur.

Abnormal heart rhythms may occur in elderly patients taking carbamazepine, but they are otherwise rare. Carbamazepine can also affect the body's ability to control fluid and salt balance. *Swelling of the ankles* is sometimes seen; *fluid retention* and *decreased sodium concentration* in the blood, though more serious, occur less frequently.

Allergic skin reactions occur in about 10 percent of patients. Those who experience a rash should stop treatment with carbamazepine, alert their treating physician quickly, and have it monitored closely. Some patients may have a more serious allergic skin condition known as

Stevens-Johnson syndrome, which produces extensive skin loss. This condition, however, is relatively rare.

Nausea is a frequent side effect early in carbamazepine treatment; it usually improves with time or if the patient takes the medication along with food. Carbamazepine is metabolized in the liver and commonly induces an *increase of liver enzyme activity*. Serious *inflammation of the liver or the pancreas* is rare.

Carbamazepine can interfere with the ability of the bone marrow to produce new blood cells, causing a *decrease in the white blood cell count or in the platelet count*. Serious deficiencies of these blood cells are quite rare (affecting only about 1 in 40,000 patients), but laboratory monitoring of blood counts is required. Patients should be alert to possible problems with their white blood cell count or platelet count if they develop infection, fever, sore throat, bruising, or increased sensitivity of the skin to sunlight. The blood count should be checked if these symptoms appear.

Interactions of Carbamazepine with Prescription Drugs. A large number of interactions with other medications have contributed to carbamazepine's decreasing use as a mood stabilizer. These are summarized in the accompanying box.

Lamotrigine (Lamictal)

Lamotrigine is a drug approved for the treatment of epilepsy. Improved mood has been observed in some patients receiving the drug for epilepsy. Based on preliminary reports it appears to be a promising agent in that both acute mania and depression seem to respond favorably. There are limited data available regarding the effectiveness of lamotrigine for prophylaxis of manic-depressive illness.

Efficacy of Lamotrigine. The largest of several nonblinded studies of lamotrigine involved seventy-five patients.[28] Eighty-four percent of the patients with hypomania, mania, or mixed states improved. In one controlled study that compared lamotrigine to lithium or olanzapine (fifteen patients in each group), lamotrigine appeared to be equally as

Drugs That May Interact with Carbamazepine

Drugs that may cause increased carbamazepine blood levels:

1. antibiotics
   - erythromycin and similar antibiotics
   - isoniazid
   - triacetyloleandomycin

2. antidepressants
   - fluoxetine
   - fluvoxamine
   - nefazodone
   - sertraline

3. others
   - cimetidine
   - diltiazem
   - propoxyphene
   - verapamil
   - viloxazine

Drugs that may cause decreased carbamazepine blood levels:
   - phenobarbital
   - phenytoin
   - primidone

Drugs that may work less well in combination with carbamazepine:

1. antidepressants
   - tricyclic antidepressants
   - buproprion
   - nefazodone
   - fluvoxamine

2. antipsychotics

3. dicumarol

4. doxycycline

5. epilepsy medications
   - ethosuximide
   - phenobarbital
   - phenytoin
   - valproate

6. oral contraceptives

7. pregnancy tests

8. steroid anti-inflammatory drugs

9. theophyllin

10. thyroid hormone

11. warfarin

efficacious as both of the other drugs.[29] Two other small, controlled studies[30] did not show a benefit of lamotrigine over placebo in acute mania.

In the largest of the open trials of lamotrigine,[31] 68 percent of the patients presenting with depression improved. In one controlled trial comparing two different doses of lamotrigine to placebo,[32] significant improvements in mood were noted.

Administration of Lamotrigine.   Lamotrigine is marketed by Glaxo Wellcome as Lamictal. It is available in 25, 100, 150, and 200 mg tablets. It is also available in 5 and 25 mg chewable tablets for children. The usual dosage range is 50–300 mg. The dosage of lamotrigine should be increased very gradually over several weeks in order to reduce the risk of skin irritation. The half-life is about fifteen to twenty-four hours, and the medication is usually taken twice per day.

Side Effects of Lamotrigine. *Headache, dizziness, incoordination, insomnia,* and *sleepiness* may occur early in treatment and are usually mild. In the large trials conducted to study epilepsy, *rash* developed in about 10 percent of patients. Several different kinds of rash may occur, usually within the first two months of treatment. Serious rash (Stevens-Johnson syndrome or toxic epidermal necrolysis) reportedly occurs in 0.3 percent of adults (3 per 1,000) and 1 percent of children. It is generally agreed that lamotrigine should be discontinued if any rash develops, since it is impossible to predict which rashes will become serious. *Nausea* is usually mild and limited to the early phase of treatment.

Interactions of Lamotrigine with Prescription Drugs. Valproate doubles the half-life of lamotrigine, so the dose of lamotrigine must be reduced if these drugs are used together. Carbamazepine, phenobarbital, and phenytoin cause reduced blood levels of lamotrigine. Sertraline (Zoloft) may cause an increase in lamotrigine level.

Topiramate (Topamax)

Efficacy of Topiramate. Topiramate is a new drug approved for the treatment of epilepsy. Because its neurochemical profile somewhat overlaps that of valproate, it has been studied preliminarily for manic-depressive illness. There are five published studies on the use of topiramate in this illness.[33] All were uncontrolled pilot studies. In general, they suggest that 30 to 60 percent of patients improve with topiramate. The largest of these studies[34] involved fifty-four patients. Sixty-three percent of those with manic symptoms improved, compared to only 27 percent of patients presenting with depression. Larger controlled studies with topiramate are needed.

Administration of Topiramate. Topiramate is marketed by Ortho-McNeil as Topamax. It is available both as 25, 100, and 200 mg tablets and as 15 or 25 mg "sprinkle capsules" that can be mixed with food for use in children. To avoid side effects, the dose of topiramate should be increased gradually over several weeks. The usual dosage range is 100–400 mg per day. The half-life is about twenty-one hours, but the drug is usually given twice per day.

Side Effects of Topiramate. *Sleepiness, fatigue, dizziness* and complaints of *decreased concentration* are common at the start of therapy, but these usually decrease with time. Occasionally, patients develop a *worsening of psychotic symptoms* on topiramate. *Numbness and tingling in the hands and feet* or *ringing in the ears* occur occasionally and are usually mild. However, the numbness and tingling can be quite unpleasant for some patients. There is an increased risk of *kidney stones* with topiramate treatment.

One side effect of topiramate actually appears to be an advantage: It is one of the few psychotropic medications available that appears to cause *weight loss* rather than weight gain. In existing studies with topiramate, patients have lost an average of about ten pounds during the trial. In addition to weight loss, patients may notice mild *nausea* or *decreased appetite.*

Interactions of Topiramate with Prescription Drugs. Blood levels of diphenylhydantoin (Dilantin) are increased with topiramate therapy. Oral contraceptives work less well when combined with topiramate. Co-administration of valproate or carbamazepine may make topiramate less effective.

Gabapentin (Neurontin)

Gabapentin was approved for the treatment of epilepsy in 1993. The drug is under evaluation for manic-depressive illness because of its reported calming effects in patients with epilepsy.

Efficacy of Gabapentin. Several open and retrospective studies have reported on the efficacy of gabapentin when it is used along with other psychotropic medications in the treatment of acute mania, mixed states, and depression.[35] Conversely, two controlled studies have failed to demonstrate that gabapentin is better than placebo for the treatment of manic-depressive illness, either in conjunction with other medications[36] or as the sole agent.[37] Both of the latter studies, however, have methodological limitations that prevent a definitive answer regarding the efficacy of gabapentin. Some patients, especially those with anxiety, aggression, or rapid cycling, may nevertheless respond to treatment with gabapentin.

Administration of Gabapentin. Gabapentin is marketed by Parke-Davis as Neurontin. It is available in 100, 300, and 400 mg capsules. The usual dosage range is 900–2,400 mg per day in three divided doses. The dose should be titrated slowly upward over several weeks to avoid side effects. Gabapentin has a very wide margin of safety and does not require laboratory monitoring.

Side Effects of Gabapentin. Gabapentin has a very favorable side-effect profile. It may cause *blurred vision, dizziness, clumsiness,* and *sedation,* but these are usually transient or improved by a reduction in dose.

Interactions of Gabapentin with Prescription Drugs. Since gabapentin is not metabolized by the liver, it has very few interactions with other medications. Antacids may counteract the effects of gabapentin.

Calcium Channel Blockers

Calcium channel blockers are a group of medications approved for the treatment of high blood pressure, heart failure, angina pectoris, and cardiac arrhythmias. There are several types of calcium channel blockers available,[38] but verapamil and nimodipine have received the most attention for manic-depressive illness. Although there is still reason to study calcium channel blockers, they are considered to be a third-line choice for mood stabilization.[39]

Efficacy of Calcium Channel Blockers. Verapamil has been the most widely studied compound in this group. In two small studies of acute mania, verapamil is associated with modest improvements in comparison to placebo,[40] but a study using the most careful design reported no benefit of verapamil over placebo.[41] In comparison to lithium, verapamil has been shown to be less effective. However, some lithium refractory patients may respond to verapamil, and some patients may respond more rapidly to verapamil than to lithium.

Nimodipine is another calcium channel blocker that enters the brain more easily than verapamil. It has been investigated in two controlled studies, which showed positive effects in some patients, especially those with rapid cycling.

Administration of Calcium Channel Blockers.   Verapamil is available in generic preparations. It is also marketed as Calan (Searle) in 40 mg tablets. The usual dose is 80–160 mg three times per day. Covera (Searle), Isoptin (Knoll), and Verelan (Schwarz) are sustained-release preparations of verapamil available in 120, 180, 240, and 360 mg tablets. The usual dose is 120–480 mg once per day.

Nimotop (Bayer) is available in 30 mg capsules. The usual dose is 30–60 mg four times per day.

Liver function tests should be checked periodically with these medications; otherwise, no specific laboratory monitoring is necessary.

Side Effects of Calcium Channel Blockers.   Calcium channel blockers are associated with side effects caused by dilatation of blood vessels. These may include *dizziness, low blood pressure, headache, flushing, nausea, pins-and-needles sensations,* and *water retention.* Such effects are generally mild but may be unpleasant enough to warrant discontinuation for some patients.

Interactions of Calcium Channel Blockers with Prescription Drugs. Calcium channel blockers may decrease the effectiveness of lithium, quinidine, disopyramide, flecainide, carbamazepine, cyclosporine, and theophylline. They may also potentiate the effects of digoxin and beta blockers.

The effectiveness of calcium channel blockers may be reduced by rifampin, phenobarbital, and sulfinpyrazone.

Since grapefruit juice inhibits the enzyme that metabolizes calcium channel blockers, it should be avoided by patients who are taking these medications.

Essential Fatty Acids

Essential fatty acids cannot be synthesized by the body and must therefore be obtained in the diet. Important components of nerve cell function, these acids are present in high concentration in certain plant oils and in fish. There is some evidence that patients with mood disorders and schizophrenia may have abnormally low levels of essential fatty acids[42] and that supplementation of the diet with these oils may have beneficial effects on symptoms. In one small controlled trial using omega–3 fatty acids, Andrew Stoll et al.[43] were able to show a reduced relapse rate in a group of thirty patients with unstable manic-depressive illness. Future research is necessary to determine whether this is a strong effect observed in larger populations. Although fish oil capsules are widely available in health food stores and are quite safe, patients should consult with their treating physician prior to taking these capsules.

9

MEDICATIONS: ANTIDEPRESSANTS, ANTIPSYCHOTICS, AND BENZODIAZAPINES

Of all the ills which flesh is heir to, there is perhaps none so dreadful as insanity. Utter poverty, hideous deformity, mutilation of limbs, deafness, blindness, all these, sad as they are, leave alive the human affections, and admit the consolations of sympathy and love; while insanity not only makes man utterly dependent upon others for the supply of his physical wants, but it strips him of the noblest attributes of humanity.

SAMUEL GRIDLEY HOWE,
"Insanity in Massachusetts" (1843)[1]

Many individuals with manic-depressive illness can be treated with mood stabilizers alone for much, or even all, of the course of their illness. Many others, however, require medications in addition to the mood stabilizers. This is especially true for individuals with severe forms of manic-depressive illness and those with rapid cycling. The most commonly used adjunctive medications are antidepressants, antipsychotics, and benzodiazepines.

Antidepressants

There is an alarming lack of good scientific data to guide the choice of medications for the treatment of the depressed phase of manic-depressive illness. This is the case because researchers have tended to assume that studies of unipolar depression were generalizable to the depressed phase of manic-depressive illness. In addition, patients with manic-depressive illness are often excluded from studies of new antidepressants because they are taking other psychotropic medications or have high rates of substance abuse, anxiety, or other problems.

Selective serotonin reuptake inhibitors (SSRIs) and other new antidepressants, such as buproprion and venlafaxine, are generally considered to be the first-line choices for the depressed phase of manic-depressive illness. Most clinicians do not prescribe antidepressants alone for manic-depressive illness but instead prescribe them in combination with a mood stabilizer. This is because antidepressants have the potential to provoke a manic episode in some patients (see below). Following a description of the SSRIs and other new antidepressants, a description of tricyclic antidepressants (TCAs) and monoamine oxidase inhibitors (MAOIs) will be given.

Selective Serotonin Reuptake Inhibitors (SSRIs)

Efficacy of SSRIs.   There is a large literature demonstrating the efficacy of SSRIs in major depression.[2] The SSRIs are probably not more efficacious than older antidepressants, but they are generally much safer and better tolerated.

In contrast to the large literature on major depression, there are very few published studies specifically addressing the depressed phase of manic-depressive illness. In one such study, J. B. Cohn et al.[3] compared fluoxetine to imipramine (a TCA) and to placebo in eighty-nine patients with manic-depressive illness. Fluoxetine produced a good response in 60 percent of the patients, a proportion significantly better than for imipramine (40 percent) or placebo. In a trial comparing paroxetine and imipramine to placebo,[4] both drugs produced a better response than placebo but did not differ significantly from each other. However, paroxetine was much easier to tolerate than imipramine.

The SSRIs are considered to be among the primary treatments for manic-depressive illness. These drugs have a very favorable side-effect profile and, along with buproprion and MAOIs, have been less frequently associated with worsening of manic symptoms. (This issue is further discussed under "Switch Rate" below.)

TABLE 9.1   SSRIs and Their Properties

Drug Name	Trade Name/ Manufacturer	Strengths	Half-Life	Usual Dosage
fluoxetine	Prozac/Lilly	capsules: 10 and 20 mg concentrate: 20 mg per teaspoon	4–6 days	10–80 mg once per day
fluoxetine hydrochloride	Prozac Weekly/ Lilly	capsules: 90 mg	4–6 days	90 mg once per week
sertraline	Zoloft/Pfizer	tablets: 25, 50, and 100 mg	26 hours	50–200 mg once per day
paroxetine	Paxil/Smith-Kline-Beecham	tablets: 10, 20, 30, and 40 mg concentrate: 10 mg per teaspoon	21 hours	20–50 mg once per day
fluvoxamine	Luvox/Solvay	tablets: 25, 50, and 100 mg	15 hours	50–300 mg per day in two divided doses
citalopram	Celexa/Parke-Davis	tablets: 20 and 40 mg	33 hours	20–60 mg once per day

Administration of SSRIs.   Available SSRIs and their properties are listed in Table 9.1. As of this writing, all are relatively expensive and no generic forms are available. However, fluoxetine will soon be available in generic form.

Side Effects and Relative Merits of SSRIs.   The most common side effect associated with SSRIs is *nausea*. This occurs in 10 to 25 percent of patients and is most noticeable with fluvoxamine. It can be counter-acted by taking the medications with food.

Other common side effects, reported in 10 to 25 percent of patients, include *headache, insomnia, sleepiness, nervousness, tremors, increased sweating, dry mouth,* and *loose bowel movements.* Usually these symptoms are mild and subside after the first few weeks of treatment. Occasionally, however, they may be severe enough to make SSRIs difficult to tolerate. Citalopram has the lowest incidence of these side effects in published trials.

Sexual dysfunction for both males (usually delayed orgasm) and females (decreased sexual drive) are reported much more commonly in clinical practice than in published studies. This effect, which can be troublesome for patients, is handled by using the lowest possible dose of SSRIs, switching to another class of antidepressant, or, as a last resort, adding other medications to improve sexual function.

Other side effects that are reported more rarely include *palpitations* or *abnormal heart beat, bruising* or *increased tendency for bleeding,* and *decreased concentration of sodium* in the blood.

SSRIs and other antidepressants can cause the *serotonin syndrome.* This syndrome occurs when too much serotonin is released in the brain and peripheral nervous system. The symptoms of serotonin syndrome include chills, headache, diarrhea, profuse sweating, confusion, and restlessness. If this syndrome occurs, the patient should stop all antidepressant medications and see the treating physician without delay. The serotonin syndrome, though rare, occurs more commonly in people who are taking multiple medications that affect the serotonin system.

Many patients who abruptly stop taking SSRIs experience a mild but unpleasant withdrawal syndrome. This usually consists of anxiety, dizziness, poor concentration, and vivid dreams. It is most common in association with drugs that have a short half-life and do not have a breakdown product that also affects the serotonin syndrome (paroxetine, fluvoxamine, citalopram). These drugs should be discontinued gradually over one or two weeks. Withdrawal symptoms are less common with fluoxetine and sertraline.

Interactions of SSRIs with Prescription Drugs.   The SSRIs bind quite strongly to blood plasma proteins. Thus, they may displace and change the available concentration in the blood of other drugs that are highly protein-bound. Fluvoxamine and citalopram have the lowest degree of protein binding and should probably be chosen for patients taking other drugs that are highly protein-bound, such as digoxin and warfarin.

The SSRIs also inhibit the various members of the cytochrome P450 family of enzymes in the liver. The cytochrome P450 enzymes are necessary for the metabolism of many other drugs, and if they are inhibited by SSRIs, the levels of the other prescribed drugs may increase. This effect has been reported for tricyclic antidepressants, antipsychotics, anti-anxiety medications, beta-blockers, antiarrythmic agents, carbamazepine, antidiabetes medications, and cough medications. Usually these medications can be used in combination with SSRIs, but they require careful monitoring. Terfenidine, astemizole, and cisapride should not be used in combination with fluvoxamine. And none of the SSRIs should be used in combination with MAOIs.

Buproprion and Other New Antidepressants

Buproprion (Wellbutrin) is also rated as a first-line choice for the treatment of manic-depressive illness.[5] This rating has evolved mostly from clinical experience, as direct evidence from controlled studies is lacking. In one study comparing buproprion to desipramine (a TCA), the two drugs showed equivalent efficacy in reducing depressive symptoms, but there was less risk for provocation of mania with buproprion.[6] Buproprion does not appreciably alter the serotonin system but works mainly through the dopamine and norepinephrine systems. Its side-effect profile, therefore, differs from that of the SSRIs. Buproprion has a very low incidence of weight gain and sexual dysfunction. The most common side effects of buproprion are *dry mouth, constipation, headaches,* and *insomnia.* Compared to other antidepressants, there is an increased risk for *seizures* with buproprion. This risk is more common with doses above 400 mg, and seizures probably occur with a frequency of about 4 per 1,000 treated patients.

Venlafaxine (Effexor) has also been rated highly for the treatment of manic-depressive illness.[7] As with most other antidepressant drugs, controlled studies of venlafaxine's efficacy in manic-depressive illness are lacking. Jay Amsterdam et al.[8] compared venlafaxine treatment in a group of patients with mild manic-depressive illness (bipolar II disorder) to the same treatment in a group of patients with major depression. Both groups showed improvement, and there were no observed switches to mania. Venlafaxine is a serotonin reuptake inhibitor but at higher doses also blocks the reuptake of norepinephrine. Because of its neurochemical properties, it has several advantages over SSRIs and TCAs. First, the clinical response to venlafaxine is directly correlated with dose, a relationship that is not observed for most other antidepressants; thus it may have superior efficacy at higher doses and may produce a response in patients who have not done well with SSRIs. Second, venlafaxine may alleviate the symptoms of depression more rapidly than other antidepressants. Third, venlafaxine has fewer effects on liver enzymes and can be used more easily in combination with other medications. Venlafaxine has a favorable side-effect profile and a lower incidence of sexual dysfunction than SSRIs. At higher doses, however, its use may be associated with hypertension.

Reboxetine is a selective inhibitor of norepinephrine reuptake. It is not yet available in the United States but can be obtained in Canada and Europe. Compared to SSRIs, reboxetine may be more effective in patients with pronounced fatigue and lack of energy when depressed; it also may have a better side-effect profile. At present, there are no available published data regarding the use of reboxetine in manic-depressive illness.

Nefazodone (Serzone) blocks a particular type of serotonin receptor in addition to serotonin reuptake blockade, whereas *mirtazapine (Remeron)* blocks serotonin receptors and norepinephrine receptors and produces serotonin reuptake blockade. These drugs are rated as secondary choices for manic-depressive illness,[9] but there are no published data available regarding their efficacy in this disorder. Both drugs have several advantages over the SSRIs. They are quite sedating and are therefore often helpful for patients with severe insomnia. They also produce less nausea and may rapidly alleviate anxiety. The sedative properties of these drugs can also be viewed as disadvantageous by some patients, who experience this effect as unpleasant. Weight gain is more common with mirtazapine than with SSRIs. Nefazodone potently inhibits liver enzymes and thus may cause problems when combined with other drugs.

These new antidepressants are summarized in Table 9.2.

Tricyclic Antidepressants

Tricyclic antidepressants (TCAs) have been available for the treatment
of depression since the 1950s. However, as with the SSRIs, there are
very few published reports on the specific effects of TCAs in manic-
depressive illness. Imipramine (Tofranil) and maprotiline (Ludiomil)
have been found to be superior to placebo in at least one controlled
trial.[10] Disadvantages of TCAs include a greater likelihood of increased
cycling frequency and precipitation of mania relative to SSRIs or
MAOIs,[11] decreased efficacy relative to SSRIs and MAOIs, a greater

TABLE 9.2   New Antidepressants and Their Properties

Drug Name	Trade Name/ Manufacturer	Strengths	Half-Life	Active Metabolites	Usual Dosage
buproprion	Wellbutrin/ Glaxo-Wellcome	tablets: 75 and 100 mg; sustained-release tablets: 100 and 150 mg.	14 hrs / 21 hrs	Yes	150–400 mg/day tablets: three doses/day; sustained-release: two doses/day
venlafaxine	Effexor/ Wyeth-Ayerst	tablets: 25, 37.5, 50, 75, and 100 mg; sustained-release capsules: 37.5, 75, and 100 mg	11 hrs	Yes	75–225 mg/day; tablets: three doses/day; sustained-release: two doses/day
mirtazapine	Remeron/ Organon	tablets: 15, 30, and 45 mg	20–40 hrs	Yes	7.5–45 mg at bedtime
nefazodone	Serzone/ Bristol-Myers Squibb	tablets: 50, 100, 150, 200, and 250 mg	11–24 hrs	Yes	200–600 mg/day in two divided doses

TABLE 9.3   TCAs and Their Most Common Side Effects

Generic Name	Brand Name	Usual Dose (mg/day)	Sedation	Anticholinergic Properties*	Weight Gain
amoxapine	Ascendin	200–300	+	+	+
desipramine	Norpramin	100–200	+	+	+
nortriptyline	Pamelor	75–150	+	+	+
protriptyline	Vivactil	15–40	+	+	+
clomipramine	Anafranil	100–200	++	+++	+
maprotiline	Ludiomil	100–150	++	++	++
amitriptyline	Elavil	100–200	+++	+++	++
doxepin	Sinequan	100–200	+++	++	++
imipramine	Tofranil	100–200	+++	++	++

* Anticholinergic properties include dry mouth, constipation, blurred vision, and heart rhythm abnormalities.

likelihood of lethal consequences if taken in overdose, and frequent unpleasant side effects. Advantages of TCAs include the potential for monitoring blood levels to guide treatment for some of the drugs and low cost (all of these drugs are available in generic forms). Though not prescribed commonly in current practice, the TCAs are regarded as second- or third-line therapy for manic-depressive illness. Because they are used infrequently, we will not review all of their properties here; however, a detailed discussion of the TCAs can be found in *Principles and Practice of Psychopharmacotherapy* (1997), by Philip Janicak et al.[12] Table 9.3 provides a summary of the TCAs and their most common side effects.

Monoamine Oxidase Inhibitors (MAOIs)

Monoamine oxidase is an enzyme that occurs in two different forms in the body: Monoamine oxidase A mainly breaks down serotonin and norepinephrine, and monoamine oxidase B mainly breaks down dopamine. Drugs that inhibit these enzymes (MAOIs) are effective antidepressants. Currently available MAOIs are nonselective and block both forms of the enzyme.

Efficacy of MAOIs. Compared to TCAs, the MAOIs have a reputation for better efficacy and for lower risk of producing a switch to mania in patients in the depressed phase of manic-depressive illness. This reputation is supported by a few controlled studies.[13] Tranylcypromine has been studied most thoroughly and is considered a worthwhile choice if patients have not responded to an SSRI and one of the newer antidepressants. In fact, experts in the field consistently rate the MAOIs as a good second-line choice, ahead of TCAs.[14]

Administration of MAOIs. Phenelzine and tranylcypromine are the two MAOIs currently available for clinical use in the United States. Phenelzine is marketed by Parke-Davis as Nardil. It is available in 15 mg tablets, and the usual dosage is 45–90 mg per day in three divided doses. Tranylcypromine is marketed by Smith-Kline-Beecham as Parnate. It is available in 10 mg tablets. The usual dosage is 30–60 mg per day in three divided doses.

Moclobemide is a new MAOI that is selective for MAO-A and is reversible. Its efficacy is equal to that of imipramine for the depression phase of manic-depressive illness,[15] and unlike the other MAOIs it does not require a special diet. Unfortunately, moclobemide is not available in the United States. Selegiline is selective for MAO-B and is currently used for the treatment of Parkinson's disease. Although some preliminary reports suggest that it may help with depressive symptoms, the effect appears to be modest, and selegiline is not widely used for this purpose. Three other selective and reversible MAOIs are in development: brofaromine, cimoxatone, and toloxatone.

Side Effects of MAOIs. Commonly reported side effects include *insomnia, sleepiness, nervousness, low blood pressure* on standing suddenly, *sweating, weight gain,* and *sexual dysfunction.* These are usually mild and transient. MAOIs may contribute to the *serotonin syndrome* (see section on side effects under SSRIs). Treatment with MAOIs is inconvenient because a special diet is required when taking these medications. MAOIs block the degradation of a substance called tyramine, which is found in certain foods. Decongestants found in over-the-counter cold preparations also contain substances that are usually broken down by MAO. If tyramine or decongestants are taken in sufficient quantities, elevated blood pressure can occur. Very elevated blood pressure, or hypertensive crisis, has been observed with these drugs and can be fatal. If followed carefully, a low-tyramine diet will drastically reduce the risk for elevated blood pressure. The necessary food restrictions while taking MAOIs are given in the accompanying box.

Patients can learn to monitor their blood pressure at home when on these medications. The blood pressure should be checked on a regular basis and immediately if new symptoms such as headache, personality change, or confusion develop. If the blood pressure is elevated, patients should go to the emergency room, where there are medications available to reduce the blood pressure quickly. Patients taking an MAOI should discuss any new medication with their treating physician or pharmacist prior to beginning treatment. They should also consider wearing an alerting bracelet that identifies them as taking an MAOI in case they need emergency treatment.

Patients with significant cardiovascular, cerebrovascular, or liver disease should not take MAOIs.

Interactions of MAOIs with Prescription Medications.   The half-life of MAOIs is relatively short (a matter of hours). However, once the drug binds to monoamine oxidase, the enzyme is irreversibly inhibited. It takes about two weeks for new enzymes to be manufactured by the body, so the effects of MAOIs are quite long-lasting. This explains why it is best to avoid other drugs with the potential to affect dopamine, norepinephrine, or serotonin for two weeks after taking an MAOI. (Drugs that have this potential are TCAs, SSRIs, stimulants, buspirone, and L-dopa.) As mentioned above, over-the-counter decongestants should be avoided as well. Toxic effects can also be observed if MAOIs are combined with meperidine (Demerol) and dextromethorphan (found in cough syrups). Finally, MAOIs may counteract the effects of drugs used for the treatment of diabetes.

Food Restrictions While Taking MAOIs

Foods to be avoided while taking MAOIs:

- cheese (except cream cheese)
- overripe aged fruit
- fava beans
- sausage and salami
- sherry, liqueurs
- sauerkraut
- monosodium glutamate

- pickled or smoked fish, poultry, and meats
- meat extracts
- brewer's yeast
- beef and chicken liver
- fermented products
- red wine

Foods to be used in moderation while taking MAOIs:

- coffee
- chocolate
- colas
- tea
- soy sauce
- beer, alcohol-free beers, other wines
- sour cream

- avocados
- eggplant
- plums
- raisins
- spinach
- tomatoes
- yogurt

Stimulants

Stimulant drugs are used for the treatment of attention deficit disorder, narcolepsy, and other sleep disorders. They are also sometimes used for the treatment of depression when patients have not responded to other medications. In fact, the stimulants should be reserved for those

TABLE 9.4   Stimulants and Their Properties

Drug	Trade Name/ Manufacturer	Strengths	Half-Life	Usual Dose
dextroamphetamine/ amphetamine	Adderall/ Shire Richwood	tablets: 5, 10, 20, and 30 mg	Varied	5–60 mg/day in divided doses
pemoline	Cylert/Abbott	tablets: 18.75, 37.5, and 75 mg	12 hrs	56.25–75 mg once per day
dextroamphetamine sulfate	Dexedrine/Smith-Kline-Beecham	capsules: 5, 10, and 15 mg; tablets: 5 mg	12 hrs	5–60 mg/day in divided doses
methamphetamine	Desoxyn/ Abbott	tablets: 5, 10, and 15 mg	5 hrs	20–25 mg/day in divided doses.
methylphenidate	Ritalin/ Novartis	tablets: 5, 10, and 20 mg; sustained-release tablets: 20 mg	tablets: 4 hrs; sustained-release: 12 hrs	20–60 mg/day
	Methylin/ Mallinckrodt	tablets: 5, 10, and 20 mg	4 hrs	20–60 mg/day
modafinil	Provigil/ Cephalon	tablets: 100 and 200 mg	15 hrs	100–200 mg/day

patients who have not responded to several classes of antidepressant drugs. Many of these drugs are effective for the treatment of major depression, but few data are available regarding their use in manic-depressive illness. One open study has suggested positive effects with methylphenidate.[16]

Several forms of stimulants are available, as summarized in Table 9.4.

Side effects of stimulants include *loss of appetite, weight loss, headache, insomnia, dizziness, tremor, dry mouth, increased heart rate, increased blood pressure,* and *agitation.* There is a slightly elevated risk of *seizures* with these medications. *Elevated liver enzymes* may occur, especially with pemoline. Except for the new drug modafinil, stimulants are controlled substances because they can become *habit-forming.* This is especially true of methamphetamine. When stimulants with a short half-life are used, *"rebound" depression* or agitation can occur as the drug is eliminated from the body. This effect may sometimes feel like a severe "crash" in mood. Prolonged use of high-dose stimulants can lead to *paranoia* and to *mania.* These drugs should be used cautiously in patients with a history of frequent or severe mania accompanied by psychosis.

Many stimulants are less effective if taken with food and, indeed, are counteracted by large amounts of vitamin C. Stimulants may change the metabolism of other antidepressants, anticonvulsants, and blood pressure medications, so these combinations need to be followed carefully.

Thyroid Supplementation

As described in Chapter 7, subtle abnormalities in thyroid hormone physiology may occur in patients with mood disorders. Even if thyroid hormone levels are normal on routine clinical tests, some physicians will try adding thyroid hormone to other antidepressants and mood stabilizers. Studies of supplemental thyroid hormone in major depression have shown response rates ranging from 30 to 50 percent.[17] There are no controlled studies of thyroid augmentation in manic-depressive illness. However, in one open study involving eleven rapid cycling patients, ten improved, including those who presented with mania.[18] Fortunately, supplemental thyroid hormone is well tolerated and has few side effects.

St. John's Wort and Other Herbal Remedies

Herbal and other complementary medical therapies have gained in popularity in recent years. St. John's wort has been used by approximately 17 percent of the U.S. population, mostly for the treatment of depression.[19] The nine controlled studies that have been performed on patients using St. John's wort as a treatment for depression demonstrated modest improvements in mood symptoms. Overall, about 60 percent of patients receiving St. John's wort responded well, compared to 24 percent receiving placebo. However, a recent large study of this compound showed no benefit in cases of major depression,[20] and no studies have been published on the use of St. John's wort in manic-depressive illness.

Side effects include *allergic reactions, nausea, dry mouth, sedation, headache,* and *photosensitivity.* In addition, the *serotonin syndrome* has been reported in cases where St. John's wort was combined with other antidepressants.

Although St. John's wort may be a viable option, patients must consult a physician before using it. Which of the many compounds present in the herb are most active and what the dosage limits should be are not yet known.

Many people have also sought relief from depression by taking Kava, Ginkgo biloba, and Valerian. However, there are no controlled data available on the use of these compounds for the treatment of manic-depressive illness.

Switch Rate

The use of antidepressant drugs alone to treat the depressed phase of manic-depressive illness is probably not safe. It has been estimated in uncontrolled studies that 31 to 70 percent of patients in the depressed phase of manic-depressive illness will experience a switch to manic symptoms when prescribed an antidepressant.[21] Although there are no prospective controlled studies to use as a guide, this rate of switching to mania is probably higher than would be expected from the natural course of the illness. It is also possible that the sole use of antidepressants can increase the frequency of mood cycles. Preliminary studies have suggested that buproprion, SSRIs, and MAOIs produce a switch to mania less commonly than TCAs. The risk for switching to mania is probably greater in women than in men and in patients who already have a history of rapid cycling. For these reasons, antidepressants should be prescribed in combination with a mood stabilizer.

Antipsychotics

As noted in Chapter 3, some individuals with manic-depressive illness also have delusions, hallucinations, or prominent disorders in thinking. Such symptoms are also found in schizophrenia. When they occur in manic-depressive illness, the person is diagnosed as having manic-depressive illness *with psychotic features.* Drugs used to treat these symptoms are called antipsychotics; they are sometimes also referred to as neuroleptics or major tranquilizers, but *antipsychotics* is the best term because it describes their action. Antipsychotics can be categorized in terms of either the older first-generation or typical antipsychotics and the newer second-generation or atypical antipsychotics.

First-Generation, or Typical, Antipsychotics

The typical antipsychotic drugs were initially used to relieve symptoms of anxiety prior to surgery or anesthesia. In the 1950s researchers observed that these drugs had a particularly noticeable effect on symptoms such as hallucinations and delusions. All of the typical antipsychotic drugs share the ability to block dopamine receptors, and although these drugs affect many other neurochemical systems, dopamine blockade remains the best predictor of their potency.

Typical antipsychotics have been used for many years to control the acute symptoms of mania and are probably as effective as lithium for this problem.[22] The use of typical antipsychotic drugs as prophylactic treatments for future episodes of mania has not been studied adequately. However, the long-term addition of an antipsychotic to a mood stabilizer is not uncommon in clinical practice. Several studies have suggested that 40 to 70 percent of outpatients with manic-depressive illness are currently being prescribed antipsychotics and that 90 to 100 percent of patients with manic-depressive illness have a history of exposure to antipsychotics.[23] Antipsychotics are often prescribed for long-term use in patients who have very disabling or frequent psychosis during manic periods or who are incompletely responsive to a regimen of one or more mood stabilizers. Antipsychotic drugs are probably not especially helpful for acute depression that is not accompanied by psychotic symptoms and may in fact increase the chance for more depressive episodes when prescribed for the long term.[24]

The first-generation or typical antipsychotic drugs are analogous to the TCAs in that they are less regularly used today. This is mainly due to the many possible side effects of these drugs. Nevertheless, these drugs have been widely used, are safe for most people if monitored carefully, and are very inexpensive.

These drugs are called "typical" because they all share the ability to produce *movement disorder side effects*, also known as *extrapyramidal side effects (EPS)*. All of the typical antipsychotics can produce acute EPS, but this condition is most common with "high potency" drugs (see Table 9.5). Most forms of acute EPS can be eliminated by reducing the dose of antipsychotics or by adding "anti-Parkinson's" medications (such as Cogentin, Artane, Symmetrel, or Benadryl). Patients with mood disorders are more likely to have EPS than patients with schizophrenia.[25]

The most common type of EPS is *parkinsonism,* in which the patient develops symptoms similar to those seen in Parkinson's disease. These symptoms, which are a direct result of blocking dopamine receptors, include tremor, stiffness of the muscles, and slowness of movements and speaking. They are found in up to 60 percent of patients taking typical antipsychotics on careful examination and can be quite unpleasant.

Acute dystonic reactions are another form of EPS. These reactions are characterized by acute muscle spasms of the tongue, face, or neck muscles. Most common in young males, they may occur in up to 20 percent of patients receiving these drugs.

Akathisia is an uncomfortable feeling of restlessness or the need to keep moving. Patients usually notice this form of EPS in the legs, causing them to feel as though they must keep pacing or walking. Akathisia may also occur in about 20 percent of patients.

A dangerous but rare form of EPS is the *neuroleptic malignant syndrome (NMS).* This syndrome is characterized by severe muscle rigidity; unstable heart rate, blood pressure, and breathing rate; confusion; fever; elevated white blood cell count; and elevated levels of muscle enzymes. It occurs most commonly when high-potency antipsychotics are prescribed in high doses or when the dose is rapidly escalated. If

TABLE 9.5 Antipsychotics and Their Properties

	Generic Name	Brand Name	Usual Dose (mg/day)	EPS	Anticholinergic Effects and Sedation
High Potency	fluphenazine	Prolixin	2–20	+++	+
	trifluoperazine	Stelazine	5–30	+++	++
	haloperidol	Haldol	5–20	+++	+
	thiothixene	Navane	5–30	+++	+
	perphenazine	Trilafon	2–60	+++	++
Low Potency	chlorpromazine	Thorazine	200–600	++	+++
	thioridazine	Mellaril	200–600	++	+++
	mesoridazine	Serentil	20–200	++	+++
	molindone	Moban	20–100	++	++
	loxapine	Loxitane	20–100	++	++

this syndrome is suspected, antipsychotic drugs should be stopped and emergency medical treatment sought.

Tardive dyskinesia (TD) is the most feared of the movement disorder side effects. It usually occurs after prolonged exposure to antipsychotics. TD is characterized by repetitive, involuntary, twisting movements, usually of facial muscles. It appears as forced chewing, blinking, or lip and tongue movements. These movements can affect the limbs and trunk of the body. In the majority of cases the movements slowly fade away once the drug is discontinued, but in a minority of cases they remain for long periods, even after antipsychotic treatment has been discontinued. TD has been associated with all of the typical antipsychotic drugs.

Among the many other side effects of antipsychotics, the most frequently seen are *anticholinergic side effects* (which are more common with "low potency" antipsychotics), *sedation, weight gain, abnormal menstrual periods and discharge of breast milk in women, seizures,* and *heart rhythm abnormalities.*

Haloperidol and fluphenazine are available in long-acting "depot" preparations, which allow an intramuscular injection of the medication every two to four weeks. These preparations can be very useful for patients who are unable to take regular oral medication or who are not compliant with treatment recommendations. Patients with manic-depressive illness receiving a depot formulation of an antipsychotic as a prophylactic treatment may have fewer mood swings than those treated with intermittent oral doses of antipsychotics.[26]

Table 9.5 provides a summary of the typical antipsychotics and their properties.

Second-Generation, or Atypical, Antipsychotics

Clozapine (Clozaril). Clozapine was the first "atypical antipsychotic" introduced into clinical practice in the United States. It was soon followed by risperidone, olanzapine, and quetiapine. These drugs are considered "atypical" because they have a low propensity for causing EPS and may have improved efficacy in treating the symptoms of schizophrenia.

In a group of small, uncontrolled studies, clozapine has been reported as efficacious for acute mania, mixed states, rapid cycling, and the depressed phase of manic-depressive illness.[27] And in a randomized study that evaluated clozapine as a long-term prophylactic treatment,[28] patients receiving clozapine experienced significant improvements in manic symptoms and psychotic symptoms compared to standard treatments and were able to take lower doses of other medications. These studies suggest that clozapine may be effective in patients who have not tolerated or responded well to mood stabilizers such as lithium, valproate, or carbamazepine, or to typical antipsychotic drugs. Because of clozapine's many side effects, its use should be limited to those patients who have not done well with these other treatment strategies.

Clozapine is marketed by Novartis as Clozaril and can also be obtained in a generic form. It is available in 25 and 100 mg tablets and is administered twice per day. Because of its side effects, which the body must accommodate, it is usually begun at a low dosage (25 mg per day) and increased gradually (25 mg every few days). The usual dosage range is 50–600 mg per day. It may take two to six months to see the full clinical response to clozapine.

Blood levels of clozapine can be measured as a way to help determine dosing. According to one study, 64 percent of patients with a blood level greater than 350 ng/ml respond to treatment, compared to only 22 percent of patients with blood levels below this value.[29]

A complete blood count must be obtained weekly during the first six months of treatment with clozapine and biweekly thereafter. *Agranulocytosis*, a severe drop in the white blood cell count, is the most feared side effect of clozapine, appearing in up to 1 percent of patients treated with this drug. It can arise at any time but is most likely to occur within two and six months of starting treatment. If the white blood cell count begins to drop, clozapine can be discontinued and for most people the blood count will return to normal. If it does not, hospitalization and treatment with drugs to stimulate the bone marrow production of white blood cells is necessary.

There is an increased risk for *seizures* with clozapine treatment—a risk directly related to the dose of clozapine used. About 0.7 percent of patients may experience seizures for every 100 mg of clozapine prescribed. If seizures occur in patients who have responded well to clozapine, valproate should be the first choice for an antiseizure medication. Clozapine combined with carbamazepine may increase the risk for agranulocytosis.

Clozapine treatment may also be associated with *sedation, drooling, urinary incontinence,* and *anticholinergic side effects* (see above). These side effects often subside with time. Patients may experience a sudden drop in blood pressure when standing up (*orthostatic hypotension)* and *rapid heart beat.* These side effects are potentially dangerous and need to be monitored carefully. Patients may also experience benign *fever* in the first few weeks of therapy. *Weight gain* is a significant problem, which may also become associated with diabetes mellitus and elevation of blood cholesterol and triglycerides. Inflammation of the pancreas (*pancreatitis*) and inflammation of the heart muscle (*myocardiditis*) are rare side effects.

Clozapine should not be used concurrently with other drugs (such as carbamazepine) that suppress bone marrow function. The combination of clozapine with benzodiazepines (Valium-like drugs) may cause low blood pressure and passing out; these drugs should be combined with caution. Clozapine, because it is highly bound to blood proteins, may cause an increase in blood levels of warfarin or digoxin. Drugs that are metabolized by the same liver enzyme that metabolizes clozapine (cytochrome P450 2D6)—such as cimetidine, erythromycin, propafenone, flecainide, and encainide—may cause elevated blood clozapine levels. Likewise, drugs that inhibit these liver enzymes—such as quinidine—may cause increased clozapine levels. Phenytoin may cause decreased clozapine levels. Since clozapine also shares a liver enzyme with caffeine, the clozapine level may be markedly elevated in individuals who ingest large amounts of caffeine.

Risperidone (Risperdal).   Risperidone was the second second-generation antipsychotic to be introduced in the United States. A number of open, naturalistic studies (observation of treatment without placebo control) have been conducted on risperidone in manic-depressive illness.[30] Taken together, these studies suggest that risperidone may be effective for all phases of manic-depressive illness, including mood states that do not include psychotic symptoms, with an overall response rate of about 55 percent. In some of the studies, risperidone was used alone; in others, it was added to existing mood stabilizers. Two controlled studies of risperidone for acute mania have also been conducted. In one, risperidone was observed to be as good as haloperidol or lithium over a one-month period.[31] In the other, 57 percent of patients receiving risperidone responded well in a three-week trial, compared to 38 percent receiving placebo.[32]

Risperidone is marketed by Janssen as Risperdal. It is available in 0.25, 0.5, 1.0, 2.0, 3.0, and 4.0 mg tablets. The usual dosage is 1–4 mg per day. It can be taken once or twice per day. No laboratory monitoring is necessary with risperidone.

Compared to clozapine and olanzapine, risperidone is less likely to produce *weight gain*. At doses greater than 4–6 mg per day, however, it may produce *extrapyramidal side effects* at a frequency similar to that seen with typical antipsychotics, especially in elderly patients or in patients with concomitant brain disease. A number of reports further suggest that risperidone can worsen *mania* in some patients.[33] This finding has since come under question, but it is probably safest to the use risperidone in conjunction with a mood stabilizer rather than as the sole treatment. Other side effects include *dizziness, somnolence, elevated prolactin level,* and *abnormal body temperature regulation. Priapism* (sustained, painful erection of the penis) has been reported only rarely.

As with clozapine, drugs that are metabolized by or that inhibit the liver enzyme known as cytochrome P450 2D6 may cause increased levels of risperidone.

Olanzapine (Zyprexa).   There have been three controlled studies of olanzapine for acute mania. These studies allowed olanzapine to become the third drug approved by the FDA for the treatment of mania. Two of the studies compared olanzapine to placebo.[34] In both, olanzapine treatment was associated with an improvement in manic symptoms. About two-thirds of patients treated with olanzapine responded to treatment, compared with about one-third of patients treated with placebo. Olanzapine was associated with a good response in patients with and without psychotic symptoms accompanying mania. Depressive symptoms also seemed to improve with olanzapine treatment.

In the third study, olanzapine was compared to lithium.[35] It was observed to be equivalent to lithium on most measures of mania and superior to lithium on one measure. However, the patients in this study had blood lithium levels lower than those recommended for acute mania.

Olanzapine is marketed by Eli Lilly as Zyprexa. It is available in 2.5, 5, 7.5, and 10 mg tablets. The usual daily dosage is 5–20 mg taken once per day. No laboratory monitoring is necessary.

The most worrisome side effect of olanzapine is *weight gain.* This can be quite profound for patients treated with olanzapine for long periods (20 to 30 pounds). Weight gain is probably related to a change in the way the body metabolizes high-calorie foods. In fact, olanzapine treatment may be associated with diabetes mellitus, diabetic ketoacidosis, and elevation of cholesterol and triglyceride levels.

Weight gain with olanzapine is worse if the drug is combined with lithium or valproate.

The side effects commonly observed in association with olanzapine are *somnolence, dizziness,* and *dry mouth. Extrapyramidal side effects,* though rare, have been seen in patients with concomitant brain illnesses or injury.

Olanzapine is metabolized though several different enzyme pathways, so it can be combined safely with most drugs. Carbamazepine causes a decrease in olanzapine blood levels, whereas, caffeine, like clozapine, may cause a marked increase in olanzapine blood levels.

Quetiapine (Seroquel).   There are few uncontrolled and no controlled trials evaluating the use of quetiapine for manic-depressive illness. In preliminary case reports, quetiapine seems to be helpful for both manic and depressive symptoms.[36]

Quetiapine is marketed by Zeneca Pharmaceuticals as Seroquel. It is available in 25, 100, and 200 mg tablets. The usual dosage is 150–750 mg per day in two divided doses. Quetiapine is usually begun at a low dosage, which is gradually raised over a period of several days. No laboratory monitoring is necessary with this drug.

The most common side effects of quetiapine are *dizziness, postural hypotension, dry mouth,* and *upset stomach.* Quetiapine is associated with a very low incidence of EPS. Quetiapine may also be associated with *weight gain* and *increased cholesterol and triglyceride levels.*

Increased doses of quetiapine may be required for patients who are also taking phenytoin. Decreased doses of quetiapine may be required for patients taking ketoconazole, itraconazole, fluconazole, and erythromycin.

Ziprasidone (Geodon).   Early in 2001, ziprasidone was approved by the FDA for the treatment of schizophrenia. In one controlled study, ziprasidone was found to be superior to placebo for the treatment of mania.[37] Fifty percent of patients treated with ziprasidone improved, compared to 36 percent of patients receiving placebo. Details regarding the administration of ziprasidone and its side effects are not yet fully available. What has been established, however, is that it combines some features of antipsychotic drugs and antidepressants, so it may be advantageous for depressive symptoms. It also appears to cause less weight gain than other antipsychotics. A major concern about ziprasidone, which has not yet been fully explored, is the degree to which it can alter the electrical conduction system of the heart, leading to dangerous arrhythmias. For this reason, patients taking ziprasidone are advised to have periodic EKGs.

Benzodiazepines

Efficacy of Benzodiazepines

Benzodiazepines, such as diazepam (Valium), are widely prescribed for anxiety and insomnia. There are many different benzodiazepines available; because they differ from each other mainly in the way they are absorbed into and eliminated from the body, they will be described together. Although some benzodiazepines, such as clonazepam and lorazepam, have been studied specifically for the treatment of acute mania,[38] these drugs are now rarely used alone for this purpose. Benzodiazepines are often prescribed in conjunction with mood stabilizers or other drugs during acute manic periods in order to treat agitation, anxiety, or sleeplessness. As patients become more stable, the benzodiazepines are usually withdrawn over several weeks.

Administration of Benzodiazepines

Benzodiazepines and their properties are summarized in Table 9.6. All are available as generic drugs, but brand-name forms are also listed.

Benzodiazepines with a short half-life are best suited for easing acute situational anxiety and for helping patients sleep in the early part of the night. Intermediate or long-acting drugs are more effective when agitation and anxiety are consistent features of the illness. Many benzodiazepines also have active metabolites, which may themselves remain in the body for long periods of time. Of the drugs listed in the table, only lorazepam is reliably absorbed after intramuscular injection, so this drug is frequently used for patients who cannot or will not take oral medications. Unlike most other drugs used in psychiatry, benzodiazepines produce their effects almost immediately.

TABLE 9.6   Benzodiazepines and Their Properties

Drug Name	Brand Name	Half-Life	Usual Dosage (mg/day)
triazolam	Halcion	short (less than 6 hrs)	0.125–0.5
clorazepate	Tranxene	short	15–30
flurazepam	none	short	15–30
alprazolam	Xanax	intermediate (6–20 hrs)	0.75–1.5
lorazepam	Ativan	intermediate	2–6
oxazepam	none	intermediate	30–60
temazepam	none	intermediate	10–30
chlordiazepoxide	Librium	intermediate	15–40
diazepam	Valium	long (more than 20 hrs)	4–20
clonazepam	Klonopin	long (more than 20 hrs)	1.5–3

Side Effects of Benzodiazepines

Sedation is the most common side effect. Patients taking regular doses of benzodiazepines often feel sleepy, slowed down, and *uncoordinated. Amnesia* (loss of memory) occurs frequently with intravenous administration of these drugs but may also occur in people taking oral forms. Amnesia is a desirable property of benzodiazepines when they are used as a form of anesthesia prior to medical or surgical procedures, but it is not desirable for patients taking them to ease psychiatric symptoms. In elderly patients, the incoordination produced by benzodiazepines may lead to worrisome *falls;* it also impairs one's ability to drive or operate machinery. Another potential problem is that benzodiazepines are *habit-forming.* If taken for long periods, patients will develop tolerance to these medications and require higher doses to produce the desired effects. For this reason, benzodiazepines are best used for short periods of time. Because patients may become dependent on these drugs, discontinuation of their use can be associated with a *withdrawal syndrome* not unlike that seen with alcohol. Therefore, benzodiazepines must be discontinued slowly. Benzodiazepines are very dangerous if taken in *overdose* or in combination with other central nervous system depressants, especially alcohol. Suicidal patients should be given very limited supplies of these drugs. Some patients may become "disinhibited" while taking benzodiapines, paradoxically becoming more impulsive, aggressive, or hostile.

Interactions of Benzodiazepines with Prescription Drugs

Benzodiazepines have relatively few interactions with other drugs. Cimetidine and disulfiram cause increased blood levels of benzodiazepines. Antacids, tobacco, and rifampin cause decreased effectiveness of benzodiazepines. And benzodiazepines themselves may increase the blood level of digoxin.

10

MEDICATIONS:
TREATMENT STRATEGIES

I can't help clinging to the idea that some essential physical thing, like salt
or iron or semen or some unguessed at holy water is either missing [in
insane individuals] or is present in too great [a] quantity.

F. SCOTT FITZGERALD,
in a letter to Zelda Fitzgerald's psychiatrist (ca. 1934)[1]

Even after the medications for treating manic-depressive illness have
been mastered by the treating physician, deciding which ones to use,
and in what order, is still problematic. Because of the paucity of
research on the treatment of this illness, we are still at the try-it-and-see-
if-it-works stage. At some point in the future, thanks to an emerging field
of study called *pharmacogenomics*, we will be able to use a person's
genes to predict their response to a specific drug; but that time is still a
long way off.

Treatments for the Different Phases of
Manic-Depressive Illness

What follows is a brief overview of general principles for treatment.
Many attempts have been made to develop an algorithm for the treatment of manic-depressive illness. But no such algorithm can satisfacto-
rily address the needs of individual patients; indeed, the treatment of
this illness must evolve as a collaborative and individualized program
designed by the patient, the treating physician, and the family.

189

Acute Mania

A number of agents have demonstrated efficacy for use as first-line monotherapy in acute mania. These include lithium, valproate, carbamazepine, first-generation antipsychotics, olanzapine, and clozapine. Of these drugs, lithium has yielded the best results; it is thus probably still the leading choice for typical mania. Valproate is also commonly preferred by clinicians today because of its greater convenience of use, safety, and efficacy. However, the long-term efficacy of valproate has still not been stablished.

Patients with a history of poor response to lithium should be given a trial of one of the other agents. Lithium may not be the best first-line choice for patients with "dysphoric" or "mixed" mania, psychosis, a history of rapid cycling, a history of depression rather than mania as a first episode, a history of many prior manic episodes, or a history of substance abuse.

Although it is preferable to prescribe only one drug, in the acute stage of mania supplemental medications are usually necessary. For patients with significant agitation or insomnia, a benzodiazepine, most commonly clonazepam or lorazepam, can be prescribed.

If possible, it is best to avoid using antipsychotic drugs for the control of agitation. However, if a patient has hallucinations or delusions, an antipsychotic should be prescribed. Some physicians prefer to use one of the newer second-generation antipsychotics (preferably olanzapine, risperidone, or quetiapine) to avoid the risk of movement disorder side effects (i.e., extrapyramidal side effects, or EPS). However, the first-generation antipsychotics, if employed in judicious doses, may be equally safe and beneficial and are certainly less expensive.

It is not uncommon to prescribe a mood stabilizer, a benzodiazepine, and an antipsychotic together for acute mania. For patients who do not respond well to this combination, most experts recommend a combination of mood stabilizers (e.g., lithium combined with valproate or carbamazepine). If the patient still does not respond, a novel anticonvulsant (e.g., gabapentin, topiramate, or lamotrigine), other antipsychotic drugs, or electroconvulsive therapy can be tried. Clinicians, patients, and families often feel rushed to alter the treatment strategy for patients who are not responding well. This can lead to unpredictable problems and side effects. It is probably best to wait several days before attempting a major change in strategy.

Depression

Patients with depression who also have a history of mania should not be treated with an antidepressant as monotherapy. Likewise, patients presenting with depression who have a family history of mania are at risk of developing mania when prescribed an antidepressant alone. Therefore, the first-line approach to treating depression in such patients is to prescribe lithium or valproate. An antidepressant (usually paroxetine, buproprion, or venlafaxine) can be added if there is not a good response. If the response continues to be inadequate, the antidepressant drug can be changed, lithium and valproate can be used in combination, lamotrigine can be added to lithium or valproate, or thyroid supplementation can be tried. Electroconvulsive therapy or trials of clozapine or stimulants should be considered a last resort.

Rapid Cycling

For rapid cycling patients, most recommendations for treatment are similar to those given above under "Acute Mania." However, valproate is probably preferable to lithium as a first-line mood stabilizer. For episodes of mania in patients already taking a mood stabilizer, a second mood stabilizer should be added. Lamotrigine may turn out to be particularly effective in this setting. Rapid cycling patients who are currently depressed may be treated with an antidepressant in conjunction with a mood stabilizer. However, it is not uncommon to encounter "brittle" patients, who become hypomanic when given an antidepressant and depressed when these drugs are withdrawn. In this setting, combinations of two or more mood stabilizers, novel anticonvulsants, or second-generation antipsychotics can be tried.

Maintenance Treatment

For patients who have had successful treatment with lithium or valproate for the acute phase of illness, these drugs should be continued.
For patients who have had more than two episodes of mania and
patients who have had a particularly severe manic episode, mood stabilizers should be continued indefinitely. Mood stabilizers should probably also be continued indefinitely for patients with one episode of mania
and a strong family history of manic-depressive illness.

For patients who have had manic-depressive illness with severe psychotic features, an antipsychotic drug should be continued indefinitely.
If possible, a second-generation antipsychotic (olanzapine, risperidone,
or quetiapine) should be used, since it will be taken over a long period.

When patients have been stabilized for a reasonable length of time,
benzodiazepines should be slowly tapered and withdrawn. Likewise,
antidepressant drugs can be tapered and withdrawn if depressive symptoms have been resolved for six to twelve months and there is no history
of frequent or severe recurrent depressions.

Frequently Asked Questions About Medications

Above and beyond the scientific evidence for the efficacy of the drugs
described above, there is a great need to improve our understanding of
how drug treatments affect patients' lives. Here are some questions that
commonly arise.

Do I Really Need to Take All of These Medications?

If there is an incomplete response to an initial medication, or if intolerable side effects occur, it is relative easy to try an additional medication.
In fact, it is very common in clinical practice to see an incomplete or
partial response to an initial choice of medication, and in such cases,
most physicians, rather than completely abandon the initial strategy,
prescribe an "adjunctive" drug in addition to the existing medication.
This procedure—known as *polypharmacy*—is frequently used in other
branches of medicine as well but is particularly common in psychiatry.

It has been estimated that 28 to 75 percent of psychiatric patients take multiple psychotropic medications.[2] Polypharmacy is very common for patients with manic-depressive illness.

During periods of acute mania, "atypical mania" (mixed or dysphoric mania or mania combined with psychosis), and depression, it is very likely that patients will need more than one medication. During maintenance treatment, the need for multiple medications should decrease, but medications that were initially effective may begin to lose their efficacy. For example, in one large study of lithium used as maintenance treatment, the proportion of patients retaining normal mood was 85 percent, 52 percent, and 37 percent after one, three, and five years of lithium monotherapy, respectively.[3]

There is a rational approach to this combining of medications, which will continue to be necessary until more perfect treatments and prevention strategies have been developed. Specifically, when medications are combined, they should have complementary, rather than duplicated, mechanisms of action with the other prescribed medications. For example, there is poor support for the use of multiple antipsychotics, multiple benzodiazepines, or multiple antidepressants, whereas there is good support for combining drugs from different classes (e.g., a mood stabilizer, an antipsychotic, and an antidepressant) depending on the phase of the manic-depressive illness. There is also some support for combining mood stabilizers with different mechanisms of action[4] as described above (e.g., lithium in combination with valproate or carbamazepine).

As the number of medications goes up, however, patients and physicians need to increase their level of monitoring. The risk of side effects, such as incoordination, falling, and impaired thinking, is greater when multiple medications are being taken, especially by elderly and very young patients.

Do I Need to Take These Medications for the Rest of My Life?

For most people with manic-depressive illness, the illness is best conceptualized as a chronic, life-long problem that needs to be closely monitored, similar to diabetes or epilepsy. Most patients who have manic-depressive illness will need some form of medication for the remainder of their lives. As mentioned above, mood stabilizers, such as lithium, valproate, or carbamazepine, should be continued indefinitely for those who have had a good response to these drugs and who have had more than one episode of mania or a severe and debilitating form of mania. This recommendation has been accepted by physicians for the following reasons: About 50 percent of patients with manic-depressive illness will experience another episode of mood disturbance within five months of stopping lithium,[5] there is a significant risk of hospitalization and suicidal acts following discontinuation of lithium, recurrent mood symptoms following withdrawal of lithium may be less likely to respond to lithium treatment,[6] and the period of time between episodes of mood disorder may get shorter if lithium is discontinued.[7]

The length of time that antidepressants and antipsychotics should be continued is less certain. If patients have had relatively brief, or relatively few, episodes of psychotic symptoms, then antipsychotic drugs can be tapered and discontinued over several weeks. The discontinuation of antipsychotics should probably take place six to twelve months after psychotic symptoms have been stabilized. For patients who consistently have psychotic symptoms when they are experiencing mania or depression, antipsychotics should be continued indefinitely. Likewise, if patients have had relatively brief, or relatively few, episodes of depression, antidepressant drugs should be tapered and discontinued six to twelve months after depressive symptoms have improved.

For patients with treatment-resistant manic-depressive illness or rapid cycling, it is not uncommon to require almost constant medication adjustments to optimize mood state and functional capacity. Most patients with these clinical problems will need to see their physician regularly—at least monthly—to fine-tune the combination of medications they are taking.

What If I Am Pregnant or Breast-Feeding?

The use of psychotropic medications during pregnancy is a particularly challenging problem. On the one hand, medications may cause problems for the developing fetus and are best avoided. On the other hand, severe recurrence of psychiatric illness poses a significant risk to the mother and the fetus. In order to make a recommendation for medications during pregnancy, physicians require a clear understanding of the level of risk. Several kinds of risk are associated with pregnancy. First, there is a risk that the baby will have malformations of the body or organs (*teratogenic risk*). Second, infants exposed to medications may experience a toxicity that manifests as a difficult birth process or postnatal period. Finally, there is a chance that psychotropic drugs may produce subtle behavioral, learning, or psychiatric problems in exposed infants.

Following is a review of the available data on the risks associated with the main medications used in the treatment of manic depression.

Lithium. Exposure of the fetus to lithium may result in malformations of the heart. The most commonly reported abnormality is known as *Ebstein's anomaly* (improper formation of the right ventricle of the heart and the tricuspid valve). This abnormality can cause heart failure in newborn infants; for some, it may be fatal. In certain cases it can be corrected with surgery. The risk for this abnormality with lithium exposure during the first trimester of pregnancy is between 1 per 2,000 (0.05 percent) and 1 per 1,000 (0.1 percent). Although this risk is quite low, it is ten to twenty times greater than that seen in the general population.[8] Fetal exposure to lithium has also been associated with decreased muscle tone at birth, abnormal thyroid function, and abnormal kidney function, although such cases appear to be rare. Little information is available regarding the long-term behavioral effects of fetal lithium exposure. No significant problems were noted in a five-year follow-up study of sixty children.[9]

Current recommendations for lithium use during pregnancy are as follows.[10] Women who are taking lithium should carefully use a birth control method until they are ready to conceive. When a woman is ready to become pregnant, she should gradually taper and discontinue lithium (over six months) if she has had few episodes of mood disturbance and long intervening periods of normal mood. During the pregnancy, she should have very close follow-ups with her treating physician. If lithium use is required, it can be restarted during the second or third trimester, when the risk to the baby is lower. For women with more frequent or debilitating episodes of mood disturbance, physicians still usually attempt to discontinue lithium during the first trimester. Antipsychotic drugs, preferably haloperidol or perphenazine at the lowest effective dose, can be substituted for lithium in women with very unstable manic-depressive illness. Hospitalization and electroconvulsive therapy can also be used safely. Some women will not be able to taper or discontinue lithium during pregnancy. These women should have ultrasound examinations performed on the fetus at the sixteenth, seventeenth, or eighteenth week of pregnancy. For women who stay on lithium during pregnancy, the dose of lithium should be decreased by about one-third just before delivery; because there is a reduction in blood volume following delivery, blood lithium levels can climb to dangerous levels if this is not done.

After the birth of the baby, the risk for mood problems in the postpartum period is quite high. Women who were taking lithium before pregnancy and who restart lithium after the baby is born are less likely to have episodes of mood disturbance.[11] However, the decision to restart lithium depends in part on whether or not the mother plans to breast-feed.

Women who require lithium therapy to control manic-depressive illness should avoid breast-feeding because lithium is excreted in breast milk, and there are insufficient data to determine the level of risk to the baby. The concentration of lithium in these secretions is about one-half that found in the mother's blood. The nursing infant's blood lithium level may range from one-tenth to one-half of the mother's level.[12] Some babies—especially those who become sick or dehydrated—can develop signs of lithium toxicity even when the blood level is within the adult therapeutic range.

Other Mood Stabilizers.   There are very few data regarding the risk to babies born to mothers taking anticonvulsants (valproate, carbamazepine, gabapentin, topiramate, lamotrigine) for manic-depressive illness. What has been established, however, is that women with epilepsy give birth to infants with physical malformations more frequently than women without epilepsy. Part of this increased risk may be due to medications. Spina bifida and other "neural tube defects" are common with carbamazepine and valproate exposure during the first trimester, affecting, respectively, 1 percent and 3–5 percent of births to women taking these drugs. Both drugs are also associated with an increased risk for malformation of oral and facial structures. The use of multiple anticonvulsants increases the risk even more. Finally, there are reports, albeit conflicting ones, as to whether fetal exposure to anticonvulsants leads to later behavioral problems or lower IQ. For the reasons just discussed, it is recommended that women not take these medications for manic-depressive illness during pregnancy. Those who nevertheless elect to take valproate or carbamazepine during pregnancy, or who are exposed to these drugs inadvertently, need to take folate supplements. They also need to undergo fetal ultrasound examination and measurement of serum -fetoprotein (a marker for birth defects).

Anticonvulsants are excreted in breast milk, but their risks to the baby are not well understood. Valproate and carbamazepine, which are present in trace quantities in breast milk, are regarded by the American Academy of Pediatrics as safe during breast-feeding; they may be safer than lithium during this period. However, it is possible that even trace amounts of Valproate and carbamazepine may affect the developing brain, so women who are taking these medications may elect to avoid breast-feeding.

Antidepressants.   Of all the data on prenatal exposure to selective serotonin reuptake inhibitors (SSRIs), the largest quantity is devoted to the study of fluoxetine. The several prospective studies of prenatal exposure to fluoxetine that have been completed suggest that there is no increased risk of major malformations with this drug.[13] However, there may be an increased risk for minor physical malformations and admission to special-care nurseries.[14] Nevertheless, if an antidepressant is required during pregnancy, an SSRI may be used if close observation and psychotherapy are insufficient as treatment options.[15]

Data regarding prenatal exposure to buproprion, venlafaxine, mirtazapine, nefazodone, monoamine oxidase inhibitors (MAOIs), and stimulants are so limited that these drugs are probably best avoided during pregnancy.

A number of studies have looked at the safety of tricyclic antidepressants (TCAs) during pregnancy. These studies are not conclusive, but they suggest that the risk for congenital malformations is low. After birth, infants who were exposed to TCAs *in utero* may experience a withdrawal syndrome characterized by jitteriness, irritability, and seizures. Infants may also experience anticholinergic side effects, including slowed bowel function and urinary retention. For these reasons, mothers taking antidepressants during pregnancy should have them tapered and discontinued about one week prior to delivery, if possible.

With regard to long-term behavioral consequences of prenatal exposure to antidepressants, I. Nulman et al.[16] were unable to show that prenatal exposure to TCAs or to fluoxetine led to problems with intelligence, language, or behavior in children ranging from sixteen to eighteen months of age.

SSRIs and TCAs are excreted in breast milk and may be present in higher concentrations than in maternal blood. In studies of the blood of breast-feeding infants, the concentrations of SSRIs, especially fluoxetine, may become quite high. The degree of accumulation of other SSRIs and whether these drugs can adversely affect the baby are not known. The concentration of TCAs in infant serums tends to be very low. Amitriptyline, nortriptyline, desipramine, and clomipramine are probably safe during breast-feeding, but doxepin may be associated with respiratory depression. The safest course is to avoid breast-feeding if antidepressants cannot be discontinued.

Antipsychotics. The use of first-generation antipsychotics during pregnancy appears to be associated with a low risk for major congenital malformations. However, most of the data on antipsychotic exposure pertain to women who took relatively low doses of these medications for brief periods in order to treat nausea or vomiting. One particular class of antipsychotics, the *aliphatic phenothiazines* (e.g., chlorpromazine), may be more likely to cause malformations than the piperazine phenothiazines (e.g., trifluoperazine and perphenazine).[17] For these reasons, the safest course is to try to avoid such drugs, if possible—especially during the first trimester. But the first-generation antipsychotics are probably safer during pregnancy than lithium and other mood stabilizers and can be used for very unstable cases of manic-depressive illness.

Some infants who were exposed to first-generation antipsychotics *in utero* may experience extrapyramidal side effects (EPS), jaundice, or intestinal problems at birth.[18] As with the TCAs, these drugs should be tapered and discontinued five to ten days before delivery to prevent such problems.

The studies in this area, though limited, suggest that infants exposed to first-generation antipsychotics did not have problems with intelligence during a four-year follow-up period; however, these studies included women who were taking relatively low doses of the drugs.[19]

The concentration of first-generation antipsychotics in breast milk tends to be very low, but data regarding the effects of these drugs on infants exposed during breast-feeding are limited. In some cases, breast-feeding infants have been reported to develop extrapyramidal side effects. Therefore, if these drugs are required, the safest course is to avoid breast-feeding.

Also limited are data on the use of second-generation antipsychotics during pregnancy and breast-feeding. Until more data are accumulated, these drugs are probably best avoided by new and expectant mothers.

Benzodiazepines. The use of benzodiazepines during the first trimester of pregnancy is associated with a slightly increased risk for cleft palate and cleft lip. Data suggest that the risk for malformations is even lower during later stages of pregnancy. Of the available benzodiazepines, lorazepam appears to accumulate least in the fetal tissues. At birth, infants who have been exposed to these drugs may have impaired temperature regulation, decreased breathing, decreased muscle tone, and feeding problems. Pregnant women who are taking these medications regularly should have them tapered and discontinued several days prior to delivery. Long-term effects of benzodiazepine exposure on later intelligence and behavior appear to be slight, but here, too, the data are very limited. Most benzodiazepines are present in low concentration in breast milk and may be used judiciously during breast-feeding. Mothers taking large doses or taking benzodiazepines on a regular long-term basis may notice lethargy, sedation, or decreased feeding in their babies. Breast-feeding is best avoided by such women.

Should Treatment Be Different for the Very Old and the Very Young?

Elderly patients need to be medicated with special care. They metabolize drugs quite differently from young people because they often have altered cardiovascular, kidney, and liver functions. Physicians need to have complete and accurate histories of medical conditions and prescribed medications for elderly people. It is common for very elderly patients to be prescribed many medications by different doctors and to lack a clear understanding or memory of how to take them. For this reason, it is important to maintain an accurate and up-to-date medication list and to have an organized system for medication dispensing.

In general, elderly people can be prescribed all of the aforementioned psychotropic medications. But there are several additional rules of thumb: Doses should be very low at the beginning of treatment and should be increased gradually. All attempts should be made to avoid complicated polypharmacy, which increases the risk for falls, confusion, and other side effects. And elderly people should be monitored more frequently to ensure that their medication regimen is as safe and as simple as possible.

The best treatments for manic-depressive illness in children are not well understood. As discussed in Chapter 12, for many years psychiatrists believed that this disorder presented only in adulthood. It is becoming increasingly clear that children, too, may suffer from this illness. Most of the mood stabilizers used in adults are also effective for children, as are the antidepressants and antipsychotic drugs. However, children need more regular and more careful monitoring than adults. Children tend to metabolize and eliminate medications more rapidly than adults, so they need more individually tailored drug regimens. The physician must also seek consensus between the child's requirements and those of the parents—an especially difficult task with many adolescents. A lack of consensus often translates into a lack of compliance with medication prescriptions.

Finally, child psychiatrists must pay close attention to the self-image of children who are prescribed medications, as they may be treated differently by peers and teachers. Children with manic-depressive illness are also at increased risk for substance abuse, poor school performance, and legal difficulties. These problems often require the involvement of a multidisciplinary team in the treatment of such children.

11

NONMEDICATION
ASPECTS OF TREATMENT

There's not a string attuned to mirth
But has its chord in melancholy.

THOMAS HOOD,
"Ode to Melancholy" (1827)[1]

Medications are essential—indeed, the most important aspect of the treatment of manic-depressive illness—but they are not sufficient. With medications alone, many patients will do moderately well, but many will not. If nonmedication aspects of treatment are added, most patients do well.

Finding a Good Doctor

Managing the medication and nonmedication aspects of treatment for manic depression requires a good doctor. The question is how to find one.

The doctor is needed to order diagnostic tests and establish a clear diagnosis (see Chapter 4) as well as to prescribe medications.

The best way to find a good physician is to use personal contacts in the medical profession: Doctors, nurses, psychologists, and psychiatric social workers will know who the competent physicians are in the community. An alternative but often satisfactory way to find a good doctor is to ask members of the local NAMI or National DMDA chapter (see Appendix D) or members of a support group.

A less helpful way is to ask for a referral from a local medical society or chapter of the American Psychiatric Association; such organizations list all physicians who ask to be so listed and, in some cases, identify physicians against whom malpractice charges are pending. Physicians who have been disciplined by their state medical board or the federal government are listed in *Questionable Doctors,* which is published by the Public Citizen's Health Research Group in Washington, D.C. (*www.citizen.org*). In addition, the state medical board will usually supply, upon request, information regarding a physician's education and whether the physician has been disciplined or formally charged with misconduct.

Is it essential for the physician treating a person with manic-depressive illness to be a trained psychiatrist? No, there are many internists, neurologists, and family practitioners who have taken an interest in psychiatric disorders and are competent to treat them. Is it essential that the physician be board certified? *Board certified* means that the physician passed an examination in a given specialty sometime in the past. However, if the physician neglected to keep up with new information after passing the examination, he or she may be incompetent even though board certified; thus, board certification is not always a reliable indicator.

What about international medical school graduates? As practiced in the United States, especially in public clinics, psychiatry comprises a large proportion of international medical graduates. The level of competence of these physicians ranges (as with graduates of American medical schools) from extremely competent to totally incompetent. The same criteria should be utilized in evaluating an international medical school graduate as in evaluating an American medical school graduate, but with one addition: language. Adequate language skills are essential for diagnosing manic-depressive illness, assessing symptoms, and conveying information to the patient and family; if the physician lacks the necessary language skills, good care is much less likely to take place.

In many cases, the problem of finding a good doctor is moot because the person's insurance company, managed-care contract, or public clinic restricts the choice. Much of the time, the person is given a short list of approved physicians and asked to select one. In such cases, the person should obtain as much information as possible about the individuals on the list in order to identify the best choice.

Ideally, what should a patient look for in a doctor? A good doctor will have many of the characteristics listed in the accompanying box. Establishing that the doctor is knowledgeable and up-to-date is essential. Patients and their families should therefore not hesitate to ask open-ended questions such as "What do you think about lamotrigine as a mood stabilizer?" and "Do you know how lithium works?" and "How important is it to monitor the thyroid function when taking lithium?" The more knowledgeable patients and their families are, the easier it will be for them to assess the competence of a physician for treating this illness.

Finally, it is important for a doctor to convey hope. This ineffable quality is crucial, especially during the depression phase of the illness. Hope does not mean a promise of cure, which is unrealistic, but it does signal to the patient that things will ultimately improve and that the physician will work collaboratively with the person to make sure they do. Martha Manning, who suffered from severe depression and at times was on the verge of suicide, described the hope engendered by her

---

A Good Doctor . . .

- Is knowledgeable and up-to-date about current medications and research
- Is not afraid to say "I don't know"
- Works collaboratively with the patient as a partner, not as a king and loyal subject
- Welcomes input from family
- Is available, returns calls, has adequate emergency and weekend coverage
- Is not afraid to make changes when necessary or to try new approaches
- Conveys hope

psychiatrist and her therapist in this way: "Each time I entered their offices I gave silent testimony to the possibility of breaking out of hell."[2]

Building a Support Network

Having a support network is desirable for everyone, but for those with manic depression, it is especially important. Being able to draw on the understanding of trusted friends can increase the patient's chances of doing well. Such friends should feel free to give the patient feedback, such as "I'm worried about your excess energy; I wonder if you shouldn't check with your doctor." These are the people who can be called upon in a crisis.

Research indicates that people with manic-depressive illness who have a support network do better. According to one study of fifty-nine individuals, those with low social support had more continuing symptoms and took longer to recover during a six-month period following an acute episode. This was especially true for people who were recovering from an episode of depression rather than mania.[3]

For a person who has an inadequate support network of family and friends, joining a support group is highly recommended. Such groups exist in most communities; the best way to find them is by contacting the local NAMI or National DMDA chapter (see Appendix D), asking a physician, or calling the local mental health center. Mary Ellen Copeland, in *The Depression Workbook,* provides instructions on how to start a new support group.[4]

The main function of support groups is usually summarized as "sharing and caring." Indeed, support group members are able to talk freely about their symptoms and problems. Other group members offer advice and support. Getting direct feedback from others who are afflicted with the same illness is very useful, as is hearing how other people are coping with problems similar to one's own. The extent of such "sharing and caring" is illustrated by the following comment from a group member:

> We share our ups and downs at meetings and elsewhere. We get to know the "signs"—weight loss, talkativeness, spending sprees, no sleep; or if

someone doesn't answer the phone, cancels appointments. We've exchanged house keys. We have a telephone lifeline system. When someone is manic it is also a great reminder to the rest of us.[5]

Many support groups combine "sharing and caring" with a formal educational and/or social function. Speakers may be invited, or books (see Appendix A) and videos (see Appendix C) may be discussed. Social activities may range from a social hour following the meeting to joint dinners or trips. Many people with manic-depressive illness develop their closest and most important friendships with people they meet in their support group.

Psychotherapy

Can individuals with manic-depressive illness benefit from psychotherapy? Some certainly do. Kay Jamison, for example, wrote that she "cannot imagine leading a normal life without both taking lithium and having had the benefits of psychotherapy. . . . It makes some sense of the confusion, reins in the terrifying thoughts and feelings, returns some control and hope and possibility of learning from it all."[6] Others advocate psychotherapy for individuals with manic-depressive illness as a means of monitoring patients' symptoms and motivating them to continue taking their medication.

Psychotherapy, however, is not essential, and many patients do fine without it—especially if they have a strong support network or are actively participating in a support group. Francis Mondimore, in *Bipolar: A Guide for Patients and Families,* admonishes: "I can't stress enough that *every bipolar patient needs psychotherapy* at one point or another,"[7] but this is simply not true. Many patients benefit from it, but for others it is not necessary.

Several forms of psychotherapy have been advocated for individuals with manic-depressive illness. However, none of them are of much value unless the person is also taking medication. Patty Duke, in *A Brilliant Madness,* described the futility of psychotherapy before she started lithium: "Before taking lithium, trying to participate in therapy was like trying to fly a jet without ever having been on a plane. There was nothing wrong with the intellectual part of my brain. I understood the words the psychiatrist was saying. They just didn't compute."[8] Duke had tried psychoanalytic psychotherapy, which is one of the least helpful forms of psychotherapy for individuals with manic-depressive illness or any other severe psychiatric disorder. In *A Season in Hell*, Percy Knauth described his own experience with psychoanalytic psychotherapy as a treatment for his severe depression:

> It began to dawn on me that I didn't really have anyone to talk *to;* he was only somebody to talk *at*. No matter what I said, I scarcely ever got what I would consider to be an enlightening reply. Whenever I paused in my monologue, waiting for an answer from him, he usually said only, "Please go on." He was an extraordinary listener, so quiet, so unobtrusive that he could easily have traded places with his own shadow. . . . I could hear my own self talking as we sat in the dimness of his consultation room, and my words were strange and foreign to my ears, as if completely unrelated to my problem.[9]

Cognitive Therapy. Cognitive therapy was developed in the 1960s by Aaron Beck and his colleagues at the University of Pennsylvania for individuals with depression and anxiety disorders. In contrast to psychoanalytic psychotherapy, which assumes that *unconscious* thoughts are the most important determinant of behavior, cognitive therapy assumes that *conscious* thoughts are the most important.

Cognitive therapy thus emphasizes changing the person's conscious thought patterns. As summarized by Peter Whybrow in *A Mood Apart*, "the basic postulate is that, given accurate information, the brain can 'think' its way back to health. . . . The brain can learn to be objective about itself and replace old destructive schema with new, and constructive, thinking patterns."[10] This is carried out in a collaborative, interactive dialogue between the cognitive therapist and the patient.

Therapy sessions usually start by mutually setting a therapy agenda and often end with homework assignments. A major goal of therapy sessions is to help patients identify and monitor what are called "automatic negative thoughts" (ANTs) and to provide techniques for dealing with them. The patient, in essence, is asked to learn new patterns of thinking, substituting new positive patterns for the old negative ones with the help of behavioral techniques and positive reinforcement. As such, cognitive therapy has overtones of Norman Vincent Peale's popular book *The Power of Positive Thinking* (1952).

Although cognitive therapy has been widely used for the treatment of depression and anxiety disorders, its use for the treatment of manic-depressive illness is comparatively new. Four small studies of its effectiveness have been carried out.[11] According to one of these studies, at the termination of cognitive therapy and six months afterward, the patients had better medication compliance and fewer hospitalizations compared with the controls. The other three studies showed improvement in depressive symptoms and social functioning. In addition, a book has been published on the use of cognitive therapy in manic-depressive illness: Dominic Lam et al., *Cognitive Therapy for Bipolar Disorder: A Therapist's Guide to Concepts, Methods and Practice* (1999). This book is reviewed in Appendix A.

The ultimate role of cognitive therapy for the treatment of manic-depressive illness is still to be determined. There are major methodological problems in the studies done to date, including questions regarding the extent to which patients' improvement is due to better medication compliance rather than to a change in thought patterns. The optimal timing and duration of the therapy also need to be determined. Nevertheless, cognitive therapy appears to be a useful adjunct to medication for at least some people with manic-depressive illness.

Interpersonal and Social Rhythm Therapy.   Another form of psychotherapy for manic-depressive illness is interpersonal and social rhythm therapy (IPSRT), an adaptation of interpersonal therapy developed for the treatment of depression. IPSRT evolved from the disturbances in body rhythms theory of manic-depressive illness (discussed in Chapter 7). According to Ellen Frank and her colleagues, "we formulated IPSRT at a time when there was a great deal of interest in the relationship between stressful life events and bipolar episodes onset. . . . [O]ur research group was particularly interested in the effects of those life events that caused a significant disruption in social rhythms."[12]

In IPSRT, patients are asked to track both their mood states and their activities on a daily basis. For example, using a "social rhythm metric" chart, they record the exact time they eat dinner and go to sleep each day. They also develop an "interpersonal inventory" of their social network, including all existing and potential conflicts and stresses that may upset their daily rhythms and emotional stability. The therapist then helps the patients develop strategies for minimizing the conflicts, thus stabilizing their daily rhythms.

Preliminary studies on IPSRT have suggested that it helps patients stabilize their daily routines and achieve clinical remission more quickly.[13] It may also help prevent recurrences of depressive episodes. How much of its effect comes from improved medication compliance remains to be determined. Since the studies of IPSRT have been carried out by the group that developed it, these studies need to be replicated by other groups.

Family Therapy.   Since the effects of manic-depressive illness almost inevitably spill over onto other family members, family therapy is often useful. The need for family therapy was well described by a woman known to Patty Duke:

> After a few months of seeing a psychiatrist on my own and gaining some insight into what I was like to live with, I didn't know where to start making amends—or how. How could I apologize to my children for the ball games I never went to, for the school nights I missed, for shutting them out of my room and my life when they needed me most? How could I tell my husband that I couldn't help the affairs I had, the scenes I caused, the embarrassment I brought him? I was so ashamed, it felt overwhelming. I also needed to know what they were feeling. How angry were they? Could I make it up to them or was too much chipped away? And I wanted them to know what I was still going through, the terror I still have about going out of control again.[14]

Since family members are usually an integral part of a person's support network, educating them about that person's illness will almost inevitably improve the overall outcome of the illness. An educated family is better able to understand the person's symptoms and the need for medication and to identify the early signs of relapse.

One particular form of family therapy that has been promoted for manic-depressive illness is *family-focused treatment*.[15] This family therapy usefully focuses on the education of the family and the development of communication and problem-solving skills. The main problem with family-focused treatment, however, is that it is structured on the outmoded theoretical underpinnings of "expressed emotion," a blame-the-family approach that has been largely discredited.[16]

Several studies have been carried out on the effectiveness of family therapy on manic-depressive illness. Although these studies all have major methodological shortcomings, they suggest that such therapy can be helpful in improving medication compliance and reducing rehospitalization rates.[17]

Group Therapy.   Group therapy is on the same continuum as the support groups described above. The major difference is that group therapy is led by a professional group leader and costs money, whereas support groups are led by their members and cost nothing except possibly a nominal fee to rent the meeting room. Like support groups, therapy groups may include any combination of education, interpersonal problem solving, and support. Studies of the efficacy of group therapy have suggested that they may be helpful in improving medication compliance, lessening symptoms, and decreasing hospitalization.[18]

In summary, psychotherapy in one form or another may help some people with manic-depressive illness, but it is not needed by everyone. All forms of psychotherapy appear to be at least somewhat effective. At least some of their effectiveness is related to the fact that each improves medication compliance, which may be the common denominator. It is not clear whether any particular form of psychotherapy for manic-depressive illness is any better than another, or whether any of them have effective ingredients beyond the four basic ones associated with all psychotherapies: a shared worldview, the personal qualities of the therapist, the expectations of the patient, and an improved sense of mastery by the patient.[19]

Reducing Stress

Given that severe stress is thought to be a risk factor for relapse in manic-depressive illness (see Chapter 6), reducing stress is clearly in patients' best interest. There are many ways to reduce stress; one or more of the following should be included in the treatment regimen of everyone with this illness.

1. *Exercise:* Exercise is important for all people, but even more important for those with manic-depressive illness. It reduces tension in the muscles; increases endorphins, which elevate mood; increases the supply of oxygen to the brain; and suppresses the appetite, thereby making weight control easier. The human animal was not constructed to be sedentary.

Exercise comes in many forms and can be accomplished individually or in groups, outdoors or indoors, depending on the person's interests and fitness. The most important thing is to do it regularly and at least twice a week. Exercise unquestionably makes individuals with manic-depressive illness feel better. Mary Ellen Copeland, who surveyed almost 100 patients with manic-depressive illness while writing *The Depression Workbook,* reported: "There was universal agreement among study participants that exercise makes them feel better. If they are depressed, exercise improves their mood. If they are manic, gentle exercise, such as a leisurely walk, helps them calm down."[20]

2. *Relaxation:* Relaxation techniques can also be used to reduce stress. Many such techniques are available, including meditation, yoga, and massage. In addition to reducing stress, relaxation techniques increase patients' sense of control, which is often weakened during episodes of mania or depression. Kathy Cronkite, in *On the Edge of Darkness,* described how she uses what she called "forced relaxation": "If I can cancel all obligations that aren't imperative and take the time to sit in the hammock and stare at the sky, have my husband take the kids while I soak in a hot tub, or put on Bach and do a little needlework, the rest of my life will seem less overwhelming."[21]

3. *Diet:* Like exercise, eating well is important for all people, but even more so for those with a chronic illness. Although no controlled studies have been done, many individuals with manic-depressive illness

strongly believe that when they restrict their intake of alcohol and caffeine, they do better. It is also important to eat regularly scheduled meals, specifically as a means of keeping one's daily clock in rhythm.

4. *Psychotherapy:* Psychotherapy, in one or more of the forms discussed above, may be useful for reducing especially those stresses that are primarily interpersonal in origin. It is indeed difficult to control the symptoms of manic-depressive illness when, for example, one's spouse is threatening to initiate divorce proceedings. Individual, family, or group therapy may help by improving interpersonal relations and thus reducing these stresses.

Mood Charts

Mood charts have been widely hailed by patients and professionals alike as one of the most helpful nonmedication forms of treatment. Following are some of their uses:

1. They help the person regularize their daily schedule by recording moods at the same time every day.

2. They improve the person's insight into their illness by allowing them to view the fluctuations in their moods over time.

3. They help identify early warning signs that the person may be in the early stages of a relapse into depression or mania.

4. They provide a record for the physician and other members of the person's treatment team to use when assessing possible medication changes.

5. They help identify either monthly (e.g., premenstrual) or seasonal periodicities in mood fluctuations, thus making predictions of future problems feasible.

Several methods of mood charting have been developed for adults and children with manic-depressive illness. The simplest versions require that persons record their daily mood (e.g., from 1: very depressed to 10: manic) on a calendar. For children, the recording is usually done by a parent in consultation with the child. More complex versions involve both retrospective and prospective charting of moods on a form that also has space for recording the person's daily medication, major stressors, and hours of sleep. One such form is the Life Chart Manual for Recurrent Affective Illness; now widely used, it was developed at the National Institute of Mental Health by Gabriele Leverich and Robert Post. This type of record can be extremely helpful to the treating physician. Life Chart Manuals can be obtained by contacting the National Depressive and Manic-Depressive Association (National DMDA) by mail (730 N. Franklin Street, Suite 501, Chicago, IL 60610-7204), by phone (1-800-826-3632 or 312-642-7243), by fax (312-642-7243), or online (*www.ndmda.org*).

Electroconvulsive Therapy

Electroconvulsive therapy (ECT), which was developed in the 1930s for the treatment of schizophrenia, involves the application of an electrical charge to the brain to induce a seizure. Its major use now is for the treatment of severe depression, especially when this condition is complicated by catatonia or other psychotic features, and when the patient is seriously suicidal. It is also indicated for the treatment of severe mania in cases where it does not respond to standard anti-manic medications.[22]

In ECT, the electrical stimulus may be applied to both sides of the brain (bilateral) or to only one side (unilateral), usually the nondominant right side. Bilateral ECT is considered to be more effective but also causes more memory loss. Short-term memory loss and confusion immediately following the procedure are the most common side effects. If the patient is taking carbamazepine (Tegretol) or other mood stabilizers that have anti-seizure properties, these medications are discontinued prior to the ECT treatment, since they would block its effectiveness.

ECT has been vilified by the Scientologists and other anti-psychiatry groups (see Chapter 16), and legislation has been introduced to ban it in several states, including Texas and California. Anti-ECT forces claim that ECT damages the brain and causes a multitude of irreversible side effects. Popular but inaccurate depictions of ECT in movies such as *One Flew over the Cuckoo's Nest* have contributed to the bad press that "shock therapy" regularly receives.

In fact, multiple studies on ECT have shown conclusively that it does not alter brain structure or cause other brain damage[23] and that its side effects have been markedly exaggerated. Because of its bad press, ECT is underutilized in cases of severe, suicidal depression in which it can be, literally, lifesaving. A 1993 review of ECT use concluded: "After 55 years, ECT remains unsurpassed in safety, efficacy, and speed of onset in the treatment of severe depression and possibly in several other psychiatric disorders. Although not without side effects (what is?), ECT is cost-effective, and unquestionably it can save lives and diminish suffering."[24]

During the same year, the *New England Journal of Medicine* labeled ECT "a modern medical procedure" that "has been refined to the point of being the treatment of choice for selected patients."[25] One such patient was talk-show host Dick Cavett, who underwent ECT for severe depression and then publicly announced that "ECT was miraculous. . . . It was like a magic wand."[26]

Insurance Issues

The treatment of manic-depressive illness can be very expensive, especially if hospitalization is needed. And for individuals who often have gotten themselves thousand of dollars into debt on a manic spending spree, the additional cost of treatment can be catastrophic.

Until a decade ago, insurance companies often did not cover the medical costs of treating manic-depressive illness, because they claimed that it was a "mental" disorder, not a physical one. A series of lawsuits brought by families against the insurance companies has reduced this discrimination. Court battles in such states as Arkansas,[27] Illinois,[28] and Florida[29] have drawn attention to the problem and made it more difficult for insurance companies to deny charges.

In defense of the insurance companies, it should be pointed out that the psychiatric profession has been part of the problem. Psychiatrists have a reputation for not accurately reporting the diagnoses of patients so that insurance will cover them. A 1985 study[30] reported that "psychiatrists form a disproportionately large segment of the total" physicians who were suspended from the Medicaid and Medicare programs because of fraud and abuse. And psychiatrists played major roles in the private psychiatric hospital insurance scandals of the early 1990s. (For a detailed discussion, see Joe Sharkey's *Bedlam: Greed, Profiteering, and Fraud in a Mental Health System Gone Crazy*.)[31]

Also contributing to resistance to insurance parity for psychiatric conditions are the vague outer limits of psychiatric diagnoses as defined by the American Psychiatric Association. Almost anybody can qualify for one or another diagnosis and therefore theoretically become eligible for insurance benefits for psychotherapy or hospitalization. This problem was summarized in December 1999 in an editorial in the *Wall Street Journal*:

> The reason "parity" doesn't exist is that, beyond treatment of obvious disorders, "mental health" is a vague and open-ended term. The difficulty has been abuse of mental-health insurance by both individuals and the "provider network" who gamed insurance plans to make endless payments for dubious benefits of apparently marginal problems, all the while lobbying to gain coverage for an ever-expanding definition of mental illness.[32]

The obvious solution to the insurance problem is to limit parity to those psychiatric conditions for which there is convincing evidence that they are indeed diseases—a category that includes manic-depressive illness. This solution would go a long way toward alleviating the restricted coverage faced by so many families.

Many individuals with manic-depressive illness do not have to worry whether their insurance company will pay—because they don't have insurance. A 1998 study of 525 individuals with schizophrenia and manic-depressive illness who were being admitted to hospitals for the first time reported that 44 percent had no insurance at all.[33] For such individuals, the most important thing to do is to establish eligibility for Medicaid benefits; such benefits are automatic for those who qualify for Supplemental Security Income (SSI).

SSI and SSDI

The majority of individuals with manic-depressive illness are able to be self-supporting, especially if they stay on their medication. A minority, however, are not able to be self-supporting and require some kind of subsidy. Except for a few families who can afford to support the ill family member themselves, most such individuals are supported by SSI or by Old Age, Survivors and Disability Insurance (OASDI), usually referred to as SSDI.

SSI, a program to provide income for needy aged, blind, and disabled persons, is administered by the Social Security Administration, which defines *disability* as "an inability to engage in any substantial gainful activity by reason of any medically determined physical or mental impairment which . . . has lasted, or can be expected to last, for a continuous period of not less than twelve months." SSDI is a similar program, except that to be eligible the person must have worked prior to becoming ill and accumulated sufficient credit under Social Security. SSDI benefits vary according to how long the person had worked before becoming ill, whereas SSI benefits vary from state to state depending upon how much that state supplements the federal SSI payment; approximately half of the states provide some supplement. SSI and SSDI are the most important sources of financial support for individuals with manic-depressive illness in the United States. In 1999 a total of 1.3 million people were receiving SSDI because of mental impairment (not including mental retardation), and 1.4 million more were receiving SSI for the same reason. These 2.7 million people accounted for 27 percent and 31 percent of all recipients of SSDI and SSI, respectively, and "mental impairment not including mental retardation" was the single largest category of medical disability for both SSDI and SSI.

Applications to establish disability and receive SSI and SSDI funds should be made at the local Social Security office. For SSI, the person's assets and other income are taken into consideration in determining eligibility. If the person has savings worth more than $2,000, he or she may not be eligible; in computing assets, a home, car, and basic household goods do not count toward the $2,000. The application for SSI or

SSDI is evaluated by a team consisting of a disability examiner and a physician; they may request additional medical information or an examination of the applicant in selected cases. When evaluating the application, they pay special attention to evidence of a restriction of daily activities and interests, deterioration in personal habits, marked impairment in relating to other people, and the inability to concentrate and carry out instructions necessary to hold a job. Thus, whatever medical records are pertinent to establishing disability should be submitted with the original application. Assessing eligibility for SSI and SSDI is necessarily a subjective task, and studies have reported disagreement among reviewers as much as 50 percent of the time. A decision on an initial application usually takes three to six months; approximately half of all initial applications are denied.

If the applicant is denied SSI or SSDI, he or she has the right to appeal. This must be done within sixty days of the denial, at which time additional evidence of disability can be included. The initial reconsideration of the appeal occurs in the local Social Security office and results in approval only 15 percent of the time. However, the applicant may appeal again, and this time the hearing is before an Administrative Law Judge of the Bureau of Hearings and Appeals of the U.S. Department of Health and Human Services. At this level a higher percentage of appeals is approved. Further appeals are possible if taken to the Appeals Council Review Board and then to a U.S. district court. It is clear that persistence in pressing a legitimate claim for SSI or SSDI benefits will often result in success.

For applicants who are approved for SSI or SSDI benefits, payments are made retrospectively from the date of the initial application. Since the appeals process can take a year or longer, it is not unusual for SSI and SSDI recipients to receive, as their initial payment, a check for thousands of dollars. For individuals who are not capable of managing their own funds, especially those with concurrent substance abuse, it is customary for the Social Security Administration to appoint a representative payee who may be a family member, case manager, or other person. (Further discussion is provided in Chapter 13, under "Assisted Treatment.")

People with manic-depressive illness usually require assistance with SSI and SSDI applications and the appeals process. Social workers who file these applications on a regular basis are often helpful, especially in ensuring that the correct clinical information is included so that the patient's degree of disability can be assessed fairly. Persons applying for SSI or SSDI for psychiatric disability for the first time would be wise to use the services of a knowledgeable social worker. Application forms and appeals processes are confusing even for people whose brains are working perfectly.

SSI payments, but not SSDI payments, are reduced when the disabled recipient lives with his or her family. In theory this restriction takes account of the person's room and board; but in reality it penalizes people with mental disabilities for living at home. Many families resent this discriminatory aspect of the SSI program and claim that they must pay expenses in behalf of the disabled person just as surely as a boarding-house operator does. SSI payments are also stopped if a person is hospitalized for more than ninety days. A portion of the SSI monthly payment is intended for the disabled person to use as spending money for clothes, transportation, laundry, and entertainment. The amount of spending money varies by state.

It is important for persons with manic-depressive illness to establish eligibility for SSI or SSDI benefits if they can. Even if they have other income, thereby reducing the monthly SSI check to a small amount, it is still worthwhile. The reason is that eligibility for SSI or SSDI also establishes eligibility for other assistance programs that can be worth much more than the SSI or SSDI benefits by themselves. Such programs include Medicaid, Medicare, vocational rehabilitation services, food stamps, and some housing and rental assistance programs of the Department of Housing and Urban Development. In some states, eligibility for SSI or SSDI automatically confers eligibility for these other programs; in other states a separate application must be submitted.

As of January 2001, the federal monthly payment for SSI was $530 for an individual and $796 for a married couple; approximately half of all states provide a state supplement to these amounts. Individuals on SSI can earn up to $65 per month without losing any SSI income. For persons earning more than $65 per month, SSI benefits are reduced by $1 for each additional $2 earned. In 2000, Congress passed legislation making it possible for SSI recipients who are trying to return to full-time employment to retain their Medicaid benefits; previously these benefits were automatically lost, thereby presenting a major disincentive for SSI recipients to return to work.

Individuals with manic-depressive illness who do not receive support from their families or from the SSI and SSDI programs must rely on other income. Many of these people, especially if they are living in public shelters, utilize public assistance or welfare checks. Individuals who were in the military at the time they first became ill often qualify for disability payments from the Veterans Administration; these may total over $2,000 a month when all benefits are included.

Food stamps, another supplementary source of support for persons with mental disabilities, are often underutilized. To be eligible, a person must have an income below the poverty level. The amount of food stamps a person can receive varies by state and with income. It also varies with the cost of food and thus, of late, has been rising along with food prices. Food stamps can be obtained through local welfare or social services offices.

12

MANIC-DEPRESSIVE ILLNESS IN CHILDREN AND ADOLESCENTS

Here rests his head upon the lap of Earth
A youth to fortune and to fame unknown.
Fair Science frown'd not on his humble birth
And Melancholy mark'd him for her own.

THOMAS GRAY (1742)[1]

Manic-depressive illness in children made its unofficial debut during the 1990s. At the beginning of the decade, some clinicians doubted whether manic-depressive illness even existed in children. By its end, an out-pouring of research on clinical and treatment aspects of this condition had led to numerous scientific papers, three books (*The Bipolar Child* in 1999 and *Bipolar Disorders: A Guide to Helping Children and Adolescents* and *The Life of a Bipolar Child* in 2000; see Appendix A), and Internet websites specifically devoted to this illness (see Appendix B).

There is no longer any doubt that manic-depressive illness occurs in children. The question now is how often it occurs. Studies of adults with manic-depressive illness have reported that 20 to 40 percent first developed their symptoms during childhood.[2] An example is Margot Kidder, the actress who played Lois Lane in four Superman films and was subsequently diagnosed with manic depression. As a child of 10 or 11, she wrote in her diary about her fears: "I knew I was different, had these mind flights that other people didn't seem to have. And I had deep depressions."[3] At age 14, Kidder attempted suicide.

The incidence of manic-depressive illness among children is a source of lively debate. It has been claimed that approximately one-fifth of all severely disturbed children who are referred for psychiatric care have a diagnosis of manic depression.[4] It has also been claimed that childhood manic-depressive illness is more common in the United States than in some other countries because of more widespread use of stimulants and antidepressants, which are alleged to precipitate episodes of mania in childhood.[5] This claim of higher incidence in the United States has not been confirmed.

Clinical Aspects

The following is a typical case of manic-depressive illness with a childhood onset:

> A 13-year-old girl was brought to her pediatrician for an evaluation. Family history was positive for manic-depressive illness in the father. One year previously she had been diagnosed with attention deficit hyperactivity disorder (ADHD) and started on methylphenidate (Ritalin). Her ADHD symptoms had improved markedly on this medication. At this time, her mother was concerned because she had begun sleeping much less and had increased energy, sometimes doing housework all day long. She had also shown a marked recent increased interest in boys. Clinically, she was restless, talkative, and flirtatious and had an elevated mood. A preliminary diagnosis of manic-depressive illness was made, and she was started on lithium. Despite therapeutic levels of lithium, her mood continued to escalate for the next few weeks, she became increasingly irritable, and she started experiencing auditory hallucinations. Lithium was stopped and valproate (Depakote) begun. Her symptoms improved markedly except for impulsivity. Clonidine was added, and she stabilized on the combination treatment.[6]

Studies of children with manic-depressive illness suggest that the earlier the age of onset of the illness, the less typical are the symptoms. In young children, for example, discrete episodes of mania are rare. More common are such symptoms as continuous irritability, temper tantrums, poor frustration tolerance, impulsivity, aggressive behavior, and hyperactivity.[7]

In some children, symptoms of manic-depressive illness are evident even prior to starting school. Writer Danielle Steel, in *His Bright Light,* published an excellent account of the onset of manic-depressive illness in her son, describing his irritability and his being constantly at odds with those around him. Others, too, have noted this characteristic: "Bipolar children seem to be out of sync. Not only are they bothered tremendously by sensations, odors, and noises, but they seem to have great difficulty making shifts from one context to another."[8]

Temper tantrums in such children may become extreme "affective storms" or rages. The children may punch holes in the wall, destroy property, or attack other children or adults. According to one study, "several children when irritable used knives to threaten others, to stab the furniture or floor, or to cut off a cat's tail."[9] As one boy, age 8, put it: "When my moods shift, I am never prepared. It feels all tight around me. During a rage, I feel as though the real me is over on the stairway watching myself, but I'm powerless to stop it."[10] This account is somewhat similar to descriptions of seizures given by people with epilepsy; indeed, there are many similarities between the two conditions, not the least of which is that many of the same drugs are effective in treating both manic-depressive illness and epilepsy (see Chapter 8).

Another major characteristic of childhood-onset manic depression is the frequency of mixed states, with simultaneous symptoms of mania and depression (see Chapter 2) and rapid cycling (see Chapter 3). Some researchers claim that "the earlier the onset [of manic-depressive illness], the greater the frequency of mixed states."[11] One study reported that 84 percent of childhood-onset manic depression "had a mixed presentation."[12] Such clinical presentations make a correct diagnosis more difficult, as "it can be very misleading to see a happy child laughing in the office in the context of a miserable history (e.g., school suspensions, family fights)."[13]

The mixed states and rapid cycling of childhood-onset manic depression can also be very confusing for families: "Thus, children may be having a laughing fit and happily doing an arts and crafts project when, without any environmental prompt, they will suddenly become miserable and acutely suicidal, talking about wanting to shoot themselves."[14] Mitzi Waltz provides a similar description in her excellent book on children with manic-depressive illness: "They are very emotional, swinging from extreme happiness to extreme anger. . . . In these children, strange behavior and moods occur out of the blue. This pattern of waxing and waning, and of changing moods and behavior, is the key to diagnosis."[15]

Upon reaching adolescence, children with manic-depressive illness—as well as children who experience the onset of their illness at this time—are more likely to exhibit such classic symptoms as grandiosity, flights of ideas, hypersexuality, and suicidal thoughts and behavior. One adolescent girl with flights of ideas "wished she had a button on her forehead to turn off her thoughts."[16] A five-year follow-up study of fifty-four individuals with adolescent-onset manic depression found that eleven had made "suicide attempts sufficient in severity to require medical attention."[17] Wild driving and other daredevil behaviors are also common problems. Delusions and hallucinations are more common in older children with manic-depressive illness. The delusions may be grandiose or persecutory; one 9-year-old boy, when sent to the principal's office for disobeying his teacher, informed the principal that he could not be punished "because he was President Clinton's son."[18]

The neurological malfunctions in children with manic-depressive illness become clear when one listens to them recount their experiences. The difference between manic depression with onset in adulthood and manic depression with onset in childhood is that in the latter case, the brain is still developing. In childhood, the brain is still learning to integrate sensory modalities (e.g., hearing and vision), modulate emotions and motor activity, focus attention for increasingly longer periods, and respond to the challenges of socialization. The brain dysfunction that produces the symptoms of manic-depressive illness may interfere with many of these normal developmental processes, besetting the child not only with a mood disorder but also problems integrating sensations, modulating emotions and motor activity, paying attention, and socializing.

The causes of childhood- or adolescent-onset manic depression are unknown. Research is following the same lines of inquiry as those for adult-onset manic depression, and most researchers assume that they are the same disease. However, the question of why some people develop this disorder at age 8 whereas others do not develop it until age 18 or 28 or even older remains completely unanswered.

Diagnostic Aspects

Can we predict which disturbed child will later develop manic-depressive illness? The answer is, Not with any degree of certainty. According to recent research, the five early childhood symptoms most likely to predict later manic-depressive illness are grandiosity, suicidality, rapid thoughts, irritability, and hyperactivity. The problem, however, is that any of these symptoms may also be present in other childhood disorders.

The most controversial matter surrounding the diagnosis of childhood-onset manic depression is its relationship to attention deficit hyperactivity disorder (ADHD). ADHD confuses the issue because its symptoms, including hyperactivity, agitation, impulsivity, distractibility, talkativeness, and poor concentration, are also found in manic-depressive illness. Research indicates that approximately three-quarters of children and adolescents with manic-depressive illness also qualify for a diagnosis of ADHD; and, conversely, that approximately one-quarter of children with ADHD also meet diagnostic criteria for manic-depressive illness.[19] Studies of the relatives of children with manic-depressive illness and ADHD have also reported higher than expected incidences of individuals with the opposite condition—that is, more ADHD relatives in families with manic-depressive illness and vice versa.[20]

The overlapping syndromes of childhood manic-depressive illness and ADHD have produced much controversy regarding their relationship. Are children with ADHD being misdiagnosed with manic-depressive illness? Are children with manic-depressive illness being misdiagnosed with ADHD? Do some children have both disorders, and, if so, is it because the disorders are genetically linked in some way? Definitive answers to such questions are not yet available. Researchers do know, however, that in children with symptoms of both manic-depressive illness and ADHD, the combination disorder tends to be severe and produces more hospitalizations, more social disability, and more difficulties in treatment.

Childhood-onset manic depression may be confused with other childhood conditions as well. If repetitive behaviors are present and social skills impaired, the child may be incorrectly diagnosed as having a pervasive developmental disorder such as Rett's syndrome (which predominantly affects young girls and involves repetitive behaviors as well as impaired language development, coordination, and social skills) or Asperger's disorder (which involves impaired social skills and repetitive behaviors). If delusions or hallucinations are present, the question that inevitably arises is whether the child has childhood-onset schizophrenia. In many cases where delusions or hallucinations are present in a child or adolescent, it is not possible to say definitively whether the individual has manic-depressive illness or schizophrenia; indeed, the question can be answered only by observing the course of the illness and the child's response to medications.

A similar problem is faced when children or adolescents become severely depressed. Do these individuals have a major depressive disorder that may recur in the future, or will they eventually develop hypomania or mania and therefore be diagnosed with manic-depressive illness? There is no way to answer this question definitively except by observing, in each case, the course of the illness over time.

The symptoms of childhood manic-depressive illness may also overlap with those of oppositional defiant disorder or conduct disorder. Children with oppositional defiant disorder have temper tantrums, are often irritable and aggressive, and exhibit significant impairment in their social and school functioning; those with conduct disorder are aggressive, destroy property, are unable or unwilling to follow rules, and exhibit significant impairment in their social and school functioning.

Adolescent-onset manic depression often includes anxiety as a prominent symptom and therefore may be confused with anxiety disorders, such as generalized anxiety disorder, panic attacks, or agoraphobia. One study reported that more than half of adolescents with mania also met diagnostic criteria for an anxiety disorder.[21] Adolescent-onset manic depression in young women may also be misdiagnosed as borderline personality disorder because of such symptoms as impulsivity, irritability, rapid mood changes, aggressive behavior, self-mutilating behavior, and suicide gestures. Some researchers have even claimed that borderline personality disorder is a type of mood disorder, directly linked clinically and genetically to manic-depressive illness.[22]

Further confusing the issue is the fact that abuse of alcohol and street drugs occurs frequently among adolescents with manic-depressive illness. Does the 15-year-old boy who is using amphetamine have substance abuse with mania secondary to the amphetamine, or does he have manic-depressive illness with secondary substance abuse? Since adolescents who are developing the symptoms of manic-depressive illness commonly use alcohol and street drugs in their attempts to self-medicate, sorting out cause and effect in such individuals can be a Herculean task.

For parents who are dealing with the complex issues involved in this diagnosis, it is useful to construct a history using the children's version of the Life Chart Method, developed by Robert Post, Gabriele Leverich, and their colleagues at the National Institute of Mental Health. Parents are asked to retrospectively rate behaviors and symptoms such as the following:

Impulsivity

Temper tantrums

Hyperactivity

Skips school

Inappropriate sexual behavior

Excessively talkative

Stealing

Fighting

Excessive risk taking

Lack of remorse

Racing thoughts

Periods of sadness

More withdrawn than usual

Unusually clingy and dependent

Irritability

Sleeps less than usual

Increased aggression

Decreased attention span

Unusually happy and enthusiastic

Unreasonably and excessively self-confident

Disregard for authority

Destruction of property

Trouble with the law

Frequent lying

Bizarre behavior

Low self-esteem/ sense of worthlessness

Cries more easily than usual

Less active and energetic than usual

Excessive guilt   More anxious (tense/
                                        worried) than usual
Change in appetite   Suicidal thinking
Suicidal gesture or serious   Physical complaints
    suicide attempt
Sleeps more than usual   Obsessive thoughts
Night terrors   Does not talk or respond
Paranoid thinking   Hearing voices

The parents then maintain a daily rating of the child's behaviors on a graph, noting activated behaviors (e.g., impulsiveness, aggressiveness) above the baseline and withdrawn behaviors (e.g., depression, anxiety) below the baseline. The children's Life Chart Method can be obtained by contacting the National Depressive and Manic-Depressive Association (National DMDA) by mail (730 N. Franklin Street, Suite 501, Chicago, IL 60610-7204), by phone (1-800-826-3632 or 312-642-7243), by fax (312-642-7243), or online (*www.ndmda.org*).

Given the severity of manic-depressive illness in children and adolescents, as well as the diagnostic overlap with other disorders, it is important to clarify the diagnosis as early as possible in the course of the illness. For many of the reasons cited above, however, this is not always possible. Even the most skilled psychiatric professionals may occasionally render a misdiagnosis.

Treatment Aspects

Given this diagnostic ambiguity, it is not surprising that the treatment of manic-depressive illness in children and adolescents is less clearly delineated than that in adults. The one treatment recommendation on which there appears to be general agreement is that mood stabilizers are the drugs of choice. Lithium, valproate (Depakote), and carbamazepine (Tegretol) are all widely used to treat the illness in children and adolescents, and all three appear to be effective—although a double-blind, placebo-controlled trial has been carried out only for lithium. A large multi-site, double-blind treatment trial comparing lithium and valproate is currently under way, but the results are not yet known.[23] For treatment trials, the minimum period in which to ascertain effectiveness is six weeks for valproate and carbamazepine and eight weeks for lithium.[24]

It also seems increasingly clear that many children and adolescents with manic-depressive illness do not respond to a single mood stabilizer. In clinical practice, combinations such as lithium and valproate, lithium and carbamazepine, and valproate and carbamazepine are commonly used. To date, however, controlled trials have not been done on such combinations. The choice of drugs for the treatment of this illness in children and adolescents remains largely a guessing game. The choice of medications is also dependent on what the person will agree to take; medication noncompliance among adolescents with manic-depressive illness is an even greater problem than among adults (see Chapter 13).

In addition to mood stabilizers, low doses of antipsychotic medications are often helpful in controlling symptoms in children and adolescents with manic-depressive illness. Second-generation antipsychotics such as olanzapine (Zyprexa) and risperidone (Risperdal) are used most widely (see Chapter 9), although almost no controlled studies have been done on them in this age group.

The use of antidepressants and stimulants to treat child and adolescent manic-depressive illness is more controversial. Many clinicians believe that these medications may exacerbate symptoms of mania or even cause the illness to evolve into a rapid cycling subtype. Such allegations, though not verified by any controlled studies, have made many clinicians cautious about prescribing antidepressants unless depression is a major symptom. Similarly, clinicians are cautious about using stimulants such as methylphenidate (Ritalin) unless the presence of ADHD has clearly been established. When the symptoms of both manic-depressive illness and ADHD are present, the general recommendation is to treat the manic depression first with a mood stabilizer and then to add a stimulant if it is still needed.[25]

Another aspect of the treatment of manic-depressive illness in children and adolescents is *early treatment*. There is a belief, as yet unsubstantiated, that treating individuals very early in the course of their illness will minimize the development of more severe symptoms and ameliorate the long-term course of the illness. A study by Robert Findling and

Joseph Calabrese, at Case Western Reserve University in Cleveland, is now under way to test this theory: Children and adolescents who have at least one parent with manic-depressive illness and who are showing the earliest symptoms of the illness are being started on a mood stabilizer and will then be followed clinically for several years.

Still other modalities of treatment may be useful for children and adolescents with manic-depressive illness. Examples include occupational therapy, for improving motor skills; speech therapy, for improving language development; sensory integration therapy, for integrating modalities such as vision and hearing; and auditory integration training, for modulating sounds that may be perceived as too loud. Also potentially useful are various forms of psychotherapy (see Chapter 11) and peer support groups, especially during the teen years. Various diets (e.g., gluten-free, ketogenic, additive-free food) have been tried, but their effectiveness has not yet been established. Regular exercise, on the other hand, is almost always useful.

It is also important to remember that children and adolescents spend at least half their waking hours in school and related activities; thus, the school must be involved in the treatment plan. Under the Individuals with Disabilities Education Act passed by Congress in 1975, public schools are responsible for providing an Individualized Education Program (IEP) for each child who is disabled. The categorization of disability is complex and varies somewhat from state to state, but most children with manic-depressive illness qualify for an IEP under the disability category of either "seriously emotionally disturbed" (SED) or "other health impaired" (OHI). Establishing disability and getting a realistic and satisfactory IEP for a child with manic-depressive illness can be a complicated process; educational consultants or attorneys are often helpful. Two recent books, *The Bipolar Child* and *Bipolar Disorders: A Guide to Helping Children and Adolescents* (see Appendix A), contain detailed and helpful guidelines regarding the IEP process.

Finally, since manic-depressive illness in childhood affects the person's entire family, the family must become an integral part of the treatment plan. Guilt, shame, denial, fear, anger—all are present and must be faced on virtually a daily basis. Family members of all ages are affected by this illness, a fact clearly described by Danielle Steel in *His Bright*

Light: Her son's illness has profoundly affected not only Steel herself but also his brothers and sisters. Especially helpful for families in this situation is an interactive website established in 2000 by the Child and Adolescent Bipolar Foundation (*www.bpkids.org*), which provides updated information, online support groups, chat rooms, and helpful suggestions. For additional websites on manic-depressive illness, see Appendix B.

13

TEN SPECIAL PROBLEMS

Of all the calamities to which human nature is subjected, insanity may justly be considered the most deplorable.

ANDREW DUNCAN (1812)[1]

Manic-depressive illness is a difficult disorder not only for patients and their families but also for those who are called upon to treat it. Because the brain, rather than the heart or liver, is the organ affected, manic-depressive illness carries with it a host of special, and often very difficult, problems. Some of these, such as the seduction of mania, are unique to manic-depressive illness, whereas others, such as medication noncompliance or assisted treatment, are also major problems for individuals with schizophrenia and major depression.

Concurrent Alcohol and Drug Abuse

Drug and alcohol abuse is the single largest and most complex problem for individuals with manic-depressive illness. The concurrent abuse of these substances by individuals with manic depression turns what is already a big problem into a *giant* problem. Even worse, this concurrent abuse has become much more severe in recent years, as almost all individuals with manic-depressive illness have been deinstitutionalized from public psychiatric hospitals and are living in the community, where they have ready access to alcohol and drugs. Indeed, drug dealers quickly discovered this vulnerable population and are known to turn up on the doorsteps of those affected on the same day that SSI, SSDI, or welfare checks arrive in the mail.

233

**Special Problems Associated with
Manic-Depressive Illness**

- Concurrent alcohol and drug abuse
- Assaultive and violent behavior
- Medication noncompliance
- Assisted treatment
- Homelessness
- Arrests and jailings
- Suicide
- Sex and AIDS
- Confidentiality
- The seduction of mania

It is important to separate concurrent alcohol and drug abuse by individuals with manic-depressive illness from mania *caused* by street drugs. In the latter case, the drugs produce a temporary clinical picture that looks like, but is not really, manic-depressive illness: When the drugs are stopped, the mania goes away. In the former case, the drugs are additional to the underlying manic-depressive illness: When the drugs are stopped, the illness does not go away.

The magnitude of concurrent alcohol and drug abuse has been assessed in several surveys. For example, the Epidemiologic Catchment Area (ECA) study, carried out between 1980 and 1984, estimated that 56 percent of individuals with manic-depressive illness abuse or are dependent on alcohol or drugs at some point during their lifetime (61 and 48 percent for bipolar I and bipolar II, respectively).[2] And the National Comorbidity Survey (NCS) estimated that 71 percent of individuals with manic-depressive illness (bipolar I) "reported at least one lifetime substance abuse disorder."[3]

Even when the substance abuse disorders are restricted to alcohol and drug *dependence,* the magnitude of the problem is impressive. Alcohol or drug dependence is more serious than abuse because it includes such aspects as tolerance (requiring increasing doses of the substance), withdrawal symptoms when the substance is stopped, and increasing time spent obtaining the substance. Thus, quantifying alcohol or drug dependence provides a measure of the most difficult patients. In the ECA study, 32 percent of individuals with manic-depressive illness (bipolar I) had been dependent on alcohol and 28 percent had been dependent on drugs, with much overlap between the two groups.[4] These numbers support the widely held belief that concurrent alcohol and drug problems are a major problem for individuals with manic-depressive illness.

One other aspect of concurrent alcohol and drug abuse is of interest. Although women in general have a much lower rate of substance abuse than men, the rate for women with manic-depressive illness is proportionately much greater than for men with this illness. Thus, women who have manic-depressive illness are at major risk for also having alcohol and/or drug problems.

Why manic-depressive illness and substance abuse so often go hand in hand is not known. Indeed, remarkably little research has been carried out on this problem (see Chapter 16). Several theories have been proposed, however. According to one, there is a shared genetic predisposition to both manic-depressive illness and substance abuse. Another theory postulates the presence of shared neurochemical pathways in both disorders: In cases where a person has one disorder, the shared neurochemical pathway becomes activated and produces the second disorder. A third theory holds that chronic substance abuse (especially drug abuse) can *cause* manic-depressive illness, although there are no data to support such a causative relationship. A fourth theory emphasizes that the pursuit of pleasurable and high-risk behavior is a symptom of mania and hypomania. And a fifth theory suggests that individuals with mania and depression turn to alcohol and drugs as a way of self-medicating. Finally, it should be remembered that both substance abuse and manic-depressive illness are relatively common, so one would expect them to occur together merely by chance.

The effects of concurrent alcohol and drug abuse are very destructive. Since substance abuse often masks the diagnosis, individuals who abuse alcohol or drugs may be labeled for several years merely as substance abusers before anyone realizes they also have underlying manic-depressive illness. In addition, studies have shown that individuals with manic depression who concurrently abuse alcohol and drugs are more likely to have dysphoric mania and other mixed states, rapid cycling, slower recovery rates, poorer response to lithium, poorer medication compliance, more relapses and hospitalizations, poorer social recovery and job success, and higher rates of suicide.[5] In short, substance abuse on top of manic-depressive illness can be a disaster.

Less often discussed is one other effect of concurrent alcohol and drug abuse on individuals with manic-depressive illness: the increased propensity of affected individuals toward violent behavior. In a study of seventy-four men with schizophrenia and thirty men with major affective disorders (eighteen with manic-depressive illness and twelve with major depression) who were followed for two years, "33 percent of the patients with major affective disorders and only 15 percent of those with schizophrenia had committed crimes, most violent." Among those who had committed crimes, "more of them had, prior to the offence, at least one positive urine analysis for drug use. . . . Drug use during the follow-up period seems to be more strongly related to criminal offending among subjects with major affective disorders than among those with schizophrenia."[6] As further discussed below, this finding is consistent with other studies reporting that substance abuse is a major risk factor for violent behavior among individuals with severe psychiatric disorders.

The treatment of alcohol and drug abuse is problematic in any case—but especially so for individuals with manic-depressive illness. It is widely believed that, for such individuals, lithium is less effective as a mood stabilizer than valproate and carbamazepine, but scientific studies in support of this belief are lacking. Also yet to be established is whether the newer drugs used to decrease alcohol craving have any special value for individuals with manic-depressive illness. On the other hand, it is known that self-help groups, such as Alcoholics Anonymous and Narcotics Anonymous, are helpful to some individuals. It is also known that many individuals with alcohol and drug abuse are unable to stop using alcohol or drugs unless they are faced with visible consequences, legal or otherwise. In such cases, random urine screens are advisable as they can be effective in controlling the person's addiction.

Assaultive and Violent Behavior

Assaultive and violent behavior by individuals with manic-depressive illness has become an increasingly prominent problem in recent years. In a National Alliance for the Mentally Ill (NAMI) survey of 1,401 families carried out in 1991,[7] in which 29 percent of the severely mentally ill family members had been diagnosed with manic-depressive illness (bipolar disorder), 11 percent of the mentally ill individuals had harmed someone within the past year and 12 percent more had threatened to harm someone. One of the most surprising findings was that severely mentally ill women were responsible for almost as much assaultive behavior as were the severely mentally ill men.

Manic-depressive illness has special characteristics that increase the chances of assaultive or violent behavior. Prominent among these is irritability, as described in Chapter 2. Mania itself may predispose an individual to assaultive behavior, as may mixed states, in which manic and depressive symptoms coexist. According to Kay Jamison, "Nearly 50 percent of all manic episodes are characterized by at least one act of physical violence [against objects or people]; this proclivity to violence is further compounded by the drinking that frequently accompanies mania."[8]

It should be strongly emphasized that most individuals with manic-depressive illness are no more dangerous than anyone else in the general population. The assaultive and violent behavior attributable to manic-depressive illness is carried out by a very small percentage of those affected, some of whom have a history of repeated assaults. It should be equally strongly emphasized that individuals with severe mental disorders, including manic-depressive illness, are responsible for only a small fraction of the total violence in society.

For the victims of violent acts committed by those with manic depression, as well as for those affected, it is of little consolation that such acts are comparatively rare. Assaultive and violent behavior by individuals with manic-depressive illness often lead to tragically fatal consequences for the target of the violent act:

Maryland 1996: Donald Levin, diagnosed with manic-depressive illness, shot to death his mother and father. Mr. Levin's illness was well controlled by lithium and antipsychotics, but he had stopped taking them.[9]

Ohio 1998: Tyron Wotring, diagnosed with manic-depressive illness, beat to death his housemate. According to his mother, Mr. Wotring had stopped taking his medication.[10]

Missouri 1999: Mary Karch, diagnosed with manic-depressive illness, killed her infant daughter and attempted to kill her young son. She had recently stopped taking her lithium because of side effects.[11]

The consequences are also sometimes fatal for the person with manic-depressive illness:

Texas 1995: Police were called to the home of Matthew Morgan, diagnosed with manic-depressive illness, because he was destroying his parents' property. Mr. Morgan, who had stopped taking his medication, held the police at bay for three hours but was shot to death when he charged them with an axe.[12]

South Carolina 1999: Police were called to a grocery store where Kenneth Davis, diagnosed with manic-depressive illness, was threatening a store clerk with a knife. Mr. Davis, who had stopped taking his lithium and was abusing cocaine, had threatened other individuals twice within the preceding week. When Mr. Davis threatened the police officer with the knife, he was shot to death by the police.[13]

There is evidence that the number of mental illness–related acts of violence has risen in recent years. For example, a recent survey of homicides in which two or more persons were killed and the homicide was not associated with a crime (e.g., robbery) or domestic violence reported that in the last decade "the incidence of these rampage killings appears to have increased."[14] The report also noted that "more than half" of the perpetrators of these multiple homicides "had histories of serious mental health problems—either a hospitalization, a prescription for psychiatric drugs, a suicide attempt, or evidence of psychosis."

Can we predict who will become violent? The best predictors of violence among all individuals are a past history of violent behavior and the abuse of alcohol and/or street drugs. Among individuals with manic-depressive illness, too, these are the strongest predictors. A third predictor, however, is failure to take medication needed to remain stable and nonpsychotic. The reasons for which individuals with manic-depressive illness do not take their medication are many. They are discussed below under "Medication Noncompliance."

What to Do If a Person with Manic-Depressive Illness Threatens to Become Assaultive

- Don't underestimate the risk. People who are acutely manic, especially if also delusional and abusing alcohol or street drugs, are capable of extreme violence and are not predictable.

- Discuss the situation with the person's case manager, social worker, and/or psychiatrist. Make sure they are aware of the person's threatening or assaultive behavior. If possible, put your concerns in writing to them: Written notification is much more difficult to ignore.

- Safe-proof your house or apartment. Have a room to which you can retreat if needed; it should have a secure lock and a telephone. Do not allow firearms in the house.

- Clearly spell out the consequences for the person if he or she does become assaultive (e.g., no longer being able to live at home). Be prepared to carry out those consequences.

- Minimize alcohol and/or street drug use by the person in whatever ways are possible. Substance abuse is often a trigger for assaultive behavior.

- If threatened, remain calm, keep conversation to a minimum, and exit the situation.

- Do not hesitate to call the police. Have a Crisis Information Form already filled out for such emergencies, ready to hand to the police when they arrive. It should include the person's

name, age, diagnosis, treating psychiatrist or clinic with telephone number, current medications, and summarized past history of violent behavior and/or arrests.

Medication Noncompliance

The failure to take medication regularly is a major problem—often *the*
major problem—for people with manic depression. One study suggested that approximately half of all such individuals stop taking their
medication during a one-year period;[15] another study found that half
discontinued their medication over a two-year period.[16] This behavior
leads in many cases to relapse of symptoms, rehospitalization, psychotic
behavior that lands the person in jail, manic spending sprees, sexual
indiscretions, homelessness, assaultive behavior, and even suicide.
Understanding the reasons for medication noncompliance is therefore
crucial to managing the illness.

There are nine major reasons for medication noncompliance in
manic-depressive illness, with the first five being the most important.

Major Reasons for Medication
Noncompliance in Manic-Depressive Illness

1. The seduction of mania

2. Lack of awareness of illness

3. Side effects of medication

4. Denial of illness

5. Depression

6. Delusions

7. Cognitive deficits

8. Fears of becoming dependent

9. Poor doctor-patient relationship

1. *The seduction of mania:* As discussed separately later in the chapter, for many people with manic-depressive illness this is the major rea-

son they stop taking their medication. Sometimes the decision to stop their medication in order to resume being manic is conscious, but often it is partially or completely unconscious.

2. *Lack of awareness of illness:* Manic-depressive illness, like schizophrenia, affects circuits in the frontal areas of the brain and adjacent cingulate region that are essential for self-reflection. These are the brain areas we use when we think about ourselves and look at ourselves from the outside. They are the areas that are active when we say to ourselves "You are being too self-centered," "You are being too lazy," "You are being taken advantage of," and so on.

It is known that circuits in these areas of the brain are often damaged by the disease process of manic-depressive illness, just as they can be damaged by strokes, Alzheimer's disease, and other neurological illnesses. When this happens to patients with neurological illnesses, it is referred to in medical terms as *anosognosia*—an appropriate term to use in psychiatry as well.

Multiple studies have measured awareness of illness in individuals with manic-depressive illness and in individuals with schizophrenia (see Chapter 2). As it turns out, the findings on both groups are similar: Approximately one-third of those with manic-depressive illness have moderate or severe lack of awareness of their illness compared to approximately one-half of the individuals with schizophrenia. Studies have also found that most individuals with manic-depressive illness show substantial improvement in their awareness of illness once they are treated, and that the improvement is much more impressive for them than for individuals with schizophrenia.[17]

Lack of awareness of illness is highly correlated with a failure to take medication, as might be expected: "If I'm not sick, why should I take medication?" The authors of this book have been told by noncompliant patients many times: "Doc, if you think this medicine is so great, then you can take it, but there is nothing wrong with me!"

Attempts to improve awareness of illness are under way. Two hundred years ago, Benjamin Rush urged his insane patients "to write their thoughts and secrets on paper in the hope that when they saw what they had written they would be shocked into rejecting their pathological ideas."[18] More recent efforts include videotaping individuals during periods of psychosis and then playing the tape back to them when they are in remission in the hopes that they will acknowledge the reality of their illness. It is still too early to know whether such methods are effective, however.

3. *Side effects of medications:* Lithium, other mood stabilizers, antidepressants, and antipsychotics all have side effects (as detailed in Chapters 8 and 9). For many individuals with manic-depressive illness, the side effects may be intolerable and so they stop taking the medication. It is very important, therefore, to utilize psychiatrists and other mental illness professionals who are sensitive to what their patients say about the side effects they are experiencing. Finding such professionals, however, is easier said than done.

4. *Denial of illness:* In contrast to lack of awareness of illness, which is anatomically based, denial of illness is a psychological phenomenon that affects everyone. We all engage in denial of unpleasant facts, although some of us are more skilled at it than others. Individuals with a tendency toward hypomania or mania are especially susceptible to this behavior, because their grandiosity suggests to them that they do not really need the medication. Taking medication once or twice a day is a painful reminder that they are sick, and if they stop taking it, they can fool themselves, at least temporarily, into believing that they are no longer sick.

5. *Depression:* Studies have shown a high correlation between the symptoms of depression and medication noncompliance.[19] Feelings of hopelessness often accompany depression, such that the person quickly descends into a "What's-the-use?" frame of mind. Since episodes of depression are central to manic-depressive illness, this is a relatively common cause of medication noncompliance.

6. *Delusions:* Occasionally, individuals with manic-depressive illness discontinue their medication because of delusional beliefs. Examples of such beliefs include paranoid delusions that they are being poisoned, or that their psychiatrist is an agent of the CIA, and grandiose delusions that they themselves are psychiatrists or famous scientists and therefore are more knowledgeable than their treating psychiatrist.

7. *Cognitive deficits:* Individuals with more severe forms of manic-depressive illness occasionally fail to take their medication because of

confusion and disorganization. These symptoms may occur, for example, in rapid cyclers as they alternate between mania and depression. Confusion may also be exacerbated by the large number of medications sometimes given to individuals with manic-depressive illness; even in persons whose brain is working normally, it would be difficult to keep track of them all.

8. *Fears of becoming dependent:* Some individuals with manic-depressive illness stop taking medication because of the mistaken belief that they will become addicted. This belief may be especially uncomfortable for males, who are culturally expected to be strong and to do-it-by-yourself.

9. *Poor doctor-patient relationship:* As detailed in Chapter 11, it is difficult to find competent and caring mental illness professionals. Moreover, because individuals with manic-depressive illness have a reputation for being medically difficult to treat, many of the best professionals avoid them. It is therefore common to find great dissatisfaction among patients with their treating psychiatrist, psychologist, social worker, and/or case manager. And when the patient gets angry with them, one way to "show them" is to stop taking the medication they have urged the person to take. The patient is the one who is hurt, of course, but such logic does not usually enter into decisions based on spite.

How can medication noncompliance be reduced? First, education of affected individuals and their families is essential: Studies have shown that a remarkably high percentage of patients do not know why they are taking their medication, what the medications are supposed to do, and how to take them. Second, pill containers with separate compartments for each day can be helpful. Finally, automated systems using computer technology are being developed that remind patients what medications they should take and when. Also under development are home monitoring kits for measuring lithium levels that will help improve compliance by giving patients immediate feedback.

Anything that can be done to improve the doctor-patient relationship will also improve medication compliance. Often this will involve finding a new doctor or other mental illness professional. Medication for manic-depressive illness should be approached as a joint venture, with the risks and benefits clearly spelled out; it should also be the subject of an ongoing dialogue between the patient and physician.

For many individuals who have limited awareness of their illness, however, no amount of education or cajoling will be effective. In such cases, some form of assisted treatment becomes necessary.

Assisted Treatment

For individuals with manic-depressive illness who have clearly demonstrated their need for medication but who will not take it regularly owing to lack of awareness of their illness or some other reason, assisted treatment is often necessary. They may have demonstrated their need for treatment by being assaultive, by becoming incarcerated or homeless, or by demonstrating in other ways that they are unable to care for themselves.

Assisted treatment often evokes opposition, because it infringes on civil liberties. Nobody should be forced to take medication, it is said. That may be true for individuals with heart disease or lung cancer, because their brain is assumed to be intact and capable of making rational choices. But in cases of manic-depressive illness and other neurological diseases, the person's brain is the organ affected—and it is often impaired. How can a person make a rational decision about taking medication when the part of the brain that governs self-awareness is damaged? How can a person make such a decision when he or she is not even aware of being sick?

It should be added that, for hundreds of years, laws have permitted assisted treatment under the concept of *parens patria,* the obligation of the state to act as a father for those who are incapable of looking after themselves. This concept is regularly invoked in behalf of individuals with brain dysfunctions such as Alzheimer's disease, strokes, brain tumors, and severe mental retardation; it is equally applicable to individuals with manic-depressive illness whose brain dysfunction often produces significant and measurable impaired awareness of illness.

An example of the importance of assisted treatment is the case of Daniel Ellis, a graphic designer in Des Moines, Iowa, who has manic-depressive illness. When he takes his medication, he is said to be both kind and productive. However, in 1993, during a period when he was not taking his medication, he attempted to drown a 3-year-old boy in a river. The court ordered that some procedure to monitor Ellis's medication be put in effect, but the order was not carried out. In 1998, when he was again not taking his medication, Ellis drove his car at 70 miles per hour through a stop sign and killed an elderly man. Ellis was found not guilty by reason of insanity, and, again, the court ordered a medication-monitoring procedure to be established.[20]

Many forms of assisted treatment are available, including the following.

1. *Outpatient commitment:* In situations involving outpatient commitment, a court orders the person to comply with a treatment plan as a condition for living in the community. If the person does not comply, he or she can be involuntarily returned to the hospital. Studies in North Carolina and elsewhere have demonstrated the effectiveness of outpatient commitment in reducing both rehospitalizations and violent behavior by mentally ill individuals.[21]

2. *Conditional release:* This is basically the same as outpatient commitment except that the legal authority is vested in the director of the psychiatric hospital or mental health center. Conditional release is widely used in New Hampshire, where a study showed it to be effective in improving medication compliance and decreasing violent behavior by mentally ill individuals.[22]

3. *Representative payee:* To assist with money management, a person's SSI, SSDI, or VA disability check can be assigned to the patient's family, case manager, or psychiatric clinic as the representative payee. The payee can then require the person to comply with a treatment plan as a condition for receiving the money.

4. *Guardianship:* Guardianship or conservatorship occurs when a court appoints an individual to make decisions for another individual who is believed to be mentally incompetent. The guardian can order the person to comply with a treatment plan and to be involuntarily hospitalized if he or she fails to do so.

Guardianship is widely used for persons with mental retardation and neurological disorders such as Alzheimer's disease, but it is much less used in cases involving severe psychiatric disorders.

5. *Benevolent coercion:* This category covers a variety of situations in which a mentally ill person is given the choice between complying with a treatment plan or being involuntarily hospitalized or jailed. It is used, for example, when a mentally ill individual is charged with a misdemeanor offense; the judge then gives the person a choice between accepting a suspended sentence that includes compliance with a treatment plan or going to jail. Benevolent coercion is used quite widely, especially in states where outpatient commitment is difficult to implement.

6. *Assertive case management:* Assertive case management is utilized in programs such as Assertive Community Treatment (often abbreviated as ACT or PACT) teams, which are widely used in Michigan, Wisconsin, Delaware, Rhode Island, and New Hampshire. Mental illness professionals on an ACT team actively follow the patients for whom they are responsible by visiting them in their homes and making sure they take their medication. In many cases, they also become the patients' representative payees (described above). Studies have shown that, in cases where ACT teams are used, individuals with manic-depressive illness and other severe mental disorders have a low rate of rehospitalization.

7. *Advance directives:* This form of assisted treatment works only for individuals who regain awareness of their illness when they are being treated. The mentally ill person signs a legal document while in remission that instructs his family or treatment team to hospitalize him or otherwise make sure he follows his treatment plan if he starts to relapse again. It binds the mentally ill person to the plan even if he loses awareness of his illness, just as Ulysses' crew bound him to the mast, at his request, while they were sailing past the island of the deadly seductive Sirens. Advance directives are therefore sometimes referred to as "Ulysses contracts."

A common problem for those supervising assisted treatment is finding out whether or not patients are taking their medication. Blood can be checked for lithium levels, but that merely indicates whether a person took lithium within the previous day or two; unannounced random blood lithium checks are therefore more likely to be effective in ensuring medication compliance. This will become easier to do as home-monitoring kits using the fingerstick method become available for monitoring lithium. For individuals taking other kinds of mood stabilizers, it is possible to mix substances such as riboflavin or isoniazid with the pill or capsule and then to take urine samples to monitor medication compliance. If the person is also taking antipsychotic medications, it is useful to know that some of these (e.g., haloperidol, fluphenazine) come in a long-acting injectable form that needs to be given only every two to four weeks. Meanwhile, research is under way to develop slow-release forms of antipsychotic medication that can be implanted beneath the skin and released slowly over many months, as with long-acting, implantable contraceptives.

What is the effect on individuals with manic depression who lack awareness of their illness of being forced to take medication? Opponents of assisted treatment have alleged that the effects are devastating and drive those so treated permanently away. Yet studies done on assisted treatment have found it to be remarkably benign in most cases. In one such study,[23] twenty-seven outpatients who "had felt pressured or forced to take medications within the past year" were asked to express their feelings about the forced treatment. Among the twenty-seven, nine were positive, nine expressed mixed views, six said they had no feelings about it, and only three reported a negative effect. In another study,[24] thirty patients who had been forcibly medicated during their psychiatric hospitalization were asked about it after being discharged. Retrospectively, eighteen of them said that being forced to take medication was a good idea, nine disagreed, and three were unsure.

For many mental illness professionals and other people, however, coercive treatment for individuals with manic-depressive illness is anathema. They maintain that it contravenes beliefs about civil liberties, the rights of individuals to privacy, and the freedom of speech and thought. The American Civil Liberties Union and the Bazelon Center for Mental Health Law in Washington, D.C., have staunchly opposed laws allowing forced treatment and have obtained court rulings in some states that have made such treatment virtually impossible.

What these well-meaning but misguided advocates have failed to understand is that approximately one-third of all individuals with manic depression have little awareness of their illness. When such individuals refuse medication they are doing so as a result of illogical or irrational thought processes. The right to be free of the symptoms of a brain disease must be weighed against the individual's right to privacy. Safeguards to prevent *abuse* of forced treatment must, of course, be built into the system; this can be done using public defenders and individuals who have been mentally ill themselves to monitor the system. As articulated by one observer, psychiatric patients "will suffer if a liberty they cannot enjoy is made superior to a health that must sometimes be forced on them."[25] The right to privacy must also be weighed against the needs of the patient's family and society as a whole, especially in cases involving individuals who become assaultive or violent when not taking medications.

To focus attention on the consequences of failing to treat large numbers of individuals with severe mental disorders, the Treatment Advocacy Center in Arlington, Virginia, was founded in 1998. Funded by private donations, it promotes the use of assisted treatment when needed and is working with many states to revise their outdated statutes. In fact, the Treatment Advocacy Center is the only national organization that has addressed the issue of assisted treatment. It can be accessed on the Internet at *www.psychlaws.org* and is also listed in Appendix D.

Homelessness

Individuals with severe psychiatric disorders, including manic-depressive illness, are at increased risk of becoming homeless. That their mentally ill son or daughter may become homeless is, indeed, one of the biggest fears for aging parents who are the principal caregivers for their child.

Estimates of the total number of homeless individuals in the United States at any one time range from 250,000 to 550,000. A median estimate of 400,000 is consistent with most research. Numerous studies have also assessed the percentage of homeless individuals who have a severe psychiatric disorder such as schizophrenia, manic-depressive illness, or severe depression with psychotic features. The consensus of these studies is that approximately one-third of all homeless individuals have a severe psychiatric disorder, although this percentage may be higher among those living on the streets, in parks, or in abandoned buildings. Thus, at any given time in the United States, there are approximately 125,000 to 150,000 severely mentally ill individuals who are homeless; many of them have a secondary diagnosis of alcohol or drug abuse in addition to their severe mental illness.

How many of these individuals have manic-depressive illness? In the 1980s, surveys that addressed this diagnostic question were carried out in four cities. A survey of shelter residents in Philadelphia reported sixty-seven individuals with schizophrenia, three with manic-depressive illness, and seven with major depression.[26] In Boston, the numbers were twenty-three, four, and three;[27] in Los Angeles, twelve, eight, and sixteen;[28] and in Baltimore, fourteen, nine, and twenty-one.[29] All four surveys used similar DSM-III diagnostic criteria for manic-depressive illness (see Chapter 3), although their results varied widely. It would appear, then, that there are at least three homeless individuals with schizophrenia for each homeless individual with manic-depressive illness, a ratio that accords with anecdotal accounts from within the homeless population itself. Given a total population of 125,000 to 150,000 severely mentally ill individuals who are homeless, *it seems reasonable to conclude that there are approximately 25,000 individuals with manic-depressive illness who are homeless at any given time in the United States.*

Guillermo Descalzi is one such individual. Described by the *Washington Post*[30] as once having been a "superstar correspondent for Univision TV . . . whose face and voice were known to millions of Spanish-speaking viewers across the Americas" and "able to sprinkle his conversation with quotes from Toynbee and Cervantes and Genesis,"

Descalzi made $150,000 per year and lived in a house in elegant Chevy Chase with his wife and children.

Despite his skills, Descalzi was "long given to fits of temper" and "had been diagnosed as a manic-depressive but refused to take his medication." His illness, combined with increasingly severe alcohol and drug abuse, led him to be fired from a succession of jobs. By 1995 he was living in an abandoned, burned-out house where "sometimes chunks of roof fall on him at night [and] sometimes he smears his body with toothpaste to keep away the mosquitoes." During the day, "he roams the streets, panhandling or peddling junk items, passing time with the drunks and crack-heads." His once-brilliant mind is now preoccupied with conversations with God and comments such as "We are all trying to punch holes through the fabric of space, woven by the master weaver." In exchange for a meal, "he will expound eloquently, if at times incoherently, on the themes that have come to obsess him."

Homeless men with manic-depressive illness, like Descalzi, are often able to protect themselves on the streets. For homeless women with manic-depressive illness, it is a different story. A 1995 study in Washington, D.C., of "99 episodically homeless, seriously mentally ill women" (16 percent of whom had manic-depressive illness) found that one-third "reported at least one sexual assault while homeless. . . . For episodically homeless women with serious mental illness, the lifetime risk for violent victimization is so high that rape and physical battery are normative experiences."[31]

A poignant example is that of Susan Fuchs. Intelligent, attractive, and a college graduate, she also had "a bipolar affective disorder, manic, severe with psychotic features," according to her psychiatric records. Though repeatedly involuntarily hospitalized in New York by her family, she adamantly refused follow-up care and medication. In fact, she did not think her family was trying to help her, believing instead that "aliens had taken over her relatives' bodies." Although she had been sexually assaulted several times and had made at least one suicide attempt, her family's persistent efforts to get help for her were to no avail. On July 22, 1999, Susan Fuchs's "half-naked body" was found in Central Park, "her head smashed in with a rock."[32]

Arrests and Jailings

For individuals with manic-depressive illness, arrests and jailings are common features of their lives. In the aforementioned NAMI survey of 1,401 randomly selected families,[33] in which 29 percent of the respondents' mentally ill family members had been diagnosed with manic-depressive illness, it was reported that 20 percent of these relatives had been arrested within the previous five years and 40 percent had been arrested sometime during their lifetime.

The vast majority of such arrests are for misdemeanors usually associated with the person's untreated mental illness. In Tennessee, for example, a man with manic-depressive illness stole a car and told the police that he did so "because the car was green and I am green."[34] And in Kentucky, a man with manic-depressive illness stole a yacht moored at a public dock, then drove it around the lake until it ran out of gas.[35]

Once in jail, individuals with severe psychiatric disorders remain there approximately three times longer than arrestees who are not mentally ill. In Gainesville, Florida, for example, a woman diagnosed with manic-depressive illness was held in the Alachua County Jail for five months in 1996 on a charge of trespassing at the offices of a law firm. And in Fort Wayne, Indiana, a woman with manic-depressive illness was held for four months in 1991 with no charges whatsoever against her; she had been committed to the Richmond State Hospital, which had no beds available, and so she was held in jail until a bed opened up.

Another noteworthy finding is how frequently people with manic-depressive illness are returned to jail and rotate between being jailed and being psychiatrically hospitalized. A 1992 survey of mentally ill persons in jail[36] reported such cases as a woman with manic depression who had been arrested for misdemeanors forty-nine times in five years in Washington state, a man with manic depression who had been jailed thirty-five times and hospitalized twenty times in Wisconsin, and a man with manic depression who had been jailed eighty-two times and hospitalized three times in California. The principal reason for this revolving-door phenomenon is the failure of the mental illness treatment system to follow up and ensure that such individuals receive the medication they need to remain well (see the section above on "Assisted

Treatment"). The sister of a man with manic-depressive illness who had been jailed on misdemeanor charges fourteen times and hospitalized sixteen times in Ohio explained the situation as follows: "Mental health persons say he is not psychotic enough to be hospitalized; the legal system says he is too psychotic to be in the streets. He is caught between two systems. He falls between the cracks."[37]

For those whose brain is working normally, being held in jail is stressful enough. For those in a manic state, it is extremely difficult. Other prisoners and the jail staff are affected as well. The aforementioned survey of mentally ill persons in jail described one individual who "paced the floor screaming curses for three solid days, day and night" and another who "did considerable damage to the jail and never slept, continuously hollering and keeping all prisoners awake." As an official in the California county jail succinctly summarized it, "the bad and the mad don't mix."[38]

How many individuals with manic-depressive illness are in jails in the United States at any given time? In mid-1998 American jails and prisons held more than 1.8 million inmates, with predictions that the total would surpass 2 million by 2001. A 1999 Department of Justice report identified 16.2 percent of all jail and state prison inmates as mentally ill; two-thirds of these had previously been admitted to a mental hospital or treatment program.[39] Earlier studies of severe mental illness in jail reported that between 8 and 16 percent of prisoners had a severe psychiatric disorder, not including those with alcohol or drug abuse alone. Thus it is reasonable to estimate that, at present, at least 10 percent of all inmates, or approximately 200,000 individuals, have a severe psychiatric disorder.

Studies reporting a diagnostic breakdown of inmates with severe psychiatric disorders are limited. Two conducted prior to 1985 suggested that approximately 12 percent of mentally ill inmates had a diagnosis of manic-depressive illness,[40] but a 1991 study of Chicago's Cook County Jail[41] reported the figure to be 20 percent (based on DSM-III-R criteria). If it is assumed that 15 percent of all severely mentally ill inmates have manic-depressive illness, *the implication is that there are approximately 30,000 individuals with manic-depressive illness in America's jails and prisons at any given time.* As noted above, these individuals often cycle in and out of jails and prisons, spending time in psychiatric hospitals and being homeless between incarcerations.

Suicide

Given the severe and persistent ideas of suicide that flood the minds of many individuals with manic-depressive illness, it is not surprising that some attempt to kill themselves. A subset of these attempts succeed. Exactly how often this occurs remains a matter of debate.

Traditionally, it has been said that between 25 and 50 percent of people with manic depression attempt suicide during the course of their illness and that approximately 15 percent of all people with this illness succeed in killing themselves. However, many of the studies on which these figures are based were carried out on patient samples that included both manic-depressive illness and major depression. Others were carried out prior to the widespread use of lithium, and there is now substantial evidence that lithium has decreased the suicide rate.[42] Finally, many of the studies with the highest estimates included very small numbers of individuals. For example, the commonly cited claim that nearly one-half of those with bipolar disorder will try to kill themselves at least once is based on findings from the National Comorbidity Study carried out in the United States between 1990 and 1992, which sampled only twenty-nine cases of manic-depressive illness.[43]

The current rate of attempted suicide among individuals with manic-depressive illness appears to be approximately 25 percent, but that number depends on what one considers a suicide attempt to be. If a depressed person takes an overdose of pills and then calls 911, or drives 95 miles an hour in heavy traffic, or has unprotected sex with a prostitute, are these suicide attempts? Recently, there has been considerable publicity regarding depressed persons who provoke law enforcement officials into shooting them, a situation often described as "suicide-by-cop"; many of these instances clearly are suicide attempts.

The lifetime rate of completed suicide among individuals with manic-depressive illness appears to be substantially less than the 15 percent rate usually quoted. A twenty-six-year follow-up of 215 individuals with manic-depressive illness in Switzerland, for example, reported a completed suicide rate of 7 percent.[44] A study in Denmark that ascertained the number of suicides over a twenty-one-year period among 40,000 individuals with manic-depressive illness and major depression also reported a 7 percent rate.[45] And a recently published analysis of all studies published on this question concluded that the life-time risk of suicide for individuals with manic-depressive illness and major depression combined was 6 percent.[46]

Such studies, however, do not tell the whole story. How many individuals with manic depression commit suicide surreptitiously in single-car accidents, or by going for a swim and drowning? How many "accidental" heroin overdoses by people with concurrent manic-depressive illness are not really accidental? Since many insurance policies do not pay benefits to survivors when the death is caused by suicide, there is a strong financial incentive by patients and their families to make it appear to have been a natural death.

When all factors are considered, it appears that the lifetime rate of serious suicide attempts among individuals with manic-depressive illness is approximately 25 percent and the rate of completed suicides is approximately 10 percent. Any disease with a 10 percent mortality rate is a very serious and costly disease.

Are there risk factors or predictors of suicide associated with such individuals? The following factors appear to be relevant and should be considered when evaluating the suicidal potential for any individual with this illness.

1. *Family history of suicide:* The stronger the family history of suicide, the greater the risk.

2. *Personality:* Impulsiveness, aggressiveness, and risk-taking personality characteristics make suicide more likely.

3. *Substance abuse:* Concurrent alcohol abuse is a strong risk factor.[47] The use of tobacco, cocaine, and heroin are also risk factors, but much less clear are the data on marijuana, stimulants such as amphetamine, and hallucinogens such as LSD.[48]

4. *Clinical factors:* The severity of the person's depression—especially the depth of feelings of hopelessness and the magnitude of sleep disturbance—is a major predictor of suicide risk. The presence of agitation and anxiety increases this risk. Suicide attempts during periods of mania are

rare, although their incidence rises markedly in the period immediately following a manic episode. Be especially alert for a sudden improvement in the person's condition following a severe depression; it may merely be the calmness and peace-of-mind that follows a definitive decision to kill oneself. Vladimir Nabokov captured this feeling in one of his short stories:

> He began writing anew, but it came out cold and rhetorical. He sealed the letter and neatly wrote the address.
>
> He felt a strange lightness in his heart. He would shoot himself at noon, and after all, a man who has resolved to kill himself is a god.[49]

5. *Social network and responsibilities:* The more socially isolated the person is, the greater their risk for suicide. Individuals who have people dependent on them (e.g., a child at home under age 18 or elderly parents for whom they are responsible) are less at risk for suicide.

6. *Recent loss or stressors:* The recent death of a parent, divorce, termination of an important relationship, bankruptcy, or loss of a job—any of these events may be the proverbial straw that breaks the camel's back and precipitates suicide.

7. *Response to medication:* As expected, individuals whose symptoms are poorly controlled by medication are at greater risk for suicide than those who have a good response. Lithium, for example, probably saves many lives each year.

8. *Seasonal occurrence:* A review of sixty-one studies carried out by Frederick Goodwin and Kay Jamison[50] found a marked peak for suicides during the spring months (March, April, May, and June), with May being the maximum, and a secondary but much smaller peak in the fall (October, November, and December). However, recent data from England suggest that this seasonal variation in suicides has markedly diminished in the last several years.[51]

If family members or friends suspect that a person with manic-depressive illness is suicidal, what should they do? They should *ask* and they should *act.* Asking about suicidal thoughts and plans is very important. Often, such individuals are relieved that someone has asked, because they are unable to raise the issue themselves. And as they prepare for the suicide, they simultaneously hope that something will happen to make it

Risk Factors That Increase the Chances of Suicide Among Individuals with Manic-Depressive Illness

1. Family history of suicide

2. Impulsive, risk-taking personality

3. Alcohol, tobacco, cocaine, or heroin abuse

4. Severe depression, especially hopelessness and marked sleep disturbance with agitation and anxiety

5. Social isolation, with nobody dependent on them

6. Recent loss

7. Poor response to medication

8. Spring (especially May) or fall

unnecessary. Tracy Thompson captured these mixed feelings in her excellent book *The Beast: A Journey Through Depression:* "Even at this stage, my preparations were like strapping on a parachute in an airplane that was about to crash; the whole time I was preparing to hurl myself out the door, I clung to the hope that something would happen at the last minute to forestall that terrible necessity."[52]

Some people are afraid to ask about suicidal thoughts or plans because they believe "it will just put thoughts into their head." But this is simply not true; for most people who are severely depressed, the thoughts are already there. They need to be given an opportunity to express the thoughts to another person. One study of successful suicides in individuals with manic-depressive illness found that 39 percent "had even explicitly communicated their intent to health care personnel during the last 3 months."[53]

As noted earlier, if family or friends suspect that a person with manic-depressive illness may be suicidal, they should also act. One way to do so is to remove the person's planned modalities for committing suicide,

What to Do If You Believe Someone Is Suicidal

Ask

- Ask if the person is thinking of harming himself or herself.
- Ask if the person has a plan.
- Ask if the person has made preparations to carry out the plan.

Act

- Act by taking away the means of committing suicide (e.g., pills, weapons).
- Act by notifying the person's psychiatrist.
- Act by instituting hospitalization, either voluntary or involuntary, if necessary.
- Act as if it is an emergency; it often is.

such as a gun or pills. Another way is to ensure that the treating psychiatrist is aware of the person's suicidal intentions and is aggressively treating the person's depression. If the psychiatrist is reluctant to do anything, family members should put their advice and admonitions in a registered letter to the psychiatrist, adding, if necessary, that they have consulted a lawyer about the case. The psychiatrist will get the message. In some cases, involuntary commitment to a psychiatric unit may be necessary to ensure the person's safety until antidepressant medication can take effect or ECT can be started.

Despite the best efforts of all concerned, however, some individuals with manic-depressive illness will commit suicide. If family and friends have done what they could to help, they should not feel guilty or blame themselves. Suicide in manic-depressive illness is the ultimate tragedy in what is already a tragic disease. But its effects on those left behind can also be devastating and lifelong. Danielle Steel, in *His Bright Light*, describes this poignantly in reaction to her son's suicide; years after his death, she has left his room intact and continues to celebrate his birthday.

Sex and AIDS

Sex is a special problem for individuals with manic-depressive illness because, during periods of hypomania or mania, they may become hypersexual. The ensuing sexual activity may occur with minimal forethought, resulting in pregnancy, divorce, or AIDS. Exacerbating the problem is the high incidence of concurrent substance abuse among people with manic-depressive illness (discussed above).

A recent study in New Zealand reported that individuals with manic depression were 2.5 times more likely to engage in "risky sexual behavior" than were normal controls.[54] Such behavior was defined in terms of having had three or more sexual partners in the past year and "never or only sometimes" using a condom. Individuals with manic-depressive illness were also 4.4 times more likely than normal controls to have had sexually transmitted diseases, a rate higher than that among individuals with substance abuse disorders or antisocial personality disorder. A similar study in the United States found that 35 percent of individuals with manic-depressive illness had had multiple sexual partners in the preceding six months and that the majority had not used condoms or had used them inconsistently.[55]

The incidence of unwanted pregnancies in women with manic-depressive illness is also reported to be very high. According to one authority, "the rate of children born to psychotic women is estimated to have tripled since deinstitutionalization first began in the United States."[56] Also alarming is the recent report that women with manic-depressive illness, compared to women who are not mentally ill, are 4.4 times more likely to give birth to offspring who have mental retardation.[57] Although the present authors know of no research on induced abortions specifically among women with manic-depressive illness, a study of women with severe mental illnesses reported that 31 percent had had one or more such abortions.[58]

The high rate of unprotected sex, sexually transmitted diseases, and concurrent substance abuse among individuals with manic-depressive illness suggests that they have an increased risk for being infected with HIV and of developing AIDS. A study of seventy-four individuals with this illness voluntarily admitted to psychiatric hospitals in New York City reported that four (5.4 percent) were HIV positive.[59] Another study ascertained the degree of knowledge about AIDS among thirty-one individuals with manic-depressive illness, major depression, and schizoaffective disorder: 37 percent said that a person could get AIDS from toilet seats, 50 percent said that AIDS could be transmitted by kissing, and 33 percent did not believe that condoms help prevent AIDS.[60]

The importance of contraception and AIDS education for such individuals is obvious. Condoms are the first choice for contraception because they provide protection not only against AIDS and other sexually transmitted diseases but also against pregnancy; however, many men will not use them. Two methods of long-term contraception have been approved by the Food and Drug Administration and are now available for use by women. One involves injections of medroxyprogesterone acetate (Depo-Provera), which need to be given only every three months. The other involves progestin implants beneath the skin (Norplant), which last for five years but have significant adverse effects. Although both methods can produce some menstrual irregularities, they are highly effective contraceptives for many women.

AIDS education courses for individuals with severe psychiatric disorders have been developed by Robert Goisman and his colleagues at the Massachusetts Mental Health Center in Boston[61] and by Jeffrey Kelly and his colleagues at the Medical College of Wisconsin in Milwaukee.[62]

Confidentiality

Confidentiality can pose a major problem in the context of sharing information about individuals with manic-depressive illness. Ideally, such information should be selectively shared not only between mental health professionals and family members but also among various government agencies, such as a mental health center and the psychiatric unit in the local jail.

One family member of an individual with manic-depressive illness described the problem as follows:

Unfortunately, the hospitals and crisis centers available in the state are so absorbed with patient rights that they often discount the families of adults with the illnesses. The patient has the right to privacy. The family has no right to know and subsequently is lacking the information necessary to be protected and to help the ailing person. You don't know if the person got his or her medication, if he or she missed appointments, or if a change in medication could be causing the current breakdown. . . . Crisis centers and hospitals will not tell relatives if the person has been in for treatment or if that person is safely in residence. Other than calling the morgue hourly, there is no way to know if that person is dead or alive. There is no way to know if you can let your children play in the yard without fear of a manic person arriving and doing any number of things to harm a child's body or mind.[63]

Laws regarding the release of medical information are state laws and thus differ somewhat from state to state. They are designed to protect the physician-patient relationship, but they are not absolute. For example, if an individual with manic-depressive illness confides to his or her psychiatrist a plan to kill somebody, most states require the psychiatrist to warn the intended victim. Confidentiality can thus be overridden when it is in the best interest of either the patient or the public, although courts differ on how this rule should be interpreted.

There is strong evidence supporting the importance of sharing information between mental health professionals and families of individuals with manic-depressive illness. With such information, families are able to support their ill relative more effectively; for example, by monitoring symptoms of relapse and medications, they can reduce the incidence of relapses and rehospitalizations.[64] Information sharing among government agencies is also important; for example, when an individual with manic-depressive illness who is being followed by a mental health center is incarcerated in the local jail, it is exceedingly useful for the medical personnel of the jail to have access to information regarding the diagnosis and medications being taken by the individual.

Although the sharing of such basic information sounds like common sense, all too often it does not occur. A 1998 survey of family members of individuals with severe mental illnesses reported that one-third of the members were not even given general information (e.g., diagnosis, medications) when they asked for it.[65] Indeed, when family members call psychiatric units of general hospitals to inquire how their relative is doing, they are often told such things as "I'm sorry, but because of confidentiality laws, we cannot even verify that your relative is a patient in this hospital."

There is increasing agreement that the confidentiality laws are out of date and being misinterpreted and/or abused by mental health professionals in ways that are not in the best interests of patients or of society. For example, such laws usually state that permission of the patient must be given before any medical information can be released. However, as noted in Chapter 2, approximately 40 percent of individuals with manic-depressive illness have impaired awareness of their illness. Such individuals are unlikely to give permission to release information about their illness if they do not believe they have an illness. Other individuals with manic depression may have delusions that their family is allied with the Mafia or is trying to kill them; these individuals, too, are unlikely to give permission to release information to their families. Confidentiality laws in most states do not take into account such clinical realities.

Confidentiality laws are also misinterpreted by mental health professionals. Some of these professionals erroneously believe that they cannot release any information without the written consent of the patient. Others hide behind such laws, claiming that they cannot release any information when in fact they can. This occurs especially in cases of inadequate treatment or malpractice, when the mental health professional or hospital claims confidentiality as an excuse not to release clinical information that may result in a lawsuit. Confidentiality may also be used as a smokescreen by mental health professionals who have been trained in outdated Freudian or family interaction theories and who believe that patients' manic-depressive illness was caused by their "sick" family; in such cases, the family is often viewed by the mental health professional as the enemy.

The key to resolving confidentiality problems is to recognize that, for many individuals with manic-depressive illness, the relatives are not *merely* relatives but also essential members of the treatment team—especially now that patients are no longer hospitalized for long periods of time but, rather, are treated in the community, often in the family's home. Relatives have become increasingly sophisticated about the disease and its treatment and frequently know as much as the mental illness professionals themselves. When relatives are accepted as legitimate care providers, the issue of confidentiality becomes easier to resolve.

Pioneering work on the development of release-of-information forms, including a protocol to guide confidentiality problems, and confidentiality staff training programs have been carried out by the Department of Mental Health in Riverside County, California, and adopted in other counties. The protocol, in particular, emphasizes the benefits of family involvement and the fact that mental illness professionals can (and should) accept information *from* the families at any time. If the individual with manic-depressive illness refuses to consent to any release of information, mental illness professionals can still provide much information to the family by speaking of hypothetical cases rather than about the specific individual.

If you are a family member in this situation, be sure to familiarize yourself with the confidentiality statutes governing the release of information in your state. When faced with an uncooperative professional, appeal first to the professional's supervisor and then, if necessary, to the supervisor's supervisor. Put your request in writing and send it by registered mail, indicating your familiarity with the state's statute and pointing out that it does not apply in this case.

If that fails, have a lawyer friend send a letter on law-firm stationery reiterating your request for information needed to provide adequate care for your relative. State clearly that you will hold the mental illness professionals and/or psychiatric care center legally responsible for any consequences of failed psychiatric care attributable to their failure to provide you with the necessary information. Most important, do not accept any less information than you would expect to be forthcoming from professionals if your family member had another brain disease, such as multiple sclerosis or Alzheimer's disease.

The Seduction of Mania

Of all the special problems raised by manic-depressive illness, none is more challenging than the seduction of mania. There is probably no person with schizophrenia, severe depression, obsessive-compulsive disorder, or panic disorder who, if given the choice, would choose to have the illness. Not so with mania! Mania is the seductress of mental disorders, the psychiatric Siren calling to the passing Ulysses of the world, encouraging them to put away their lithium and enjoy, enjoy, enjoy. The Siren, however, does not tell them that the price they pay may be disaster or even death.

After listening to individuals describe their experiences with mania, one is not surprised that they would wish to experience it again. Who would not like to have boundless energy, to need only two or three hours of sleep, to be capable of performing sexually for hours at a time, to experience music and sights more intensely than others, to feel possessed of infinite amounts of money, and, perhaps most important, to be An Important Person? People who have been manic often do not remember the resulting problems; what they recall is merely the feeling of being manic. Jacki Lyden, in *The Daughter of the Queen of Sheba*, describes this phenomenon as her mother experienced it:

> And each time, she remembered very little of what had been done or said when she was sick. Which I regret. She doesn't remember in any specific way the costumes and speeches and strange migrations, the visit to bail out a prisoner or attempts to steal a horse or set a feast for Mary Baker Eddy. What she remembers is the feeling that she could set the world on fire, that she could paint what people were thinking and feeling, that she had the physical prowess of three—that she felt wonderful. That she was brilliant. That's what she remembers.[66]

Lyden contrasts her mother's mental state when manic to the reality of her drab existence when not manic. "In her delusions, my mother fancied above all else that she had dignity and power. She could fly beyond mortal realms to inhabit all the shining positions of influence that she lacked in the real world." However, "in the hospital layer upon layer of delusions were peeled back. . . . To be only human caused fear, and doubt and mortality, and the dead weight of having run out of dreams."[67] After leaving the hospital, Lyden's mother took a job in a clothing store: "A customer was berating my mother, who waddled and lowered her head. She was not a queen, but a beast of burden."[68]

Kay Jamison has also described the seduction of mania. A brilliant writer and a psychologist who specializes in manic-depressive illness, she herself suffers from the disease, so she knows it from many angles. In *An Unquiet Mind,* she recounts its allure:

> I found myself, in that glorious illusion of high summer days, gliding, fly-ing, now and again lurching through cloud banks and ethers, past stars, and across fields of ice crystals. . . . The intensity, glory, and absolute assuredness of my mind's flight made it very difficult for me to believe, once I was better, that the illness was one I should willingly give up. Even though I was a clinician and a scientist, and even though I could read the research literature and see the inevitable, bleak consequences of not tak-ing lithium, I for many years after my initial diagnosis was reluctant to take my medications as prescribed.[69]

Jamison is especially attracted to the creative aspects of mania and describes the importance of hypomania and mania in the creation of many literary and musical masterpieces. From her own standpoint, she states: "My manias, at least in their early and mild forms, were absolutely intoxicating states that gave rise to great personal pleasure, an incomparable flow of thoughts, and a ceaseless energy that allowed the translation of new ideas into papers and projects."[70]

As a professional, however, Jamison is able to step back and view the destructive aspects of mania:

> Although manic-depressive illness is much more common in writers and artists than in the general population, it would be irresponsible to romanticize an extremely painful, destructive, and lethal disease. Most people who suffer from manic-depressive and depressive illness are not unusually creative, and they reap few benefits from their experiences of

mania and depression; even those who are highly creative usually seek relief from their suffering.[71]

Patty Duke makes the same point in her autobiography: "Of course, not all people with manic-depressive illness are creative. Many resent the focus on the creativity connection because is doesn't reflect their experience—one characterized by lost jobs, broken marriages, and fractured relationships because their moods seesawed out of control."[72]

Jamison also clearly describes the painful depths of her depressions, which usually followed her manic episodes and included a serious attempt to kill herself. Yet despite her knowledge—both personal and professional—Jamison finds the allure of mania overwhelming:

> Still, the seductiveness of these unbridled and intense moods is powerful; and the ancient dialogue between reason and the senses is almost always more interestingly and passionately resolved in favor of the senses. The milder manias have a way of promising—and, for a very brief while, delivering—springs in the winter and epochal vitalities.[73]

She has also noted that "for some patients the illness may be similar to stimulant addiction."[74]

And when Jamison asks herself "whether, given the choice, I would choose to have manic-depressive illness" again, she replies: "Strangely enough I think I would choose to have it."[75] If someone with the personal experience and professional acumen of Kay Jamison can be seduced by mania, the same is probably true of virtually anyone with this condition.

14

MANIC-DEPRESSIVE ILLNESS
AND CREATIVITY

The learned and benevolent Dr. Parr used to say of such men, that they
were certainly *cracked;* but that the crack *let in light.* . . . Such men
adopt, as true, the most improbable assertions; they are full of discover-
ies, and secrets, and novel methods in art and science, in mechanics, in
medicine, and in government.

JOHN CONNOLLY,
An Inquiry Concerning the Indications of Insanity (1830)[1]

For centuries, unique creative talent has been seen as related to mental
disturbance. The ancient Greeks thought that inspiration in the arts
derived from the gods and constituted a kind of "divine madness."
Indeed, throughout the cultural history of the Western world, artistic
and creative people have tended to be regarded as possessed, energetic,
inspired, transcendent, or unconventional. In our current culture, however, we are less likely to view these characteristics as emanating from
the gods than as similar to the symptoms of mental illnesses, especially
manic depression. In fact, a great deal has been written about this subject in recent years, although the complex relationships between creativity and mental illness have not yet been examined in a very complete
or organized manner.

Certainly many of the symptoms of mania could be considered adap-
tive or useful qualities for creative pursuits. The energy, decreased need
for sleep, heightened sensory perceptions, and rapidity of thought associated with mania seem, on the surface, to be qualities that could stimulate the production of great art, music, or writing. Even some qualities
of depression—introspection, wistfulness, the struggling against

psychic pain—have been regarded as a kind of fertilizer for creative insight. Viewing the symptoms of manic-depressive illness as a boon to creativity can be an aspect of the seduction of mania (as described in Chapter 13). But this view can also be very therapeutic for individuals affected with the illness. One successful businessman with manic-depressive illness put it this way: "We bipolars are very creative people. We are the Schumanns, Byrons and Shelleys. We love to be creative and lead."[2] And a woman with manic-depressive illness, after reading a brochure claiming that individuals with manic depression "were often highly intelligent and creative" and listing "famous fellow-sufferers," commented:

> I loved that bit. Afterwards, even when I was depressed, that part of the brochure remained a source of solace. "I might be mad, but I'm in good company," I used to say with an ironic tone: "well I've done the illness bit, now for the creative bit!" Creativity had now become something I could reasonably expect to manifest, whereas my former self-concept as a friendly, conventional country girl had not seemed to make room for such boldness.[3]

But the symptoms of mania and depression are often linked to a precipitous decline in social functioning and productivity. Although manic-depressive symptoms may spark inspiration, prolonged and singular productivity depends upon long periods of normal mental functioning. We should therefore be careful not to underestimate the price this disease exacts from its sufferers. Indeed, as Charles Lamb noted: "So far from the position holding true, that great wit . . . has a necessary alliance with insanity, the greatest wits on the contrary, will ever be found in the sanest writers. It is impossible for the mind to conceive a mad Shakespeare."[4]

Many famously creative people have been diagnosed with mania, severe depression, or both. Among them are visual artists such as Vincent Van Gogh, Michelangelo, Paul Gaugin, and Mark Rothko; writers such as Robert Lowell, Virginia Woolf, Lord Byron, and Walt Whitman; and musicians such as Hector Berlioz, Robert Schumann, and Charles Mingus. However, we could just as easily compose a list of famously creative people who did not have a history of mental illness. Such a list might include Edgar Degas, Henri Matisse, Henry Moore, Duke Ellington, George Gershwin, Arnold Schoenberg, and Fred Astaire, all of whom pursued their crafts in a steadfast and predictable manner. There are also many disputed examples such as George Frederic Handel, who is often included on lists of mentally ill artists. A prodigious and energetic composer, Handel was also probably temperamental and unconventional; but there is little direct evidence to support a diagnosis of manic-depressive illness.[5]

Several types of research have been conducted to determine if there is more than a random association between manic depression and creativity. These include biographical surveys of creative people, direct diagnostic interviews with living creative people, surveys to determine the prevalence of mental illness among the relatives of creative people, surveys to determine the prevalence of creativity among the relatives of mentally ill people, and attempts to directly measure creativity of mentally ill subjects. Studies of the socioeconomic status and achievement levels of people with manic-depressive illness are discussed in Chapter 5.

Biographical Studies of
Mental Illness in Creative People

In the nineteenth century, retrospective biographical surveys of artistic people began to be published, suggesting that there was an increased rate for mental illness, especially mood disorders, among this group. Perhaps the most prolific writer among those conducting such surveys was Cesare Lombroso,[6] who was convinced of a link between genius and insanity.

Retrospective biographical studies conducted in the twentieth century have also suggested a high rate of psychiatric disorder among writers (especially poets), visual artists, and composers.[7] Kay Jamison,[8] perhaps the best-known researcher in this field, has written most convincingly about the relationship between creativity and manic-depressive illness. She collected the personal and family histories of all major British and Irish poets born between 1705 and 1805 and found that, relative to the general population, they were approximately thirty times more likely to have had manic-depressive disorder, ten times more likely to have had cyclothymia, five times more likely to have committed suicide, and twenty times more likely to have been confined in a mental hospital.

However, several biographical studies have been less supportive of a simple association. In the late 1940s, Adele Juda[9] obtained a sample of 294 German male geniuses; 113 were artists and 181 were scientists and statesmen. She reported that "functional psychoses" occurred among 4.8 percent of the artists and 4.0 percent of the scientists—percentages that did not appear to differ from the general population using the diagnostic criteria available at the time. Although she concluded that genius and a formal diagnosis of insanity were not clearly related, psychiatric symptoms (both psychotic and neurotic) as well as suicide were more common among artistic people, especially poets.

In a similar but more contemporary study using DSM-III-R criteria, Felix Post[10] concluded that "functional psychoses" were less frequent in highly creative people than in the general population and that schizophrenia was conspicuously absent. When psychoses did occur, they could sometimes be explained by organic brain syndromes such as syphilis. Here, too, creative writers were distinguished from other creative people by their tendencies toward disruptive personality traits, severe depressive episodes, and alcoholism.

Retrospective biographical approaches to the study of this question are often quite flawed and need to be evaluated in terms of the following criteria:

- How representative of the population (of artists, scientists, bankers, etc.) is the sample reported on?

- How accurate is the psychiatric diagnosis? Was it arrived at through memoirs or writings, or was it based on objective records from psychiatrists or hospitals?

- How is creativity defined? Is an individual creative just because he or she is a writer or an artist? Or should the individual be required to achieve *eminence* as a writer or an artist to be considered creative?

- Are creative people outside of the arts used as a comparison group? Is mental illness associated with artistic creativity alone, or with other forms of creativity as well?

- How good is the statistical model for predicting a relationship between manic-depressive illness and creativity? Can factors other than mental disorder *per se*, such as exposure to drugs or psychological hardships within the family, be associated more strongly with creativity?

A careful study of the relationship of creativity to mental illness that tried to address many of the flaws in retrospective research was conducted by Arnold Ludwig,[11] who surveyed the biographies of 1,004 eminent people alive in the twentieth century. Ludwig advanced this area of study significantly for several reasons: He obtained a representative sample of eminent people that was cross-checked against two other sampling methods; he included eminent people from a wide variety of professions; he used a reliable and reproducible scale for the measurement of "greatness"; he reconstructed psychiatric diagnoses using the most up-to-date criteria (DSM-IV); he compared rates of mental illness among eminent people to rates in the general population reported in the Epidemiologic Catchment Area survey (see Chapter 1); and he used sophisticated statistical procedures to compare great people to the general population. Ludwig's results are summarized in Table 14.1.

From this survey, Ludwig concluded that mania and depression are noticeably more common among creative artists than in the general population and in the population of creative people from other fields. The relationship between artistic creativity and manic-depressive illness does not appear to be specific, however, given that alcohol abuse and drug abuse were found to be as much as four times more common in artists; schizophrenia, at least twice as common in artists; and anxiety, as much as twice as common in artists. Interestingly, mania, depression, and schizophrenia were more common in some nonartistic creative people, although to a lesser degree than in artists. The rates of alcohol abuse, drug abuse, and anxiety were not particularly elevated among the nonartistic creative people. Even though it is a retrospective

TABLE 14.1   Mental Illness and Creativity

Disorder	Prevalence in General Population[a]	Prevalence in Creative Arts[b]	Relative Risk[c]	Prevalence in Other Professions[d]	Relative Risk[c]
Any psychiatric disorder	32%	60–80%	1.9–2.5	18–29%	0.56–0.9
Alcohol abuse or dependence	14%	29–60%	2.1–4.3	1–27%	0.1–1.9
Drug abuse or dependence	8%	10–36%	1.2–4.5	0–7%	0–0.87
Major depression or dysthymia	6%	34–77%	5.7–12.8	0–34%	0–5.7
Mania	0.8%	6–17%	7.5–21.2	0–5%	0–6.3
Schizophrenia	1.5%	4–17%	2.7–11.3	0–7%	0–4.7
Generalized anxiety	9%	4–16%	0.4–1.8	0–9%	0–1

[a] according to the Epidemiological Catchment Area Study
   art, music performance, music composition, theater, writers (nonfiction, fiction, poetry)
[b] prevalence in creative groups divided by prevalence in general population
[c] architecture, business, exploration, sports, military, politics, natural sciences, social science, social
[d] activism

study, this work provides strong support for the idea that mental disturbances are overrepresented in the population of creative artists; the highest rate of mania reported for the creative artists (specifically those who work as theater performers) is more than twenty times that reported for the general population and three times that reported for other creative people.

Studies of Psychiatric Illness in Living Artists

Another way to solve the methodological problems in biographical studies is to interview contemporary creative people and assess the prevalence of psychiatric problems among them. With this procedure, researchers can use interviewing techniques designed to accommodate systematic psychiatric diagnoses and are better able to identify control groups matched for education and professional achievement. Note, however, that biographical studies tend to include small samples that are not necessarily representative of the population of artists and tend to be focused on a single type of artist.

N.J.C. Andreasen and A. Canter[12] interviewed fifteen writers and their relatives who participated in the Iowa Writers Workshop and found increased rates of depression, cyclothymia, and alcoholism relative to the general population. In an enlarged sample from the same workshop, Andreasen[13] observed significantly increased rates of manic-depressive illness and alcoholism among thirty writers. And in a study of fifty-nine women writers who had participated in the Women Writers Conference at the University of Kentucky, Ludwig[14] observed that mania and depression were more common in writers than in controls. However, as he also observed in the biographical study cited above, writers were also more likely to have other psychiatric problems, such as anxiety, panic attacks, drug abuse, and eating disorders. Ludwig further noted that the extent of creativity in both writers and in controls could be predicted not only by a history of mental disorders but also by exposure to sexual or physical abuse in childhood, mental disorders in parents, and the extent of creativity in parents.

In another study, Jamison[15] observed forty-seven prominent British writers and artists, all of whom had obtained national recognition, as evidenced by their receipt of various prizes. This study focused on the role of changing mood states in creativity rather than on a direct determination of the frequency of psychiatric diagnoses. Nevertheless, the results revealed that 38 percent of the writers had been treated for a mood disorder and 18 percent of poets had been treated for mania. In their descriptions of the creative process, these writers endorsed many mood and physiological effects (such as sleeplessness and rapidity of thought) that overlap with the recognized symptoms of mania, although they would not necessarily have received a formal diagnosis. Jamison concluded from this study and others that there is a relationship between certain aspects of manic-depressive illness and creativity that cannot be explained simply by looking for the presence of the full psychiatric disorder:

> Any attempt to arbitrarily polarize thought, behavior, and emotion into clear-cut sanity or insanity is destined to fail; it defies common sense and is contrary to what we know about the infinite varieties and gradations of disease in general and psychiatric illness in particular. . . . The assumption that psychosis is an all-or-nothing sort of phenomenon, and that it is stable in its instability, leads to tremendous confusion. . . . Lucidity is not incompatible with occasional bouts of madness, just as extended periods of normal physical health are not incompatible with occasional bouts of hypertension, diabetic crisis, hyperthyroidism, or any other kind of acute exacerbation of underlying metabolic disease.[16]

Mental Illness and Creativity in Relatives

Several of the studies mentioned above also tried to determine the prevalence of psychiatric disorders among the relatives of creative people. For example, Andreasen and Canter's 1974 study[17] found an increased rate of depression among first-degree relatives of writers. Andreasen's 1987 study[18] found an increased rate of depression and a trend toward an increased rate of manic-depressive illness among sixty parents and fifty-six siblings of creative writers; the first-degree relatives were also more likely to have achieved creative success than the relatives of normal controls. And Ludwig's 1995 study[19] found that, compared to normal controls, mothers of creative persons were more likely to have experienced alcohol abuse, drug abuse, depression, and psychoses; fathers were more likely to have had a history of alcoholism; and siblings were more likely to have had a history of drug abuse and depression.

In addition, J. L. Karlsson[20] found that first-degree relatives of psychotic individuals born in Iceland between 1881 and 1910 were more likely than the general population to be listed in the *Who's Who of Iceland* and to be considered persons of eminence according to the occupations they obtained.[21] He combined data for relatives of individuals with schizophrenia and relatives of individuals with manic-depressive illness, but reanalysis of his work by others suggests that an increased rate of eminence was more pronounced for the latter.[22]

Increased creativity among relatives may be due to increased stimulation and opportunity for creative pursuits within the family of origin rather than to an inherited effect. To examine this question, T. F. McNeil[23] studied children who had been adopted as well as both their biological and adoptive parents, for whom rates of mental illness had been determined as part of a larger Danish study of the genetics of psychiatric diseases. What he found was that "highly creative" adoptees were three times more likely than "above average" adoptees, and thirty times more likely than "low creative" adoptees, to have mental illness; and that the biological parents of highly creative children were three times more likely than the parents of "above average" children, and two times more likely than the parents of "low creative" children, to have mental illness. The adoptive parents of all three groups of children had similar rates of mental illness (about 5 percent in each case).

Direct Measurements of Creativity in People with Mental Illness

Several attempts have been made to directly quantify the degree of creativity in people with manic-depressive illness compared to controls. For example, R. L. Richards et al.[24] used the Lifetime Creativity Scale to study seventeen individuals with manic-depressive illness, sixteen with cyclothymia, and fifteen normal controls. The relatives of the patients achieved higher scores than the patients themselves, which led the authors to conclude that "[t]here may be a positive compensatory advantage . . . to genes associated with greater liability for bipolar disorder. . . . Such a compensatory advantage among the relatives of a disorder affecting at least 1% of the population could affect a relatively large group of people."

Other studies have attempted to compare creative people and those with mental illness on the speed of associations or the rapidity with which they are able to generate opposites.[25] The earliest of these studies, which focused on schizophrenia and depended in part on psychoanalytic theories of the etiology of psychosis, claimed that creative and psychotic modes of thought were very similar. These studies were flawed, however, in that they tended to draw broad conclusions from small numbers of poorly matched groups and used tests that may not have been reliable measurements of the complexity of creative thought. Several studies, moreover, have failed to find increased rapidity of thought in patients with mental illness.[26]

The Effects of Psychotropic Medications on Creativity

Many patients with manic-depressive illness worry that they will lose significant amounts of energy and creativity if they agree to treatment for their illness. This is a legitimate concern that has to be approached with care in behalf of all patients, but especially those who make their living as artists. Indeed, both patients and psychiatrists need to examine two important factors so that an individualized plan for treatment can be designed.

The first factor to consider is illness severity. What should not be underestimated is that manic-depressive illness can remove people from creative pursuits and human interactions for long periods of time and can even be fatal. Patients who have had severe mania or depression, have required hospitalization, or have made suicide attempts are at serious risk from their illness and will usually be advised to continue with long-term treatment. Although some patients may complain of missing the "highs" of mania, they will be able to sustain creative pursuits over a longer period of time if they accept reasonable treatment. Patients with less severe forms of manic-depressive illness may be able to go without medications periodically.

The second factor is the type of medication to be prescribed. Although lithium is still a standard treatment for manic-depressive illness, it has a number of possible disadvantages for creative people. Lithium may be associated with the feeling that life has become less intense or interesting, a decreased desire to face creative problems, boredom and decreased energy, and a decreased desire to socialize. Lithium may also be associated with mild impairments in mental speed, memory, and verbal ability (see Chapter 8).

Despite the possible deleterious effects of lithium on creativity, only a few studies have examined their importance and frequency. According to two studies of lithium use by artist and writers, 77 percent of the participants felt that lithium either improved or did not affect their creativity and 23 percent felt that lithium caused decreased productivity.[27] In a special issue commemorating the fiftieth anniversary of lithium in 1999, the *Australian and New Zealand Journal of Psychiatry*[28] invited five creative Australians—a member of parliament, three writers, and a psychologist—to describe the effects of lithium on their own creativity. Although this survey was not meant to be conclusive, its results were quite consistent with those of the studies quoted above: Some, but not all, of the authors found that lithium treatment improved their long-term productivity. As Neil Cole, a member of parliament and a playwright, wrote: "Lithium's mollifying effect on my mania, coupled with antidepressants, helped my creativity to blossom. . . . In my experience, people who say they don't want to take lithium because it removes their highs are often talking about their perception and not the reality of their creativity."

The negative effects of lithium on cognition and creativity can be minimized in several ways. For example, sustained-release preparations of lithium can be used, or the lithium can be limited to a single daily dose. In fact, a general means of dealing with the negative effects on cognition is to use the lowest possible dose of lithium. If low lithium levels are insufficient to contain symptoms, lithium can be combined with other drugs (mood stabilizers or atypical antipsychotics) and with competent psychotherapy. And for patients who cannot tolerate the cognitive side effects of lithium, valproate or carbamazepine, which are probably less likely to interfere with cognition, can be substituted.

In conclusion, studies have shown that there is an increased rate of manic-depressive illness among creative individuals, that there is an increased rate of mental illness among the relatives of creative people, that there is an increased rate of creativity among the relatives of mentally ill people, and that there may be increased rates of creativity among people with manic-depressive illness. All of these studies are far from perfect, and each individually can be considered flawed. Taken together, however, they suggest a reasonable conclusion: that there is a significant relationship between creativity and manic-depressive illness.

Although we know that most creative people are not mentally ill, and that the vast majority of people with manic-depressive illness are not particularly creative, the link between creativity and manic depression is an intrinsically interesting issue that deserves more detailed research. Indeed, given that this illness is at least partially explained by genetic inheritance, it is also reasonable to conclude that the capacity for modes of thought essential for creativity can be inherited, that an optimal dose of that inheritance can lead to brilliance, and that an inappropriate dose—possibly combined with other environmental factors—can lead to severe mania and depression.

15

COMMONLY ASKED QUESTIONS

> Perhaps it was something about the training I had as a child at that very vulnerable sponge-like age. Discipline and the fear of not fulfilling my obligations were so thoroughly branded into my soul that I was able to have some kind of manic, total craziness for forty-eight hours—right up to two hours before performance time—and then go to work. Once I was out in public, no one ever knew. Unfortunately, my ability to function probably delayed my diagnosis for years.
>
> PATTY DUKE (1992)[1]

When people slip into the land of manic-depressive illness, they find themselves in a strange terrain, unlike any they have previously known. The road signs are not familiar, and when people ask for directions, replies are often incomprehensible.

It is for this reason that support groups, such as those described in Chapter 11, are so important. When one enters a strange land, it is helpful to be able to talk with people who have lived there longer. Among the many questions that arise are the following.

Should I Tell People?

Whether or not people with manic-depressive illness should disclose their illness is a decision that varies widely, depending on the person, the severity of the illness, and the recipient of the information. It also varies over time, with disclosure today being much more common than even a few years ago. Despite the relatively greater acceptance of mental illness by the general public, however, stigma continues to be a major fact of life (see Chapter 16).

It is important to disclose one's illness to those who can be helpful. Included in this category, of course, are the physicians and dentists who are treating you for medical conditions, since, to prevent drug interactions, they need to know what medications you are taking. Also included, perhaps above all, are family members and close friends capable of telling you when you are relapsing and need to get help. The days of hiding manic-depressive illness from other family members are pretty well over; Uncle John's episodes of mania or Aunt Sally's episodes of depression should no longer be passed off as eccentricities.

Should you tell your boss? In most cases, the answer is yes. Having a stable work and sleep schedule is important for many individuals with manic-depressive illness, but such a schedule is difficult to maintain if you are asked to work long hours of overtime or to fly to Europe twice a month. The Americans with Disabilities Act requires that employers make reasonable accommodations for employees with disabilities, but your employer cannot do that if he or she is unaware of your illness.

What about people you are meeting for the first time? Obviously, disclosure does not need to occur at the level of "I want you to meet my friend Jane, who has manic-depressive illness." But if you intend to have a serious relationship with another, sooner or later you will want to disclose your illness. Close relationships of all kinds are built on mutual trust, and, in any case, failure to disclose your illness would expose you to the constant threat that the other person will find out anyway.

As suggested earlier, people with manic depression are becoming more open about disclosing their illness. For example, when Representative Lynn Rivers was running for Congress in Michigan in 1994, she announced that she was being treated for manic-depressive illness, and it made no difference in her successful campaign. Robert Boorstin held high-level jobs in the Clinton administration despite being very public about his manic depression. And increasingly, advocates for improved services for individuals with mental illness (see Chapter 16) are gaining credibility in their advocacy efforts by disclosing that they, too, have had manic depression or some other serious mental illness.

What Are the Chances That
Other Family Members Will Get
Manic-Depressive Illness?

Since it is widely known that genes play a role in manic-depressive illness, concern is often expressed about the chances of other family members developing this disease. This is, in fact, one of the most frequently asked questions. As discussed in Chapter 7, research opinions vary regarding the relative importance of genes in causing the disease. There are also differences in what various researchers mean by "manic-depressive illness" in other family members. Observers who count every case of depression, anxiety, and substance abuse as an extended manifestation of manic-depressive illness in other family members will obviously view the disease as much more highly heritable than will observers who restrict their view to the illness itself. Also unclear is how much of the familial pattern of manic-depressive illness is truly genetic (see Chapter 7); in some families, for example, an infectious agent could theoretically be transmitted more commonly in childhood, creating a familial pattern that appears to be genetic but in actuality is not. For all these reasons, it is more difficult than one might suppose to get a clear answer to the question "What are the chances that other family members will get manic-depressive illness?"

Despite these limitations, some facts are clear:

- *The more mental illnesses in a family, the greater is the probability that additional family members will be affected.* Sheila La Polla's family is illustrative. Her father suffered from severe depression and alcoholism, and he attempted suicide on multiple occasions. One brother was diagnosed with paranoid schizophrenia and was repeatedly hospitalized. Another was diagnosed with manic-depressive illness and committed suicide. And Ms. La Polla herself was diagnosed with manic-depressive illness.[2] Such families are not common, but they do exist. In contrast, if you come from a family in which there are no other cases of manic-depressive illness, schizophrenia, or

severe depression among close relatives, then the chances that
other family members will be affected are much lower.

- *In most families, if one member has manic-depressive illness, the
  probability that a first-degree relative will develop it is approximately 8 percent.*[3] First-degree relatives are those with whom
  you share 50 percent of your genes—namely, parents, siblings,
  and children.

- *In most families, if one member has manic-depressive illness, the
  probability that a second-degree relative will develop it is only
  slightly greater than the probability that anyone in the general
  population will develop it*—which is slightly less than 1 percent.[4] Second-degree relatives are those with whom you share
  25 percent of your genes—namely, grandparents, uncles, aunts,
  nephews, and nieces.

- *The offspring of two parents who have manic-depressive illness
  or schizophrenia have a much greater probability of developing
  one of these diseases (at least 40 percent) than the offspring of
  parents among whom only one is affected (approximately 8 percent).* Given these findings, a person with manic-depressive illness who is planning to have children should select as a partner
  a person who does not have a severe psychiatric disorder.

Geneticists are hopeful that specific genes eventually will be discovered that allow us to genetically test a person and thereby predict who
is going to develop manic-depressive illness. Theoretically, if such a test
became possible, it could even be done on fetuses. Contemplating this
possibility, researchers gave a questionnaire to forty-three individuals
with manic-depressive illness. Among them, 68 percent said that they
would be in favor of genetic testing of children to ascertain whether they
were going to get the disease, even if no prophylactic treatment were
available to prevent it. When asked about terminating pregnancies for
fetuses that were determined to be carrying the putative manic-depressive illness genes, almost nobody was in favor of termination if the

course of the illness was going to be mild, but two-thirds favored termination if the course was going to be very severe (defined as needing hospitalization for at least half of one's adult life).[5]

How Does It Affect Family Members?

Manic-depressive illness, like all serious psychiatric disorders, inevitably affects all members of the patient's family. As described by one writer: "Families are like mobiles. . . . When one member develops mental illness, it sets the whole family mobile in motion and affects each of its parts."[6] This includes the mother and father, sisters and brothers, aunts and uncles, grandmothers and grandfathers, wives and husbands, and children of the affected individuals.

One way in which manic-depressive illness affects family members is through a sense of loss. When an individual is minimally affected, it may be the loss of what he or she might have been in the absence of the illness—CEO instead of division head, professor instead of associate professor. Those outside the family may regard the person as being successful, but those within know what the person might have become were it not for the periodic episodes of mania and depression. When the individual is seriously affected, the sense of loss for family members may be profound; as one patient's relative commented: "It's like someone close died, but there's no closure. It's never over."[7] Another noted: "The problems with my daughter were like a black hole inside of me into which everything else had been drawn."[8]

A second way in which manic-depressive illness may affect family members is through anger and resentment. Parents often must give up personal time and social relationships to provide care for their sick daughter or son; if the person is severely affected, their parenting role may stretch into the indefinite future, aborting plans for a quiet retirement and time to travel. In addition, the ill person may absorb large quantities of the family's financial resources, especially if he or she undertakes shopping sprees while manic or requires expensive medications. For parents, manic-depressive illness in a daughter or son may also mean the loss of the grandchildren for which they had hoped. And if grandchildren come, the joy of having them is tempered by the reality that they, too, may become sick.

In the past, guilt and shame frequently accompanied manic-depressive illness to family gatherings. This still occurs but, fortunately, is becoming less common. As an understanding of the biological causes of manic-depressive illness has become more widespread, guilt among family members has decreased. And feelings of shame are both inappropriate and irrational; people should feel no more ashamed of having a family member with manic-depressive illness than of having a family member with Parkinson's disease or multiple sclerosis.

Finally, there is fear—an important but rarely discussed effect on family members in some cases of manic-depressive illness. As described in Chapter 13, some individuals with this illness do occasionally become dangerous, especially if they are not taking the medication necessary to control their symptoms. Diane Berger, in an account of the onset of manic depression in her son, describes her initial realization that her son might be dangerous:

> Mark's rage and nonsequiturs compelled me to face a new truth. He was completely out of control, and none of us understood it. Everyone was terrified. For the first time, I shivered at the thought that he could be violent. . . .
>
> I slowly crossed the lobby, soundlessly sat beside him, and reached for his hand. He angrily pulled it away and twisted around so I couldn't see his face.
>
> "Why can't you understand, Diane, I want to be alone." He spit out the words as one would a rotten shrimp. He had never called me by my name before. Wheeling around, he shoved his face inches from mine and menacingly locked his eyes in mine.
>
> "Don't you see, bitch, this is my life, not yours. Go away." He casually resumed reading the *Time* in his lap. For the first time, I was physically afraid. The only words that came to me were "demonic possession."[9]

In addition to these general effects is one that is specific to manic-depressive illness: The symptoms are such that they may be difficult for family members to handle. Kim Mueser and his colleagues carried out a study in which they compared the effects on family members of the symptoms of twenty-seven individuals with schizophrenia and twenty-one individuals with manic-depressive illness.[10] Surprisingly, family members of the individuals with manic depression were more troubled by many symptoms than were family members of individuals with schizophrenia. The most extreme differences between the effects of the two disorders concerned such symptoms as labile mood, overactivity, and lack of insight, but family members of individuals with manic depression were also witness to higher levels of irritability, unpredictable behavior, aggressiveness, sleeplessness, and noncompliance with medication. Even though these patients were especially severely affected, the study demonstrated that the symptoms of manic-depressive illness can be extremely burdensome for family members.

What can families do to ameliorate this burden? One way is by becoming as educated as possible about the symptoms of the illness. Another way is by setting limits on the person's behavior and making it clear that behavior such as substance abuse or threats will not be tolerated. Those who cannot accept such limits should not be allowed to live at home, or, in some cases, even to visit. It may also be necessary to establish money-management control over individuals with manic-depressive illness who are inclined to go on spending sprees. This may include taking away all credit cards and lines of credit, closing checking accounts, and putting their spending on a cash-only basis.

The most important thing families can do to lighten the burden of manic depression is to achieve acceptance of the illness. This implies not passivity but, rather, an active acceptance that the illness is real, that it is here to stay, and that one is doing everything within reason to help. Diane Berger describes such acceptance as follows:

> Mark's illness took a place in my life where it neither dominated my days nor was banished to a dark basement. It fell somewhere in the middle. It wasn't a nasty, evil secret or the consuming obsession of my life. It was a biological, medical fact of life, and I defied anyone to disapprove of my frankness about it or to impose some insidious guilt by suggesting that it wouldn't have happened if I had been a more attentive mother.

I met the common dinner party question "Where are your children?" with equal love for both my offspring.

"The oldest is an engineer living in San Francisco, and the youngest is in a hospital in Boston," I stated. If they asked why, I would explain that he was being treated for manic depression. In short, he was ill and in the hospital, and he should get funny cards and potted plants, not whispers and embarrassed silences. I had a moral obligation to treat Mark and his life with the same pride and worth as Robert's engineering accomplishments.[11]

How Does It Affect Siblings?

The sisters and brothers of those with manic depression are affected by all of the problems enumerated above. They also have some additional problems.

Shame may be especially difficult for school-age children whose older sibling has developed manic-depressive illness. Childhood peers are quick to stigmatize a person as "crazy," and sisters and brothers may become known by their relationship to their sick sibling. At an age when peer acceptance is of utmost importance, having a sibling who is "crazy" can lead to much resentment. And if the affected sibling is living at home, brothers and sisters may be reluctant to invite friends to the house because of their embarrassment.

Jealousy and resentment are also commonly experienced by siblings whose ill sister or brother has taken center stage in the family. Mother and father have less time for their well offspring, and money set aside for the siblings' college education must sometimes be diverted to pay for hospitalizations and medications.

In addition, siblings of individuals with manic-depressive illness are frequently forced to assume unwanted responsibilities. As their parents age or die, it is the brothers and sisters who must assume responsibility for cleaning up the financial and personal debris after a manic episode, or for breaking down the bedroom door to prevent a suicide attempt during a depressive episode. Sisters and brothers become *de facto* mothers and fathers for their ill siblings, an awkward situation that is often resented by all parties.

And always there is the fear. Since manic-depressive illness is known to have a significant genetic component, many sisters and brothers wake up each morning wondering whether this will be the day when their own symptoms first become manifest. Periods of hyperactivity or mild depression, which most people accept as normal ups and downs of living, become magnified in their minds. They watch themselves and each other suspiciously and wonder, month after month, year after year.

How Does It Affect Spouses?

The wives and husbands of individuals with manic-depressive illness have a special set of problems. One is the problem of separating the effects of the illness from the nonillness parameters of their relationship. For example, one husband was initially attracted to his wife specifically because "her baseline hypomania energized her personality, making her productive, efficient and fun." In fact, "her exuberance led me to the mistaken belief when we first met that she had immediately fallen madly in love with me, when in fact she was manic." After many years of marriage, he continued to view her symptoms as part of her personality:

> I am in love with my wife because of the wonderful characteristics she possesses, some of which are a reflection of her illness. Her ebullience, work ethic, energy level, and enthusiasm, wonderful parts of what initially attracted me, are a reflection of her baseline hypomania. Though I hate the illness that has brought her so much discomfort, it is a prominent part of what she is like. I am aware that the illness is part of who she is; it does not define her, but it is reflected in her.[12]

Other wives and husbands have described their marriage to a person with manic-depressive illness as being very difficult. One wife recalled the constant accommodations she and her children had to make:

> Listen, let's just get the movie Dad wants. *So what if it's in black and white and about clipper ships. Let's not set him off.*
>   Want to go out? *Let's wait for Dad to get up so we can go together. Yes, I know it's three in the afternoon and he's still in bed. . . .*

And so we coped and settled and settled and settled, until I lost myself in making do, compromising, calming everyone down, explaining away, not complaining, covering over and not wanting anything I truly wanted for myself—spiritually, emotionally, personally.

She stayed with her husband but paid a high price for doing so:

But manic depression is a thief. It steals money, hope, security, dreams and love from those it inhabits and those who live with them. How do you trust the man who is supposed to help protect the children when you realize he's the most dangerous thing in your life?[13]

How Does It Affect Children?

Children of a parent or parents with manic-depressive illness may be profoundly affected by the illness. Even more important, they may think that they are the cause of their parent's illness. Mary Ellen Copeland, whose mother spent eight years hospitalized for manic-depressive illness, recalled: "As a child, I always thought it was my fault my mother got sick. I didn't know what I had done to cause her illness but I thought that if I said the right thing to her she would get well and stay well. The only trouble was, whenever I was alone with her, I didn't know the words to say."[14]

Linda Sexton, daughter of poet Anne Sexton, described her mother's mental illness, "which lived among us like a fifth person," and her own sense of blame:

I averted my eyes with shame when she told me how hard I was to care for: perhaps my ugly nature was to blame for my mother's difficulties with being a mother. . . . At night I lay awake in the dark to plead my case with God. *If I am very good tomorrow could you please make my Mommy better? If I eat all the broccoli on my plate will you help me not to make a mistake?*[15]

Such parents are often viewed by their children as fragile and unreliable, as Sexton poignantly observed: "My mother had been hospitalized in a terrible place, my mother had left me, my mother—the center of my small universe—was as fragile and precarious as the translucent Limoges my Nana kept on high shelves at her house."[16]

Jacki Lyden, whose mother also had manic-depressive illness, recalled the unpredictable quality of her mother's behavior in *Daughter of the Queen of Sheba:* "I knew my sisters and I were growing up like bumper cars in an arcade—the brakes applied harshly and erratically here, and no brakes or direction at all there, and all the time spinning around and hitting the edges."[17]

Patty Duke, in *A Brilliant Madness,* similarly described the effects of her manic-depressive illness on her children:

> On the other hand, I can only surmise how frightening it must have been for them to live with the kind of unpredictability that characterized our way of life. They referred to what used to happen to me as "Mom's freakouts." And I have heard them say how scary it felt because they didn't know when I was going to lose it, when I would send something flying through the air or take to my bed. . . .
>
> When I have spoken to groups of people who are concerned about the effect of their illness on their children, they often ask me which I think are worse for the kids: the manias or the depressions. I tell them that neither, of course, is easy, but at least with the manias, my children knew there would be an end within a reasonable period of time. They knew that the mania would stop.[18]

Kathy Cronkite, in *On the Edge of Darkness,* noted how difficult parental periods of severe depression are on the children:

> Depressives are not able accurately to observe the effect that they have on their children. It's almost like walking around in a cloud, or feeling like the light is only halfway up. Or they may think that things are going okay, but they're really missing the nuance of experience for their children.
>
> When the parent is not available for the child, the child experiences that as rejection, thinking that perhaps it has something to do with him, or the way that he's behaving or not behaving. He feels that he may be to blame for the parent's behavior.[19]

Patty Duke also recalled the effects of her periods of depression:

> But once I was in bed, behind closed doors, they didn't know what I was
> thinking or maybe what I had taken. Nobody ever went into Mommy's
> room; I was just sort of in there like Mrs. Bates at the motel. No matter
> that I had attempted or threatened suicide in the past and never suc-
> ceeded, I don't think the kids ever get used to it. In the back of their
> heads they have to wonder if maybe this time it'll really happen.[20]

We mentioned earlier that as the children get older, they often
become *de facto* parents to their own parents. Jacki Lyden's account of
how her mother's illness followed her and her sisters into adulthood is
illustrative:

> My mother is a worm in our brains that makes us crazy, Kate and Sarah
> and I. . . . She calls my sisters and me laughing in the middle of the
> night, talking about people we don't know.
>   "I feel helpless," Sarah told me on the phone from Denver. "I'm angry
> at God or whoever. I can't clean up after her anymore. I feel like her
> problems are my problems, just like when I was in law school. I wake
> up, I'm with her. I go to bed, I'm with her. I've got my own family now.
> I'm supposed to be independent." . . .
>   My grandmother would call me at all hours of the day and night to say
> that my mother had deposited a basket of kittens at a car dealership in
> lieu of payment, or purchased a carload of lingerie, or legally changed
> her name so that it somehow matched the name of a department store.
> . . .
>   For just like that, our lives had a way of falling prey to her guile, as my
> mother herself fell, a slippage, a breath, nothing very great, no time to
> look back, to grab each other's hands. Just my mother turning around to
> say, "I must be dreaming," and our lives fell away at a touch, mine with
> hers—throughout my life as a college student, girlfriend, journalist in
> Belfast or Baghdad, Chicago or London.[21]

The most effective way to minimize the effects of parental manic-
depressive illness on children is to educate them. No child is too young

to be told that something is wrong with Mommy's or Daddy's brain, that it is not the child's fault, and that other adults are taking charge of the situation. We constantly underestimate how much children are able to understand about such matters. Not knowing and not being told is much more frightening to children than the facts of the disease itself.

16

ISSUES FOR ADVOCATES

They say, "Nothing can be done here!" I reply, "I know no such word in the vocabulary I adopt."

DOROTHEA DIX (1848)[1]

In advocating for individuals with severe mental illnesses, Dorothea Dix set a standard that has never been equaled. Tirelessly, over more than thirty years, she visited hundreds of jails and workhouses to identify inmates who were mentally ill. She then testified before state legislators, haranguing them, embarrassing them, and ultimately provoking them into building additional state psychiatric hospitals. In speaking to the Massachusetts legislature in 1843, for example, she apologized for being "obliged to speak with great plainness, and to reveal many things revolting to the taste. . . . But truth is the highest consideration. . . . Men of Massachusetts, I beg, I implore, I demand. . . . Raise up the fallen; succor the desolate; restore the outcast; defend the helpless."[2] By the end of her career, Dix had brought about the building or enlargement of more than thirty psychiatric hospitals.

Given the continuing sad state of affairs for individuals with severe psychiatric disorders today, we need another Dorothea Dix—in fact, probably several of them. Where are those today who would decry the number of mentally ill individuals among the homeless? Or the number in jails and prisons? Where are those who would publicly chastise state and county governments for shirking their duty to provide adequate public psychiatric services? Who would demand that research on these illnesses be improved, and that the National Institute of Mental Health be required to do its job? Most voices today are inexplicably silent. But if one listens

293

carefully, the echoes of Ms. Dix's voice can sometimes be heard on the now-abandoned wards of the hospitals she brought into being.

Advocacy Organizations

Three national organizations have played the most significant role in providing support groups and advocating for better treatment for individuals with manic-depressive illness: the National Alliance for the Mentally Ill (NAMI), the National Depressive and Manic-Depressive Association (National DMDA), and the Treatment Advocacy Center (TAC). Addresses for these organizations are listed in Appendix D.

1. *NAMI:* The roots of NAMI go back to 1976, when psychiatrist Richard Lamb assisted families in San Mateo County, California, in organizing advocacy efforts to improve county services for their family members afflicted with severe psychiatric disorders. Families in other states began similar efforts, leading in 1979 to a national conference in Madison, Wisconsin—the official birthplace of the National Alliance for the Mental Ill, which became NAMI. NAMI today has over 1,000 chapters and offers support groups and education to its members. Many state chapters have developed advocacy efforts to improve services, and national NAMI lobbies Congress on relevant legislative and research issues.

2. *National DMDA:* The National Depressive and Manic-Depressive Association was founded in 1986 on behalf of individuals with depression and manic-depressive illness. It has 275 local chapters, whose main function is to operate support and education groups for individuals affected with these illnesses. It also occasionally becomes involved with other issues such as its September 1999 conference on the design of clinical trials to test new medications.

3. *TAC:* Formed in 1998, the Treatment Advocacy Center emphasizes the consequences of failing to treat individuals with manic-depressive illness and schizophrenia. Such consequences include homelessness, incarceration, being victimized, or committing violent acts. TAC focuses on changing state laws so that individuals can be treated before they suffer such consequences of non-treatment. This effort is especially directed at those mentally ill individuals who,

because of their brain dysfunction, are not aware they are ill. TAC works with groups that wish to change state laws to make treatment more available and, in 1999, was instrumental in effecting passage of an assisted treatment statute (Kendra's Law) in New York State.

Scientologists, Antipsychiatrists, and "Consumer Survivors"

One reason for the limited advocacy efforts on behalf of individuals with severe psychiatric disorders in the United States is the presence of countervailing forces—a small but vocal coalition of Scientologists, antipsychiatrists, and "consumer survivors." These disparate and often interdependent groups are united by their hatred of psychiatry in general and their opposition to any form of assisted treatment in particular. Many of their members are intellectual descendants of Thomas Szasz, who taught that mental illnesses do not really exist, and Ronald Laing, who claimed that psychosis is a growth experience. These groups often attempt to intimidate individuals and organizations that provide advocacy for individuals with manic-depressive illness, schizophrenia, and other severe psychiatric disorders.

The Scientologists channel their opposition to psychiatry through their Citizens Commission on Human Rights (CCHR), which proclaims on its letterhead that it was "established by the Church of Scientology in 1969 to investigate and expose psychiatric violations of human rights." Not known for its subtlety, CCHR also disseminates publications with titles such as "Betraying Women: Psychiatric Rape," "Psychiatry: Victimizing the Elderly," "Psychiatry's Role in the Creation of Crime," and "Psychiatry: Destroying Religion."

The efforts of CCHR are based on the teachings of L. Ron Hubbard, the founder of Scientology, whose main book was entitled *Dianetics: The Modern Science of Mental Health*. Scientologists see psychiatry as a rival that must be destroyed. According to one published account, "Hubbard taught that the psychotic person is a 'potential trouble source' who is connected to forces opposed to Scientology. People who behave as psychotics are 'unethical' and 'immoral.'" Hubbard also taught that the "forces" behind psychiatry are extraterrestrial, claiming that "Earthlings are the pawns of aliens" and that "the psychiatric establishment—which always looked askance at his theories—was not just a present-day evil but a timeless one. In a distant galaxy, alien 'psychs' [as Hubbard called them] devised implants that would ultimately wreck the spiritual progress of human beings."[3] In effect, psychiatrists were the Darth Vaders of Hubbard's universe.

All of this sounds like harmless nonsense until one realizes that many Scientologists actually believe it. Even more unsettling is the fact that, by making financial demands on members and recruiting celebrities such as John Travolta and Tom Cruise, the Scientologists have assembled enormous monetary resources to finance their antipsychiatry crusade and provide support to other groups and individuals who oppose psychiatry. The Scientologists' opposition to psychiatric treatment also has occasional fatal consequences. For example, in 1995, when a woman Scientologist in Clearwater, Florida, developed acute mania, other Scientologists confined her and failed to seek psychiatric care; she died seventeen days later. A civil wrongful-death suit filed against Scientology by the woman's estate is pending.

One prominent antipsychiatrist who has been linked to Scientology's Citizens Commission on Human Rights is Thomas Szasz. The CCHR website lists Szasz as a "founder," and its letterhead lists him as a "Founding Commissioner," although Szasz himself has disavowed this relationship. Another antipsychiatrist who has been linked to Scientology is Peter Breggin, author of *The Psychology of Freedom* and *Toxic Psychiatry*. According to a published account, "Breggin admits that he was once an ally of the group [Scientologists] and that his wife was a member."[4] Breggin, who trained under Szasz, has also written, in the context of mental illness, that "the difference in believing in the divinity of Christ and believing in oneself as Christ is merely a difference in religious point of view."[5] In place of psychiatric medications, which Breggin has labeled "the worst plague of brain damage in medical history," he advocates the use of "therapy, empathy and love." Breggin's methods for promoting good mental health early in life are equally questionable; he has written that "permitting children to have sex among themselves would go a long way toward liberating them from oppressive parental authority."[6]

Szasz and Breggin are revered by the "consumer survivors," a small group of former psychiatric patients opposed to psychiatric medications and any form of assisted psychiatric treatment. Much of their rhetoric has a Scientology ring to it. "MadNation" proclaims itself to be "People Working Together for Social Justice and Human Rights in Mental Health." Another such group is the Support Coalition. One of its co-directors, Janet Foner, is also the "main leader for Mental Health Liberation in the Re-Evaluation Counseling Communities." Re-Evaluation Counseling was founded by an ex-Scientologist and, like Scientology, presents its teachings as an alternative to psychiatry. Much of the "consumer survivor" movement is funded by the federal Center for Mental Health Services, which certainly qualifies as one of the strangest cases of misuse of federal money in existence today.

It is important for advocates of individuals with manic-depressive illness to understand the position of Scientologists, antipsychiatrists, and "consumer survivors" because these groups frequently oppose efforts to improve services or to provide treatment for those who need it most. Organized psychiatric advocacy groups are too often silent when confronted by the distortions and misinformation of the Scientologists and other antipsychiatry groups. Some people are also reluctant to counter erroneous public statements by "consumer survivors," because of a misplaced belief that it is politically incorrect to argue with ex-patients. This, of course, is nonsense; for every "consumer survivor," there are a hundred individuals with manic-depressive illness or schizophrenia who are quietly working to provide support for others so afflicted and to improve psychiatric services. The "consumer survivors" speak for no one but themselves.

Research Funding and the
National Institute of Mental Health

The failure to adequately fund research on manic-depressive illness is one of the major scandals of American psychiatry. It is the main reason why so little is known about the causes of this disease and why better treatments are not available.

The primary responsibility for disease-related research in the United States is vested in the National Institutes of Health (NIH), within which the National Institute of Mental Health (NIMH) is supposed to take responsibility for research on manic-depressive illness, schizophrenia, and other psychiatric disorders. Recent evaluations of NIMH's research efforts have documented just how badly NIMH has failed to carry out this responsibility.

According to an evaluation of NIMH's 1997 research grants, for example, just 3.5 percent of these grants targeted any aspect of manic-depressive illness and only 0.8 percent (17 out of 2,029 research grants) targeted clinical or treatment aspects of this illness.[7] A follow-up study of 1,342 NIMH new research grants funded in 1999 found that 2.4 percent related to any aspect of manic-depressive illness and only 0.5 percent (7 out of 1,342 research grants) targeted clinical or treatment aspects of this illness. And during 1999, at the same time that NIMH was funding only 7 research grants on clinical or treatment aspects of manic-depressive illness, it was also funding 7 new grants to study pigeons, 8 new grants to study songbirds, and 4 new grants to study fish.[8] Clearly, something is fundamentally wrong with the priorities of this federal agency, and individuals with manic-depressive illness bear the consequences of these misplaced priorities.

The failure of NIMH to support research on manic-depressive illness can certainly be criticized on clinical and humanitarian grounds. But it can also be criticized on economic grounds. As we noted in Chapter 1, using 1991 data, the annual cost of manic-depressive illness in the United States was estimated to be $7.6 billion in direct costs (e.g., hospitalization, outpatient visits) and an additional $37.6 billion in indirect costs (e.g., lost wages). Increasing costs for individuals with manic-depressive illness and other severe psychiatric disorders are a major reason why federal costs for SSI and SSDI are rising so rapidly. That the federal agency responsible for research is allocating such a small share of its budget on a disease that is costing the federal government so much money is both illogical and irresponsible.

Improvements in treatment would be extremely cost-effective. For example, Richard Wyatt and his colleagues estimated that between

1970 and 1991 the use of lithium saved over $170 billion, or $8 billion per year, in the cost of treatment for individuals with manic-depressive illness.[9] Even minor treatment advances would save additional money. But if NIMH is not supporting research on such advances, these savings will never occur.

Some small signs of improvement at NIMH have recently emerged in response to public criticism. In 2000, NIMH initiated a Systematic Treatment Enhancement Program for Bipolar Disorder (STEP-BD) to evaluate specific drugs for treating manic-depressive illness—a program featuring multi-site clinical trials that will involve twenty clinical facilities and up to 1,500 patients. This is the kind of research NIMH should have been supporting all along. But whether it signals a truly new direction for NIMH or is mere window-dressing to appease public critics remains to be seen.

Whatever the outcome, advocacy efforts to increase NIMH's support for research on manic-depressive illness is sorely needed. Individuals with manic-depressive illness and their families should demand, through their elected representatives in Congress, a shift in NIMH priorities to reflect the true needs of the nation. Consideration should also be given to the possibility of merging NIMH with the National Institute of Neurological Diseases and Stroke (NINDS) to create a single National Brain Research Institute that could more effectively focus on brain diseases such as manic-depressive illness.

Stigma and Public Education

Stigma is a major problem for individuals with manic-depressive illness. It reduces self-esteem, hinders them from making and keeping friends, and often limits job opportunities. Devaluation and discrimination are dual afflictions that all mentally ill persons must confront on a regular basis.

The good news is that in recent decades the public has developed a much greater understanding of psychiatric disorders. According to the 1999 *Mental Health: A Report of the Surgeon General*, Americans have "achieved greater scientific understanding of mental illness" since the

1950s.[10] The bad news, according to the same report, is that "in comparison with the 1950s, the public's perception of mental illness more frequently incorporated violent behavior."[11]

The reason for this apparent paradox—greater scientific understanding, yet also greater fear—is increased publicity about episodes of violence. Such episodes are the single largest source of stigma against individuals with manic-depressive illness and other psychiatric disorders. As described in Chapter 13, homicides and other violent acts committed by mental ill persons have become not only more frequent but also more highly publicized. In almost all cases, these people were not receiving treatment at the time of their violent act. Such episodes were less frequent in the 1950s, at the time the original stigma surveys were done, because at that time most individuals with severe psychiatric disorders were confined to state psychiatric hospitals. Massive deinstitutionalization, followed by the failure of the mental health system to ensure that the discharged patients received treatment, has brought about the present sad state of affairs.

Other recent research has confirmed the relationship between violent behavior committed by individuals with severe psychiatric disorders and increased stigma against all individuals with mental illnesses. For example, a study using university volunteers demonstrated that merely reading a newspaper article reporting a violent crime committed by a mental patient led to increased "negative attitudes toward people with mental illnesses."[12] And in Germany, following highly publicized attacks on prominent officials by individuals with severe mental illnesses, researchers found a measurable "marked increase in desired social distance from mentally ill people immediately following [the] violent attacks." The increased social distance and consequent stigma slowly decreased over time but had not returned to baseline two years later.[13]

Individuals with manic-depressive illness are painfully aware of the relationship between episodes of violence and increasing stigma. In Salt Lake City in 1999, for example, a mentally ill man killed two people in a church library. According to a news account of the incident, "within hours Valley Mental Health began getting calls from frightened clients. 'Clients were just sobbing,' said a spokesperson. 'They were afraid that the public would want to retaliate against them."[14] A single such episode of violence can set back local efforts to reverse stigma for years.

What can be done to combat stigma? The most important measure is to decrease the incidence of violence committed by mentally ill persons—and this can be done only by addressing the treatment issue. As long as literally hundreds of thousands of individuals with untreated severe psychiatric disorders continue to wander the streets, periodic episodes of violence are inevitable. The ultimate answer to the stigma problem, then, is the greater utilization of various forms of assisted treatment to ensure that mentally ill individuals receive the medication they need to control the symptoms of their illness (see Chapter 13).

Another way to combat stigma is through public education. The number of people who are unaware of the biological basis of manic-depressive illness, and who tell people with mania or severe depression to "just snap out of it," is still shockingly high.

Indeed, education is one of the most important advocacy activities for individuals with manic-depressive illness, their families, and mental illness professionals. Such education can be carried out in schools, churches, and synagogues, and through community organizations such as the Lions, Kiwanas, or Rotary Club. Education can also be achieved through letters to the local newspaper, articles written by or about individuals with manic-depressive illness, and local radio and television programs. In all of these venues, the most effective and creditable spokespersons are the ill individuals themselves.

Exemplary Individual Advocates

One of the most encouraging developments in recent years in bringing about a brighter future for people with manic-depressive illness has been the emergence of an increasing number of individuals with this disorder who are public advocates. Such individuals have a credibility that organizations cannot achieve.

An example from the 1950s is Jim Piersall, a well-known Boston Red Sox baseball player who chronicled his experience with manic depression in a book titled *Fear Strikes Out:* "We don't have to talk about our sickness in whispers or prowl about on the edge of society with our hands to our ears to block out the whispers of others," he wrote.[15] Piersall started one of the first support and advocacy groups for people affected with this disorder. But it was during the 1990s that a dramatic increase occurred in the number of such individuals who emerged as public advocates. A few of them—including actress Patty Duke, professional golfer Bert Yancey, and psychologist-writer Kay Jamison—were public figures prior to identifying themselves as having manic-depressive illness. Most, however, had not previously been well known.

There are now literally scores of individuals with manic-depressive illness actively working to improve services, making treatment more available, educating the public, decreasing stigma, and increasing research. Their growing numbers provide much hope for the future. We have selected five such advocates as examples; they are models for others to follow.

1. *Donna Orrin* had completed two years of university when she was initially diagnosed with manic-depressive illness in 1972. Over the next twenty years, she was hospitalized more than thirty times for periods ranging from one week to six months and was placed in four different group homes. One of Donna's social workers told her that, at best, she might be able to work as a part-time store clerk.

Donna, however, is not a person who gives up easily. Between her recurrent episodes of mania and depression, she completed her university degree, earned a master's degree in social work from the University of Michigan, and took a position as a social worker in state and private psychiatric hospitals. Slowly, her illness stabilized through her strict adherence to medication, her participation in cognitive behavioral therapy, and her increasing ability to manage stress in her life.

In the early 1990s, Donna began educating others about manic-depressive illness. She started her own business (Creative Connections, P.O. Box 7044, Ann Arbor, MI 48107) and began giving talks to various groups about manic depression and recovery. To date, she has provided over a hundred workshops and presentations in thirteen states to family groups, consumer groups, mental illness professionals, law students, and others; co-produced an award-winning documentary on recovery issues; created a public service announcement for radio with the Michigan governor's wife; and written a handbook on consumer involvement in mental illness policy-making that was distributed to every community mental health agency in Michigan. Donna has also contributed articles about recovery to many local, state, and national publications.

At present, Donna is continuing these advocacy efforts and working part-time for the Washtenaw County Community Mental Health agency. Periodically, she still experiences symptoms of her illness but has learned how to minimize these by adjusting her medication and dealing with stress. She has not been hospitalized in over eight years.

2. *Jonathan Stanley* first became manic following his second year in college. During the episode of depression that followed, he was diagnosed as having manic-depressive illness. He denied it and refused medication. He subsequently had additional and increasingly severe episodes of mania and depression, which eventually led to severe mania with delusions. Paranoid, Jon became convinced that Navy intelligence agents were spying on him and hitting him with radioactive rays in an attempt to kill him. While acutely manic, he climbed onto a milk crate in a New York City deli and proceeded to disrobe. This resulted in his involuntary hospitalization, followed by a slow recovery over many months.

Finally stabilized on medication, Jon completed college. He then went to law school, working afterward as an attorney with the County Attorney's Office for Henrico County, Virginia. However, he became increasingly interested in using his experiences to help others. When the Treatment Advocacy Center (*www.psychlaws.org*) opened in 1998, Jon was recruited to be its assistant director.

Since that time, Jon has become a national expert on mental health laws. He helped draft a model law for assisted treatment that is being considered for use in several states, and he provides legal consultation to legislators and others in many states and even a few Canadian provinces. He played a key role in the 1999 passage in New York State of Kendra's Law, which makes it easier to get treatment for individuals with severe psychiatric disorders who are unaware of their illness—as he was at one time. He has also given talks to numerous groups regarding the need to modify mental health laws, served as a guest lecturer at a course entitled "Mental Illness and the Law" at George Mason

University Law School, and co-authored papers on this topic for submission to professional journals.

Jon's professional focus is on increasing care for mentally ill individuals who are so overcome by their illness as to be rendered unaware of it. As he explained in one published interview: "When people lose the ability to choose what's right for themselves, civil rights end up protecting the right to be sick, the right to be homeless, and the right to be in jail."[16] He has continued to successfully manage his illness with medications and recently got married.

3. *Bill Lichtenstein* was an award-winning print and broadcast journalist before he was diagnosed with manic-depressive illness in 1986. He had worked for seven years producing investigative reports for ABC News, for such programs as *20/20, Nightline,* and *World News Tonight.* However, it was while he was producing *Jimmy Breslin's People* for ABC-TV that his thinking processes began to break down over a three-week period. As his hypomania grew into mania, Bill stopped sleeping, became suspicious and later paranoid, and suffered delusions that his apartment was bugged and that he was receiving special messages on his TV. Finally, his girlfriend and boss walked him over to the St. Lukes/Roosevelt Hospital emergency room, where he was admitted for three weeks. Although he was diagnosed with manic depression, the stigma of his mental illness created a significant barrier to his staying in treatment. Upon hearing of his diagnosis, many of his former network news colleagues and close friends stopped returning his calls; a job offer from a local TV news department also evaporated. Two more hospitalizations followed over the next four years, before Bill found the local DMDA chapter and learned that he was not alone. By the early 1990s, he was working hard to recover—specifically, by finding the right medication and talk therapy treatment.

Since his recovery, Bill has put his skills to work in educating the public, especially as president of Lichtenstein Creative Media (*www.LCMEDIA.com*). Visiting a local bookstore, he found few books offering support to people struggling with manic depression; he also came to realize that most documentaries on the subject featured people who were sick—highly symptomatic—but had little to offer in the way of insight into the illness or hope for recovery. Starting in 1992, he produced *Voices of an Illness*, a three-part public radio documentary series featuring people with schizophrenia, manic-depressive illness, and severe depression who described the onset of their illnesses as well as their recovery—telling their own stories in their own words. Hosted by Jason Robards, Patty Duke, and Rod Steiger, respectively, the series won twenty-three major broadcast awards, including a George Foster Peabody Award—television and radio's highest honor—and was described as "remarkable" by *Time* magazine. In 2001, Bill, along with his wife, June Peoples, released *West 47th Street*, a cinéma vérité documentary film that follows four individuals with severe psychiatric disorders in New York City over three years. The film made its World Premiere in Paris at the prestigious Cinéma du Réel International Film Festival in March of that year. The couple also produces *The Infinite Mind*, a weekly public radio program on manic-depressive illness, schizophrenia, and other brain disorders, hosted by former director of the National Institute of Mental Health Fred Goodwin and heard on over 150 public radio stations.

4. *Ed Francell Jr.* first developed manic-depressive illness at age 18, during his final year in high school. In the intervening twenty years, he has had three hospital admissions and been treated with a total of twenty-five different medications as he and psychiatrists searched for the best combination. His illness has been complicated by intermittent panic attacks and breakthrough depressions and hypomanias.

Despite his illness, Ed completed a bachelor's degree at Indiana University and obtained a master's degree in social work from the University of Cincinnati. He then devoted himself to improving services for individuals with psychiatric disorders, working for five years in two Georgia Community Mental Health Centers where, among other things, he assisted in developing thirteen continuous treatment teams, including four Assertive Community Treatment (ACT) teams; wrote successful housing grants; developed a Medicaid case rate for Georgia ACT teams; established targeted outcomes; and trained staff. He has given talks to over thirty different groups, focusing on consumer education and the importance of medication, and has published articles in psychiatric journals. For his tireless efforts to improve psychiatric services, he has received a NAMI Consumer of the Year Award and a NAMI Georgia Consumer Empowerment Award.

5. *Charles "Chuck" Sosebee* recalls having experienced symptoms of mental illness at age 21, but he remained undiagnosed and untreated for ten years. At age 31, he underwent a severe depression, necessitating voluntary hospitalization. Following discharge, he stopped taking his medications, which led to a relapse, multiple suicide attempts, involuntary rehospitalizations, and eventual homelessness in California. Through a homeless outreach program, he received intensive case management, a diagnosis of manic-depressive illness (bipolar II), and stabilization on appropriate medication.

In 1998 he was appointed to his county's Mental Health Board, and in 1999 he became a director of the Southern Region of the California Association for Local Mental Health Boards and Commissions and founded—and led—California Clients for LPS Reform, which has grown to over 300 members, to help change the state commitment laws. (LPS stands for "Lanterman-Petris-Short"—a 1968 act passed in California regarding involuntary treatment.) Currently he also serves on the NAMI–California Board of Directors and the NAMI Consumer Council and is employed as coordinator of Consumer Outreach and Education for NAMI–San Diego. Chuck believes that involuntary treatment saved his life and that it should be available for those who need it. He has been an outspoken opponent of "consumer survivor" groups (described above), saying that they have outlived their time: "It's old thought," he says. "Today treatment works, if you can get it. And I want it to be available before I try to kill myself." Chuck recently received the California Psychiatric Association's Family and Patient Advocacy Award for his advocacy efforts.

APPENDIX A:
REVIEW OF BOOKS

The following are brief summaries of books about manic-depressive illness, including a few about severe depression, listed alphabetically. Those of special interest are marked with an asterisk. Many of these books are in print, and those that are not can often be purchased over the Internet (*www.bookfinder.com*).

Adamec, Christine. *How to Live with a Mentally Ill Person: A Handbook of Day-to-Day Strategies.* New York: John Wiley and Sons, 1996.

This is a solid and practical how-to book by a professional writer whose daughter developed a severe psychiatric illness. It utilizes a positive, "cheerleading" approach "to energize you and give you the hope you need." Included are a multitude of practical suggestions, such as a model "Crisis Information Form" to be prepared ahead of time for emergency admissions or if you have to call the police. The author emphasizes the importance of accepting the illness and moving on, of not being bogged down by the "myth of the 'before' person" or the "ghost of patient past." She also emphasizes the importance of a sense of humor, exemplified by a woman with schizophrenia who "went to a Halloween party dressed as a Cogentin tablet, a medication to counter the side effects in antipsychotic medication." Above all, says Adamec, "never give in, never give in, never, never, never, never. . . . "

Alvarez, Alfred. *The Savage God: A Study of Suicide.* New York: W. W. Norton, 1990. Originally published in 1971.

Alvarez's history of suicide, one of the first books on the subject, is widely quoted. An English poet and literary critic, Alvarez himself attempted suicide, an experience he chronicles in the final chapter of the book. The initial chapter is a long account of Sylvia Plath's life, and this is followed by chapters on suicide throughout history. As a history, the book fulfills its mission and is well written. Alvarez, however, was writing before modern research on depression and manic-depressive illness had been carried out, and he was largely unaware of the medical and biological antecedents of suicide.

Amador, Xavier, and Anna-Lisa Johanson. *I Am Not Sick, I Don't Need Help! Helping the Seriously Mentally Ill Accept Treatment.* Peconic, N.Y.: Vida Press, 2000.

This is the first book that attempts to address the question of why some individuals with schizophrenia and manic-depressive illness will not take the medication they need to remain well. Both of the authors are related to severely mentally ill individuals and have "been there." In addition, Amador has pioneered much of the recent research on unawareness of illness (see Chapter 2 of the present volume). Most important, both authors provide readers with a concrete, step-by-step plan to improve awareness of illness in the person with schizophrenia or manic-depressive illness. This plan may not work all the time, but it is well worth trying before turning to involuntary hospitalization and various forms of assisted treatment (see Chapter 13 of the present volume).

Barondes, Samuel H. *Mood Genes: Hunting for Origins of Mania and Depression.* New York: Oxford University Press, 1998.

For aficionados of genetics, this is an interesting and well-written summary of research on genetic aspects of manic-depressive illness. Barondes, a professor of psychiatry at the University of California at San Francisco, knows his subject well. He has also published a book illustrating molecular and genetic research in psychiatry, *Molecules and Mental Illness* (New York: Scientific American Library, 1993), which nicely complements the book under discussion. *Mood Genes* weaves together the histories of individuals who have manic-depressive illness with accounts of the relevant research. Included is historical information of much interest on key researchers, such as John Cade and Emil Kraepelin, and readable accounts of the most important genetic research, such as the Amish study and the Costa Rica study. Also included are sections on the genetic aspects of Huntington's and Alzheimer's diseases. The author is an enthusiastic and devout believer that genetics research is the road to the promised land, and he is not discouraged by the washed-out byways that appear to be slowing this trip.

Berger, Diane, and Lisa Berger. *We Heard the Angels of Madness: One Family's Struggle with Manic Depression.* New York: William Morrow, 1991. Paperback by Harper-Trade, 1992.

This is the story of a young man who developed manic-depressive illness at age 19. Although the book was written by his mother and sister, it incorporates the young man's recollections as if written by him. He had a relatively rapid onset with multiple psychotic features, including auditory and visual hallucinations. One of the strongest aspects of the book is the juxtaposition of the son's recollections of his hallucinations and his mother's account of what the family was observing. The mother candidly describes her continuing denial of her son's illness despite overwhelming evidence to the contrary. The difficulty experienced by the family in achieving a realistic understanding of the problem was further exacerbated by a series of incompetent psychiatrists (five in a ten-month period) until finally a competent one was found. The book is well written and helpful, with a foreword by Alexander Vuckovic that is both sensitive and articulate.

Bernheim, Kayla F., Richard R. J. Lewine, and C. T. Beale. *The Caring Family: Living with Chronic Mental Illness.* New York: Random House, 1982.

Although this was one of the first books written for family members of someone with a severe mental illness, its message is as useful today as when it was published. The authors discuss such common reactions as guilt, shame, fear, anger, and despair and offer suggestions for resolving them. They also discuss "chronic mental illness" as a whole, effectively focusing on individual and family dynamics as a consequence of the illness.

Bradley, Lynn. *Manic-Depression: How to Live While Loving a Manic Depressive.* Houston, Texas: Emerald Ink Publishing, 2000.

This is a chatty, advice-over-coffee book written by a woman who, for thirty years, has been married to a man with manic-depressive illness. For someone living with an affected spouse, it is modestly useful. The author has a nice sense of humor and is not afraid to take on some of the tough issues, such as how she dealt with her husband's sexual dysfunction, brought about by his antidepressant medication. For a nonspouse, however, this book has little to offer. In addition, it is poorly put together, with multiple errors; our copy even had duplicate pages.

Buckley, Peter F., and John L. Waddington (eds.). *Schizophrenia and Mood Disorders: The New Drug Therapies in Clinical Practice.* Oxford: Butterworth-Heinemann, 2000.

This book is written for psychiatrists but contains useful and accessible information for consumers and families. Antipsychotic drugs, antidepressants, and mood stabilizers are described in seventeen short chapters. The chapters contain some detail on basic science and the mechanism of action of these drugs, but the bulk of the text concerns data on efficacy and side effects. The book closes with a useful section, "Key Issues in Clinical Psychopharmacology," that deals with such issues as drug interactions, pregnancy, substance abuse, and violence.

Carlson, Trudy. *The Life of a Bipolar Child: What Every Parent and Professional Needs to Know.* Duluth, Minn.: Benline Press, 2000.

This book is a mother's laudable attempt to salvage something useful from the suicide of her 14-year-old son. However, it has major limitations, and the title is somewhat misleading. In fact, very little of the book discusses manic-depressive illness *per se;* most of it deals with depression, attention deficit hyperactivity disorder (ADHD), anxiety disorder, and suicide, each of which may or may not be an aspect of manic-depressive illness in children. Over one-third of the book is a detailed account of the development of the author's son, who had all of the above problems and can be presumed to have had an underlying manic-depressive illness, since he appeared to respond to lithium in his final months. Much of the book was published in 1995 as

The Suicide of My Son. The brief material on manic-depressive illness, comprising notes from a 1997 conference, was then added but not integrated into the original manuscript. The result, which is not very satisfactory, limits the book's usefulness.

Clooney, Rosemary. *This for Remembrance.* New York: Playboy Press, 1977. Written with Raymond Strait.

Rosemary Clooney was a major pop singer in the 1950s, married to actor Jose Ferrer and friends with Bing Crosby et al. The first third of this book, which recounts her episodes of mania during periods when she was on singing tours, is neither insightful nor well written. Clooney was eventually hospitalized and, in keeping with the times, went into psychoanalysis. The remaining two-thirds of the book consists of a rather dull autobiography that may be of interest to 50s aficionados but contains virtually no information about Clooney's illness.

Copeland, Mary Ellen. *The Depression Workbook: A Guide for Living with Depression and Manic Depression* (1992) and *Living with Depression and Manic Depression: A Workbook for Maintaining Mood Stability* (1995). Oakland: New Harbinger Publications.

These companion workbooks have been popular with families and have much to commend them. They offer information and practical tips for improving your life if you have a mood disorder. Included are such topics as diet, exercise, meditation, light therapy, and enhancing one's self esteem, and extensive discussion of the benefits of psychotherapy, especially cognitive therapy. Both books include a question-and-answer format with space to take notes. Of the two, the first is better. These workbooks also have shortcomings. The major one is that they are geared toward depression alone, saying relatively little about mania or psychosis; the reason for this is probably that the author apparently suffers from bipolar disorder II and her own depressions have been much more troublesome than her hypomanias. The books include almost nothing about medications; indeed, the first mentions only lithium as a mood stabilizer. Concurrent substance abuse also gets only brief mention. The books oversell psychotherapy, especially cognitive therapy, as essential—again, based on the author's personal experience. Finally and inexplicably, the second workbook recommends several antipsychiatry groups as useful resources.

Court, Bryan L., and Gerald L. Nelson. *Bipolar Puzzle Solution: A Mental Health Client's Perspective.* Philadelphia: Taylor and Francis, 1996.

Although this book has an odd title and an unusual format, many individuals diagnosed with manic-depressive illness for the first time will find it moderately helpful. Court, the primary author, has manic-depressive illness, whereas Nelson is a psychiatrist who provides commentary. The book's question-and-answer format utilizes 187 questions asked by affected individuals in manic-depressive illness support groups. Court provides a nice example of self-education about his disease and, in doing so, offers a good model for others. The information he supplies is factually accurate (if sometimes incomplete) and includes practical advice on varied issues. The main limitation of the book is its organization, which despite the inclusion of an index, makes finding specific material difficult. Listing all 187 questions in the table of contents would have improved it.

Cronkite, Kathy. *On the Edge of Darkness: Conversations About Conquering Depression.* New York: Doubleday, 1994. Paperback by Delta Books, 1995.

This book contains a series of brief essays on various aspects of depression by Kathy Cronkite, actors and journalists who have suffered from depression (e.g., Rod Steiger, Mike Wallace, William Styron), and psychiatrists. Occasional nuggets are tucked away in its pages, but on the whole it is verbose, uneven, and fitful. The book's main value is to reassure people that even the famous get depressed and that stigma should not keep anyone from seeking help.

Custance, John. *Wisdom, Madness and Folly: The Philosophy of a Lunatic.* New York: Pellegrini and Cudahy, 1952.

This book is of historical interest. It apparently was the first book written by an individual with manic-depressive illness in which the writer attempted to describe and catalog the symptoms of his manias and depressions. Chapter 2, in which Custance describes his periods of mania, has been quoted by others and is useful. Chapter 3, which describes his symptoms of depression, is considerably weaker. Not much can be said for the remainder of the book. "John Custance" was a pseudonym for a well-educated British scholar who had studied theology, philosophy, and the archetypes of Carl Jung in great depth. After the onset of his illness, at age 36, he studied his own symptoms and attempted to fit them into Jung's schema. Much of the book was written while Custance was hospitalized in a manic or hypomanic phase, and it reads accordingly. Jung even contributed a preface, in which he complained about the lack of progress on the "psychological investigation of the psychoses" and the reluctance of psychiatrists to accept his theories. Custance summarizes his book as "a series of parallels between the mystical intuition and the manic consciousness as I have experienced it. . . . I have perhaps shown that there is a wisdom in 'madness' which has not yet been fully explained." As such, the book can be seen as a forerunner of the writings of Ronald Laing a decade later, in which Laing described schizophrenia as a growth experience. Such nonsense occasionally still surfaces in the writings of individuals who try to "make sense" of their psychotic symptoms.

Dally, Peter. *The Marriage of Heaven and Hell: Manic Depression and the Life of Virginia Woolf.* New York: St. Martin's Press, 1999.

This is one of the latest contributions to a long list of works describing Virginia Woolf's mental illness and is probably of interest only to avid Woolf readers. The main body of the book does not add much to the existing literature or to Virginia Woolf's own descriptions of her illness; in fact, the book reads like a very long list of family relationships and stressful life events and a calendar of mood symptoms. There is little new information regarding the historical understanding of manic-depressive illness or its relationship to creativity. The best part of the book is the Appendix, "Mania, Madness and Creativity," although this material is better covered in some of the other works listed here.

*Duke, Patty, and Gloria Hochman. *A Brilliant Madness: Living with Manic-Depressive Illness.* New York: Bantam Books, 1992.

This excellent book was co-authored by actress Patty Duke and science writer Gloria Hochman. Duke provides a candid, powerful account of her own illness, from her first episode of mania at age 19 to a definitive diagnosis at age 35, at which time she started taking lithium. Even though she did not have psychotic symptoms, Duke illustrates how painful and destructive episodes of mania and depression can be, both for the individual affected and for her family and friends. She was fortunate in being a good lithium responder and in finding a competent and sympathetic psychiatrist. She deals directly with the question of creativity and refuses to romanticize the illness in any way. Hochman's chapters alternate with those by Duke and provide factual information regarding what was known about manic-depressive illness at the time the book was written. She did her homework well, interviewing many psychiatric experts, and synthesizes the material in a format that is pleasant to read and easy to understand. The writing throughout the book is of high quality. Overall, this is an essential book for manic-depressive illness libraries.

Fawcett, Jan, Bernard Golden, and Nancy Rosenfield. *New Hope for People with Bipolar Disorder.* Roseville, Calif.: Prima Health, 2000.

For someone who is being confronted by the diagnosis of manic-depressive illness for the first time, this is a modestly useful book. It is easy to read and does not include too much detail. However, for individuals looking for in-depth information, it is not satisfactory. The description of symptoms is surprisingly inadequate, given the fact that one of the three authors has manic-depressive illness. The chapter on causes is almost completely restricted to genes. The chapter on medication does not provide as much information as most families want, and the chapter on psychotherapy is virtually restricted to cognitive behavioral therapy. In addition, none of the tough issues are addressed, such as lack of insight as a cause of noncompliance or the problem of violence as a cause of stigma. In summary, the book is an adequate appetizer, but most readers will then want to also order a main course.

Fieve, Ronald R. *Moodswing.* New York: Bantam Books, 1997.

Originally published in 1975, this book is primarily of historical interest, being one of the first published for lay readers about manic-depressive illness. Although the book is advertised as a "second revised edition," the revisions are both superficial and incomplete, and much of the book reads as it did in 1975. It is understandable that Fieve wishes to emphasize the importance of lithium, since he played a significant role in its original promotion in the United States. Less understandable, however, is why carbamazepine and valproate should barely be mentioned in a book that claims to have been revised in 1997. In another example of how out-of-date the book is, the author describes the dexamethasone suppression test as a "new diagnostic test." This test is, in fact, long gone. The style of the book is also much more suited to the 1970s, relying as it does on clinical vignettes with a paucity of facts or other hard data. Families and patients are no longer satisfied with vignettes and vague or unsupported generalizations but, rather, want the facts laid out in a comprehensive manner. In *Moodswing,* there is far too little of that to satisfy most readers.

Fink, Max. *Electroshock: Restoring the Mind.* New York: Oxford University Press, 1999.

This is a useful book for individuals and their families who are contemplating electroconvulsive therapy (ECT) as a treatment for severe depression or mania that has not responded to medications. Aimed at lay persons, the book details the procedure, its side effects, and its use in various psychiatric conditions. Included is an extensive discussion of the controversies surrounding ECT and an extensive bibliography for those who want additional information. The author also maintains an informational website (*www.electroshock.org*).

Goldberg, Joseph F., and Martin Harrow (eds.). *Bipolar Disorders: Clinical Course and Outcome.* Washington, D.C.: American Psychiatric Press, 1999.

This multi-authored textbook focuses on clinical and treatment aspects of manic-depressive illness. Its intended audience is psychiatrists who are doing research on, or specializing in the treatment of, this illness. Several chapters cover nonresponsiveness to medications and difficult clinical problems such as mixed states and rapid cycling. Other chapters are devoted to special problems that often accompany manic-depressive illness, such as alcoholism and anxiety.

Goodwin, Frederick K., and Kay Redfield Jamison. *Manic-Depressive Illness.* New York: Oxford University Press, 1990.

When this book was published in 1990, it was very important, since it was the first such textbook focusing exclusively on manic-depressive illness. It is heavy, literally—over four pounds in weight and more than 900 pages long—and thus not a book you curl up with at the beach. However, it covers everything published about every aspect of this disorder up until the late 1980s. Given research and treatment developments since that time, many sections are now out of date. The authors are revising it, and a second edition is tentatively scheduled for publication in 2002.

Gorman, Jack M. *The Essential Guide to Psychiatric Drugs,* 3rd ed. New York: St. Martin's Press, 1997.

This is a general guide to psychiatric drugs that has been popular with patients and families since the first edition was published in 1990. It includes not only a summary of each drug used for schizophrenia, manic-depressive illness, depression, and other psychiatric disorders but also chapters on issues of special interest, such as "Sex and Psychiatric Drugs" and "Psychiatric Drugs and Pregnancy." The book is user friendly and well organized, making it easy to find what you are looking for.

Hall, Laura Lee. *Genetics and Mental Illness: Evolving Issues for Research and Society.* New York: Plenum Press, 1996.

This is a useful volume for those with a specific interest in the genetics of severe psychiatric disorders. There are good overviews of genetic research in general and of the nature-nurture controversy in particular; the section on genetic counseling is especially thoughtful. The chapter on the inheritance of mood disorders, by Drs. Ming Tsuang and Stephen Faraone, includes summaries of family, twin, and adoption studies as well as current genetics research. The research discussed in the book was current at the time it was written in the mid-1990s, but this is an area that is changing rapidly.

Hatfield, Agnes B., and Harriet P. Lefley. *Surviving Mental Illness: Stress, Coping and Adaptation.* New York: Guilford Press, 1993.

Eminently practical and well written, this book will be useful for families trying to sort out the myriad problems confronting them when a family member becomes seriously mentally ill. One of its main purposes is to emphasize the importance of understanding what the sick person is experiencing; toward this end, it includes some helpful personal accounts by Frederick Frese, Esso Leete, and Daniel Link.

Hoffman, Jack, and Daniel Simon. *Run Run Run: The Lives of Abbie Hoffman.* New York: G. P. Putnam's Sons, 1996.

Abbie Hoffman was a major radical figure in the 1960s, renowned for such things as proposing a pig named Pigasus for president at the 1968 convention, being arrested for selling cocaine, and founding the Yippies. From his 30s onward, he was also "a classic, textbook-perfect manic-depressive," according to this biography by his brother and publisher. Episodes of mania or depression occurred once or twice a year for almost thirty years, with manic episodes lasting three months or longer. He also had psychotic features, believing "that the doctors had inserted a transmitting device." He responded well to lithium but took it only intermittently, having been seduced by his manias: "The world through the lens of his mania was a playground in which he could do anything. Abbie used to say: 'There's no drug in the world that could take you to that level.' His mania was something Abbie was born with, and it was something he didn't want to lose, couldn't imagine living without, and was unable and perhaps unwilling to control." Except for readers with a historical interest in the 1960s radical movement, this biography is not very satisfactory. Despite his colorful public persona, Hoffman was in reality an egotistical, thoughtless, and rather dreary individual. And when he finally and inevitably commits suicide, the reader is left with a strong impression of an illness largely untreated and a talented life wasted.

Isaac, Rael Jean, and Virginia C. Armat. *Madness in the Streets.* New York: Free Press, 1990. Paperback by the Treatment Advocacy Center, 2000.

This is an important history of the "mental health" movement that details how so many individuals with serious mental illnesses ended up homeless and on the streets. There is enough blame to go around for just about everyone involved in the "mental health" scene, but the lawyers with the American Civil Liberties Union and the Bazelon Center for Mental Health Law collect (and deserve) the largest share. Well-written and depressing, this history is essential to understand if we expect to improve things.

*Jamison, Kay. *An Unquiet Mind.* New York: A. A. Knopf, 1995. Paperback by Random House, 1997.

This is an excellent subjective account of what it is like to have manic-depressive illness. Exceptionally well written, the book describes the allure of mania and the depths of depression. Even more important, the author shares her experiences with stigma and her disclosure of her illness to professional colleagues. If the book has a shortcoming, it is the author's conclusion that, given the choice, she would still opt to have been affected with the illness. Given her own narrow escape from death through suicide and the interpersonal corpses that litter her landscape, it is difficult to understand this conclusion. Nevertheless, the book is essential reading for those affected with manic-depressive illness and their families and friends.

*Jamison, Kay. *Night Falls Fast: Understanding Suicide.* New York: A. A. Knopf, 1999.

This book takes its place alongside Alfred Alvarez's classic study of suicide *The Savage God,* but in many ways it is better. Jamison skillfully and lyrically mixes what is known about suicide with narrative accounts of those who tried and those who succeeded. Among the areas covered are a history of suicide, its genetic and neurochemical roots, seasonal patterns, methods, and the effect of suicide on the individual's survivors. Jamison knows whereof she speaks, since she, like Alvarez, made a serious suicide attempt. When she recovered, she went to church and asked: "Where had God been? I could not answer the question then, nor can I answer it now. I do know, however, that I should have been dead but was not—and that I was fortunate enough to be given another chance at life, which many others were not."

Janicak, Philip G., John M. Davis, Sheldon H. Preskorn, and Frank J. Ayd. *Principles and Practice of Psychopharmacotherapy*, 2nd ed. Baltimore: Williams and Wilkins, 1997.

This book is a detailed text written by some of the founding fathers of psychopharmacology. Mainly designed for psychiatrists, it is very clinically oriented, containing little information on neurobiological models of disease or molecular mechanisms of drug action but covering all of the major pharmacological treatments used in psychiatry. Chapters on antipsychotics, antidepressants, mood stabilizers, and electroconvulsive therapy are informative for both clinicians and consumers. Especially useful are the chapters on evaluation of study designs for clinical trials and those on the treatment of special clinical populations (e.g., pregnant women, the very old, and the very young).

Karp, David. *Burden of Sympathy: How Families Cope with Mental Illness*. New York: Oxford University Press, 2000.

Karp, a professor of sociology at Boston College, suffered from severe depression himself. Based on sixty intensive interviews he did with family members of individuals with schizophrenia, manic-depressive illness, and severe depression, he has written an excellent book "about the social tango between emotionally ill people and those who try to help them." In examining the lives of the family members, he demonstrates that "sustaining an appropriate level of involvement with a mentally ill child, parent, sibling, or spouse is extraordinarily difficult." Karp writes well and, perhaps because of his own experience with depression, captures the essence of caring and caregivers.

Knauth, Percy. *A Season in Hell*. New York: Harper and Row, 1975.

This is a slim and modestly useful account of severe depression. Percy Knauth was a successful writer and journalist when, at age 57, he became severely depressed. The book chronicles his attempts to come to terms with his disease, including a futile bout with psychoanalytically oriented psychotherapy, before he discovered antidepressant medication. Written in 1975, it is one of the first modern-day accounts of depression but pales when juxtaposed to William Styron's *Darkness Visible*.

Lam, Dominic H., Steven H. Jones, Peter Hayward, and Jenifer A. Bright. *Cognitive Therapy for Bipolar Disorder: A Therapist's Guide to Concepts, Methods and Practice*. Chichester: John Wiley and Sons, 1999.

For those with an interest in the treatment of manic depression through individual psychotherapy in general, and cognitive therapy in particular, this is a useful and well-written manual. It focuses on specific symptoms and details the various strategies a therapist can use. The authors present data on a small outcome study showing the efficacy of cognitive therapy. As discussed in its tenth chapter, however, the ultimate role of cognitive therapy for the treatment of manic-depressive illness is still to be determined.

Lefley, Harriet P. *Family Caregiving in Mental Illness.* Thousand Oaks, Calif.: Sage Publications, 1996.

This is the most recent of several good books Lefley has written to bridge the gulf of understanding between families (she has a mentally ill child) and psychiatric professionals (she is also a psychologist). She is thus admirably qualified to help each side understand the problems faced by the other. Previously, she co-edited *Families as Allies in Treatment of the Mentally Ill* (Washington, D.C.: American Psychiatric Press, 1990) and *Helping Families Cope with Mental Illness* (New York: Harwood Academic Publishers, 1994). If the mental illness professional with whom you are dealing does not understand the family burden of having a severely psychiatrically ill family member, this book would make a nice present.

Ludwig, Arnold M. *The Price of Greatness: Resolving the Creativity and Madness Controversy.* New York: Guilford Press, 1995.

This is a very readable and interesting synthesis of the author's long experience in this field. Ludwig, who is a professor of psychiatry at the University of Kentucky, describes a detailed study of 1,004 creative individuals from the twentieth century and concludes that manic-depressive illness and other mental disturbances are more common in the creative artists (see Chapter 14 of the present volume). He also provides excellent information on factors other than mental illness that may predict great achievement and useful discussions of the statistical complexities involved in this kind of work.

*Lyden, Jacki. *Daughter of the Queen of Sheba.* New York: Houghton Mifflin, 1997. Paperback by Penguin Books, 1998.

This is an important book describing three sisters who have a mother with chronic mania. "I knew my sisters and I were growing up like bumper cars in an arcade," says the author, and she recounts the various tragicomedies that inevitably resulted. A brutal stepfather complicates the picture, and the reader is left with the impression that he, in fact, caused more long-term damage than their manic mother. Especially poignant are the accounts of attempts to get the mother treated that failed because of stringent commitment laws. The book is lyrically written, despite a disjointed narrative style that appears to be mirroring the illness it is portraying.

Manji, Husseini K., Charles L. Bowden, and Robert H. Belmaker (eds.). *Bipolar Medications: Mechanisms of Action.* Washington, D.C.: American Psychiatric Press, 2000.

This textbook is intended primarily for researchers on manic-depressive illness. Its nineteen multi-authored chapters provide detailed discussions about various mechanisms by which lithium and other mood stabilizers may function in the brain. It is an excellent, up-to-date summary for individuals with this research interest but is not likely to appeal to laypersons unless they have a background in neuroscience or psychopharmacology.

*Manning, Martha. *Undercurrents: A Therapist's Reckoning with Her Own Depression.* New York: HarperCollins, 1994.

This is an exceptionally well-written and engaging account of severe depression, told by a psychologist who herself experienced it. With self-deprecating humor and insight, Manning chronicles her slow descent from normality and assumed invincibility, ever deeper, until she arrived at "a room in hell with only your name on the door." Failing to respond to all available antidepressant medications, she was left with only two exits: suicide or a trial of electroconvulsive therapy (ECT). Manning opted for the latter, and responded to a short course. Her description of the experience of undergoing ECT is one of the strongest and most useful sections of the book and serves as an important counterpoint to Ken Kesey's *One Flew Over the Cuckoo's Nest.* This is followed by details of her slow recovery and the effect of her depression on her family, friends, and acquaintances. Insightful, thoughtful, and funny-sad, Manning's book is among the best accounts available of what it is like to experience severe depression.

Marsh, Diane T. *Serious Mental Illness and the Family: The Practitioner's Guide.* New York: John Wiley, 1998.

This is the best book available for mental illness professionals providing care for individuals with severe mental illnesses. The author, a psychologist who specializes in treating individuals with these illnesses and their families, also authored the useful *Families and Mental Illness: New Directions in Professional Practice,* published in 1992. As the author notes, *Serious Mental Illness and the Family* "is designed to assist practitioners in developing the competencies necessary for working with families. . . . " Although the book is aimed at mental health professionals, families will find its sections on siblings, spouses, and offspring of seriously mentally ill individuals especially useful. Another very worthy book in this genre is Harriet P. Lefley and Dale L. Johnson (eds.), *Families as Allies in Treatment of the Mentally Ill* (Washington, D.C.: American Psychiatric Press, 1990).

Marsh, Diane T., and Rex Dickens. *How to Cope with Mental Illness in Your Family: A Self-Care Guide for Siblings, Offspring, and Parents.* New York: Jeremy P. Tarcher/Putnam, 1997.

This is an excellent book on how severe psychiatric disorders affect other members of the family and, above all, what to do about it. The authors, a psychologist specializing in severe psychiatric disorders and a man whose mother and three siblings have been affected, are longtime members of NAMI. Their book is a synthesis of what they have been told by hundreds of families, including extended personal accounts that they published in an earlier book, *Anguished Voices.* The emphasis in *How to Cope* is on self-help and coping skills. Most important, the authors emphasize the tremendous variability of the effects of having a family member with a severe psychiatric disorder. On one end are devastation, divorce, and what has been called "a funeral that never ends." On the other end is the young woman described by Marsh and Dickens who remembers "standing up in second grade and sharing the mental condition of my brother as my contribution to Show and Tell. I thought it was the most unique thing about my life and certainly better than any hamster!"

Millet, Kate. *The Looney-Bin Trip.* New York: Simon and Schuster, 1990.

This is a useful book, though not in ways the author intended. Millet is a radical feminist and writer whose previous books, especially *Sexual Politics,* were highly praised. In this book, she describes her episodes of recurrent mania and involuntary hospitalization in 1980, the sequelae to her having stopped taking the lithium that had kept her stable since the onset of her manic-depressive illness in 1973. The book is useful because Millet is a gifted writer who articulates the many reasons patients stop taking their medication. There are the side effects ("six years of hand tremor in public places") and the need to deny her illness ("by going off lithium I could erase the past, could prove it had never happened"). Stopping her lithium would make her "whole, not a cracked egg, not an imperfect specimen." She also stopped lithium because "I hate drugs; chemical stuff really does play with your mind," although as she writes this, she lights up another cigarette and reaches for her Pernoud. For a radical feminist and civil libertarian, taking medication symbolized social control as well: "But lithium represented collusion; when I stopped I was no longer cooperating in some social and emotional way. . . . It stopped the shame, the compliance." Pathetically, Millet even reaches out to the ghost of Ronald Laing: "But what if there were something on the other side of crazy, what if across that line there were a certain understanding, a special knowledge?" Millet also articulates the seduction of mania ("a certain speed of thought, certain wonderful flights of ideas") and selective recall of her manic behavior ("like my notorious inexhaustible energy these days: the proof of my manic state for some, for me only an index of my insecurity"). And when it is all over, sadly, Millet has learned nothing. Manic-depressive illness, she says, is merely a "general superstition. . . . I say it doesn't exist." There is no understanding of its tragedies: "Why not hear voices? So what?" And there is no appreciation of the lost lives and wasted talent, including her own.

Mondimore, Frances M. *Bipolar: A Guide for Patients and Families.* Baltimore: Johns Hopkins University Press, 1999.

As one of the first books written for individuals with manic-depressive illness and their families, *Bipolar* has been most welcome. Its descriptions of the symptoms of the illness and its diagnosis are comprehensive and readable, and the case histories are useful. Treatment is also well covered, with the exception of the author's insistence that *every* individual with manic-depressive illness requires psychotherapy: "Finally, I can't stress enough that *every bipolar patient needs psychotherapy* at one point or another" (italics in original). However, what is known about possible causes of manic-depressive illness is less well covered and poorly organized (e.g., the discussion of kindling theory is buried in a section entitled "Practice Mood Hygiene," and the chapter on bipolar disorder in children and adolescents is remarkably brief). The book is also weak in terms of practical advice on how to handle day-to-day problems (e.g., the brief section on medication compliance emphasizes denial but includes no discussion at all on anosognosia—unawareness of one's illness because of brain damage caused by the illness). Finally, the resources section at the end of the book could have been much expanded (e.g., only six books are listed, some of which are useful only to psychiatric professionals).

Orum, Margo. *Fairytales in Reality: My Victory over Manic Depression.* Sydney: Pan Macmillan Australia, 1996.

The foreword to this book describes it nicely as "essentially a love story about the brain—girl meets brain, girl loses brain, girl finds brain." Margo Orum was 31 when she suffered the first of what would become six manic episodes and three depressive episodes over seven years. Her account emphasizes how her behavior while manic interfered with and destroyed many of her most important personal relationships. The writing is pedestrian, but the story is worthwhile. Now stabilized on lithium, Ms. Orum has become a psychologist.

Ostwald, Peter. *Schumann. The Inner Voices of a Musical Genius.* Boston: Northeastern University Press, 1985. This is a carefully researched and well-written biography of the nineteenth-century German composer. Although it may be most attractive to music lovers, it contains moving and detailed accounts of Schumann's experience with his manic-depressive illness and how the illness affected his friends, family, and musical productivity. The author, an academic psychiatrist at the University of California at San Francisco at the time he wrote the book, is an accomplished musician himself. He writes sensitively about relationships between creativity and mental illness, but some of the formulations concerning Schumann's illness are overly speculative and psychoanalytic.

Papolos, Demetri, and Janice Papolos. *Overcoming Depression,* 3rd ed. New York: HarperPerennial, 1997.

Written by a psychiatrist and a journalist who are also husband and wife, *Overcoming Depression* is somewhat mistitled. The book includes discussions of both depression alone and manic-depressive illness, and the mixture is at times confusing. Among its many strengths are coverage of treatments (e.g., the "integrated treatment approach," which includes both medications and education and involves family members) and details on hospitalization, insurance, and Medicaid coverage. Shortcomings include no data on prevalence or other epidemiological aspects, no figures on genetic risks, insufficient data on childhood and adolescent aspects, and no chapter notes, making it impossible to identify specific studies referred to in the text.

*Papolos, Demetri, and Janice Papolos. *The Bipolar Child: The Definitive and Reassuring Guide to Childhood's Most Misunderstood Disorder.* New York: Broadway Books, 1999.

Written by the same husband-and-wife team who wrote *Overcoming Depression,* this was the first book published specifically on manic-depressive illness in childhood. In researching the book, the authors utilized the listserv of a network of families whose children had been given this diagnosis; thus, over a year's period, they had almost daily contact with approximately 200 families. The strongest parts of the book reflect this input and include many practical suggestions (e.g., have the child take his medicine at the same time his parents take their vitamins and other medications so he doesn't feel he is any different). Coverage of medications is very good, as are practical sections such as developing a symptom checklist. The book occasionally becomes long-winded (e.g., on theories of childhood development), and there are references but no specific chapter notes; but despite these shortcomings, it is a very useful book for families.

Piersall, Jim, and Al Hirshberg. *Fear Strikes Out: The Jim Piersall Story.* Boston: Little, Brown and Co., 1955. Republished by the University of Nebraska Press, 1999.

What would happen if a major-league baseball player became overtly manic in the middle of the season and no lithium or other mood stabilizer was available? Jimmy Piersall, a promising rookie outfielder with the Boston Red Sox, faced exactly this experience in 1952. He had a family history of severe mental illness (his mother had undergone multiple admissions to a state psychiatric hospital), had been hypomanic since his late teens, and had severe, persistent headaches. Finally, at age 22, he became overtly manic, on the ballfield, in full view of every baseball fan in America. What does a manic baseball player do? Jimmy Piersall got into countless arguments with umpires, got thrown out of games, got into fistfights with teammates, clowned around on the field, and ran backward around the bases after hitting a homerun. On one occasion, called out on strikes, he took a squirt gun out of his pocket, cleaned off home plate, and then said to the umpire: "Now maybe you can see it!" Finally, he was involuntarily hospitalized for seven weeks and treated with ECT. He fully recovered and resumed his baseball career. Especially interesting are Piersall's efforts after recovery to help a fledgling patient self-help group in Chicago called "Fight Against Fears." He did so publicly and became probably the first out-of-the-closet, ex-mental-patient athlete. He was thus not only a very good baseball player but also a very good person.

Preston, John D., et al. *Consumer's Guide to Psychiatric Drugs.* Oakland, Calif.: New Harbinger Publications, 1998.

This guide to drugs used for treating severe psychiatric illnesses is similar to Gorman's *The Essential Guide to Psychiatric Drugs,* but each book has different strengths. The first half of *Consumer's Guide* discusses general issues (e.g., "Managing Your Medications," "Seeking Treatment"), whereas the second half offers an extensive description of each drug listed alphabetically along with a directory by brand names that makes it user friendly. Also included is a useful chapter, "Nonpharmaceutical Approaches," that discusses such treatments as melatonin and St. John's wort.

Rosen, Laura E., and Xavier Amador. *When Someone You Love Is Depressed: How to Help Your Loved One Without Losing Yourself.* New York: The Free Press, 1996.
   Written by two psychologists, this is one of the best of numerous books written for individuals who are depressed; an especially helpful feature is its focus on other family members who are affected by the person's depression. Although it is not targeted specifically at manic-depressive illness, many such individuals suffer from recurrent depression, and in such cases this book will be useful.

Russell, L. Mark, Arnold E. Grant, Suzanne M. Joseph, and Richard W. Fee. *Planning for the Future: Providing a Meaningful Life for a Child with a Disability After Your Death,* 3rd ed. Evanston, Ill.: American Publishing Company, 1995.
   For anyone who is trying to plan for the future of a mentally disabled family member, this is essential reading. The authors cover everything from SSI, SSDI, Medicaid, Medicare, and other government benefits to wills, trusts, estate planning, power of attorney, and nursing home expenses. The book is replete with detailed examples and includes sample letters of intent. It has been especially popular among parents who worry about what will happen to their mentally ill child after they are gone.

Schatzberg, Alan F., and Charles B. Nemeroff (eds.). *The American Psychiatric Press Textbook of Psychopharmacology,* 2nd ed. Washington, D.C.: American Psychiatric Press, 1998.
   This complex, multi-authored text on the entire field of psychopharmacology may be useful for readers seeking detailed discussions of the major mental illnesses and their treatment. Included are individual chapters on the major medications used in psychiatry that describe basic neuroscience and pharmacological properties related to these drugs, as well as a section on the neurobiology of the major mental illnesses that provides a good review of research findings accumulated up to the date of publication. A final section describes the relative merits of the various pharmacological treatments and side effects.

*Sexton, Linda Gray. *Searching for Mercy Street: My Journal Back to My Mother, Anne Sexton.* Boston: Little, Brown and Company, 1994.
   Like Jacki Lyden's *Daughter of the Queen of Sheba,* this is a daughter's account of growing up with a mother who had manic-depressive illness. In this case, the mother was a Pulitzer Prize–winning poet, and Linda Sexton gives new meaning to the term *dysfunctional family* as she describes her mother's periods of mania and depression, nine suicide attempts, multiple hospitalizations, and their effect on herself and other members of her family. The family rarely took trips or vacations "because Mother is too unpredictable. . . . [F]or us there was always the sense that we were about to slip over the edge, that a day's depression could turn quickly into a suicide attempt or a

hospitalization." Friends at school taunted Linda, saying, "Your Mother is crazy"; she dared not ask friends to her house. Most painful was Linda Sexton's sense of blame and responsibility for her mother's condition. "I keep seeing my own small face, so desperate and so afraid, overwhelmed with the responsibility I feel toward keeping Mother sane." Sexton describes her mother as being "as fragile and precarious as the translucent Limoges my Nana kept on high shelves at her house." The book's major deficiency is the author's limited understanding of the biological nature of her mother's illness. This is due to Linda Sexton's own psychoanalysis and consequent Freudian perspective, but also to the fact that Anne Sexton's manic-depressive illness was made much worse by concurrent severe alcoholism and narcissistic personality disorder. Her remarkable self-indulgence and malicious intrusiveness into her daughter's life both exacerbated and confused the effects of her underlying illness. Indeed, when Anne Sexton finally killed herself at age 45, the effect on those closest to her was predominantly one of relief. Because of her alcoholism and personality disorder, Anne Sexton's family was never certain how much to blame her for her illness while she was alive; not surprisingly, her daughter is still not certain now that her mother is dead.

Soares, Jair C., and Samuel Gershon (eds.). *Bipolar Disorders: Basic Mechanisms and Therapeutic Interpretation*. New York: Marcel Dekker, 2000.

   This is a textbook summarizing what is known about the biological causes of manic-depressive illness. The authors are themselves researchers and very knowledgeable, and most chapters are comprehensive, well written, and well edited. The book is not airplane reading, comprising as it does 580 pages of detailed information covering virtually every aspect of contemporary research. As it is also up to date, serious scholars and researchers on causation could do no better than to use it as their starting point.

*Steel, Danielle. *His Bright Light: The Story of Nick Traina*. New York: Dell Publishing, 1998.

   This is an exceptional book about Danielle Steel's son, Nick, who developed manic-depressive illness in his early teens. As an entry on the *New York Times* bestseller list, it has probably done more to educate the public about childhood-onset manic-depressive illness—"baby bipolar," as the author calls it—than all other such books put together. *His Bright Light* poignantly describes Nick's earliest symptoms and Steel's feelings that something was wrong with him even early in his childhood. But parents are not trained to know how to understand such things, and Steel gives a detailed if painful account of her on-the-job training. Most devastating is the incompetence of most of the mental health professionals to whom she turned for help; the mental health profession is depicted as more dysfunctional than her son. In the end, and almost inevitably, Nick kills himself at age 19 despite his mother's best efforts. The devastation wrought by this suicide occupies the final pages—the endless sadness, the sense of loss, the continued annual celebration of her son's birthday. It is as if Nick did not die once but is dying a thousand times, endlessly. Such is the cruel outcome of this disease in all too many cases.

*Styron, William. *Darkness Visible: A Memoir of Madness.* New York: Vintage Books, 1990.

This national bestseller deserves all the acclaim it has received. Styron details the onset of severe depression at age 60 with a precision and lucidity unmatched in personal accounts of this illness. He was predisposed to depression by his genes (his father had been hospitalized), early childhood experiences (his mother died when he was 13), long-standing abuse of alcohol, and addiction to benzodiazepines. Styron chronicles his descent from the earliest signs of decline ("the shadows of nightfall seemed more somber, my mornings were less buoyant") to the deeper depths ("my brain . . . had become less an organ of thought than an instrument registering, minute by minute, varying degrees of its own suffering") and finally to the very bottom ("death . . . was now a daily presence, blowing over me in cold gusts"). Just short of suicide, Styron was finally hospitalized, and he recovered with antidepressant medication. The result is this book, a traveler's guide to Hell, and we are fortunate that Styron lived to write it.

Swados, Elizabeth. *The Four of Us: A Family Memoir.* New York: Farrar, Strauss and Giroux, 1991. Paperback by Penguin Books, 1993.

This is an extraordinary account of how severe mental illness can devastate an entire family. The son is officially diagnosed with schizophrenia but appears to have the schizoaffective type or even manic-depressive illness. The effects of the disease's malignant ripples are stunning, as the young man spirals downward to a failed suicide attempt, throwing himself beneath a subway train, then into homelessness. It is beautifully written, brutally honest, and profoundly depressing. Recommended for reading on sunny days in pleasant gardens.

Taylor, Robert. *Distinguishing Psychological from Organic Disorders: Screening for Psychological Masquerade.* New York: Springer Publishing Co., 2000.

This is an updated, second edition of an excellent book. The author lays out a method for mental illness professionals to use to distinguish organic brain diseases (e.g., brain tumors) from schizophrenia, manic-depressive illness, and other psychiatric conditions. Taylor's method is lucid, eminently practical, and remarkably easy to implement, and any professional who reads this book will be a better clinician for it. The book should also be required reading for all mental illness professionals in training.

Thompson, Tracy. *The Beast: A Journey Through Depression.* New York: Plume, 1995.

This is a solid and useful account of chronic, recurrent depression. The author, a successful journalist with the *Washington Post,* experienced the onset of periodic depression as a teenager, but her illness went untreated for twenty years. Thompson is completely forthcoming, and her descriptions of how depression affected her personal relationships are especially useful. Except for being long-winded at times, the book is well written and engaging.

Torrey, E. Fuller. *Out of the Shadows: Confronting America's Mental Illness Crisis.* New York: John Wiley and Sons, 1997. Paperback edition, 1998.

This book details the consequences of our failed mental illness treatment system, including those confronting individuals with schizophrenia and manic-depressive illness who are homeless, in jails and prisons, victimized, or who commit violent acts because they are not being treated. Much of the blame goes to the thought-disordered funding system and laws, and the book offers a blueprint for solving these problems. *Out of the Shadows* is, in some respects, a sequel to *Nowhere To Go: The Tragic Odyssey of the Homeless Mentally Ill* (New York: Harper and Row, 1988), which gives more of the historical background of the disaster that we call contemporary mental illness services.

Torrey, E. Fuller, Ann E. Bowler, Edward H. Taylor, and Irving I. Gottesman. *Schizophrenia and Manic-Depressive Disorder: The Biological Roots of Mental Illness as Revealed by a Landmark Study of Identical Twins.* New York: Basic Books, 1994. Paperback edition 1996.

This is the report of a study of sixty-six pairs of identical twins; in twenty-seven pairs, one had schizophrenia and the other was well, and in eight pairs, one had manic-depressive illness and the other was well. The twins were intensively examined in terms of developmental history, minor physical anomalies, and fingerprint patterns, undergoing PET scans and neurological, neuropsychological, MRI, and blood studies in an effort to identify nongenetic causes of the disease. As one twin researcher wrote, identical twins are "'experiments' which nature has conducted for us, starting in each case with identical sets of genes and varying environmental factors." And as "experiments," they are indeed both interesting and useful.

*Waltz, Mitzi. *Bipolar Disorders: A Guide to Helping Children and Adolescents.* Sebastopol, Calif.: O'Reilly and Associates, 2000.

This is an eminently practical, up-to-date, and helpful book for young persons with manic-depressive illness and their families. The author, a freelance writer, has one child with childhood-onset manic depression and another child with a pervasive developmental disorder. Her broad, on-the-job training comes through clearly, and she includes many useful comments from affected children and their families. The sections on diagnosis, medications, and schools are especially strong. Weaknesses include an inadequate table of contents, occasional minor factual errors (e.g., the amygdala is connected to the basal ganglia but, contrary to the author's description, is not part of it), and an inadequate section on causes. However, the book's assets far outweigh its liabilities, and it is strongly recommended. It is well written and occasionally lyrical: "Bipolar kids are like ships tossed on crashing waves of mood and action, and these dangerous icebergs lurk just below the surface."

Wasow, Mona. *The Skipping Stone: Ripple Effects of Mental Illness on the Family*. Palo Alto: Science and Behavioral Books, 1995.

This is a lyrical summary of 100 interviews done with family members of individuals with a serious mental illness. Mona Wasow is a social worker and the mother of a son who is severely mentally ill. "The ripple effect of mental illness on the entire family is enormous," she states, and proceeds to document this effect on the siblings, spouses, grandparents, and children of affected individuals. Her chapters on grief, coping, and hope are excellent, as when she explains that "trying to capture the essence of grief in writing is like trying to capture the wind in a box or the ocean in a glass." And her understanding of these illnesses is beautifully and brutally frank: "But let us be honest with ourselves: the tortures of hallucinations, the failure to connect with people, and the anxieties, desperate isolation, and loneliness of people with serious mental illness take a staggering toll."

Weiden, Peter J., Patricia L. Scheifler, Ronald J. Diamond, and Ruth Ross. *Breakthroughs in Antipsychotic Medications: A Guide for Consumers, Families and Clinicians*. New York: W. W. Norton and Company, 1999.

This book focuses primarily on the second-generation antipsychotics and includes valuable summaries of clozapine, risperidone, olanzapine, quetiapine, and ziprasidone. It also includes fact sheets on such adverse effects as weight gain, sedation, and sexual difficulties. The major drawback of the book is its uncritical enthusiasm for the newer drugs and its implicit assumption that virtually everyone with psychotic symptoms should be switched from first-generation medications to these medications. As is becoming increasingly clear, the second-generation antipsychotics have their own set of problems and many patients are better off with the older drugs.

Whybrow, Peter. *A Mood Apart: The Thinker's Guide to Emotion and Its Disorders*. New York: BasicBooks, 1997. Paperback by HarperCollins, 1998.

This is an especially well-written tome on the basic biology of mood disorders. Given its heavy content, the book is surprisingly engaging. With a chatty style, the author weaves didactic information amidst case histories, and the reader can skip sections that become ponderous (e.g., the physiology gets a bit heavy from time to time). The book focuses on the biology of moods, emphasizing depression and manic-depressive illness; it also includes some discussion of the workings of medications for these disorders.

Winerip, Michael. *9 Highland Road*. New York: Vintage Books, 1994.

Michael Winerip, a respected reporter for the *New York Times,* spent two years hanging around a group home on Long Island. The result of his observations there is an engaging, lively, and well-written narrative that captures the home's ambience, including the struggles and joys of its residents diagnosed with severe psychiatric disorders. Winerip writes: "Listening to Anthony's explanations when he was psychotic was like trying to understand one of your dreams the next morning." Perhaps the book's greatest contribution is to illustrate that individuals with severe psychiatric disorders need more than medication to reclaim their lives. They also need friends, guidance, support, and people who believe in them. A good group home, such as Winerip is describing, provides those things and is an optimal living situation for many people with this diagnosis.

Wolpert, Louis. *Malignant Sadness: The Anatomy of Depression.* New York: Free Press, 1999.

This is a modestly useful but rather dry account of depression. Its author, a Ph.D. professor of biology in London, experienced a severe depressive episode late in life. Finding little useful information available, he set out on "a personal quest to try and understand the nature of depression." This book is the result, one-quarter personal account and three-quarters what he learned. The book is strongest when Wolpert talks about himself, but he does so with reluctance. He acknowledges that his depression may have been caused by a medication he had recently started for heart problems. But rather than pursuing this line of inquiry and detailing the frequency with which late-life depression is caused by medications, he embarks on a library quest to summarize everything written about the subject. As such, his account reads like class notes from Depression 101—necessary to graduate but rather dull.

Woolis, Rebecca. *When Someone You Love Has a Mental Illness: A Handbook for Family, Friends, and Caregivers.* New York: Jeremy P. Tarcher/Perigee Books, 1992.

This is a handy book to have around because of its numerous Quick Reference Guides for such subjects as "Handling Your Relative's Anger," "Dealing with Bizarre Behavior," "Preventing Suicide," and "Rules for Living at Home or Visiting." It does not provide long discourses on the various subjects but instead tells you what to *do.* It is a practical book par excellence.

APPENDIX B:
SELECTED WEBSITES

The Internet offers an overwhelming number of websites with information about manic-depressive illness. Ask a search engine to look for *manic-depression* or *bipolar disorder*, and it will produce 10,000 to 20,000 matches. Not all information on these websites is accurate, however. Even more confusing is the fact that sites are constantly appearing and disappearing.

In general, websites maintained by nonprofit groups provide more accurate information than do websites run by for-profit groups. Some pharmaceutical companies maintain websites that include useful information on nonmedication aspects of manic-depressive illness but, not surprisingly, biased information regarding medications. Other companies and groups have websites that include bulletin boards, mailing lists, and chat rooms through which families and consumers can get in touch with one another. Such websites can be used for advocacy purposes.

The Internet can also be used to search for published articles about a specific topic and, in many cases, to then access the articles online. This is becoming increasingly easy to do. For example, the National Library of Medicine (NLM) website, *http://www.nlm.nih.gov/medlineplus/*, offers free access to MEDLINE, a database with references and abstracts from more than 4,300 biomedical journals, dating back to 1966. From the NLM website, click on "Other Resources," then on "MEDLINE," and then enter a query term, with or without various limits. For example, if you enter the term *lithium*, you will receive citations to over 20,500 articles. Using the Boolean operator "AND" to further refine your search with the term *hypothyroid* and limiting your search to the years 1990 to 2001 will yield 62 articles, 48 of which have an abstract that you can access by clicking on the author link. Full-text versions of some of the 62 articles are also available. Articles not available online may be found at your local library and may also be ordered via NLM's Loansome Doc service (you must establish an agreement with a health science library in your area to use this service and you may be charged a fee); click on "Related Resources: Order Documents" for information on how to do so.

Following are some selected websites that include useful information on manic-depressive illness. The list is not to be considered inclusive, and readers should remember that such sites are constantly changing.

www.mentalhealth.com: This is a private website maintained and personally funded by Phillip W. Long, M.D., a Canadian psychiatrist. It is very comprehensive and easily navigated. Note: It should not be confused with *www.mentalhealth.org,* which is a much less helpful website maintained by the Center for Mental Health Services under the U.S. Department of Health and Human Services.

www.psychlaws.org: This is the website of the Treatment Advocacy Center and is privately funded by foundations and individual donations. It focuses specifically on problems associated with the failure to treat individuals with manic-depressive illness and other severe psychiatric disorders. Most of the information on this website is not available elsewhere.

www.citizen.org/eletter/: This website is sponsored by the Public Citizen's Health Research Group and the Treatment Advocacy Center, neither of which accepts pharmaceutical company support. It provides unbiased, up-to-date information on medications used to treat manic-depressive illness and other severe psychiatric disorders and includes instructions for reporting adverse drug reactions by phone or fax or via the Food and Drug Administration's MedWatch website, *www.fda.gov/MedWatch/.*

www.bpkids.org: This is the website of the Child and Adolescent Bipolar Foundation (CABF), a nonprofit organization that specializes in early-onset manic-depressive illness.

www.ndmda.org: This is the website of the National Depressive and Manic-Depressive Association (National DMDA), a nonprofit organization. It includes a directory of chapters and support groups.

www.nami.org: This website provides a list of local NAMI support groups, a useful consumer e-mail list, and abundant information on various advocacy efforts. NAMI is funded by dues and donations from its members.

www.frii.com/~parrot/bip.html: This website, maintained by Joy Ikelman, includes lists of famous people who have suffered from manic-depressive illness and depression, a bibliography that can be used to further investigate these individuals' struggles with the disorder, and evaluations of related plays, films, documentaries, and other works of fiction and nonfiction.

www.electroshock.org: This website is maintained by Max Fink, a psychiatrist, to provide information about electroconvulsive therapy (ECT) as a treatment for depression and mania.

www.med.jhu.edu/drada/other_org.html: This is the website of the Depression and Related Affective Disorders Association and is maintained by individuals and families in cooperation with the Department of Psychiatry at the Johns Hopkins University School of Medicine.

www.mhsource.com/narsad.html: This is the website of the National Alliance for Research on Schizophrenia and Affective Disorders (NARSAD).

www.antenna.nl/lithium/englishweb/index_e/html: This is the website of the Lithium Plus Working Group," an organization of psychiatrists and families in the Netherlands.

www.psycom.net/depression.central.html: This website serves as a clearing-house for information on mood disorders.

www.mhsource.com/bipolar: This website is part of the broader Mental Health InfoSource website and includes an electronic newsletter, transcripts and slides from recent professional conferences, and clinical treatment informa-tion, including treatment guidelines. Related sites include *www.mhsource.com/interactive/chat.html,* which offers consumer and pro-fessional chat rooms, and *www.bipolarchild.com/articles.html,* a website sponsored by Demetri and Janice Papolos and based on their book *The Bipolar Child* (see Appendix A).

www.harbor-of-refuge.org: This website offers peer support for individuals with manic-depressive illness and their families.

www.a-silver-lining.org: This website offers chat rooms and bulletin boards, a newsletter, a bookstore, news articles, and links to related resources.

www.patientcenters.com/bipolar: This website includes useful articles excerpted from Mitzi Waltz's *Bipolar Disorders: A Guide to Helping Chil-dren and Adolescents* (see Appendix A) as well as links to publications, advo-cacy groups, related websites, and information on medications and special issues pertaining to manic-depressive illness.

www.centerwatch.com/patient/studies/cat20.html: This website lists centers across the country that are conducting clinical trials on manic-depressive ill-ness and includes detailed profiles of the centers.

www.bipolarworld.net: This website provides both general information and the chance for personal involvement with others through its message board, poetry pages, art gallery, and "ask the doctor" forum.

www.pendulum.org: This website provides, among other things, information on diagnostic criteria, medications, alternative treatments, and ways of deal-ing with stress.

www.mhsanctuary.com/bipolar: This website serves both as a clearinghouse for information on manic-depressive illness and as a support group for individ-uals and families, with links to self-care, a file of frequently asked questions, individual and family bulletin boards and chat rooms, and related personal stories.

www.bpso.org: This website is intended for "bipolar significant others." It includes general information that is available to the general public and a peer-support mailing list that is restricted to members only.

healthscout.com: This is a commercial, for-profit, general medical website that sells medications and other health items. It is specifically useful for locating recent research and general news articles about manic-depressive illness. (Be aware, however, that the reliability and validity of mental illness research by the general news media is variable.) This site also includes detailed information about all drugs, including contraindications, adverse reactions, dosage, and how supplied.

APPENDIX C:
REVIEW OF VIDEOTAPES BY KATIE PETRAY, PROGRAM DIRECTOR, NAMI ILLINOIS FAMILY-TO-FAMILY EDUCATION

The thirteen videotapes on manic-depressive illness and severe depression listed here were selected from a total of thirty videos I recently reviewed. Many of these videos were featured at the Film Festival during the 2000 NAMI National Conference. Undoubtedly, other very good videos on the subject have been produced of which I am unaware.

These "favorites" are videos designed to educate and encourage parents and their loved ones to seek treatment. They provide insights into the problems of living with manic-depressive illness and the impact this illness has on families. Especially meaningful to viewers are the consumers' own stories about what it's like to fight the symptoms of the illness.

Many interesting segments include pertinent information about scientific advances and call attention to newer medications. All videos are listed alphabetically. They may be purchased as indicated or may be borrowed at local libraries or through NAMI-affiliate lending libraries.

Breaking the Dark Horse: A Family Copes with Manic Depression. 1995.
   Viewers follow the moving story of a woman's lifelong struggle with mental illness from early childhood to adulthood. Strengthened by a family who learns to accept and understand, Mindy faces her illness and takes responsibility in working toward recovery.
   Writer's Group, P.O. Box 82, Isle of Palms, SC 29451. 803-886-4795. 30-min. videotape, $24.95 plus $3.95 shipping.

Claire's (My) Story. 1994.
   Claire addresses the facts, fears, and fiction of depression. Interspersed with lively graphics and music, the video teaches adults and children to recognize symptoms, understand treatment, and work together to overcome this serious disorder.

333

Wellness Reproductions Publishing, Inc., 23945 Mercantile Road, Beachwood, OH 44122-5924. 1-800-669-9208 or 216-831-9209. 48-min. videotape, $99.95 plus $9.95 shipping.

Coping with Depression. 1990.

Mary Ellen Copeland, M.S., a person with manic-depressive illness, describes the causes and treatment of depression and manic depression. The author strives to empower others with insight, energy, and hope, offering techniques and strategies to keep depressive episodes at bay.

Courage to Change, P.O. Box 1268, Newburgh, NY 12551-1268. 1-800-440-4003. 48-min. videotape, Cat. #61228BS, $44.95 plus $9.95 shipping.

Dark Glasses and Kaleidoscopes: Living with Manic Depression. 1997.

Join host Tony Dow for an exploration of the symptoms and treatment of manic depression through the honest, emotional testimony of individuals and families who live with this illness. The video provides information, answers, and hope for those who suffer. Treatment is available; and for over 80 percent of individuals who receive it, treatment is successful.

Abbott Laboratories. Contact: National DMDA, 730 North Franklin Street, Suite 501, Chicago, IL 60610. 1-800-826-3632. 33-min. videotape, $5.00 plus $4.25 shipping.

Day for Night: Recognizing Teen Depression (DRADA). 1999.

This video highlights interviews with teenagers who are dealing with clinical depression and bipolar disorder. These teens and their families and friends offer an in-depth look at the symptoms and treatment of teenage depression. The goal is to provide education, support, and hope to teens suffering from this serious, yet very treatable, illness.

DRADA Meyer 3-181, 600 North Wolfe Street, Baltimore, MD 21205. 410-729-7940. E-mail: drada@jhmi.edu 26-min. videotape, $60.00 plus $3.00 shipping.

Dead Blue: Surviving Depression. 1998.

CBS correspondent Mike Wallace, clinical psychologist Martha Manning, Ph.D., and Pulitzer Prize–winning author William Styron speak candidly while recalling real-life experiences in dealing with depression. This is a glowing, impressive film that reminds us that we are all vulnerable to this illness and that awareness is the beginning of wisdom.

America Undercover Documentary for HBO TV. Contact: HBO Video Productions, P.O. Box 60577, Burbank, CA 91510. 888-442-6843. 60-min. videotape, $24.98 plus $3.95 shipping.

Depression: Kay Jamison. 1997.

Gain insight into the harrowing ordeal of manic-depressive illness. Kay Jamison delves into the battle against manic depression and other mental diseases. She discusses her own extraordinary struggle with the illness and reveals lesser known aspects of the disease, such as its crushing physical manifestations and genetic origins.

Great Minds of Medicine Series. Contact: WGBH-Unapix/Miramar, 200 Second Avenue West, Seattle, WA 98119. 1-800-245-6472. 48-min. videotape, $79.95.

Depression: On the Edge, 1997.

Designed for teens by teens, this video, part of the PBS Teen Series "In the Mix," follows a group visiting Pierre, South Dakota. Teens describe the difference between everyday blues ("feeling down") and clinical depression. The messages are that depression can't be "fixed on one's own"; it helps to "get the facts"; and "suicide is preventable." Teens, schools, families, hospitals, and professionals all need to work together to promote better understanding.

PBS Teen Series, "In the Mix." Contact: Castle Works, 114 E. 32nd Street, New York, NY 10016. 212-684-3940. 1-800-597-9448. www.castleworks.com. 30-min. videotape, $59.95, plus $4.00 shipping.

A Different Journey: Parents for NBD. 1998.

This video captures the essence of young families and their struggles with mental illness. Here the youth themselves, whose vivid descriptions of what it's like to live with a neurobiological brain disorder (NBD), also known as a mental illness, are the ones who promote advocacy efforts for children with these disorders. Senator Pete Domenici from New Mexico encourages communication with legislators to help change laws and lessen the stigma that surrounds children who have emotional or behavioral differences.

Parents for Behaviorally Different Children PBDC, Video Project, 5905 Marble N.E., Ste. 8, Albuquerque, NM 87110. 1-800-273-7232. 11-min. videotape, $12.00 plus $2.00 shipping.

Learning to Live with Bipolar Disorder. 2000.

This is an inspirational video that features the testimony of five persons who face bipolar illness openly and share their experiences as they venture forward on the road to recovery. Their frank discussions about, and recognition of, the benefits of medication and support are an encouragement to other consumers and families in their efforts to educate themselves and build strong support networks.

Produced through an Abbott Laboratories grant. Contact: NAMI Resource Publications, P.O. Box 753, Waldorf, MD 20064. Fax 301-843-0159. www.NAMI.org. 30-min. videotape, $10.00 plus $4.00 shipping.

No More Shame: Understanding Depression. 1995.

Ellen Kelley and her family provide us with the reality of depression and emphasize how important it is to recognize the symptoms and seek treatment. Medication, therapy, and the reduction of life stressors can greatly impact depression. Graphics and computer animations assist the viewer to better understand how the brain functions.

University of Pittsburgh and WQED. Contact: Films for the Humanities and Sciences, P.O. Box 2053, Princeton, NJ 08543. 1-800-257-5126. Cat. #5826. 20-min. videotape, $89.95 plus 5.95 shipping.

Straight Talk About Bipolar Disorder. 1999.

This videotape features an interview with Christopher Heather, R.N., Ph.D., Ohio. Designed for the "lay" person, it provides an easy-to-understand, comprehensive, "straight-talking" overview of manic depression offering current information and insight into the illness.

American Video Productions Co., 7116-D Pippin Road, Cincinnati, OH 45239. 513-522-5700. 56-min. videotape, $16.00 (includes shipping).

When Physicians Commit Suicide: Reflections of Those They Leave Behind. 1999.

Survivors of physicians who have committed suicide talk about their experience, describing their feelings, their relationship with the deceased, the circumstances of the death, and their healing. This is a moving video intended to further diminish the stigma associated with mental illness among physicians.

Michael F. Myers, MD, Dept. of Psychiatry, St. Paul's Hospital, Vancouver, BC V6Z 1Y6 Canada. 604-631-5498. 24-min. videotape, $25.00 plus $7.50 shipping.

APPENDIX D: USEFUL RESOURCES

The following are some useful resources for information regarding manic-depressive illness.

Education and Advocacy

NAMI (formerly called the National Alliance for the Mentally Ill)
Colonial Place Three
2107 Wilson Blvd., Suite 300
Arlington, VA 22201-3042
703-524-7600
Helpline: 1-800-950-6264
www.nami.org

Begun in 1979, NAMI is the nation's largest advocacy organization for individuals with severe mental illnesses, including schizophrenia, manic-depressive illness, major depression, obsessive-compulsive disorder, and severe anxiety disorders. Its members include people with serious mental illness and their families. Membership costs $25 and includes a subscription to the bimonthly *NAMI Advocate,* which provides much helpful information. NAMI's more than 1,200 state and local affiliates offer excellent education and support; to contact the affiliate closest to you, click on "Affiliates" at the NAMI website, *www.nami.org*. NAMI also has a toll-free Helpline, which serves as an information and referral service about mental illness issues. The annual NAMI convention is another good place to learn about manic-depressive illness. NAMI accepts donations.

National DMDA (National Depressive and Manic-Depressive Association)
730 North Franklin, Suite 501
Chicago, IL 60610-3526
312-642-0049
1-800-82-NDMDA
www.ndmda.org

Begun in 1986, the National DMDA has 275 chapters that function primarily to conduct support groups and educate the public about depression and manic-depressive illness. Membership costs $20 per year and includes the *National DMDA Newsletter.*

DRADA (Depression and Related Affective Disorders Association)
Johns Hopkins University Medical Center, Meyer 3-181
600 North Wolfe Street
Baltimore, MD 21205
1-410-955-4647
www.med.jhu.edu/drada

Allied with the Department of Psychiatry at Johns Hopkins University School of Medicine in Baltimore, DRADA provides education and support groups for individuals with depression or manic-depressive illness. Membership costs $30 per year and includes a quarterly newsletter, *Smooth Sailing.*

TAC (Treatment Advocacy Center)
3300 N. Fairfax Drive, Suite 220
Arlington, VA 22201
1-703-294-6001
www.psychlaws.org

This legal advocacy organization was formed in 1998 to bring attention to and correct the consequences of the failing mental illness treatment system. TAC specifically focuses on people with manic-depressive illness, schizophrenia, and other severe mental illnesses who are homeless, in jails or prisons, being victimized, or at risk of suicide or committing violent acts because they are not being treated and works to reform legal systems that prevent them from getting treatment. The Center is a resource for individuals seeking to reform assisted treatment laws in their own states. Its free bimonthly newsletter (*Catalyst*) and its website, *www.psychlaws.org,* include much useful information; there is also a free online newsletter. From the website, subscribe to the newsletter by clicking on "Join Us" and completing the "TAC Network Form." TAC accepts donations but does not accept funding from pharmaceutical companies.

Research-Related Resources

Stanley Foundation Research Programs
5430 Grosvenor Lane, Suite 200

Bethesda, MD 20814
1-301-571-0770
www.stanleyresearch.org

Begun in 1989, the organization known as Stanley Foundation Research Programs is, with the exception of the federal government, one of the two largest providers of research funds for manic-depressive illness and schizophrenia. It also funds the Stanley Laboratory of Developmental Neurovirology at the Johns Hopkins University Medical Center in Baltimore and the Laboratory of Brain Research at the Uniformed Services University of the Health Sciences in Bethesda, Maryland. It is funded predominantly by Mr. and Ms. Theodore Stanley, and it accepts donations.

NARSAD (National Alliance for Research on Schizophrenia and Affective Disorders)
60 Cutter Mill Rd., Suite 404
Great Neck, NY 11021
1-516-829-0091
www.narsad.org

Begun in 1986, NARSAD is one of the two largest providers of funds for depression, manic-depressive illness, and schizophrenia research outside of the federal government. It also funds research on other major psychiatric disorders. Its newsletter includes useful accounts of current research. NARSAD welcomes help in raising funds for research and accepts donations.

Useful Publications

Bipolar Disorders is a quarterly journal aimed at researchers covering all aspects of the causes, clinical course, and treatment of manic-depressive illness. The cost is $103 per year. Order from Munksgaard, International Publishers Ltd., 350 Main Street, Malden, MA 02148.

The *Journal of Affective Disorders* is a monthly journal aimed at researchers covering depression and anxiety disorders as well as manic-depressive illness. The cost is $199 per year. Order from Elsevier Science, P.O. Box 945, New York, NY 10159.

Hospital and Community Psychiatry is a monthly journal of the American Psychiatric Association. This is the best single source of information on psychiatric services. The cost is $51 per year. Order from the APA, 1400 K Street, N.W., Washington, DC 20005 (phone 202-682-6000, fax 202-682-6850, e-mail *apa@psych.org*).

NOTES

Epigraph

1. Roy Porter (ed.), *The Faber Book of Madness* (London: Faber and Faber, 1991), pp. 12–13, quoting Pinel.

Preface

1. C. Krauthammer and G. L. Klerman, "Secondary mania: Manic syndromes associated with antecedent physical illness or drugs," *Archives of General Psychiatry* 35: 1333–1339, 1978.

Chapter 1

1. John Crammer, *Asylum History: Buckinghamshire County Pauper Lunatic Asylum—St. John's* (London: Gaskell, Royal College of Psychiatrists, 1990), p. 39, quoting Millar.

2. "Famous (Living) People Who Have Experienced Manic Depression," *http://www.frii.com/~parrot/living.html*, accessed January 29, 2001.

3. Ray Buck, "Police Say Underwood Tried Suicide," *Fort Worth Star Telegram*, January 7, 2001.

4. "Health care reform for Americans with severe mental illnesses: Report of the National Advisory Mental Health Council," *American Journal of Psychiatry* 150: 1447–1465, 1993.

5. J. C. Anthony, M. Folstein, A. J. Romanoski, et al., "Comparison of the Lay Diagnostic Interview Schedule and a standardized psychiatric diagnosis," *Archives of General Psychiatry* 42: 667–675, 1985.

6. R. C. Kessler, K. A. McGonagle, S. Zhao, et al., "Lifetime and 12-month prevalence of *DSM-III-R* psychiatric disorders in the United States: Results from the National Comorbidity Survey," *Archives of General Psychiatry* 51: 8–19, 1994.

7. R. C. Kessler, personal communication to Dr. Torrey, February 3, 1995.

8. R. C. Kessler, D. R. Rubinow, C. Holmes, et al., "The epidemiology of DSM-III-R bipolar I disorder in a general population survey," *Psychological Medicine* 27: 1079–1089, 1997.

9. J. Unützer, G. Simon, C. Pabiniak, et al., "The treated prevalence of bipolar disorder in a large staff-model HMO," *Psychiatric Services* 49: 1072–1078, 1998.

10. D. A. Regier, W. E. Narrow, D. S. Rae, et al., "The de facto US mental and addictive disorders service system: Epidemiologic Catchment Area prospective 1-year

prevalence rates of disorders and services," *Archives of General Psychiatry* 50: 85–94, 1993.

11. Ibid.

12. Kessler et al., "The epidemiology of DSM-III-R."

13. M. Weissman, M. L. Bruce, P. J. Leaf, et al., "Affective Disorders," in L. N. Robins and D. A. Regier (eds.), *Psychiatric Disorders in America: The Epidemiologic Catchment Area Study* (New York: Free Press, 1991).

14. Ibid.

15. M. A. Burnam, R. L. Hough, J. I. Escobar, et al., "Six-month prevalence of specific psychiatric disorders among Mexican Americans and non-Hispanic whites in Los Angeles," *Archives of General Psychiatry* 44: 687–694, 1987; M. Karno, R. L. Hough, M. A. Burnam, et al., "Lifetime prevalence of specific psychiatric disorders among Mexican Americans and non-Hispanic whites in Los Angeles," *Archives of General Psychiatry* 44: 695–701, 1987.

16. J. W. Eaton and R. J. Weil, *Culture and Mental Disorders: A Comparative Study of the Hutterites and Other Populations* (Glencoe, Ill.: Free Press, 1955).

17. E. F. Torrey, "Prevalence of psychosis among the Hutterites: A reanalysis of the 1950–53 study," *Schizophrenia Research* 16: 167–170, 1995.

18. V. L. Nimgaonkar, T. M. Fujiwara, M. Dutta, et al., "Low prevalence of psychoses among the Hutterites, an isolated religious community," *American Journal of Psychiatry* 157: 1065–1070, 2000.

19. J. A. Egeland, "An Epidemiologic and Genetic Study of Affective Disorders Among the Old Order Amish," in D. F. Papolos and H. M. Lachman (eds.), *Genetic Studies in Affective Disorders* (New York: John Wiley and Sons, 1994), pp. 70–90.

20. M. M. Weissman, R. C. Bland, G. J. Canino, et al., "Cross-national epidemiology of major depression and bipolar disorder," *JAMA* 276: 293–299, 1996.

21. A. L. Smith and M. M. Weissman, "Epidemiology," in E. S. Paykel (ed.), *Handbook of Affective Disorders* (London: Churchill Livingstone, 1992), pp. 111–129.

22. E. S. Gershon, and J. H. Liebowitz, "Sociocultural and demographic correlates of affective disorders in Jerusalem," *Journal of Psychiatric Research* 12: 37–50, 1975.

23. C.-N. Chen, J. Wong, N. Lee, et al., "The Shatin Community Mental Health Survey in Hong Kong. II: Major findings," *Archives of General Psychiatry* 50: 125–133, 1993.

24. J. H. Boyd and M. M. Weissman, "Epidemiology of affective disorders," *Archives of General Psychiatry* 38: 1039–1046, 1981; M. M. Weissman, K. R. Merikangas, and J. H. Boyd, "Epidemiology of Affective Disorders," in J. E. Helzer and S. B. Guze (eds.), *Psychiatry. Vol. 2: Psychoses, Affective Disorders, and Dementia* (New York: Basic Books, 1986), pp. 105–118.

25. M. Shepherd, "Historical epidemiology and the functional psychoses," *Psychological Medicine* 23: 301–304, 1993.

26. Winifred F. Courtney, *Young Charles Lamb, 1775–1802* (New York: New York University Press, 1982), pp. 108, 110, quoting Lamb's letters to Coleridge.

27. Ibid., pp. 114, 115.

28. John Haslam, *Observations on Madness and Melancholy* (London: Callow, 1809), pp. 33, 37, 42–44.

29. Ibid., pp. 159–161.

30. J. Baillarger, "De la folie à double forme," *Annales Medico-Psychologiques* 6: 367–391, 1854, as cited in F. K. Goodwin and K. R. Jamison (eds.), *Manic-Depressive Illness* (New York: Oxford University Press, 1990), p. 59.

31. Emil Kraepelin, *Manic-Depressive Insanity and Paranoia* (1896), G. M. Robertson (ed.), R. M. Barclay (trans.) (New York: Arno Press, 1976; reprint of 1921 edition), p. 1.

32. Pliny Earle, "Popular fallacies in regard to insanity and the insane," *Journal of Social Science* 26: 107–117, 1890.

33. U.S. Bureau of the Census, *Insane and Feeble-Minded in Institutions, 1910* (Washington, D.C.: Government Printing Office, 1914).

34. E. S. Gershon, J. H. Hamovit, J. J. Guroff, et al., "Birth-cohort changes in manic and depressive disorders in relatives of bipolar and schizoaffective patients," *Archives of General Psychiatry* 44: 314–319, 1987. See also E. S. Gershon, "Genetics," in F. K. Goodwin and K. R. Jamison (eds.), *Manic-Depressive Illness* (New York: Oxford University Press, 1990), pp. 373–401.

35. K. Lasch, M. Weissman, P. Wickramaratne, et al., "Birth-cohort changes in the rates of mania," *Psychiatry Research* 33: 31–37, 1990.

36. J. Angst, "Switch from depression to mania—a record study over decades between 1920 and 1982," *Psychopathology* 18: 140–154, 1985.

37. See, for example, G. L. Klerman, and M. M. Weissman, "Increasing rates of depression," *JAMA,* 261: 2229–2235, 1989; Cross-National Collaborative Group, "The changing rate of major depression: Cross-national comparisons," *JAMA* 268: 3098–3105, 1992.

38. R. J. Wyatt and I. Henter, "An economic evaluation of manic-depressive illness—1991," *Social Psychiatry and Psychiatric Epidemiology* 30: 213–219, 1995.

39. S. Durrenberger, T. Rogers, R. Walker, et al., "The high costs of care for four patients with mania who were not compliant with treatment," *Psychiatric Services* 50: 1539–1542, 1999.

40. *Annual Statistical Supplement to the Social Security Bulletin* (Washington, D.C.: Social Security Administration, 1986 and 1999).

Chapter 2

1. Roy Porter, *The Faber Book of Madness* (London: Faber and Faber, 1991), pp. 12–13, quoting Pinel.

2. Emil Kraepelin, *Manic-Depressive Insanity and Paranoia* (1896), G. M. Robertson (ed.), R. M. Barclay (trans.) (New York: Arno Press, 1976; reprint of 1921 edition), p. 22.

3. From *An Unquiet Mind* by Kay Jamison, copyright ©1995 by Kay Redfield Jamison. Used by permission of Alfred A. Knopf, a division of Random House, Inc.

4. Kay R. Jamison, *Touched with Fire: Manic-Depressive Illness and the Artistic Temperament* (New York: Free Press, 1993), p. 28.

5. Kraepelin, *Manic-Depressive Insanity and Paranoia*, p. 55.

6. Bill Lichtenstein, "Telling our stories," *CAMI Journal* 6: 41, 1995.

7. John Custance, *Wisdom, Madness, and Folly: The Philosophy of a Lunatic* (New York: Pellegrini and Cudahy, 1952), pp. 31–32, 37, 41, 46.

8. Rosalynn Carter, *Helping Someone with Mental Illness: A Compassionate Guide for Family, Friends, and Caregivers* (New York: Times Books, 1998), p. 45.

9. Lewis Wolpert, *Malignant Sadness: The Anatomy of Depression* (New York: Free Press, 1999), p. 26.

10. Jamison, *An Unquiet Mind*, pp. 37, 79.

11. Ibid., pp. 90–92.

12. Kraepelin, *Manic-Depressive Insanity and Paranoia*, p. 56.

13. Jim Piersall and Al Hirshberg, *Fear Strikes Out: The Jim Piersall Story* (Boston: Little, Brown and Co., 1955; republished by the University of Nebraska Press, 1999), p. 174.

14. K. T. Mueser, C. Webb, M. Pfeiffer, et al., "Family burden of schizophrenia and bipolar disorder: Perceptions of relatives and professionals," *Psychiatric Services* 47: 507–511, 1996.

15. John Haslam, *Observations on Madness and Melancholy* (London: Callow, 1809), p. 41.

16. Kraepelin, *Manic-Depressive Insanity and Paranoia*, p. 6.

17. Sylvia Nasar, *A Beautiful Mind: A Biography of John Forbes Nash, Jr., Winner of the Nobel Prize in Economics, 1994* (New York: Simon and Schuster, 1998; paperback by Touchstone Books, 1999), p. 136, quoting Paul Samuelson about Weiner.

18. Kraepelin, *Manic-Depressive Insanity and Paranoia*, p. 14.

19. Jamison, *An Unquiet Mind*, pp. 67, 72.

20. Kraepelin, *Manic-Depressive Insanity and Paranoia*, p. 13.

21. Ibid., p. 15.

22. Reprinted with permission from *Daughter of the Queen of Sheba* by Jacki Lyden, Hodder Headline 1999. (New York: Houghton Mifflin, 1997; paperback by Penguin Books, 1998), p. 35.

23. Kraepelin, *Manic-Depressive Insanity and Paranoia*, pp. 31, 61.

24. From *A Brilliant Madness: Living with Manic-Depressive Illness* by Patty Duke and Gloria Hochman, copyright © 1992 by Patty Duke. Used by permission of Bantam Books, a division of Random House, Inc., p. 132. (Hereafter referred to as Duke, *A Brilliant Madness*.)

25. Custance, *Wisdom, Madness, and Folly*, p. 30.

26. Samuel Beckett, *Not I*, in *Collected Shorter Plays* (New York: Grove/Atlantic, Inc., 1984), p. 220.

27. Custance, *Wisdom, Madness, and Folly*, p. 44.

28. Jamison, *An Unquiet Mind*, p. 67.

29. Haslam, *Observations on Madness and Melancholy*, p. 42.

30. Demetri Papolos and Janice Papolos, *Overcoming Depression*, 3rd ed. (New York: HarperPerennial, 1997), p. 28, quoting Yancey.

31. Duke, *A Brilliant Madness*, p. 18.

32. Kraepelin, *Manic-Depressive Insanity and Paranoia*, p. 21.

33. Lyden, *Daughter of the Queen of Sheba*, p. 176.

34. M. A. Taylor and R. Abrams, "The phenomenology of mania: A new look at some old patients," *Archives of General Psychiatry* 29: 520–522, 1973.

35. R. Freedman and P. J. Schwab, "Paranoid symptoms in patients on a general hospital psychiatric unit," *Archives of General Psychiatry* 35: 387–390, 1978.

36. Kraepelin, *Manic-Depressive Insanity and Paranoia*, p. 57.

37. Duke, *A Brilliant Madness*, p. 13.

38. Kraepelin, *Manic-Depressive Insanity and Paranoia*, p. 27.

39. Jamison, *An Unquiet Mind*, p. 74.

40. Duke, *A Brilliant Madness*, p. 28.

41. Jamison, *An Unquiet Mind*, p. 67.

42. Custance, *Wisdom, Madness, and Folly*, pp. 44, 48.

43. Alan A. Stone and Sue Smart Stone, *The Abnormal Personality Through Literature* (Englewood Cliffs, N.J.: Prentice-Hall, 1966), p. 106.

44. Kraepelin, *Manic-Depressive Insanity and Paranoia*, p. 66.

45. Wolpert, *Malignant Sadness*, p. 27.

46. Duke, *A Brilliant Madness*, p. 18.

47. Kraepelin, *Manic-Depressive Insanity and Paranoia*, p. 58.

48. Piersall, *Fear Strikes Out*, pp. 157, 173, 178.

49. Kraepelin, *Manic-Depressive Insanity and Paranoia*, p. 6.

50. William Styron, *Darkness Visible: A Memoir of Madness* (New York: Vintage Books, 1990), p. 44.

51. Ibid., p. 43.

52. Martha Manning, *Undercurrents: A Therapist's Reckoning with Her Own Depression* (New York: HarperCollins, 1994), p. 56.

53. Jamison, *An Unquiet Mind*, p. 217.

54. Ibid., p. 110.

55. Kraepelin, *Manic-Depressive Insanity and Paranoia*, p. 75.

56. Manning, *Undercurrents*, p. 112.

57. Ibid., p. 88.

58. Percy Knauth, *A Season in Hell* (New York: Harper and Row, 1975), p. 6.

59. Quoted in Peter Whybrow, *A Mood Apart: The Thinker's Guide to Emotion and Its Disorders* (New York: BasicBooks, 1997; paperback by HarperCollins, 1998), p. 23.

60. Wolpert, *Malignant Sadness*, p. 129.

61. Manning, *Undercurrents*, p. 70.

62. Kay R. Jamison, *Night Falls Fast: Understanding Suicide* (New York: A. A. Knopf, 1999), p. 84, quoting Jarrell.

63. Excerpt from "The Sickness Unto Death," from *The Awful Rowing Toward God*, by Anne Sexton. Copyright © 1975 by Loring Conant Jr., executor of the Estate of Anne Sexton. Reprinted by permission of Houghton Mifflin Company. All rights reserved.

64. Wolpert, *Malignant Sadness*, p. 61.

65. Tracy Thompson, *The Beast: A Journey Through Depression* (New York: Plume, 1995), p. 3.

66. Styron, *Darkness Visible*, p. 17.

67. Manning, *Undercurrents*, p. 99.

68. Styron, *Darkness Visible*, p. 37.

69. Ibid., p. 58.

70. Kraepelin, *Manic-Depressive Insanity and Paranoia*, pp. 6, 16.

71. Styron, *Darkness Visible*, p. 14.

72. Wolpert, *Malignant Sadness*, p. 156.

73. Thompson, *The Beast*, p. 11.

74. Knauth, *A Season in Hell*, p. 50.

75. Thompson, *The Beast*, p. 145.

76. Bert Kaplan, *The Inner World of Mental Illness* (New York: Harper and Row, 1964), p. 84, quoting Brooks.

77. Styron, *Darkness Visible*, pp. 50, 53.

78. Wolpert, *Malignant Sadness*, p. 65, quoting Tolstoy.

79. Alfred Alvarez, *The Savage God: A Study of Suicide* (New York: W. W. Norton, 1990; originally published in 1971), pp. 103, 269, 291.

80. Emily Dickinson, "After Great Pain," poem no. 341, ca. 1862. Reprinted by permission of the publishers and the Trustees of Amherst College from *The Poems of Emily Dickinson*, Ralph W. Franklin, ed., Cambridge, Mass.: The Belknap Press of Harvard University Press, Copyright 1998 by the President and Fellows of Harvard College. Copyright 1951, 1955, 1979 by the President and Fellows of Harvard College.

81. Kraepelin, *Manic-Depressive Insanity and Paranoia*, p. 82.

82. Knauth, *A Season in Hell*, p. 35.

83. Styron, *Darkness Visible*, p. 5.

84. Jamison, *An Unquiet Mind*, p. 110.

85. Kraepelin, *Manic-Depressive Insanity and Paranoia*, pp. 36, 77.

86. Manning, *Undercurrents*, p. 107.

87. Styron, *Darkness Visible*, p. 18.

88. Wolpert, *Malignant Sadness*, p. 155.

89. Ibid., p. 3, quoting Solomon.

90. Dru Ann McCain, "Consumer Column," *Yuma, Arizona, AMI Newsletter*, March 1994.

91. Kraepelin, *Manic-Depressive Insanity and Paranoia*, p. 37.

92. Ibid., p. 80.

93. Ibid., p. 115.

94. Ibid., pp. 99–100.

95. Ibid., p. 99.

96. Ibid., p. 104.

97. Jamison, *An Unquiet Mind*, p. 45.

98. Kraepelin, *Manic-Depressive Insanity and Paranoia*, p. 39.

99. S. C. Dilsaver, Y. R. Chen, A. M. Shoaib, et al., "Phenomenology of mania: Evidence for distinct depressed, dysphoric, and euphoric presentations," *American Journal of Psychiatry* 156: 426–430, 1999.

100. Sheila Marie La Polla, "I am a survivor!" *California AMI Journal* 6: 49–51, 1995.

101. J. T. Dalby, "Elizabethan madness on London's stage," *Psychological Reports* 81: 1331–1343, 1997, quoting from Dekker's play.

102. "Confinement of the insane," *American Law Review* 3: 215, 1869.

103. X. F. Amador, M. Flaum, N. C. Andreasen, et al., "Awareness of illness in schizophrenia and schizoaffective and mood disorders," *Archives of General Psychiatry* 51: 826–836, 1994; A. Michalakeas, C. Skoutas, A. Charalambous, et al., "Insight in schizophrenia and mood disorders and its relation to psychopathology," *Acta Psychiatrica Scandinavica* 90: 46–49, 1994; C. L. Swanson, O. Freudenreich, J. P. McEvoy, et al., "Insight in schizophrenia and mania," *Journal of Nervous and Mental Disease* 183: 752–755, 1995; S. Fennig, E. Everett, E. J. Bromet, et al., "Insight in first-admission psychotic patients," *Schizophrenia Research* 22: 257–263, 1996; S. Pallanti, L. Quercioli, A. Pazzagli, et al., "Awareness of illness and subjective experience of cognitive complaints in patients with bipolar I and bipolar II disorder," *American Journal of Psychiatry* 156: 1094–1096, 1999; S. N. Ghaemi, E. Boiman, and F. K. Goodwin, "Insight and outcome in bipolar, unipolar, and anxiety disorders," *Comprehensive Psychiatry* 41: 167–171, 2000; M. Weiler, M. H. Fleisher, and D. McArthur-Campbell, "Insight and symptom change in schizophrenia and other disorders," *Schizophrenia Research* 45: 29–36, 2000; S. Pini, G. B. Cassano, L. Dell'Osso, et al., "Insight into illness in schizophrenia, schizoaffective and mood disorders with psychotic features," *American Journal of Psychiatry* 158: 122–125, 2001.

104. S. Pallanti, L. Quercioli, A. Pazzagli, et al., "Awareness of illness and subjective experience of cognitive complaints in patients with bipolar I and bipolar II disorder."

105. X. F. Amador, M. Flaum, N. C. Andreasen, et al., "Awareness of illness in schizophrenia and schizoaffective and mood disorders"; A. Michalakeas, C. Skoutas, A. Charalambous, et al., "Insight in schizophrenia and mood disorders and its relation to psychopathology"; S. Fennig, E. Everett, E. J. Bromet, et al., "Insight in first-admission psychotic patients"; S. N. Ghaemi, E. Boiman, and F. K. Goodwin, "Insight and outcome in bipolar, unipolar, and anxiety disorder."

106. Kraepelin, *Manic-Depressive Insanity and Paranoia,* pp. 22, 60.

107. Thompson, *The Beast,* p. 112.

108. Mueser et al., "Family burden of schizophrenia and bipolar disorder."

Chapter 3

1. John Haslam, *Observations on Madness and Melancholy* (London: Callow, 1809), p. 230.

2. American Psychiatric Association, *Diagnostic and Statistical Manual of Mental Disorders, Fourth Edition* (Washington, D.C.: American Psychiatric Association, 1994).

3. C. Krauthammer and G. L. Klerman, "The epidemiology of mania," in B. Shopshin (ed.), *Manic Illness* (New York: Raven Press, 1979), pp. 11–28.

4. F. K. Goodwin and K. R. Jamison, *Manic-Depressive Illness* (New York: Oxford University Press, 1990), p. 80.

5. R. T. Joffe, L. T. Young, and G. M. MacQueen, "A two-illness model of bipolar disorder," *Bipolar Disorders* 1: 25–30, 1999.

6. E. F. Torrey, R. R. Rawlings, J. M. Ennis, et al., "Birth seasonality in bipolar disorder, schizophrenia, schizoaffective disorder and stillbirths," *Schizophrenia Research* 21: 141–149, 1996.

7. Samuel H. Barondes, *Mood Genes: Hunting for the Origins of Mania and Depression* (New York: Oxford University Press), p. 45.

8. C. L. Bowden, "Classification of bipolar and related disorders: Implications for biological research in this field," in J. C. Soares and S. Gershon (eds.), *Bipolar Disorders: Basic Mechanisms and Therapeutic Implications* (Monticello, N.Y.: Marcel Dekker, Inc., 2000), p. 5.

9. M. B. Knable, E. F. Torrey, M. J. Webster, et al., "Multivariate analysis of prefrontal cortical data from the Stanley Foundation Neuropathology Consortium," *Brain Research Bulletin,* in press.

10. H. S. Akiskal, "The prevalent clinical spectrum of bipolar disorders: Beyond DSM-IV," *Journal of Clinical Psychopharmacology* 16 (Suppl. 1): 4S–14S, 1996.

11. Ibid.

12. Peter Whybrow, *A Mood Apart: The Thinker's Guide to Emotion and Its Disorders* (New York: BasicBooks, 1997; paperback by HarperCollins, 1998), p. 108.

13. R. J. Baldessarini, "A plea for integrity of the bipolar disorder concept," *Bipolar Disorders* 2: 3–7, 2000.

14. From *A Brilliant Madness: Living with Manic-Depressive Illness* by Patty Duke and Gloria Hochman, copyright © 1992 by Patty Duke. Used by permission of Bantam Books, a division of Random House, Inc., 213.

15. C. O. Cheney, "Clinical data on general paresis," *Psychiatric Quarterly* 9: 467–485, 1935.

16. E. F. Torrey and M. B. Knable, "Are schizophrenia and bipolar disorder one disease or two? Introduction to the symposium," *Schizophrenia Research* 39: 93–94, 1999.

Chapter 4

1. John Milton, *Paradise Lost* (XI, line 485), 1667.

2. C. Stasiek and M. Zetin, "Organic manic disorders," *Psychosomatics* 26: 394–402, 1985.

3. J. L. Katz, "A psychotic manic state induced by a herbal preparation," *Psychosomatics* 41: 73–74, 2000.

4. A. Meijer, Z. Zakay-Rones, and A. Morag, "Post-influenzal psychiatric disorder in adolescents," *Acta Psychiatrica Scandinavica* 78: 176–181, 1988.

5. D. Steinberg, S. R. Hirsch, S. D. Marston, et al., "Influenza infection causing manic psychosis," *British Journal of Psychiatry* 120: 531–535, 1972.

6. E. A. Weinstein, L. Linn, and R. L. Kahn, "Encephalitis with a clinical picture of schizophrenia," *Journal of the Mount Sinai Hospital* 21: 341–354, 1955.

7. K. Koehler and W. Guth, "The mimicking of mania in 'benign' herpes simplex encephalitis," *Biological Psychiatry* 14: 405–411, 1979.

8. K. N. Wiesert and H. C. Hendrie, "Secondary mania: A case report," *American Journal of Psychiatry* 134: 929–930, 1977.

9. K. Myers and D. L. Dunner, "Acute viral encephalitis complicating a first manic episode," *Journal of Family Practice* 18: 403–407, 1984.

10. N. Buhrich, D. A. Cooper, and E. Freed, "HIV infection associated with symptoms indistinguishable from functional psychosis," *British Journal of Psychiatry* 152: 649–653, 1988.

11. S. Moor and H. Skrine, "Psychosis in mycoplasma infection," *Postgraduate Medical Journal* 65: 96–97, 1989.

12. O. J. Thienhaus and N. Khosla, "Meningeal cryptococcosis misdiagnosed as a manic episode," *American Journal of Psychiatry* 141: 1459–1460, 1984.

13. G. Mapelli and T. Bellelli, "Secondary mania" (letter), *Archives of General Psychiatry* 39: 743, 1982.

14. R. B. Schwartz, "Manic psychosis in connection with Q-fever," *British Journal of Psychiatry* 124: 140–143, 1974.

15. S. Shukla, B. L. Cook, S. Mukherjee, et al., "Mania following head trauma," *American Journal of Psychiatry* 144: 93–96, 1987.

16. T. W. McAllister, "Neuropsychiatric sequelae of head injuries," *Psychiatric Clinics of North America* 15: 395–413, 1992.

17. W. A. Lishman, *Organic Psychiatry* (Oxford: Blackwell Scientific Publications, 1978), p. 234, citing the 1967 study by Achte et al.

18. R. E. Jorge, R. G. Robinson, S. E. Starkstein, et al., "Secondary mania following traumatic brain injury," *American Journal of Psychiatry* 150: 916–921, 1993.

19. W. A. Lishman, "Brain damage in relation to psychiatric disability after head injury," *British Journal of Psychiatry* 114: 373–410, 1968.

20. J. A. Wilcox and H. A. Nasrallah, "Childhood head trauma and psychosis," *Psychiatry Research* 21: 303–306, 1987.

21. P. B. Mortensen, O. Mors, M. Frydenberg, et al., "Head injury as a risk factor for bipolar disorder," submitted manuscript.

22. S. E. Starkstein, G. D. Pearlson, J. Boston, et al., "Mania after brain injury: A controlled study of causative factors," *Archives of Neurology* 44: 1069–1073, 1987.

23. M. R. Cohen and R. W. Niska, "Localized right cerebral hemisphere dysfunction and recurrent mania," *American Journal of Psychiatry* 137: 847–848, 1980.

24. R. L. Binder, "Neurologically silent brain tumors in psychiatric hospital admissions: Three cases and a review," *Journal of Clinical Psychiatry* 44: 94–97, 1983.

25. R. C. Jamieson and C. E. Wells, "Manic psychosis in a patient with multiple metastatic brain tumors," *Journal of Clinical Psychiatry* 40: 280–283, 1979.

26. J. R. Stevens, "Psychosis and the temporal lobe," *Advances in Neurology* 55: 79–96, 1991.

27. P. Flor-Henry, "Psychosis and temporal lobe epilepsy: A controlled investigation," *Epilepsia* 10: 363–395, 1969.

28. R. T. Joffe, G. P. Lippert, T. A. Gray, et al., "Mood disorder and multiple sclerosis," *Archives of Neurology* 44: 376–378, 1987.

29. D. S. Pine, C. J. Douglas, E. Charles, et al., "Patients with multiple sclerosis presenting to psychiatric hospitals," *Journal of Clinical Psychiatry* 56: 297–306, 1995.

30. S. E. Folstein and M. F. Folstein, "Psychiatric features of Huntington's disease: Recent approaches and findings," *Psychiatric Developments* 1: 193–205, 1983.

31. S. Villani and W. D. Weitzel, "Secondary mania," *Archives of General Psychiatry* 36: 1031, 1979.

32. F. C. Goggans, "A case of mania secondary to vitamin B12 deficiency," *American Journal of Psychiatry* 141: 300–301, 1984.

33. A. J. Cooper, "Hypomanic psychosis precipitated by hemodialysis," *Comprehensive Psychiatry* 8: 168–174, 1967.

34. R. G. Robinson and J. I. Travella, "Neuropsychiatry of mood disorders," in B. S. Fogel, R. B. Schiffer, and S. M. Rao (eds.), *Neuropsychiatry* (Baltimore: Williams and Wilkins, 1996), pp. 287–305.

35. Jorge et al., "Secondary mania following traumatic brain injury."

36. S. M. Strakowski and K. W. Sax, "Secondary mania: A model of the patho-physiology of bipolar disorder?" in J. C. Soares and S. Gershon (eds.), *Bipolar Disorders: Basic Mechanisms and Therapeutic Implications* (Monticello, N.Y.: Marcel Dekker, Inc., 2000), pp. 13–29.

37. A. Kiev, *Transcultural Psychiatry* (New York: Free Press, 1972), p. 87.

38. B. L. Cook, S. Shukla, A. L. Hoff, et al., "Mania with associated organic factors," *Acta Psychiatrica Scandinavica* 76: 674–677, 1987.

39. Robert L. Taylor, *Distinguishing Psychological from Organic Disorders: Screening for Psychological Masquerade* (New York: Springer Publishing Company, 2000).

40. H. C. Sox, L. M. Sox, C. H. Sox, et al., "A medical algorithm for detecting physical disease in psychiatric patients," *Hospital and Community Psychiatry* 40: 1270–1274, 1989.

Chapter 5

1. From *John Milton: Complete Poems and Major Prose*, Merritt Y. Hughes (ed.) (New York: Odyssey Press, 1957).

2. P. Dalén, *Season of Birth: A Study of Schizophrenia and Other Mental Disorders* (New York: North-Holland/American Elsevier, 1975), p. 92.

3. E. H. Hare, J. Price, and E. Slater, "Mental disorder and season of birth: A national sample compared with the general population," *British Journal of Psychiatry* 124: 81–86, 1974; E. H. Hare, "Manic-depressive psychosis and season of birth," *Acta Psychiatrica Scandinavica* 52: 69–79, 1975; E. H. Hare, "Epidemiological Evidence for a Viral Factor in the Aetiology of the Functional Psychoses," in P. V. Morozov (ed.), *Research on the Viral Hypothesis of Mental Disorders* (New York: Karger, 1983), pp. 52–75.

4. E. F. Torrey, R. R. Rawlings, J. M. Ennis, et al., "Birth seasonality in bipolar disorder, schizophrenia, schizoaffective disorder and stillbirths," *Schizophrenia Research* 21: 141–149, 1996.

5. Y. Mino, I. Oshima, and K. Okagami, "Seasonality of birth in patients with mood disorders in Japan," *Journal of Affective Disorders* 59: 41–46, 2000.

6. M. Clarke, F. Keogh, P. T. Murphy, et al., "Seasonality of births in affective disorder in an Irish population," *European Psychiatry* 13: 353–358, 1998.

7. H. C. Deng, H. F. Huang, C. J. Tsai, et al., "Seasonality of birth of affective disorders among Chinese in Taiwan" (abstract), *Biological Psychiatry* 33, 73A, 1993.

8. D. Dassa, J. M. Azorin, V. Ledoray, et al., "Season of birth and schizophrenia: Sex difference," *Progress in Neuro-psychopharmacology and Biological Psychiatry* 20: 243–251, 1996.

9. Z. Rihmer, "Season of birth and season of hospital admission in bipolar depressed female patients," *Psychiatry Research* 3: 247–251, 1980.

10. J. E. D. Esquirol, *Mental Maladies: A Treatise on Insanity* (Paris: J. B. Gallière, 1845).

11. W. C. Hood, *Statistics of Insanity* (London: Batten, 1862).

12. J. C. Bucknill and D. H. Tuke, *A Manual of Psychological Medicine* (London: Churchill, 1879).

13. E. H. Hare and S. D. Walter, "Seasonal variation in admissions of psychiatric patients and its relation to seasonal variation in their births," *Journal of Epidemiology and Community Health* 32: 47–52, 1978.

14. N. Takei, E. O'Callaghan, P. Sham, et al., "Seasonality of admissions in the psychoses: Effect of diagnosis, sex, and age at onset," *British Journal of Psychiatry* 161: 506–511, 1992.

15. M. Clarke, P. Moran, F. Keogh, et al., "Seasonal influences on admissions in schizophrenia and affective disorder in Ireland," *Schizophrenia Research* 34: 143–149, 1998.

16. G. Parker and S. Walter, "Seasonal variation in depressive disorders and suicidal deaths in New South Wales," *British Journal of Psychiatry* 140: 626–632, 1982; R. T. Mulder, J. P. Cosgriff, A. M. Smith, et al., "Seasonality of mania in New Zealand," *Australian and New Zealand Journal of Psychiatry* 24: 187–190, 1990; H. K. Sayer, S. Marshall, and G. W. Mellsop, "Mania and seasonality in the Southern Hemisphere," *Journal of Affective Disorders* 23: 151–156, 1991; I. Jones, H. Hornsby, and D. Hay, "Seasonality of mania: A Tasmanian study," *Australian and New Zealand Journal of Psychiatry* 29: 449–453, 1995.

17. D. L. Dix, "Praying a grant of land for the relief and support of the indigent and incurable insane in the United States," 1848, cited in R. Porter (ed.), *The Faber Book of Madness* (Boston: Faber and Faber, 1991), p. 8.

18. G. Lewis, A. David, S. Andreasson, et al., "Schizophrenia and city life," *Lancet* 340: 137–140, 1992; N. Takei, P. C. Sham, E. O'Callaghan, et al., "Schizophrenia: Increased risk associated with winter and city birth—a case-controlled study in 12 regions within England and Wales," *Journal of Epidemiology and Community Health* 49: 106–109, 1995; K. S. Kendler, T. J. Gallagher, J. M. Abelson, et al., "Lifetime prevalence, demographic risk factors, and diagnostic validity of nonaffective psychosis as assessed in a US community sample," *Archives of General Psychiatry* 53: 1022–1031, 1996; H. Verdoux, N. Takei, R. Cassou de Saint-Mathurin, et al., Seasonality of birth in schizophrenia: The effect of regional population density, *Schizophrenia Research* 25: 175–180, 1997; E. F. Torrey, A. E. Bowler, and K. Clark, "Urban birth and residence as risk factors for psychoses: An analysis of 1880 data," *Schizophrenia Research* 25: 169–176, 1997; M. Marcelis and J. van Os, "High rates of psychosis in urban areas: Effect of urban birth or residence?" (abstract), *Schizophrenia Research* 29: 27, 1998; P. B. Mortenson, C. B. Pederson, T. Westergaard, et al., "Effects of family history and place and season of birth on the risk of schizophrenia," *New England Journal of Medicine* 340: 603–608, 1999; E. F. Torrey, R. Rawlings, and

R. H. Yolken, "The antecedents of psychosis: A case-controlled study of selected risk factors," *Schizophrenia Research* 46: 17–23, 2000.

19. M. Weissman, M. L. Bruce, P. J. Leaf, et al., "Affective Disorders," in L. N. Robins and D. A. Regier (eds.), *Psychiatric Disorders in America: The Epidemiologic Catchment Area Study* (New York: Free Press, 1991), p. 76.

20. M. Marcelis, F. Navarro-Mateu, R. Murray, et al., "Urbanization and psychosis: A study of 1942–1978 birth cohorts in The Netherlands," *Psychological Medicine* 28: 871–879, 1998.

21. W. W. Eaton, P. B. Mortensen, and M. Frydenberg, "Obstetric factors, urbanization and psychosis," *Schizophrenia Research* 43: 117–123, 2000.

22. D. K. Kinney, D. A. Yurgelun-Todd, D. L. Levy, et al., "Obstetrical complications in patients with bipolar disorder and their siblings," *Psychiatry Research* 48: 47–56, 1993; D. K. Kinney, D. A. Yurgelun-Todd, M. Tohen, et al., "Pre- and perinatal complications and risk for bipolar disorder: A retrospective study," *Journal of Affective Disorders* 50: 117–124, 1998.

23. B. Gutiérrez, J. Van Os, V. Vallès, et al., "Congenital dermatoglyphic malformations in severe bipolar disorder," *Psychiatry Research* 78: 133–140, 1998; N. Jelovac, J. Milicic, M. Milas, et al., "Dermatoglyphic analysis in bipolar affective disorder and schizophrenia: 'Continuum of psychosis' hypothesis corroborated?" *Collegium Antropologicum* 23: 589–595, 1999.

24. E. Susser, R. Neugebauer, H. W. Hoek, et al., "Schizophrenia after prenatal famine: Further evidence," *Archives of General Psychiatry* 53: 25–31, 1996.

25. A. S. Brown, J. Van Os, C. Driessens, et al., "Further evidence of relation between prenatal famine and major affective disorder," *American Journal of Psychiatry* 157: 190–195, 2000.

26. N. E. Takei, O'Callaghan, P. C. Sham, et al., "Does prenatal influenza divert susceptible females from later affective psychosis to schizophrenia?" *Acta Psychiatrica Scandinavica* 88: 328–336, 1993; A. S. Brown, E. S. Susser, S. P. Lin, et al., "Affective disorders in Holland after prenatal exposure to the 1957 A_2 influenza epidemic," *Biological Psychiatry* 38: 270–273, 1995; A. Sacker, D. J. Done, T. J. Crow, et al., "Antecedents of schizophrenia and affective illness: Obstetric complications," *British Journal of Psychiatry* 166: 734–741, 1995; R. A. Machón, S. A. Mednick, and M. O. Huttunen, "Adult major affective disorder after prenatal exposure to an influenza epidemic," *Archives of General Psychiatry* 54: 322–328, 1997; V. Morgan, D. Castle, A. Page, et al., "Influenza epidemics and incidence of schizophrenia, affective disorders and mental retardation in Western Australia: No evidence of a major effect," *Schizophrenia Research* 26: 25–39, 1997; J. Welham, J. McGrath, and M. Pemberton, "Affective psychoses and the influenza epidemics of 1954, 1957, and 1959" (abstract), *Schizophrenia Research* 29: 19, 1998.

27. M. Hyun, S. D. Friedman, and D. L. Dunner, "Relationship of childhood physical and sexual abuse to adult bipolar disorder," *Bipolar Disorders* 2: 131–135, 2000.

28. G. S. Leverich, S. L. McElroy, T. Suppes, et al., "The role of early physical or sexual abuse on the course of bipolar illness" (abstract), *Acta Neuropsychiatrica*, 12: 162, 2000.

29. R. A. Knox, "Bean-Bayog Case Focuses on Credibility of the Patient," *Boston Globe,* September 29, 1992, pp. 1, 11, quoting McHugh.

30. O. Agid, B. Shapira, J. Zislin, et al., "Environment and vulnerability to major psychiatric illness: A case control study of early parental loss in major depression, bipolar disorder and schizophrenia," *Molecular Psychiatry* 4: 163–172, 1999.

31. P. B. Mortensen, C. B. Pedersen, M. Melbye, et al., "No association between urbanicity of place of birth, season of birth, sibship characteristics, or prenatal exposure to influenza and the risk of bipolar illness in Denmark," poster presentation at the Winter Workshop on Schizophrenia, Davos, Switzerland, February 2000.

32. B. Pfohl, D. Stangl, and M. T. Tsuang, "The association between early parental loss and diagnosis in the Iowa 500," *Archives of General Psychiatry* 40: 965–968, 1983; C. Perris, S. Holmgren, L. Von Knorring, et al., "Parental loss by death in the early childhood of depressed patients and of their healthy siblings," *British Journal of Psychiatry* 148: 165–169, 1986; R. Alnaes and S. Torgersen, "Mood disorders: Developmental and precipitating events," *Canadian Journal of Psychiatry* 38: 217–224, 1993; T. A. Furukawa, A. Ogura, T. Hirai, et al., "Early parental separation experiences among patients with bipolar disorder and major depression: A case-control study," *Journal of Affective Disorders* 52: 85–91, 1999.

33. F. K. Goodwin and K. R. Jamison, *Manic-Depressive Illness* (New York: Oxford University Press, 1990).

34. Ibid., p. 169.

35. M. Weissman, M. L. Bruce, P. J. Leaf, et al., "Affective Disorders," in L. N. Robins and D. A. Regier (eds.), *Psychiatric Disorders in America: The Epidemiologic Catchment Area Study* (New York: The Free Press, 1991), p. 76.

Chapter 6

1. William Shakespeare, *King Lear,* I, ii, 149.

2. J. A. Egeland, A. M. Hostetter, D. L. Pauls, et al., "Prodromal symptoms before onset of manic-depressive disorder suggested by first hospital admission histories," *Journal of the American Academy of Child and Adolescent Psychiatry* 39: 1245–1252, 2000.

3. Emil Kraepelin, *Manic-Depressive Insanity and Paranoia* (1896), G. M. Robertson (ed.), R. M. Barclay (trans.) (New York: Arno Press, 1976; reprint of 1921 edition), p. 12.

4. Michael Cunningham, *The Hours* (New York: Farrar, Straus and Giroux, 1998), p. 70.

5. Kraepelin, *Manic-Depressive Insanity and Paranoia,* p. 97.

6. R. E. Kendell, J. C. Chalmers, and C. Platz, "Epidemiology of puerperal psychoses," *British Journal of Psychiatry* 150: 662–673, 1987.

7. T. Reich and G. Winokur, "Postpartum psychoses in patients with manic depressive diseases," *Journal of Nervous and Mental Disease* 151: 60–68, 1970.

8. N. Coyle, I. Jones, E. Robertson, et al., "Variation at the serotonin transporter gene influences susceptibility to bipolar affective puerperal psychosis," *Lancet* 356: 1490–1491, 2000.

9. T. A. Wehr, "Sleep-loss as a possible mediator of diverse causes of mania," *British Journal of Psychiatry* 159: 576–578, 1991.

10. B. Barbini, S. Bertelli, C. Colombo, et al., "Sleep loss, a possible factor in augmenting manic episode," *Psychiatry Research* 65: 121–125, 1996.

11. C. Colombo, F. Benedetti, B. Barbini, et al., "Rate of switch from depression into mania after therapeutic sleep deprivation in bipolar depression," *Psychiatry Research* 86: 267–270, 1999.

12. John Haslam, *Observations on Madness and Melancholy* (London: Callow, 1809), pp. 257–258.

13. T. Suppes, E. B. Dennehy, and E. W. Gibbons, "The longitudinal course of bipolar disorder," *Journal of Clinical Psychiatry* 61 (suppl. 9): 23–30, 2000.

14. Peter Whybrow, *A Mood Apart: The Thinker's Guide to Emotion and Its Disorders* (New York: BasicBooks, 1997; paperback by HarperCollins, 1998), p. 118.

15. Suppes et al., "The longitudinal course of bipolar disorder."

16. Kraepelin, *Manic-Depressive Insanity and Paranoia.*

17. T. A. C. Rennie, "Prognosis in manic-depressive psychoses," *American Journal of Psychiatry* 98: 801–814, 1942.

18. P. E. Keck Jr., S. L. McElroy, S. M. Strakowsk, et al., "12-month outcome of patients with bipolar disorder following hospitalization for a manic or mixed episode," *American Journal of Psychiatry* 155: 646–652, 1998.

19. J. F. Goldberg, M. Harrow, and L. S. Grossman, "Course and outcome in bipolar affective disorder: A longitudinal follow-up study," *American Journal of Psychiatry* 152: 379–384, 1995.

20. S. L. Johnson and J. E. Roberts, "Life events and bipolar disorder: Implications from biological theories," *Psychological Bulletin* 117: 434–449, 1995.

21. K. S. Hall, D. L. Dunner, G. Zeller, et al., "Bipolar illness: A prospective study of life events," *Comprehensive Psychiatry* 18: 497–505, 1977.

22. H. McPherson, P. Herbison, and S. Romans, "Life events and relapse in established bipolar affective disorder," *British Journal of Psychiatry* 163: 381–385, 1993.

23. A. Ellicott, C. Hammen, M. Gitlin, et al., "Life events and the course of bipolar disorder," *American Journal of Psychiatry* 147: 1194–1198, 1990.

24. N. Hunt, W. Bruce-Jones, and T. Silverstone, "Life events and relapse in bipolar affective disorder," *Journal of Affective Disorders* 25: 13–20, 1992.

25. Ellicott et al., "Life events and the course of bipolar disorder."

26. F. K. Goodwin and K. R. Jamison, *Manic-Depressive Illness* (New York: Oxford University Press, 1990), p. 151.

27. B. P. Dembling, D. T. Chen, and L. Vachon, "Life expectancy and causes of death in a population treated for serious mental illness," *Psychiatric Services* 50: 1036–1042, 1999.

28. M. T. Tsuang, R. F. Woolson, and J. A. Fleming, "Causes of death in schizophrenia and manic-depression," *British Journal of Psychiatry* 136: 239–242, 1980; A. Weeke and M. Vaeth, "Excess mortality of bipolar and unipolar manic-depressive patients," *Journal of Affective Disorders* 11: 227–234, 1986; R. Sharma and H. R. Markar, "Mortality in affective disorder," *Journal of Affective Disorders* 31: 91–96, 1994; E. H. Høyer, P. B. Mortensen, and A. V. Olesen, "Mortality and causes of death in a total national sample of patients with affective disorders admitted for the first time between 1973 and 1993," *British Journal of Psychiatry* 176: 76–82, 2000.

Chapter 7

1. John Haslam, *Observations on Madness and Melancholy* (New York: Arno Press, 1976; originally published in 1809), p. 230.

2. H. Elkis, L. Friedman, A. Wise, et al., "Meta-analyses of studies of ventricular enlargement and cortical sulcal prominence in mood disorders: Comparisons with controls or patients with schizophrenia," *Archives of General Psychiatry* 52: 735–746, 1995.

3. S. M. Strakowski, D. R. Wilson, M. Tohen, et al., "Structural brain abnormalities in first episode mania," *Biological Psychiatry* 33: 602–609, 1993.

4. G. J. Moore, J. M. Bebchuk, I. B. Wilds, et al., "Lithium-induced increase in human brain grey matter," *Lancet* 356: 1241–1242, 2000.

5. E. A. Hoge, L. Friedman, and S. C. Schulz, "Meta-analysis of brain size in bipolar disorder," *Schizophrenia Research* 37: 177–181, 1999.

6. J. C. Soares and J. J. Mann, "The anatomy of mood disorders: Review of structural neuroimaging studies," *Biological Psychiatry* 41: 86–106, 1997.

7. L. L. Altschuler, J. G. Curran, P. Hauser, et al., "T2 hyperintensities in bipolar disorder: Magnetic resonance imaging comparison and literature meta-analysis," *American Journal of Psychiatry* 152: 1139–1144, 1995; P. Videbech, "MRI findings in patients with affective disorder: A meta-analysis," *Acta Psychiatrica Scandinavica* 96: 157–168, 1997.

8. P. B. Moore, D. J. Shepherd, D. Eccleston, et al., "Cerebral white matter lesions in bipolar affective disorder: Relationship to outcome," *British Journal of Psychiatry* 178: 172–176, 2001.

9. E. F. Torrey, M. Webster, M. Knable, et al., "The Stanley Foundation brain collection and Neuropathology Consortium," *Schizophrenia Research* 44: 151–155, 2000; M. B. Knable, E. F. Torrey, M. J. Webster, et al., "Multivariate analysis of pre-

frontal cortical data from the Stanley Foundation Neuropathology Consortium," *Brain Research Bulletin,* in press.

10. G. Rajkowska, L. D. Selemon, and P. S. Goldman-Rakic, "Marked glial neuropathology in prefrontal cortex distinguishes bipolar disorder from schizophrenia," *Schizophrenia Research* 24: 41, 1997; D. Öngür, W. C. Drevets, and J. L. Price, "Glial reduction in the subgenual prefrontal cortex in mood disorders," *Proceedings of the National Academy of Sciences USA* 95: 13290–13295, 1998.

11. H. P. Blumberg, E. Stern, S. Ricketts, et al., "Rostral and orbital prefrontal cortex dysfunction in the manic state of bipolar disorder," *American Journal of Psychiatry* 156: 1986–1988, 1999. A good review of functional neuroimaging in manic-depressive illness is currently lacking, but this paper gives a fairly complete list of references to other studies.

12. S. Shukla, B. L. Cook, S. Mukherjee, et al., "Mania following head trauma," *American Journal of Psychiatry* 144: 93–96, 1987; S. E. Starkstein, G. D. Pearlson, J. Boston, et al., "Mania after brain injury: A controlled study of causative factors," *Archives of Neurology* 44: 1069–1073, 1987; E. W. Larson and E. Richelson, "Organic causes of mania," *Mayo Clinic Proceedings* 63: 906–912, 1988.

13. H. A. Nasrallah, J. Tippin, and M. McCalley-Whitters, "Neurological soft signs in manic patients," *Journal of Affective Disorders* 5: 45–50, 1983.

14. H. A. Sackheim and B. L. Steif, "Neuropsychology of Depression and Mania," in A. Georgotas and R. Cancro (eds.), *Depression and Mania* (New York: Elsevier, 1988), pp. 265–289.

15. R. E. Hoffman, "Computer simulations of neural information processing and the schizophrenia-mania dichotomy," *Archives of General Psychiatry* 44: 178–188, 1987.

16. M. L. Gourovitch, E. F. Torrey, J. M. Gold, et al., "Neuropsychological performance of monozygotic twins discordant for bipolar disorder," *Biological Psychiatry* 45: 639–646, 1999.

17. T. E. Goldberg, "Some fairly obvious distinctions between schizophrenia and bipolar disorder," *Schizophrenia Research* 39: 127–132, 1999.

18. W. S. Musser, "Electroencephalogram Abnormalities in Bipolar Disorder," in J. C. Soares and S. Gershon (eds.), *Bipolar Disorders: Basic Mechanisms and Therapeutic Implications* (New York: Marcel Dekker, 2000), pp. 343–351.

19. D. F. Salisbury, M. E. Shenton, and R. W. McCarley, "P300 topography differs in schizophrenia and manic psychosis," *Biological Psychiatry* 45: 98–106, 1999.

20. A. Bertelsen, B. Harvald, and M. Hauge, "A Danish twin study of manic-depressive disorders," *British Journal of Psychiatry* 130: 330–351, 1977.

21. Ibid.; K. R. Jamison, "Manic-Depressive Illness, Genes, and Creativity," in L. L. Hall (ed.), *Genetics and Mental Illness: Evolving Issues for Research and Society* (New York: Plenum Press, 1996), pp. 111–132.

22. A. G. Cardno, E. J. Marshall, B. Coid, et al., "Heritability estimates for psychotic disorders," *Archives of General Psychiatry* 56: 162–168, 1999.

23. T. Kieseppä, T. Partonen, J. Kaprio, et al., "Bipolar I disorder in a large sample of Finnish twins," submitted for publication.

24. J. Mendlewicz and J. D. Rainer, "Adoption study supporting genetic transmission in manic-depressive illness," *Nature* 268: 327–329, 1977.

25. E. S. Gershon, "Genetics," in F. K. Goodwin and K. R. Jamison (eds.), *Manic-Depressive Illness* (New York: Oxford University Press, 1990), pp. 376–386.

26. K. S. Kendler, L. M. Karkowski, and D. Walsh, "The structure of psychosis: Latent class analysis of probands from the Roscommon Family Study," *Archives of General Psychiatry* 55: 492–498, 1998.

27. W. H. Berrettini, "Genetics of psychiatric disease," *Annual Review of Medicine* 51: 465–479, 2000.

28. Samuel H. Barondes, *Mood Genes: Hunting for Origins of Mania and Depression* (New York: Oxford University Press, 1998), p. 172.

29. Both quotes are from Kay Jamison, *Night Falls Fast: Understanding Suicide* (New York: A. A. Knopf, 1999), p. 180.

30. Ronald R. Fieve, *Moodswing* (New York: Bantam Books, 1997), p. 80.

31. Barondes, *Mood Genes.*

32. N. Risch and David Botstein, "A manic depressive history," *Nature Genetics* 12: 351–353, 1996.

33. A. Anand and D. S. Charney, "Abnormalities in Catecholamines and Pathophysiology of Bipolar Disorder," in J. C. Soares and S. Gershon (eds.), *Bipolar Disorders: Basic Mechanisms and Therapeutic Implications* (New York: Marcel Dekker, 2000), pp. 59–94.

34. W. H. Berrettini, J. I. Nurnberger, T. A. Hare, et al., "Reduced plasma and CSF gamma-aminobutryic acid in affective illness: Effect of lithium carbonate," *Biological Psychiatry* 18: 185–194, 1983; R. H. Gerner, L. Fairbanks, G. M. Anderson, et al., "CSF neurochemistry in depressed, manic, and schizophrenic patients compared with that of normal controls," *American Journal of Psychiatry* 141: 1533–1540, 1984; F. Petty, A. J. Rush, J. M. Davis, et al., "Plasma GABA predicts acute response to divalproex in mania," *Biological Psychiatry* 39: 278–284, 1996.

35. Anand and Charney, "Abnormalities in Catecholamines and Pathophysiology of Bipolar Disorder."

36. M. E. Winsberg, N. Sachs, D. L. Tate, et al., "Decreased dorsolateral prefrontal N-actyl aspartate in bipolar disorder," *Biological Psychiatry* 47: 475–481, 2000.

37. T. Kato, S. Takahashi, T. Shiori, et al., "Alterations in brain phosphorous metabolism in bipolar disorder detected by in vivo ^{31}P and ^{7}Li magnetic resonance spectroscopy," *Journal of Affective Disorders* 27: 53–59, 1993; T. Kato, H. Hamakawa, and T. Shioiri, "Choline containing compounds detected by proton magnetic resonance spectroscopy in the basal ganglia in bipolar disorder," *Journal of Psychiatry and Neuroscience* 21: 248–254, 1996; G. J. Moore, J. M. Bebchuk, J. K.

Parrish, et al., "Temporal dissociation between lithium-induced changes in frontal lobe myo-inositol and clinical response in manic-depressive illness," *American Journal of Psychiatry* 156: 1902–1908, 1999; H. K. Manji and R. H. Lenox, "Protein kinase C signaling in the brain: Molecular transduction of mood stabilization in the treatment of manic-depressive illness," *Biological Psychiatry* 46: 1328–1351, 1999; C.-G. Hahn and E. Friedman, "Abnormalities in protein kinase C signaling and the pathophysiology of bipolar disorder," *Bipolar Disorders* 2: 81–86, 1999.

38. J. D. Amsterdam, G. Maislin, and J. Rybakowski, "A possible antiviral action of lithium carbonate in herpes simplex virus infections," *Biological Psychiatry* 27: 447–453, 1990.

39. Z. F. Fu, J. D. Amsterdam, M. Kao, et al., "Detection of Borna disease virus-reactive antibodies from patients with affective disorders by Western immunoblot technique," *Journal of Affective Disorders* 27: 61–68, 1993.

40. R. H. Yolken and E. F. Torrey, "Hypothesis of a Viral Etiology in Bipolar Disorder," in J. C. Soares and S. Gershon (eds.), *Bipolar Disorders: Basic Mechanisms and Therapeutic Implications* (New York: Marcel Dekker, 2000).

41. S. L. Buka, M. T. Tsuang, E. F. Torrey, et al., "Maternal infections and subsequent psychosis among offspring," *Archives of General Psychiatry*, in press.

42. M. H. Rapaport, "Immune parameters in euthymic bipolar patients and normal volunteers," *Journal of Affective Disorders* 32: 149–156, 1994; M. Maes, E. Bosmans, J. Calabrese, et al., "Interleukin-2 and interleukin-6 in schizophrenia and mania: Effect of neuroleptic and mood stabilizers," *Journal of Psychiatric Research* 29: 141–152, 1995; S.-Y. Tsai, K.-P. Chen, Y.-Y. Yang, et al., "Activation of indices of cell-mediated immunity in bipolar mania," *Biological Psychiatry* 45: 989–994, 1999.

43. R. W. Kupka, M.H.J. Hillegers, W. A. Nolen et al., "Immunological aspects of bipolar disorder," *Bipolar Disorder* 3: 86–90, 2000.

44. M. Hornig, J. D. Amsterdam, M. Kamoun, et al., "Autoantibody disturbances in affective disorders: A function of age and gender?" *Journal of Affective Disorders* 55: 29–37, 1999.

45. E. Frank, H. A. Swartz, and D. J. Kupfer, "Interpersonal and social rhythm therapy: Managing the chaos of bipolar disorder," *Biological Psychiatry* 48: 593–604, 2000.

46. S. Esposito, A. J. Prange, and R. N. Golden, "The thyroid axis and mood disorders: Overview and future prospects," *Psychopharmacology Bulletin* 33: 205–217, 1997.

47. C. B. Nemeroff, D. L. Musselman, K. I. Nathan, et al., "Pathophysiological Basis of Psychiatric Disorders: Focus on Mood Disorders and Schizophrenia," in A. Tasman, J. Kay, and J. A. Lieberman (eds.), *Psychiatry* (Philadelphia: Saunders, 1997), pp. 258–311.

48. T. G. Dinan, L. N. Yatham, V. O'Keane, et al., "Blunting of noradrenergic-stimulated growth hormone release in mania," *American Journal of Psychiatry* 148:

936–938, 1991; J. H. Thakore and T. G. Dinan, "Blunted dexamethasone-induced growth hormone responses in acute mania," *Psychoneuroendocrinology* 21: 695–701, 1996; I. S., Shiah, L. N. Yatham, R. W. Lam, et al., "Growth hormone response to baclofen in patients with mania: A pilot study," *Psychopharmacology* 147: 280–284, 1999.

49. A. Winokur, J. Amsterdam, S. Caroff, et al., "Variability of hormonal responses to a series of neuroendocrine challenges in depressed patients," *American Journal of Psychiatry* 139: 39–44, 1982.

50. R. M. Post and S. R. B. Weiss, "The Neurobiology of Treatment-Resistant Mood Disorders," in F. E. Bloom and D. J. Kupfer (eds.), *Psychopharmacology: The Fourth Generation of Progress* (New York: Raven Press, 1995), pp. 1155–1170.

51. Ibid.

52. Ibid.

53. S. L. Johnson and J. E. Roberts, "Life events and bipolar disorder: Implications from biological theories," *Psychological Bulletin* 117: 434–449, 1995.

54. Ibid.

55. Frances M. Mondimore, *Bipolar: A Guide for Patients and Families* (Baltimore: Johns Hopkins University Press, 1999), p. 224.

Chapter 8

1. William Cowper, *Memoir of the Early Life of William Cowper, Esq.* (1816), quoted in Roy Porter, *The Faber Book of Madness* (Boston: Faber and Faber, 1991), p. 204.

2. J. F. J. Cade, "Lithium salts in the treatment of psychotic excitement," *Medical Journal of Australia* 36: 349–352, 1949.

3. N. S. Kline, "Lithium comes into its own," *American Journal of Psychiatry* 125: 558–560, 1968.

4. American Psychiatric Association, "APA practice guidelines for the treatment of patients with bipolar disorder," *American Journal of Psychiatry* 151 (suppl.): 1–36, 1994.

5. G. S. Sachs, D. J. Printz, D. A. Kahn, et al., "The expert consensus guideline series: Medication treatment of bipolar disorder 2000," *Postgraduate Medicine,* Special Report 2000 (April): 1–104.

6. J. Cookson and G. Sachs, "Lithium: Clinical Use in Mania and Prophylaxis of Affective Disorders," in P. F. Buckley and J. L. Waddington (eds.), *Schizophrenia and Mood Disorders: The New Drug Therapies in Clinical Practice* (Oxford: Butterworth-Heinemann, 2000), pp. 155–178.

7. C. L. Bowden, A. M. Brugger, A. C. Swann, et al., "Efficacy of divalproex vs. lithium and placebo in the treatment of mania. The Depakote Mania Study Group." *JAMA* 271: 918–924, 1994.

8. F.G.M. Souza and G. M. Goodwin, "Lithium treatment and prophylaxis in unipolar depression: A meta-analysis," *British Journal of Psychiatry* 158: 666–675, 1991; G. L. Zornberg and H. G. Pope, "Treatment of depression in bipolar disorder: New directions for research," *Journal of Clinical Psychopharmacology* 13: 397–408, 1993.

9. J. F. Goldberg and P. E. Keck, "Summary of Findings on the Course and Outcome of Bipolar Disorders," in J. F. Goldberg and M. Harrow (eds.), *Bipolar Disorders: Clinical Course and Outcome* (Washington, D.C.: American Psychiatric Press, 1999), pp. 275–288.

10. M. Alda and P. Grof, "Genetics and Lithium Response in Bipolar Disorders," in J. C. Soares and S. Gershon (eds.) *Bipolar Disorders: Basic Mechanisms and Therapeutic Implications* (New York: Marcel Dekker, 2000), pp. 529–544.

11. G. S. Sachs, P. F. Renshaw, B. Lafer, et al., "Variability of brain lithium levels during maintenance treatment: A magnetic resonance spectroscopy study," *Biological Psychiatry* 38: 422–428, 1995.

12. L. H. Price and G. R. Heninger, "Lithium in the treatment of mood disorders," *New England Journal of Medicine* 331: 591–598, 1994.

13. P. G. Janicak, J. M. Davis, S. H. Preskorn, et al., *Principles and Practice of Psychopharmacotherapy*, 2nd ed. (Baltimore: Williams and Wilkins, 1997), pp. 463–464.

14. A. Coppen, M. E. Bishop, J. E. Bailey, et al., "Renal function in lithium and non–lithium treated patients with affective disorders," *Acta Psychiatrica Scandinavia* 73, 574–581, 1980.

15. R. G. McCreadie and D. P. Morrison, "The impact of lithium in south-west Scotland. I: Demographic and clinical findings," *British Journal of Psychiatry* 146: 70–74, 1985.

16. T. Suppes, R. Baldessarini, G. L. Faedda, et al., "Risk of recurrence following discontinuation of lithium treatment for bipolar disorder," *Archives of General Psychiatry* 48: 1082–1088, 1991.

17. L. Tondo, R. J. Baldessarini, G. Floris, et al., "Effectiveness of restarting lithium treatment after its discontinuation in bipolar I and bipolar II disorders," *American Journal of Psychiatry* 154: 548–550, 1997.

18. P. A. Lambert, G. Cavez, S. Barselli, et al., "Action neuropsychotrope d'un novel antiepeliptique: Le depamide," *Annales Medico-Psychologiques* 1: 707–710, 1966.

19. P. E. Keck and H. K. Manji, "Current and emerging treatments for acute mania and long term prophylaxis for bipolar disorder," in *Psychopharmacology: The Fifth Generation of Progress,* in press.

20. A. Swann, C. Bowden, D. Morris, et al., "Depression during mania: Treatment response to lithium or divalproex," *Archives of General Psychiatry* 54: 37–42, 1997.

21. C. L. Bowden, J. R. Calabrese, S. L. McElroy, et al., "A randomized, placebo-controlled 12-month trial of divalproex and lithium in treatment of outpatients with bipolar I disorder," *Archives of General Psychiatry* 57: 481–489, 2000.

22. A. L. Stoll, M. Banov, M. Kolbrener, et al., "Neurologic factors predict a favorable valproate response in bipolar and schizoaffective disorders," *Journal of Clinical Psychopharmacology* 14: 311–313, 1994.

23. M. L. Prevey, R. C. Delaney, J. A. Cramer, et al., "Effect of valproate on cognitive functioning," *Archives of Neurology* 53: 1008–1016, 1996.

24. T. Okuma, A. Kishimoto, K. Inoue, et al., "Antimanic and prophylactic effects of carbamazepine on manic depressive psychosis: A preliminary report," *Folia Psychiatrica et Neurologica Japonica* 27: 283–297, 1973.

25. S. L. McElroy and P. E. Keck, "Pharmacologic agents for the treatment of acute mania," *Biological Psychiatry* 48: 539–557, 2000.

26. J. C. Ballenger and R. M. Post, "Carbamazepine in manic-depressive illness: A new treatment," *American Journal of Psychiatry* 7: 782–790, 1980; R. M. Post, T. W. Uhde, P. P. Roy-Byrne, et al., "Antidepressant effects of carbamazepine," *American Journal of Psychiatry* 143: 29–34, 1986.

27. K. D. Denicoff, E. E. Smith-Jackson, E. R. Disney, et al., "Comparative prophylactic efficacy of lithium, carbamazepine and the combination in bipolar disorder," *Journal of Clinical Psychiatry* 58: 470–478, 1997; W. Greil, W. Ludwig-Mayerhefer, N. Erazo, et al., "Lithium vs. carbamazepine in the maintenance treatment of bipolar disorders—a randomized study," *Journal of Affective Disorders* 43: 151–161, 1997.

28. C. L. Bowden, J. Calabrese, S. L. McElroy, et al., "The efficacy of lamotrigine in rapid cycling and non–rapid cycling patients with bipolar disorder," *Biological Psychiatry* 45: 953–958, 1999.

29. M. Berk, "Lamotrigine and the treatment of manic in bipolar disorder," *European Neuropsychopharmacology* 9 (Suppl. 4): S119–S123, 1999.

30. Reviewed in McElroy and Keck, "Pharmacologic agents for the treatment of acute mania."

31. Bowden et al., "The efficacy of lamotrigine in rapid cycling and non–rapid cycling patients with bipolar disorder."

32. J. R. Calabrese, C. L. Bowden, G. S. Sachs, et al., "A double-blind placebo-controlled study of lamotrigine monotherapy in outpatients with bipolar I depression," *Journal of Clinical Psychiatry* 60: 79–88, 1999.

33. Reviewed in McElroy and Keck, "Pharmacologic agents for the treatment of acute mania," and in J. C. Soares, "Recent advances in the treatment of bipolar mania, depression, mixed states, and rapid cycling," *International Clinical Psychopharmacology* 15: 183–196, 2000.

34. S. L. McElroy, T. Suppes, P. E. Keck, et al., "Open-label adjunctive topiramate in the treatment of bipolar disorders," *Biological Psychiatry* 47: 1025–1033, 2000.

35. Reviewed in L. Letterman and J. S. Markowitz, "Gabapentin: A review of published experience in the treatment of bipolar disorder and other psychiatric conditions," *Pharmacotherapy* 19: 565–572, 1999.

36. A. C. Pande, J. R. T. Davidson, J. W. Jefferson, et al., "Gabapentin in bipolar disorder: A placebo controlled trial of adjunctive therapy," *Bipolar Disorders* 2: 249–255, 2000.

37. M. A. Frye, T. A. Ketter, T. A. Kimbrell, et al., "A placebo controlled study of lamotrigine and gabapentin monotherapy in refractory mood disorders," *Journal of Clinical Psychopharmacology,* in press.

38. See N. A. Levy and P. G. Janicak, "Calcium channel antagonists for the treatment of bipolar disorder," *Bipolar Disorders* 2: 108–119, 2000.

39. G. S. Sachs, C. L. Koslow, and S. N. Ghaemi, "The treatment of bipolar depression," *Bipolar Disorders* 2: 256–260, 2000.

40. Levy and Janicak, "Calcium channel antagonists for the treatment of bipolar disorder."

41. P. G. Janicak, R. P. Sharma, G. Pandey, et al., "Verapamil for the treatment of acute mania: A double-blind, placebo-controlled trial," *American Journal of Psychiatry* 155: 972–973, 1998.

42. R. W. Edwards and M. Peet, "Essential Fatty Acid Intake in Relation to Depression," in M. Peet, I. Glen, and D. F. Horrobin (eds.), *Phospholipid Spectrum Disorder in Psychiatry* (Carnforth: Marius Press, 1999), pp. 211–221; W. S. Fenton, J. Hibbeln, and M. Knable, "Essential fatty acids, lipid membrane abnormalities, and the diagnosis and treatment of schizophrenia," *Biological Psychiatry* 47: 8–21, 2000.

43. A. L. Stoll, W. E. Severus, M. P. Freeman, et al., "Omega 3 fatty acids in bipolar disorder: A preliminary double-blind, placebo-controlled trial," *Archives of General Psychiatry* 56: 407–412, 1999.

Chapter 9

1. S. G. Howe, "Insanity in Massachusetts," *North American Review* 56: 171–191, 1843.

2. T. Dinan, J. Kelsey, and C. Nemeroff, "Selective Serotonin Reuptake Inhibitors: Clinical Use and Experience," in P. F. Buckley and J. L. Waddington (eds.) *Schizophrenia and Mood Disorders: The New Drug Therapies in Clinical Practice* (Oxford: Butterworth-Heinemann, 2000), pp. 101–108.

3. J. B. Cohn, G. Collins, E. Ashbrook, et al., "A comparison of fluoxetine, imipramine, and placebo in patients with bipolar depressive disorder," *International Clinical Psychopharmacology* 4: 313–322, 1989.

4. C. B. Nemeroff, D. L. Evans, L. Gyulai, et al., "A double blind, placebo-controlled comparison of imipramine and paroxitene in the treatment of bipolar depression," *American Journal of Psychiatry,* in press.

5. American Psychiatric Association, "APA practice guidelines for the treatment of patients with bipolar disorder," *American Journal of Psychiatry* 151 (suppl.): 1–36, 1994; Sachs et al., "The treatment of bipolar depression."

6. G. S. Sachs, B. Lafer, A. L. Stoll, et al., "A double blind trial of buproprion versus desipramine for bipolar depression," *Journal of Clinical Psychiatry* 55: 391–393, 1994.

7. Sachs et al., "The treatment of bipolar depression."

8. J. D. Amsterdam, M. B. Hooper, and J. Amchin, "Once- versus twice-daily venlafaxine therapy in major depression: A randomized double-blind study," *Journal Clinical Psychiatry* 59: 236–240, 1998.

9. Sachs et al., "The treatment of bipolar depression."

10. Ibid.

11. Soares, "Recent advances in the treatment of bipolar mania, depression, mixed states, and rapid cycling."

12. P. G. Janicak, J. M. Davis, S. H. Preskorn, et al., *Principles and Practice of Psychopharmacotherapy,* 2nd ed. (Baltimore: Williams and Wilkins, 1997).

13. Soares, "Recent advances in the treatment of bipolar mania, depression, mixed states, and rapid cycling"; M. E. Thase and G. S. Sachs, "Bipolar depression: Pharmacotherapy and related therapeutic strategies," *Biological Psychiatry* 48: 558–572, 2000.

14. Sachs et al., "The treatment of bipolar depression."

15. J. Angst and M. Stable, "Efficacy of moclobemide in different patient groups: A meta-analysis of studies," *Psychopharmacology* 106: S109–S113.

16. R. S. El-Mallakh, "An open study of methylphenidate in bipolar depression," *Bipolar Disorders* 2: 56–59, 2000.

17. R. Aronson, H. J. Offman, R. T. Joffe, et al., "Triiodothyronine augmentation in the treatment of refractory depression—a meta-analysis," *Archives of General Psychiatry* 53: 842–848, 1996.

18. M. S. Bauer and P. C. Whybrow, "Rapid cycling bipolar affective disorder. II: Treatment of refractory rapid cycling with high-dose levothyroxine: A preliminary study," *Archives of General Psychiatry* 47: 435–440, 1990.

19. G. E. Beaubrun and G. E. Gray, "A review of herbal medicines for psychiatric disorders," *Psychiatric Services* 51: 1130–1134, 2000.

20. R. C. Shelton, M. B. Keller, A. Gelenberg, et al., "Effectiveness of St. John's wort in major depression: A randomized controlled trial," *JAMA* 285:1978–1986, 2001.

21. Soares, "Recent advances in the treatment of bipolar mania, depression, mixed states, and rapid cycling."

22. Soares, "Recent advances in the treatment of bipolar mania, depression, mixed states, and rapid cycling."

23. M. A. Frye, T. A. Ketter, L. L. Altshuler, et al., "Clozapine in bipolar disorder: Treatment implications for other atypical antipsychotics," *Journal of Affective Disorders* 48: 91–104, 1998.

24. G. S. Sachs and M. E. Thase, "Bipolar disorder therapeutics: Maintenance treatment," *Biological Psychiatry* 48: 573–581, 2000.

25. Frye et al., "Clozapine in bipolar disorder: Treatment implications for other atypical antipsychotics."

26. R. Littlejohn, F. Leslie, and J. Cookson, "Depot antipsychotics in the prophylaxis of bipolar affective disorder," *British Journal of Psychiatry* 165: 827–829, 1994.

27. Reviewed in Frye et al., "Clozapine in bipolar disorder: Treatment implications for other atypical antipsychotics."

28. T. Suppes, A. Webb, B. Paul, et al., "Clinical outcome in a randomized one-year trial of clozapine versus treatment as usual for patients with treatment-resistant illness and a history of mania," *American Journal of Psychiatry* 156: 37–42, 1999.

29. P. Perry, D. Miller, S. V. Arndt, et al., "Clozapine and norclozapine concentrations and clinical response in treatment refractory schizophrenic patients," *American Journal of Psychiatry* 148: 231–235, 1991.

30. Reviewed in S. N. Ghaemi, "New treatments for bipolar disorder: The role of atypical neuroleptic agents," *Journal of Clinical Psychiatry* 61 (suppl. 14): 33–42, 2000.

31. J. Segal, M. Berk, and S. Brook, "Risperidone compared with both lithium and haloperidol in mania: A double-blind randomized controlled trial," *Clinical Neuropharmacology* 21: 176–180, 1998.

32. G. S. Sachs and the Risperidone Bipolar Study Group, "Safety and efficacy of risperidone vs. placebo as add-on therapy to mood stabilizers in the treatment of manic phase of bipolar disorder. Presented at the 38th annual meeting of the American College of Neuropsychopharmacology, December 12–16, 1999, Acapulco, Mexico.

33. See Ghaemi, "New treatments for bipolar disorder: The role of atypical neuroleptic agents."

34. M. Tohen, T. M. Sanger, S. L. McElroy, et al., "Olanzapine versus placebo in the treatment of acute mania," *American Journal of Psychiatry* 156: 702–709, 1999; M. Tohen, T. G. Jacobs, S. L. Grundy, et al., "A double-blind, placebo-controlled study of olanzapine in patients with acute bipolar mania," *Archives of General Psychiatry* 57: 841–849, 2000.

35. M. Berk, L. Ichim, and S. Brook, "Olanzapine compared to lithium in mania: A double-blind randomized controlled trial," *International Clinical Psychopharmacology* 14: 339–343, 1999.

36. Ghaemi, "New treatments for bipolar disorder: The role of atypical neuroleptic agents."

37. P. E. Keck and K. Ice, "A three week, double-blind, randomized trial of ziprasidone in the acute treatment of mania," American Psychiatric Association, Annual Meeting, Chicago, Illinois, May 2000.

38. M. A. Frye and L. L. Altshuler, "Selection of Initial Treatment for Bipolar Disorder, Manic Phase," in A. J. Rush (ed.), Mood Disorders: Systematic Medication Management (Basel: Karger, 1997), pp. 88–113.

Chapter 10

1. F. S. Fitzgerald, letter to Dr. Slocum (ca. 1934), quoted in Peter D. Kramer, "How Crazy Was Zelda?" New York Times Magazine, December 1, 1996.

2. M. A. Frye, T. A. Ketter, G. S. Leverich, et al., "The increasing use of polypharmacotherapy for refractory mood disorders: 22 years of study," Journal of Clinical Psychiatry 61: 9–15, 2000.

3. E. D. Peselow, R. R. Fieve, C. DiFiglia, et al., "Lithium prophylaxis of bipolar disorder illness: The value of combination treatment," British Journal of Psychiatry 164: 208–214, 1994.

4. L. T. Young, R. T. Joffe, J. C. Robb, et al., "Double-blind comparison of addition of a second mood stabilizer versus an antidepressant to an initial mood stabilizer for treatment of patients with bipolar depression," American Journal of Psychiatry 157: 124–126, 2000.

5. R. J. Baldessarini, L. Tondo, and A. C. Viguera, "Discontinuing lithium maintenance treatment in bipolar disorders: Risks and implications," Bipolar Disorders 1: 17–24, 1999.

6. R. M. Post, G. S. Leverich, L. Altshuler, et al., "Lithium discontinuation induced refractoriness: Preliminary observations," American Journal of Psychiatry 149: 1727–1729, 1992; M. Maj, R. Pirozzi, and L. Magliano, "Nonresponse to re-instituted lithium prophylaxis in previously responsive bipolar patients: Prevalence and predictors," American Journal of Psychiatry 152: 1810–1811, 1995.

7. M. Tohen, C. M. Waternaux, and M. T. Tsuang, "Outcome in mania: A 4-year prospective follow-up of 75 patients utilizing survival analysis," Archives of General Psychiatry 47: 1106–1111, 1990.

8. L. S. Cohen and L. L. Altshuler, "Pharmacologic management of psychiatric illness during pregnancy and the postpartum period," Psychiatric Clinics of North America 4: 21–60, 1997.

9. M. Schou, "What happened later to the lithium babies: A follow-up study of children born without malformations," Acta Psychiatrica Scandinavica 54: 193–197, 1976.

10. L. S. Cohen, J. M. Friedman, J. W. Jefferson, et al., "A reevaluation of risk of in utero exposure to lithium," Journal of the American Medical Association 271: 146–150, 1994.

11. L. S. Cohen, D. A. Sichel, L. M. Robertson, et al., "Postpartum prophylaxis for women with bipolar disorder," *American Journal of Psychiatry* 152: 1641–1645, 1995.

12. M. Schou, M. D. Goldfield, M. R. Weinstein, et al., "Lithium and pregnancy. I. Report from the register of lithium babies," *British Medical Journal* 2: 1356–1360, 1973.

13. Cohen and Altshuler, "Pharmacologic management of psychiatric illness during pregnancy and the postpartum period."

14. C. Chambers, K. Johnson, L. Dick, et al., "Birth outcomes in pregnant women taking fluoxetine," *New England Journal of Medicine* 335: 1010–1015, 1996.

15. E. Robert, "Treating depression in pregnancy," *New England Journal of Medicine* 335: 1056–1058, 1996.

16. I. Nulman, J. Rovet, D. E. Stewart, et al., "Neurodevelopment of children exposed in utero to antidepressant drugs," *New England Journal of Medicine* 336: 258–262, 1997.

17. M. J. Edlund and T. J. Craig, "Antipsychotic drug use and birth defects: An epidemiologic reassessment," *Comprehensive Psychiatry* 25: 244–248, 1976.

18. Z. N. Stowe, J. R. Strader, and C. B. Nemeroff, "Psychopharmacology During Pregnancy and Lactation," in A. F. Schatzberg and C. B. Nemeroff (eds.), *American Psychiatric Press Textbook of Psychopharmacology,* 2nd ed. (Washington, D.C.: American Psychiatric Press 1998), pp. 979–996.

19. Ibid.

Chapter 11

1. Thomas Hood, "Ode to Melancholy," in *Bartlett's Familiar Quotation,* 16th ed. (Boston: Little, Brown, 1992), p. 422.

2. Martha Manning, *Undercurrents: A Therapist's Reckoning with Her Own Depression* (New York: HarperCollins, 1994), p. 150.

3. S. L. Johnson, C. A. Winett, B. Meyer, et al., "Social support and the course of bipolar disorder," *Journal of Abnormal Psychology* 108: 558–566, 1999.

4. Mary Ellen Copeland, *The Depression Workbook: A Guide for Living with Depression and Manic Depression* (Oakland: New Harbinger Publications, 1992).

5. Ibid., p. 132.

6. Kay R. Jamison, *An Unquiet Mind* (New York: A. A. Knopf, 1995; paperback by Random House, 1997), pp. 88–89.

7. Frances M. Mondimore, *Bipolar: A Guide for Patients and Families* (Baltimore: Johns Hopkins University Press, 1999), p. 155; italics in original.

8. Patty Duke and Gloria Hochman, *A Brilliant Madness: Living with Manic-Depressive Illness* (New York: Bantam Books, 1992), pp. 123–124.

9. Percy Knauth, *A Season in Hell* (New York: Harper and Row, 1975), p. 39.

10. Peter Whybrow, *A Mood Apart: The Thinker's Guide to Emotion and Its Disorders* (New York: BasicBooks, 1997; paperback by HarperCollins, 1998), pp. 246–247.

11. Reviewed in Nancy A. Huxley, Sagar V. Parikh, and Ross J. Baldessarini, "Effectiveness of psychosocial treatments in bipolar disorder: State of the evidence," *Harvard Review of Psychiatry* 8: 126–140, 2000.

12. E. Frank, H. A. Swartz, and D. J. Kupfer, "Interpersonal and social rhythm therapy: Managing the chaos of bipolar disorder," *Biological Psychiatry* 48: 593–604, 2000.

13. Ibid.

14. Duke, *A Brilliant Madness,* pp. 176–177.

15. D. J. Miklowitz, T. L. Simoneau, E. L. George, et al., "Family-focused treatment of bipolar disorder: 1-year effects of a psychoeducational program in conjunction with pharmacotherapy," *Biological Psychiatry* 48: 582–592, 2000; David J. Miklowitz and Michael J. Goldstein, *Bipolar Disorder: A Family-Focused Treatment Approach* (New York: Guilford Press, 1997).

16. S. King, "Is expressed emotion cause or effect in the mothers of schizophrenic young adults?" *Schizophrenia Research* 45: 65–78, 2000.

17. Huxley et al., "Effectiveness of psychosocial treatments in bipolar disorder: State of the evidence."

18. Ibid.

19. E. Fuller Torrey, *Witchdoctors and Psychiatrists: The Common Roots of Psychotherapy and Its Future* (New York: Harper and Row, 1986).

20. Copeland, *The Depression Workbook,* p. 251.

21. Kathy Cronkite, *On the Edge of Darkness: Conversations About Conquering Depression* (New York: Doubleday, 1994; paperback by Delta Books, 1995).

22. Max Fink, *Electroshock: Restoring the Mind* (New York: Oxford University Press, 1999).

23. D. P. Devanand, A. J. Dwork, E. R. Hutchinson, et al., "Does ECT alter brain structure?" *American Journal of Psychiatry* 151: 957–970, 1994; C. E. Coffey, R. D. Weiner, W. T. Djang, et al., "Brain anatomic effects of electroconvulsive therapy: A prospective magnetic resonance imaging study," *Archives of General Psychiatry* 48: 1013–1021, 1991.

24. "ECT Update," *Biological Therapies in Psychiatry Newsletter* 16: 31, 1993.

25. W. Z. Potter and M. V. Rudorfer, "Electroconvulsive Therapy—A Modern Medical Procedure," *New England Journal of Medicine* 328: 882–883, 1993.

26. Shari Roan, "A New Image for Shock Therapy," *Los Angeles Times,* September 15, 1992, pp. E1, E4.

27. "Court Holds Bipolar Disorder Is Physical," *Psychiatric News,* March 4, 1988, p. 1.

28. Howard Fishman, "Illinois Lawsuit Seeks Equal Insurance Coverage for Bipolar Affective Disorder," *Psychiatric Times,* December 1989, p. 1.

29. "Reimbursement for Treatment of Bipolar Disorder Again the Focus of Court Battle," *Psychiatric News,* January 18, 1991.

30. G. Geis, P. Jaslow, H. Pontell, et al., "Fraud and abuse of government medical benefit programs by psychiatrists," *American Journal of Psychiatry* 142: 231–234, 1985.

31. Joe Sharkey, *Bedlam: Greed, Profiteering, and Fraud in a Mental Health System Gone Crazy* (New York: St. Martin's Press, 1994).

32. "Mind and Money" (editorial), *Wall Street Journal,* December 17, 1999, p. A14.

33. J. Rabinowitz, E. Bromet, J. Lavelle, et al., "Relationship and care during the early course of psychosis," *American Journal of Psychiatry* 155: 1392–1397, 1998.

Chapter 12

1. Thomas Gray, "Elegy Written in a Country Churchyard" (The Epitaph, stanza 1), 1742.

2. B. Geller and J. Luby, "Child and adolescent bipolar disorder: A review of the past 10 years," *Journal of the American Academy of Child and Adolescent Psychiatry* 36: 1168–1176, 1997.

3. BettiJane Levine, "A Woman of Steel," *Los Angeles Times,* January 30, 2001, E–1.

4. J. Wozniak, J. Biederman, E. Mundy, et al., "A pilot family study of childhood-onset mania," *Journal of the American Academy of Child and Adolescent Psychiatry* 34: 1577–1583, 1995.

5. C. G. Reichart, W. A. Nolen, M. Wals, et al., "Bipolar disorder in children and adolescents: A clinical reality?" *Acta Neuropsychiatrica* 12: 132–135, 2000.

6. Case study furnished by Robert L. Findling, M.D., of Case Western Reserve University.

7. E. L. Fergus, G. S. Leverich, D. A. Luckenbaugh, et al., "Prodromes of childhood bipolar disorder: A retrospective survey of parents' report of symptom severity each year," submitted.

8. Demetri Papolos and Janice Papolos, *The Bipolar Child: The Definitive and Reassuring Guide to Childhood's Most Misunderstood Disorder* (New York: Broadway Books, 1999), p. 18.

9. Wozniak et al., "A pilot family study of childhood-onset mania."

10. Papolos and Papolos, *The Bipolar Child,* p. 13.

11. J. Biederman, S. Faraone, E. Mick, et al., "Attention-deficit hyperactivity disorder and juvenile mania: An overlooked comorbidity?" *Journal of the American Academy of Child and Adolescent Psychiatry* 35: 997–1008, 1996.

12. Wozniak et al., "A pilot family study of childhood-onset mania."

13. Geller and Luby, "Child and adolescent bipolar disorder."

14. Ibid.

15. Mitzi Waltz, *Bipolar Disorders: A Guide to Helping Children and Adolescents* (Sebastopol, Calif.: O'Reilly and Associates, 2000), p. 18.

16. Geller and Luby, "Child and adolescent bipolar disorder."

17. M. Strober, S. Schmidt-Lackner, R. Freeman, et al., "Recovery and relapse in adolescents with bipolar affective illness: A five-year naturalistic prospective follow-up," *Journal of the American Academy of Child and Adolescent Psychiatry* 34: 724–731, 1995.

18. B. Geller, K. Sun, B. Zimerman, et al., "Complex and rapid-cycling in bipolar children and adolescents: A preliminary study," *Journal of Affective Disorders* 34: 259–268, 1995.

19. J. Biederman, R. Russell, J. Soriano, et al., "Clinical features of children with both ADHD and mania: Does ascertainment source make a difference?" *Journal of Affective Disorders* 51: 101–112, 1998.

20. Wozniak et al., "A pilot family study of childhood-onset mania."

21. M. Bashir, J. Russell, and G. Johnson, "Bipolar affective disorder in adolescence: A 10-year study," *Australian and New Zealand Journal of Psychiatry* 21: 36–43, 1987.

22. H. S. Akiskal, "The prevalent clinical spectrum of bipolar disorders beyond DSM–IV," *Journal of Clinical Psychopharmacology* 16 (Suppl. 1): 4S–14S, 1996.

23. R. L. Findling, B. L. Gracious, N. K. McNamara, et al., "The rationale, design, and progress of two novel maintenance treatment studies in pediatric bipolarity," *Acta Neuropsychiatrica* 12: 136–138, 2000.

24. R. A. Kowatch, T. Suppes, T. J. Carmody, et al., "Effect size of lithium, divalproex sodium, and carbamazepine in children and adolescents with bipolar disorder," *Journal of the American Academy of Child and Adolescent Psychiatry* 39: 713–720, 2000.

25. J. Wozniak and J. Biederman, "A pharmacological approach to the quagmire of comorbidity in juvenile mania," *Journal of the American Academy of Child and Adolescent Psychiatry* 35: 826–828, 1996.

Chapter 13

1. Andrew Duncan, *Short Account of the Rise, Progress, and Present State of the Lunatic Asylum at Edinburgh* (Edinburgh: Neill, 1812).

2. D. A. Regier, M. E. Farmer, D. S. Rae, et al., "Comorbidity of mental disorders with alcohol and other drug abuse: Results from the Epidemiologic Catchment Area (ECA) study," *JAMA* 264: 2511–2518, 1990.

3. R. C. Kessler, D. R. Rubinow, C. Holmes, et al., "The epidemiology of DSM-III-R bipolar I disorder in a general population survey," *Psychological Medicine* 27: 1079–1089, 1997.

4. Regier et al., "Comorbidity of mental disorders with alcohol and other drug abuse."

5. J. F. Goldberg, J. L. Garno, A. C. Leon, et al., "A history of substance abuse complicates remission from acute mania in bipolar disorder," *Journal of Clinical Psychiatry* 60: 733–740, 1999; M. Tohen and C. A. Zarate Jr., "Bipolar Disorder and Comorbid Substance Use Disorder," in J. F. Goldberg and M. Harrow, *Bipolar Disorders: Clinical Course and Outcome* (Washington, D.C.: American Psychiatric Press, 1999), pp. 171–184; S. M. Strakowski, M. P. DelBello, D. E. Fleck, et al., "The impact of substance abuse on the course of bipolar disorder," *Biological Psychiatry* 48: 477–485, 2000.

6. S. Hodgins, M. Lapalme, and J. Toupin, "Criminal activities and substance use of patients with major affective disorders and schizophrenia: A 2-year follow-up," *Journal of Affective Disorders* 55: 187–202, 1999.

7. D. M. Steinwachs, J. D. Kasper, and E. A. Skinner, *Family Perspectives on Meeting the Needs for Care of Severely Mentally Ill Relatives: A National Survey* (Baltimore: School of Public Hygiene and Public Health, Johns Hopkins University, 1992).

8. Kay R. Jamison, *Night Falls Fast: Understanding Suicide* (New York: A. A. Knopf, 1999), p. 190.

9. *Washington Post,* March 15, 1996, and December 13, 1997; *Washington Times,* December 2, 1997.

10. *Cleveland Plain Dealer,* November 26, 1998.

11. The Associated Press, October 8, 1999, State and Regional.

12. *Houston Chronicle,* November 26, 1998, p. A44.

13. [Rock Hill, S.C.] *Herald,* February 20, 1999, p. 1A; Associated Press State and Local Wire, February 23, 1999.

14. F. Fessenden, "They Threaten, Seethe and Unhinge, Then Kill in Quantity," *New York Times,* April 9, 2000, p. A1.

15. P. E. Keck, S. L. McElroy, S. M. Strakowski, et al., "Compliance with maintenance treatment in bipolar disorder," *Psychopharmacology Bulletin* 33: 87–91, 1997.

16. W. J. Greenhouse, B. Meyer, and S. L. Johnson, "Coping and medication adherence in bipolar disorder," *Journal of Affective Disorders* 59: 237–241, 2000.

17. See, for example, S. N. Ghaemi, E. Boiman, and F. K. Goodwin, "Insight and outcome in bipolar, unipolar, and anxiety disorders," *Comprehensive Psychiatry* 41: 167–171, 2000.

18. N. Dain, *Concepts of Insanity in the United States, 1789–1865* (New Brunswick, N.J.: Rutgers University Press, 1964), p. 20.

19. M. R. DiMatteo, H. S. Lepper, and T. W. Croghan, "Depression is a risk factor for noncompliance with medical treatment: Meta-analysis of the effects of anxiety and depression on patient adherence," *Archives of Internal Medicine* 160: 2101–2107, 2000.

20. *Des Moines Register,* March 27 and 28, 1993, and June 26, 1999.

21. M. R. Munetz, T. Grande, J. Kleist, et al., "The effectiveness of outpatient civil commitment," *Psychiatric Services* 47: 1251–1253, 1996; B. M. Rohland, "The role of outpatient commitment in the management of persons with schizophrenia," Iowa Consortium for Mental Health, Services, Training, and Research, May 1998; M. S. Swartz, J. W. Swanson, H. R. Wagner, et al., "Can involuntary outpatient commitment reduce hospital recidivism? Findings from a randomized trial with severely mentally ill individuals," *American Journal of Psychiatry* 156: 1968–1975, 1999; J. W. Swanson, M. S. Swartz, R. Borum, et al., "Involuntary out-patient commitment and reduction of violent behavior in persons with mental illness," *British Journal of Psychiatry* 176: 224–231, 2000.

22. C. O'Keefe, D. P. Potenza, and K. T. Mueser, "Treatment outcomes for severely mentally ill patients on conditional discharge to community-based treatment," *Journal of Nervous and Mental Disease* 185: 409–411, 1997.

23. A. Lucksted and R. D. Coursey, "Consumer perceptions of pressure and force in psychiatric treatments," *Psychiatric Services* 46: 146–152, 1995.

24. W. M. Greenberg, L. Moore-Duncan, and R. Herron, "Patients' attitudes toward having been forcibly medicated," *Bulletin of the American Academy of Psychiatry and the Law* 24: 513–524, 1996.

25. R. Michels, "The right to refuse psychoactive drugs," *Hastings Center Report* 3: 8–11, 1973.

26. A. Arce, M. Tadlock, M. J. Vergare, et al., "A psychiatric profile of street people admitted to an emergency shelter," *Hospital and Community Psychiatry* 34: 812–817, 1983.

27. E. L. Bassuk, L. Rubin, and A. Lauriat, "Is homelessness a mental health problem?" *American Journal of Psychiatry* 141: 1546–1550, 1984.

28. P. Koegel, M. A. Burnam, and R. K. Farr, "The prevalence of specific psychiatric disorders among homeless individuals in the inner city of Los Angeles," *Archives of General Psychiatry* 45: 1085–1092, 1988.

29. W. R. Breakey, P. J. Fischer, M. Kramer, et al., "Health and mental health problems of homeless men and women in Baltimore," *JAMA* 262: 1352–1357, 1989.

30. P. Constable, "The Man in the Street: A TV Journalist Becomes His Own Saddest Story," *Washington Post,* October 1, 1995, pp. F1, F4–F5.

31. L. A. Goodman, M. A. Dutton, and M. Harris, "Episodically homeless women with serious mental illness: Prevalence of physical and sexual assault," *American Journal of Orthopsychiatry* 65: 468–478, 1995.

32. N. Bernstein, "From Early Promise to Violent Death," *New York Times,* August 8, 1999, pp. 21–22.

33. Steinwachs et al., *Family Perspectives on Meeting the Needs for Care of Severely Mentally Ill Relatives.*

34. E. F. Torrey, J. Stieber, J. Ezekiel, et al., *Criminalizing the Seriously Mentally Ill: The Abuse of Jails as Mental Hospitals* (Washington, D.C.: Health Research Group and National Alliance for the Mentally Ill, 1992).

35. Ibid.

36. Ibid.

37. Ibid.

38. Ibid.

39. P. M. Ditton, *Bureau of Justice Statistics Special Report: Mental Health and Treatment of Inmates and Probationers* (Washington, D.C.: Department of Justice, 1999).

40. H. R. Lamb and R. W. Grant, "The mentally ill in an urban county jail," *Archives of General Psychiatry* 39: 17–22, 1982; L. A. Teplin, "The criminalization of the mentally ill: Speculation in search of data," *Psychological Bulletin* 94: 54–67, 1983.

41. K. M. Abram and L. A. Teplin, "Co-occurring disorders among mentally ill jail detainees," *American Psychologist* 46: 1036–1045, 1991.

42. R. J. Baldessarini, L. Tondo, and J. Hennen, "Effects of lithium treatment and its discontinuation on suicidal behavior in bipolar manic-depressive disorders," *Journal of Clinical Psychiatry* 60 (suppl. 2): 77–84, 1999.

43. Kessler et al., "The epidemiology of DSM-III-R bipolar I disorder in a general population survey."

44. J. Angst, "Suicides Among Depressive and Bipolar Patients," abstract of paper presented at meeting of the American Psychiatric Association, 1988. Cited in F. K. Goodwin and K. R. Jamison, *Manic-Depressive Illness* (New York: Oxford University Press, 1990), p. 230.

45. E. H. Hoyer, P. B. Mortensen, and M. Frydenberg, "Suicide and other causes of death in patients with bipolar and unipolar illness," submitted for publication.

46. H. M. Inskip, E. C. Harris, and B. Barraclough, "Lifetime risk of suicide for affective disorder, alcoholism and suicide," *British Journal of Psychiatry* 172: 35–37, 1998.

47. J. B. Potash, H. S. Kane, Y. Chiu, et al., "Attempted suicide and alcoholism in bipolar disorder: Clinical and familial relationships," *American Journal of Psychiatry* 157: 2048–2050, 2000.

48. L. Tondo, R. J. Baldessarini, J. Hennen, et al., "Suicide attempts in major affective disorder patients with comorbid substance use disorders," *Journal of Clinical Psychiatry* 60 (suppl. 2): 63–69, 1999.

49. V. Nabokov, "Wingstroke," in *The Stories of Vladimir Nabokov* (New York: Vintage Books, 1995), p. 41.

50. F. K. Goodwin and K. R. Jamison, *Manic-Depressive Illness* (New York: Oxford University Press, 1990), p. 243.

51. P. S. F. Yip, A. Chao, and C. W. F. Chiu, "Seasonal variation in suicides: diminished or vanished: Experience from England and Wales, 1982–1996," *British Journal of Psychiatry* 177: 366–369, 2000.

52. Tracy Thompson, *The Beast: A Journey Through Depression* (New York: Plume, 1996), p. 145.

53. E. T. Isometsä, M. M. Henriksson, H. M. Aro, et al., "Suicide in bipolar disorder in Finland," *American Journal of Psychiatry* 151: 1020–1024, 1994.

54. S. Ramrakha, A. Caspi, N. Dickson, et al., "Psychiatric disorders and risky sexual behaviour in young adulthood: Cross sectional study in birth cohort," *British Medical Journal* 321: 263–266, 2000.

55. F. Cournos, K. McKinnon, H. Meyer-Bahlburg, et al., "HIV risk activity among persons with severe mental illness: Preliminary findings," *Hospital and Community Psychiatry* 44: 1104–1106, 1993.

56. M. V. Seeman, M. Lang, and N. Rector, "Chronic schizophrenia: A risk factor for HIV?" *Canadian Journal of Psychiatry* 35: 765–768, 1990.

57. A. Jablensky, S. Zubrick, V. Morgan, et al., "Reproductive pathology in women with schizophrenia and affective psychoses" (abstract), *Schizophrenia Research* 29: 20, 1998.

58. J. H. Coverdale and J. A. Aruffo, "Family planning needs of female chronic psychiatric outpatients," *American Journal of Psychiatry* 146: 1489–1491, 1989.

59. M. Sacks, H. Dermatis, S. Looser-Ott, et al., "Seroprevalence of HIV and risk factors for AIDS in psychiatric inpatients," *Hospital and Community Psychiatry* 43: 736–737, 1992.

60. J. F. Aruffo, J. H. Coverdale, R. C. Chacko, et al., "Knowledge about AIDS among women psychiatric outpatients," *Hospital and Community* 41: 326–328, 1990.

61. R. M. Goisman, A. B. Kent, E. C. Montgomery, et al., "AIDS education for patients with chronic mental illness," *Community Mental Health Journal* 27: 189–197, 1991.

62. S. C. Kalichman, K. J. Sikkema, J. A. Kelly, et al., "Use of a brief behavioral skills intervention to prevent HIV infection among chronic mentally ill adults," *Psychiatric Services* 46: 275–280, 1995; J. A. Kelly, T. I. McAuliffe, K. J. Sikkema, et al., "Reduction in risk behavior among adults with severe mental illness who learned to advocate for HIV prevention," *Psychiatric Services* 48: 1283–1288, 1997.

63. L. Suhay, "Families Often Pay for Patients' Privacy: By Withholding Information, the N.J. Mental-Health System Hurts Relatives of the Sick," *The Inquirer* (Philadelphia), December 2, 1999.

64. T. B. Marshall and P. Solomon, "Releasing information to families of persons with severe mental illness: A survey of NAMI members," *Psychiatric Services* 51: 1006–1011, 2000.

65. Ibid.

66. Jacki Lyden, *Daughter of the Queen of Sheba* (New York: Houghton Mifflin, 1997; paperback by Penguin Books, 1998), p. 251.

67. Ibid., p. 36.

68. Ibid., p. 37.

69. Kay R. Jamison, *An Unquiet Mind* (New York: A. A. Knopf, 1995; paperback by Random House, 1997), pp. 90–91.

70. Ibid., pp. 5–6.

71. Kay R. Jamison, "Manic-Depressive Illness, Genes, and Creativity," in L. L. Hall (ed.), *Genetics and Mental Illness: Evolving Issues for Research and Society* (New York: Plenum Press, 1996), pp. 111–132.

72. Patty Duke and Gloria Hochman, *A Brilliant Madness: Living with Manic-Depressive Illness* (New York: Bantam Books, 1992), pp. 222–223.

73. Jamison, *An Unquiet Mind,* p. 212.

74. K. R. Jamison, R. H. Gerner, C. Hammen, et al., "Clouds and silver linings: Positive experiences associated with primary affective disorders," *American Journal of Psychiatry* 137: 198–202, 1980.

75. Jamison, *An Unquiet Mind,* p. 217.

Chapter 14

1. John Connolly, *An Inquiry Concerning the Indications of Insanity, with Suggestions for the Better Protection and Care of the Insane* (London: Taylor, 1830).

2. John D. Mudie, "Living life on the bipolar ride," *CAMI Journal* 6: 46–49, 1995.

3. Margo Orum, "Van Gogh and lithium. Creativity and bipolar disorder: Perspective of a psychologist/writer," *Australian and New Zealand Journal of Psychiatry* 33: S114–S115, 1999.

4. Charles Lamb, "The Sanity of True Genius," *Elia; and, the Last Essays of Elia* (New York: Oxford University Press, 1987), pp. 212–213.

5. W. A. Frosch, "The 'case' of George Frederic Handel," *New England Journal of Medicine,* 321: 765–769, 1989.

6. Cesare Lombroso, *The Man of Genius* (New York: Charles Scribner's Sons, 1895).

7. C. Martindale, "Father's absence, psychopathology, and poetic eminence," *Psychological Reports* 31: 843–847, 1972; W. H. Trethowan, "Music and Mental Disorder," in M. Critchley and R. E. Henson (eds.), *Music and the Brain* (London: Heinemann, 1977), pp. 398–442; J. J. Schildkraut, A. J. Hirshfeld, and J. M. Murphy, "Mind and mood in modern art. II: Depressive disorders, spirituality, and early deaths in the abstract expressionist artists of the New York School," *American Journal of Psychiatry* 151: 482–488, 1994.

8. Kay R. Jamison, *Touched with Fire: Manic Depressive Illness and the Artistic Temperament* (New York: Simon and Schuster, 1993), pp. 61–72.

9. A. Juda, "The relationship between highest mental capacity and psychic abnormalities," *American Journal of Psychiatry* 106: 296–307, 1949.

10. F. Post, "Creativity and psychopathology: A study of 291 world-famous men," *British Journal of Psychiatry* 165: 22–34, 1994.

11. A. M. Ludwig, *The Price of Greatness: Resolving the Creativity and Madness Controversy* (New York: Guilford, 1995).

12. N.J.C. Andreasen and A. Canter, "The creative writer: Psychiatric symptoms and family history," *Comprehensive Psychiatry* 15: 123–131, 1974.

13. N. C. Andreasen, "Creativity and mental illness: Prevalence rates in writers and their first-degree relatives, *American Journal of Psychiatry* 144: 1288–1292, 1987.

14. A. M. Ludwig, "Mental illness and creative activity in female writers," *American Journal of Psychiatry* 151: 1650–1656, 1994.

15. K. R. Jamison, "Mood disorders and patterns of creativity in British writers and artists," *Psychiatry* 52: 125–134, 1989.

16. Jamison, *Touched with Fire*, p. 96.

17. Andreasen and Canter, "The creative writer: Psychiatric symptoms and family history."

18. Andreasen, "Creativity and mental illness."

19. Ludwig, *The Price of Greatness*.

20. J. L. Karlsson, "Genetic association of giftedness and creativity with schizophrenia," *Hereditas* 66: 177–182, 1970.

21. J. L. Karlsson, "Creative intelligence in relatives of mental patients," *Hereditas* 100: 83–86, 1984.

22. M. S. George, J. A. Melvin, and D. Mossman, "Mental illness and creativity," *American Journal of Psychiatry* 145: 908, 1988.

23. T. F. McNeil, "Prebirth and postbirth influence on the relationship between creative ability and recorder mental illness," *Journal of Personality* 39: 391–406, 1971.

24. R. L. Richards, D. K. Kinney, I. Lunde, et al., "Creativity in manic-depressives, cyclothymes, and their normal first-degree relatives: A preliminary report," *Journal of Abnormal Psychology* 97: 281–288, 1988.

25. M. Dykes and A. McGhie, "A comparative study of attentional strategies of schizophrenic and highly creative normal subjects," *British Journal of Psychiatry* 128: 50–56, 1976; J. A. Keefe and P. A. Magaro, "Creativity and schizophrenia: An equivalence of cognitive processing," *Journal of Abnormal Psychology* 89: 390–398, 1980.

26. See, for example, A. Rothenberg, "Psychopathology and creative cognition: A comparison of hospitalized patients, Nobel laureates, and controls," *Archives of General Psychiatry* 40: 937–942, 1983.

27. M. H. Marshall, C. P. Neumann, and M. Robinson, "Lithium, creativity and manic-depressive illness: Review and prospectus," *Psychosomatics* 11: 406–408, 1970; M. Schou, "Artistic productivity and lithium prophylaxis in manic-depressive illness," *British Journal of Psychiatry* 135: 97–103.

28. "Should Van Gogh have received lithium? Some perspectives on creativity and bipolar disorder," *Australian and New Zealand Journal of Psychiatry* 33: S108–122, 1999.

Chapter 15

1. Patty Duke and Gloria Hochman, *A Brilliant Madness: Living with Manic-Depressive Illness* (New York: Bantam Books, 1992), p. 10.

2. Sheila M. La Polla, "I Am a Survivor!" *California AMI Journal* 6: 49–51, 1995.

3. Samuel H. Barondes, *Mood Genes: Hunting for Origins of Mania and Depression* (New York: Oxford University Press, 1998), p. 178.

4. Ibid., p. 179.

5. L. B. Smith, B. Sapers, V. I. Reus, et al., "Attitudes towards bipolar disorder and predictive genetic testing among patients and providers," *Journal of Medical Genetics* 33: 544–549, 1996.

6. Diane T. Marsh, Susan Pickett-Schenk, and Judith A. Cook, "Families and mental illness," *California AMI Journal* 11: 5–7, 2000.

7. Ibid.

8. Diane T. Marsh, "Families are like tea bags: The hotter the water, the stronger they become," *California AMI Journal* 11: 48–50, 2000.

9. Diane Berger and Lisa Berger, *We Heard the Angels of Madness: One Family's Struggle with Manic Depression* (New York: William Morrow, 1991; paperback by HarperTrade, 1992), pp. 34, 38.

10. Kim T. Mueser, Carmen Walsh, Margaret Pfeiffer et al., "Family burden of schizophrenia and bipolar disorder: Perceptions of relatives and professionals," *Psychiatric Services* 47: 507–511, 1996.

11. Berger and Berger, *We Heard the Angels of Madness,* p. 254.

12. James Scibilia, "In sickness and in health," *California AMI Journal* 11: 24–25, 2000.

13. Toby A. Meiner and Edie Mannion, "Enough molehills to build a mountain," *California AMI Journal* 11: 28–30, 2000; italics in original.

14. Mary Ellen Copeland, "Remembering Kate: A story of hope," *California AMI Journal* 6: 64–66, 1995.

15. Linda Gray Sexton, *Searching for Mercy Street: My Journal Back to My Mother, Anne Sexton* (Boston: Little, Brown and Company, 1994), pp. 10, 13, 21; italics in original.

16. Ibid., p. 13.

17. Jacki Lyden, *Daughter of the Queen of Sheba* (New York: Houghton Mifflin, 1997; paperback by Penguin Books, 1998), p. 117.

18. Duke, *A Brilliant Madness,* pp. 243, 245.

19. Kathy Cronkite, *On the Edge of Darkness: Conversations About Conquering Depression* (New York: Doubleday, 1994; paperback by Delta Books, 1995), p. 249.

20. Duke, *A Brilliant Madness,* p. 245.

21. Lyden, *Daughter of the Queen of Sheba,* pp. 8, 9–10, 197.

Chapter 16

1. Francis Tiffany, *Life of Dorothea Lynde Dix* (Ann Arbor: Plutarch Press, 1971), p. 82.

2. Dorothea Dix, *On Behalf of the Insane Poor* (New York: Arno Press, 1971; originally published in 1843), pp. 3, 25.

3. R. Leiby, "John Travolta's Alien Notion," *Washington Post*, November 28, 1999, pp. 61–65.

4. C. Gorman, "Prozac's Worst Enemy," *Time*, October 10, 1994, p. 65.

5. P. R. Breggin, *The Psychology of Freedom: Liberty and Love as a Way of Life* (Buffalo, N.Y.: Prometheus Books, 1980), p. 70.

6. Ibid., p. 209.

7. E. F. Torrey, M. B. Knable, J. M. Davis, et al., *A Mission Forgotten: The Failure of the National Institute of Mental Health to Do Sufficient Research on Severe Mental Illnesses* (Arlington, Va.: National Alliance for the Mentally Ill, 1999).

8. E. F. Torrey, I. I. Gottesman, J. M. Davis, et al., *Missions Impossible: The Ongoing Failure of NIMH to Support Sufficient Research on Severe Mental Disorders* (Arlington, Va.: Treatment Advocacy Center, 2000).

9. R. J. Wyatt, I. D. Henter, and J. C. Jamison, "Lithium revisited: Savings brought about by the use of lithium, 1970–1991," *Psychiatric Quarterly* 72: 149–166, 2001.

10. *Mental Health: A Report of the Surgeon General* (Washington, D.C.: Department of Health and Human Services, December 1999), p. x.

11. Ibid.

12. J. A. Thornton and O. F. Wahl, "Impact of a newspaper article on attitudes toward mental illness," *Journal of Community Psychology* 24: 17–24, 1996.

13. M. C. Angermeyer and H. Matschinger, "Violent attacks on public figures by persons suffering from psychiatric disorders: Their effect on the social distance towards the mentally ill," *European Archives of Psychiatry and Clinical Neuroscience* 245: 159–164, 1995.

14. E. Jarvik, "Mental Health Clients Fear Growing Stigma," *The Deseret News* (Salt Lake City, Utah), April 24, 1999.

15. Jim Piersall and Al Hirshberg, *Fear Strikes Out: The Jim Piersall Story* (Boston: Little, Brown and Co., 1955; republished by the University of Nebraska Press, 1999), p. 5.

16. B. Upham, "Long Road Back," *Residence Publications*, September 1999, p. 4.

INDEX

acetylcholine, 122, 124, 130
acute dystonic reactions, 178
ADHD, 57, 121, 222, 225, 229
adjunctive medications. *See*
    polypharmacy
adoption studies, 117–118, 314
adrenal gland, 130, 131fig, 132
advance directives, 246
advocacy, 293–306, 337–338
agitated depression, 20, 39–40
agitation, 175, 185, 190, 254
agoraphobia, 226
agranulocytosis, 181
AIDS, 29, 105, 258–259
akathisia, 178
alcohol
    effects of, on brain structure, 112
    restriction of, as treatment, 213
alcohol abuse. *See* substance abuse
alcohol hallucinosis, 66
alcohol-induced mood disorder, 46t
alprazolam (Xanax), 186t
Alvarez, Alfred, 36, 307
Alzheimer's disease, 109, 244, 246,
    308
American Civil Liberties Union, 247,
    315
American Psychiatric Association, 204,
    216
Americans with Disabilities Act, 280
Amish studies, 3t, 6–8, 95, 308
amitriptyline (Elavil), 69–70t, 170t, 198
amok, 78
amoxapine (Ascendin), 170t
amphetamine-induced mood disorder,
    46t

amphetamine(s), 64–65, 123–124,
    174t, 175, 227
animal models, 125, 129, 133–134
anosognosia, 241
    See also insight/lack of insight
anti-anxiety medications. *See*
    benzodiazepines
anti-Parkinson's medications, 178
anti-seizure medications. *See*
    anticonvulsants
anticholinergic side effects, 170t, 179,
    179t, 181, 198
anticonvulsants
    as adjunctive medication, 191
    as cause of mania, 69–70t
    as treatment for acute mania, 190
    interactions with other medications,
        151
    need to discontinue prior to ECT,
        214
    risks during pregnancy/while breast-
        feeding, 196–197
    See also carbamazepine; gabapentin;
        lamotrigine; topiramate; valproate
antidepressants, 163–176, 191
anti-infectious properties of, 72
as cause of mania in childhood, 222
discontinuing, 192, 194
risks during pregnancy/while breast-
    feeding, 197–198
    See also depressed phase (treatment);
        mania (treatment); MAOIs;
        SSRIs; stimulants; TCAs;
        unipolar depression (treatment)
antipsychiatry, 214, 295–297
antipsychotics, 177–185

379